Football

A History of the World Game

For Val and Duncan
and
Morag

Football

A History of the World Game

BILL MURRAY

SCOLAR PRESS

Published by
SCOLAR PRESS
Gower House
Croft Road
Aldershot
Hants GU11 3HR
England

Ashgate Publishing Company
Old Post Road
Brookfield
Vermont 05036
USA

British Library Cataloguing in Publication Data

Murray, William James
    Football: A History of the World Game
    I. Title
    796.33409

ISBN 1 85928 091 9

Typeset in 10pt Garamond by Raven Typesetters, Ellesmere Port, South Wirral and printed in Great Britain by Hartnoll's Ltd, Bodmin

Contents

Preface and Acknowledgments

This book began as a short history of association football, but grew into a much larger study, as it soon became apparent that the existing works on the subject left many gaps, while whole areas like Asia and Africa had been left virtually untouched. As the areas of study increased, and the author's questions multiplied, so too did his debt of gratitude to all those who were assailed with queries or had to listen to the latest discovery of yet another remote corner where football was the popular passion. Among the most persistently pestered in this way were my colleagues at La Trobe University, above all: David Dorward who rightly looked askance on an early draft of a chapter on Africa, Paul Rule who set me right on China and helped direct me to information on Mongolia, Barry Carr who straightened me out on some aspects of South America, Don Ferrell who discussed various issues with me to and from squash, and even on the court, John Salmond who reminded me of the role of rugby, and others too numerous to mention. In the History Office Brenda Joyce and Heather Wilkie on more than one occasion made life much easier than it might otherwise have been. In the Borchardt Library at La Trobe University I was for a while almost an attachment to the Inter-Library loans department, where Julie Marshall, Peggy Cochrane, Jacquie Joslin and Jonelle Bradley showed remarkable forbearance and even interest in what I was doing. So too did John Horacek, who despite obvious doubts about the value of sport in any form, still did his best to acquire the books I requested.

In view of my linguistic restrictions, I have a particular debt to certain people who put me in touch with, or helped me with sources other than English or French. Above all, Heidi Zogbaum of La Trobe University, for whom the delights of football were (and perhaps still are) a mystery, was of immense help with German and Spanish sources. Pierre Lanfranchi is not only a talented linguist, but a renowned football scholar: he generously put at my disposal his vast knowledge and magnificent library, and commented on early drafts of some chapters. Ulrich Matheja, while working on his own history of Eintracht Frankfurt, also read parts of early drafts, answered many queries and allowed me to consult his library and that of *Kicker* magazine. Joseph Arbena read an early draft of the chapter on Latin America and raised a few pertinent doubts: I hope what I have re-written will be closer to his approval. Geralyn Pye of Flinders University also offered me many useful suggestions on this chapter.

Colleagues at the Australian Society for Sports History have been unfailingly kind in their answers to queries and reading drafts of chapters.

Above all Philip Mosely read nearly every chapter in early draft and offered encouragement and insightful criticism; Roy Hay did the same for later drafts. Wray Vamplew and Braham Dabscheck read particular chapters. In Scotland, Bill Craw offered companionship and criticism, and in England John Williams not only gave me advice on one chapter, but extended social warmth and intellectual stimulus in Leicester. At Sports House in Sydney, John Howell and Margaret Balmer allowed me open access to their magnificent collection of football material, as well as free use of their photocopying facilities. FIFA were most courteous in replying to my correspondence, and generous in the supply of information. I have special thanks to Bill Baker, who first suggested me to another publisher for this book, and Ben Rader who read very early drafts: this debt I hope to repay soon. Richard Holt read a late draft at short notice and confirmed the changes that had to be made to bring a voluminous manuscript to publishable proportions. Alec McAulay adopted these. Once more, I have a major debt to Pat Woods, who read every chapter in its final form and, as always, gave fully of his knowledge and time.

Other debts I have mentioned in specific chapters. As in my other football books I have to record my thanks to all those who have suffered my enthusiasm for the game. For this book I must include Val, finally free of the nuisance, whose disinterest in the subject, as in all sport, was as complete as possibly could be; our son Duncan, who had a brief spell kicking a ball before taking up cycling; and our daughter Morag, who would bribe me to do something for her by offering to play football with me – now we have even been to a few games together.

And especially for this book, all those with and against whom I played soccer in Australia from the 1950s to the 1970s; most of them migrants like me, who came off the ships from various parts of Europe, bringing with us our various accents, languages and approaches to the game, latterly their offspring who all spoke in Australian accents. I had no idea at the time that they were helping me prepare this book.

WJM

Abbreviations

BJSH = *British Journal of the History of Sport*

IJSH = *International Journal of the History of Sport*

Introduction

The World Cup held in Italy in 1990 was watched by more than 26 billion people throughout the world, with well over a billion tuned in for the final, by far the greatest audience for a major sporting event to that time. One reason for this was that television was available in more homes in Asia and Africa than ever before, but the main attraction was in the game itself. Soccer, or football as it is better known over that vast expanse of the globe where it is the ruling passion, is played, watched and talked about more than any other sport: perhaps more than all other sports put together – and this long before television. When Italy hosted the 1990 games even his Holiness the Pope bowed to reality when he brought forward the time of his regular address from Saint Peter's rather than have it clash with the opening game of the tournament. Politicians had long since given up any attempt to compete with the game, and were more likely to try to harness it to their ambitions: none could ignore it.

In Bangladesh during the 1990 World Cup a breakdown in power resulted in the power station being attacked by a mob of infuriated would-be telespectators. In Khartoum, a similar calamity was averted by the good sense of the authorities who flashed a message across the screens just before the start of the opening match between Argentina and Cameroon, warning that unless all unnecessary power was switched off there might not be enough to carry the game. Immediately the capital of Sudan was swathed in darkness, and the only light to be seen was from the flickering blue images from tens of thousands of television screens. On the other side of the world, in the United States, tens of millions of Americans also sat glued to their television screens, but they were watching the baseball. The minority who were watching the World Cup had to suffer through continual commercial breaks, so badly timed that that rare commodity in soccer, a goal, was occasionally scored while some sponsor's wares were being trumpeted. Unlike the citizens of Bangladesh and Sudan, those of the United States are accustomed to having their televised sport riddled with interruptions: indeed, it has been butchered to fit in with them.

It was for such reasons that news of the United States having been chosen to host the 1994 World Cup was greeted with a certain dismay in some parts of the soccer loving world. The World Cup has been a television event since at least 1954, but it is only since 1970 and the finals in Mexico that the game has actually been altered to suit viewers on the other side of the globe; in that case playing games in the Mexican heat to suit peak viewing in Europe. Altering the time of kick off, however, is nothing compared to tearing apart the seamless garment of soccer to suit the wishes of commercial sponsors. Of all the nations in the world the citizens of the United States are probably the only ones who believe that without sponsors you cannot have television, and in some cases, perhaps, that without television you cannot have sport. Since the time of the Monroe doctrine, and perhaps before, the United States has flourished in blissful ignorance of what was going on elsewhere in the world: above all in sport, where a local baseball or American football game could be billed as a 'World Series' despite none of the competitors coming from outside the States. The Americans, of course, are as fanatical about their sport as any other country, with American football, baseball and basketball – all American inventions – far and away the most popular, as well as ice hockey (simply called 'hockey' in North America) in the northern parts in the winter season.

In choosing the United States as the venue for the 1994 World Cup, the world body for soccer, FIFA, in addition to the inevitable mercenary motives, was also hoping to show Americans the folly of their sporting ways. In no other country in the world is soccer held in such total indifference – at least at the professional level. Among American youth soccer is one of the most popular participant sports, while its women showed themselves to be the best in the world when they won the inaugural Women's World Cup held in China in 1991. Beyond this, however, there is no country less interested in the world game. In the other countries that were formerly English speaking colonies of the United Kingdom, too, it is another code of football that has entered the nation's soul, but there substantial minorities of British and other immigrants retain an interest in the game. Even if they show little interest in soccer as played in their new country, they are eager to follow the soccer they have left behind, on television or through visits from top professional clubs from Europe or Latin America.

Yet despite this, the United States has enjoyed success in soccer denied Australia, New Zealand, Canada and white South Africa: in the Olympic Games and World Cup in the 1920s and 1930s the US performed creditably, and at the World Cup in Brazil in 1950 they brought off the biggest upset in the history of professional sport when they beat England 1–0 at Belo Horizonte. This victory, however, received in disbelief throughout the soccer world, was ignored in the States. Today such an upset could not so easily be passed over: television would not allow it, and there are few victories in sport so sweet as those at the national level. Had the talented but inexperienced United States team beaten, or even drawn with Italy in the 1990 World Cup, as with a large but not impossible slice of luck they might have done, perhaps some of the millions watching baseball could have been tempted into changing channels. One thing is certain: if the United States ever does devote its sporting energies to soccer a new dimension will be added to a game that already reflects so richly a variety of cultures from all around the globe.

The story of how soccer grew out of rough and tumble village brawls, through its codification in the English universities by former pupils of the so-called 'public schools', to be taken up by the working-classes and spread around the world as Britain's 'most enduring export' is one of the most fascinating in the history of sport – and yet it is only recently that soccer has been receiving the literary and scholarly attention long lavished on baseball and cricket. The very popularity of soccer and its literary neglect stem from the same source, for the 'world game' is the game of the 'people', the game that has taken a Eusebio from the Portuguese colony of Mozambique, a Pelé from the backwoods of the Minas Gerais in Brazil, a Maradona from the slums of Argentina . . . and countless other stars from the streets of Europe to the heights of world acclaim.

More than a century ago soccer was described as 'the simplest game'. It is simple in that it is open, uninterrupted and the rules (off-side notwithstanding) are easy to interpret. And although it is difficult to master it is the easiest to organize. Soccer is difficult to master because it is the most unnatural of all the football codes: arms, for holding, striking, defending and throwing are an essential part of the body, yet in soccer, apart from the goalkeeper, they serve no purpose other than for balance and taking a throw-in. It is easy to organize in that it can be played on virtually any surface, in any climate, with a ball made of the most basic materials, and played between any two or more players. No other football is more truly *foot*ball. The ball is trapped, dribbled and kicked with the feet: head, thighs and the rest of the body except the arms supply additional skills, intriguing but less essential. Nothing is more unnatural than hitting the ball with one's head, yet despite the amusement this can occasion the uninitiated, it is a spectacular and deadly skill. No other game has one player whose role is essentially different from the rest of the team: this is the goalkeeper, and while in street games this is the position usually reserved for the most unfortunate or unpopular boy (increasingly girl, particularly in the United States), this is one of the most prestigious positions in the professional game.

All football codes stem from the same origins in what seems to be an instinctive need to compete for possession of a ball or to show off by juggling with it. It was only in the nineteenth century, beginning with soccer in 1863, that the various types of football became codified into the forms with which we are familiar today. In 1866 the rules for what became known as 'Australian Rules' football were drawn up. This indigenous Australian game, popularly known as 'Aussie Rules', is the code of football that is closest to nature, the game of the 'noble savage'. It is played on an oval pitch with the goals up to 200 yards apart, with virtually no markings other than the boundaries. It is played with eighteen players on either side scattered about the pitch; they wear short shorts, jerseys ('guernseys') with no sleeves, and without as much as a shin pad for protection. The main feature of the game is the way in which players catch the oval-shaped ball in full flight at great heights ('marking') and dispose of it with long kicks either to a team mate or another group of players, with the ultimate aim of kicking it through the tall goal posts to score a goal. This is worth six points. There is no crossbar, but smaller posts indicate near misses, which are given one point. In this exhilarating game the other features are vigorous hip and shoulder tackling, rapid hand-passing and a minimum of running with the ball, which must be bounced every ten paces. This keeps the game moving at a speed that is uninterrupted even when a player is injured and needs attention: the trainer simply runs onto the field to administer help while play goes on around him. Illegal violence is tolerated as in no other football code. It is the only football not played on a rectangular pitch, and is also remarkable for the number of females who make up the spectators. Although regarded as Australia's national game, it has failed to make much headway in two of the largest states, Queensland and New South Wales.

For those who find the Australian game somewhat anarchic, the two codes of rugby, league and union, provide a sense of order, fluid movement and tests of strength that can combine the extremes of brutal violence in the scrums and tackling with grace of movement in passing and running between and away from opponents that can be breathtaking in its beauty. Both are territorial games in which any player receiving the ball from behind is off-side and the ball cannot be propelled forward by the hand. Handling is more important than kicking, running than dribbling, with most 'goals' ('tries') coming from touch-downs in what Americans would call the 'end zone'. These can be converted by kicking over the bar for extra points. The other main means of scoring is from field goals and penalty goals, scored by kicking the ball over the crossbar. Rugby Union, codified in 1871, although it had existed in its essentials long before this, is played with fifteen on each side. It is the ruling passion in New Zealand, white South Africa, Wales, Fiji and several other Pacific islands; it is a major sport in Ireland, France, Scotland, England, parts of Australia, and has a reasonable following in Romania and Argentina. As the recent rugby World Cup showed, rugby is now played in every continent, in the USA and the former Soviet Union, in Zimbabwe and Korea. It is also proving to be particularly popular with women.

Rugby League was formed as a breakaway from Union, initially on a matter of administration and disputes over amateurism, in 1895. Called the Northern Union at first, it went on to change some of the rules. League is played with 13 a side, and has eliminated line-outs and lessened the importance of scrums and kicking for touch in favour of progress through possession. The team holding the ball when a player is tackled is allowed to retain it until the fifth tackle. It is the main football game in Queensland and New South Wales in Australia, and is also popular in parts of northern England, where it had its origins, and in France and New Zealand.

The native Irish game of Gaelic football looks like a hybrid of soccer and Australian Rules, being played with a round ball similar to that used in soccer, and like Australian Rules it has no off-side. Like Rules, too, it has vigorous but controlled bodily contact, and running with the ball is restricted, in this case by the need to kick it from toe to hand every four steps. It is played with fifteen on each side, and combines handling and kicking in about the same proportions. The game was codified in 1885, one year after the formation of the Gaelic Athletic Association, founded to preserve and popularize native Irish games. Goals are scored by propelling the ball by foot or fist through soccer type goals, complete with nets, for three points, or over the bar and between the posts for one. Like Australian Rules, the game has not prospered beyond its native land, but in recent years the similarity in the style of play of the two games has led to regular encounters between teams from Australia and Ireland playing a modified game. In the United States and Britain it is played among Irish expatriates, and teams from these countries take part in the all-Ireland championships.

American football, despite recent attempts to popularize it in Europe, is a major sport only in the United States and Canada. It bears little resemblance to any of the other football codes, and is the one in which kicking is least important. On all points it is the game furthest removed from soccer, the only similarity being in the number of players. Indeed, as soccer has spread through its simplicity and appeal to the poor, American football has developed into one of the most complex and expensive games to run and organize. An entire soccer team could be fitted out for what it costs to put one American footballer on the field. Indeed, 'gridiron' as it is commonly known outside the States, could only be American: highly technical, highly specialized, very expensive and appreciated better on television than at the actual stadium. The game itself is magnificent to watch, with players who give every semblance of being musclebound under their protective clothing suddenly bursting into feats of athleticism that combine the speed of a greyhound with the power of a tank.

Unlike soccer, where kicking is of the essence, in American football kicking can almost be an irrelevance, reduced to the kick-off, failure to gain sufficient yardage, the occasional field goal and the formality of converting (for one point) a touch-down (worth six points). Tactics dominate to such an extent that most players are programmed into pre-set plays, whereas in soccer spontaneity and individual initiative can often turn the game: once the players are on the field they are in charge. For the spectators American football provides statistics in regard to heights and weights of players, yardage gained and 'assists' that fill a need unknown to the follower of soccer. Indeed, one sometimes wonders whether this mania for statistics has been encouraged to fill in time during the commercial and other artificially induced breaks, or whether the breaks were introduced to give time to digest and argue about the statistics.

Throughout the world soccer has provided a way out of the ghetto for the poor whose only talent lay in their ability to manoeuvre a ball with exceptional skill. In the States, and in many Caribbean countries, baseball – but above all basketball – have best fulfilled that purpose. Basketball has all the advantages of soccer in regard to economic democracy, but it does not have soccer's physical democracy: in soccer the smallest player can become a star; basketball is a game for 'freaks'. Nevertheless, while many of soccer's heroes are blacks from impoverished backgrounds, in the States blacks regard soccer as a white man's Yuppie game.

Soccer is the most rudimentary of games, but around it have developed ways of playing that have given rise to a variety of styles unparalleled in any other game. This is a reflection of the various climates and many surfaces on which it is played, but even more of the different societies and cultures in which it took shape. To date, the game, despite its critics from the extreme Left who see it as the opium of the masses, has survived attempts to exploit it by those who have no great sporting interests: dictators, political systems, industrial magnates, millionaire businessmen and others with little love of the game. Or even the many who do. Today soccer faces its biggest threat, not in television which has done so much to spread its joys throughout the world, but its misuse by those who would subordinate all to its money making potential. These tensions will be present at the World Cup in the United States in 1994, but they are merely an exaggerated form of the crises that have been with the game since its origins: safeguarding the rules and controlling commercial interests.

Endnotes

There are innumerable popular histories of soccer, often lavishly illustrated, which are of varying quality. Of the more serious approaches, but still with the popular touch are:

Geoffrey Green, *Soccer: the World Game. A Popular History*, Phoenix House, London, 1953.
Percy M. Young, *A History of British Football*, Stanley Paul, London, 1968.

A history fairly exhaustive in its use of the sources for the pre-nineteenth century game, but weak on the twentieth century, is:

Morris Marples, *A History of Football*, Secker and Warburg, London, 1953.

The first history of football by an academic, which treats the game in its global context, is:

James Walvin, *The People's Game. A Social History of British Football*, Allen Lane, Harmondsworth, 1975.

Works in foreign languages purporting to be world histories, still tend to be national histories in a world context. See, for example

Antonino Fugardi. *Il calcio dalle origini ad oggi*, Cappelli, Rocca San Casciano, 1973.

Where they do give a broader context, they still rely on the basic sources in English, as in

Luciano Serra, *Storia del calcio [1863–1963]*, Libreria Antiquaria Palmaverde, Bologna, 1964.

In German there is an idiosyncratic and episodic history of football in

Dietrich Schulze-Marmeling, *Der gezähmte Fussball. Zur Geschichte eines subversiven Sports*, Verlag die Werkstatt, Göttingen, 1992.

A very short history of football in the world, but superbly illustrated, is

Alfred Wahl, *La balle au pied. Histoire du football*, Gallimard, Paris, 1990.

In contrast to the way in which football was once ignored, it is now the object of study by many academics in many countries. The range of this work can be judged from the three conferences organized by Pierre Lanfranchi at the European University Institute, in Florence:

'Le football et ses publics', 19/21 March 1989
'Le football et l'Europe', 3/5 May 1990.
'Le héros sportif dans l'Europe contemporaine', 19/21 March 1992.

Emerging from these is:

Pierre Lanfranchi (ed.) *Il calcio e il suo pubblico*, Edizione Scientifiche Italiane, Napoli, 1992

From a British perspective,

John Williams and Stephen Wagg (eds.), *British Football and Social Change. Getting into Europe*, Leicester University Press, Leicester 1991.

Of the various encyclopedias on soccer, for superb scholarship with a genuinely international coverage:

R.A. Henshaw, *The Encyclopedia of World Soccer*, New Republic Books, Washington DC, 1979.

A weakness in Henshaw is the comparative absence of players and personalities; this is the strength of

Norman Barrett (ed.), *World Soccer from A to Z*, Pan Books, London, 1973.

An excellent statistical coverage of the world game is

Guy Oliver, *The Guinness Record of World Soccer. The history of the game in over 150 countries*, Guinness Publishing, Enfield, 1992.

In English, and probably in any language, the best periodical dealing with the world game is:

World Soccer, monthly from October 1960.

Any history of soccer that attempts to show it in its international perspective must refer to the work of Brian Glanville. Glanville, who reads several languages, has not only written regularly for quality sporting journals and newspapers since the early 1950s, but has published many books on football which have included histories, biographies, anthologies, short stories and novels. References to his works, and to his work on behalf of football as a stern but sympathetic critic, are scattered throughout this book, but for a single volume covering the development of the world game see:

Brian Glanville, *Soccer. A Panorama*, Eyre and Spottiswoode, London, 1968.

An interesting survey of the history of football in its various forms is:

Nicholas Mason, *Football! The story of all the world's football games*, Temple Smith, London, 1974.

The reference to football being Britain's 'most enduring export' is from the official history of the FA:

Geoffrey Green, *A History of the Football Association*, The Naldrett Press, London, 1953.

The stories of the power failures during the World Cup come from Simon Barnes in *The Times*, 23 June 1990.

CHAPTER ONE

From Rough House to Rule of Law

Football has been played in some form or another since the beginning of recorded history: characters have been depicted kicking a ball in Egyptian relics, religious paintings, Grecian vases and cathedral detail, while references to the game can be found in the Bible, moral denunciations and legal bans. It existed in ancient China and Japan, in the Americas before the Europeans arrived, and in most European countries long before it became officially recognized. It is mentioned in the poetry of Chaucer, the plays of Shakespeare, the diaries of Pepys, and other literary works as rich as these or as rank as the crudest doggerel. From at least the middle of the seventeenth century it has enriched the language with metaphors many of which have since become cliches: for fate and fortune or warfare and politics, while in 1661 can be found one of the first references to having the ball at one's feet. The game has been described in village rivalries and folk festivals, usually in disdain, as well as in royal proclamations, usually in denunciation: for football has always been a *popular* pastime, played by ordinary folks and as such feared or despised by those able to follow more elevated pursuits. Unlike archery, riding and fencing, it had no obvious military value, and while it may have kept its adherents fit, it was just as likely to maim them, for before the formalization of football, first into the Association game in 1863 and then the codification of other kicking games in the next few decades, it was little more than a form of half tolerated mayhem.

It was out of this plethora of kicking games that the Football Association (FA) was founded to bring some sort of order, and from providing rules for a few London clubs towards the end of 1863 the Association went on to provide the administrative control and set the moral example for a game which by the early twentieth century had spread around the world. Even when a rather grandiosely entitled world body was founded in France in 1904, the International Federation of Association Football (Fédération Internationale de Football Association/FIFA) still looked to the London based Football Association as the ultimate authority in all aspects of the game. By then all the other codes of football were well established, but only the round ball code, with no handling or running with the ball, had a truly international dimension.

The first world game

'Football' was originally the word used to distinguish those games played on foot from those played on horseback. As such it covered a wide range of activities in which the only common factor was the use of a ball, the size and shape of which determined the nature of the game. If the ball was small and hard it was most likely to be thrown or hit with a club or stick. If, on the other hand, the ball was made up of some form of leather encasing hair, hay or other stuffing, it was more likely to be kicked. When the leather encased an animal bladder it could be inflated and a whole range of new skills introduced. These forms of football were usually associated with some religious, military or fertility rite, as they would be through to the present day. Again, as in the development of the game through to today, most football games were noted for their violence.

The football games of pre-Columbian America, whether of the Aztecs, Mayans or Zapotecs, seem to have been stylized and closely related to religious celebrations. They were supervised by the king or religious leader, the ball courts were close to the temple, and in what were by any standards violent societies the only violence associated with the game itself came when the losers were ritually sacrificed. This was the price of defeat in the Aztec game of *tlachtli*. These games were played with the players using various parts of their body, but not the head or forearm, to knock a solid rubber ball through rings set high in a temple wall. In the cultural holocaust that followed the arrival of Christian civilization, football was one of the many victims. From these games, rubber balls were introduced to Europe.

Further north in the American continent, football was played among the native Inuit and Indian people. In the former case the game was played on snow or ice, and closely resembled soccer. Known as *aqsaqtuk*, the object of the game was to defend one's goal against the opposition, in teams that varied in numbers and playing areas that could vary from hundreds of yards to a few miles. As such *aqsaqtuk* was similar to the familiar village games of Europe, and did indeed pit different Inuit communities against each other. Sometimes, as in the European village game, contests were between teams of married and single men. Women also participated.

When the Pilgrims arrived in the northern Atlantic coast of America in the early seventeenth century, they found the indigenous peoples playing a game of football. If we are to believe Charles C. Willoughby it was one of their favourite pastimes, and William Wood in his *New England Prospect*, published in 1634, described a game that reads something like a caricature of European village football. Certainly it shows that Wood was familiar with football from the land he had left behind. The game, called *pasuckquakkohowog*, was played on the hard sand of the beaches at low tide, usually in summer, with teams made up of large numbers of players who left their weapons on the touchlines. The games were conducted with some violence but not much quarrelling, despite the heavy betting that was placed on their outcome. The Indians of Oklahoma were also said to play a form of football in celebration of gathering in the crop.

In ancient China there was a kicking game known as *tsu chu*. Recorded as far back as 2500 BC, this is generally regarded as the earliest reference to football. During the Han dynasty (206 BC–202 AD) regular games were played to celebrate the Emperor's birthday, but in preparation for the party, training practice also served the more practical purpose of preparing soldiers for battle. In this game players tried to kick a ball through holes in silk curtains, using techniques of shielding with their chests and backs to dribble with the ball that appear to anticipate the modern game. Elsewhere in Asia, in Thailand, an old form of juggling with a ball has survived down to today. In Japan the ancient game of *kemari*, later called *kemari asobi*, involved kicking a ball through bamboo stakes clearly recognizable as goalposts. References to this game go as far back as 600 BC, linked to religious and political practices and carried out under the strict codes of the samurai tradition.

In Europe the ancient Greeks had a ball game called *epyskyros* and the Romans one called *harpastum*, but neither seems to have involved kicking. The most famous of the organized European football games was that played in Florence in the sixteenth century. The Florentine *calcio*, preserved today as a living museum piece, was played by aristocrats according to formal rules, and while it was not without its vigour, victory was less important than the elegance that went with manoeuvring the ball. In Russia a game called *kila* was played with a ball the size of a man's head, made of leather filled with hair, in which teams of eight or nine players tried to force the ball over a line. The game was played in summer and in winter on ice. In France, or at least in Britanny and parts of Normandy and Picardy, the game of *soule* was played through to the nineteenth century. This game was close to hurling, was even played by the aristocracy, and counted Henri II among its aficionados. More commonly it was played village against village, or married men against bachelors. As such it was one variant of folk football, where the pursuit of an object such as an inflated pig's bladder was the excuse for letting off steam as well as breaking a few bones and spilling some blood. The most violent practitioners of this game were noted to be the British, a reputation they and their colonial cousins would retain through the centuries: rugby, Australian Rules and American football are based on controlled violence, while in soccer, the code where bodily contact is least important, charging was a feature of the more physical British game.

A bloody and murdering practice

In the various forms of folk or village football, the game was usually played between two sets of players, often numbering in their hundreds, and the object was to force the ball, by running with it, kicking it, or by any other means, to or through previously agreed upon goals. These could be set as far apart as a mile and so involved dozens of boisterous youths and young men trampling over field and dale, across rivers or marshes, or whatever else stood between them and the goal.

The most famous of these games were those played on Shrove Tuesday, celebrating the period before Lent, or the return of spring. In Ashbourne in Derby and in Lerwick in the Orkneys, the game has survived through to today as an annual event. Christmas, Easter, May Day and other Holy Days and occasions on which festivals were held usually included football. They also had their origins in more secular rites relating to the sun and fertility, be it of field or body – some games were played between spinsters (or virgins/maids) and married women, with the married women ritually winning, or between married men and bachelors.

The violence of the British was regarded as one of their peculiar quirks as early as the seventeenth century. In 1698 the French visitor, Misson, was struck by the decorum of English football, which he described as 'a charming and useful winter exercise'. What he saw were youths juggling with a ball 'big as a head and filled with wind', so perhaps what he saw were lads practising for more serious encounters to come. Two Swiss visitors who recorded their impressions a short time after the visit of M. Misson were less impressed. They deplored the game for the damage it caused to the windows of shops and even carriages, and denounced it for the great inconvenience it caused pedestrians who risked being bowled over by the participants. Earlier in the seventeenth century, William Davenant, in his fictional *Entertainment at Rutland House* (1634), saw some benefits in this boisterousness: he had a Frenchman refer to its inconveniences for pedestrians, but attributed the courage of the Englishman to it.

By this time travellers' reports and translations from the Italian of how it was played had made the Florentine game of *calcio* well known in England. It had a long history, and in 1530 a game was played while the troops of Charles V laid siege to the city, the aristocratic youths who took part in it more concerned about dodging opponents than the missiles being lobbed over the walls. Described as good for youth to 'run, leap and wrestle', Boccalini (1612: English translation by the Earl of Monmouth, 1656) also recommended it as a political safety valve. The one Englishman who appreciated its qualities was the schoolmaster Richard Mulcaster.

Mulcaster's *Positions* of 1581 was a treatise on education which dealt at length with the advantages and even necessity of physical education for schoolboys (and girls). It was so advanced that it earned him anonymity in his own time and renown three centuries later. He believed that riding and vigorous walking, and certainly not nature alone, could take care of health, and argued that those whose occupations led to 'stillness more than ordinary' had need of 'stirring more than ordinary'. Mulcaster saw in football one means of achieving this stirring and so strengthening the limbs and aiding the better functioning of the body's organs. His readers, or those who got through his stodgy prose, were no more ready to accept Renaissance ideals of body and soul 'fined to the best' than they were earlier Greek and Roman ideals of the 'healthy mind in the healthy body'. Other views he extolled were similarly ignored: among these were his suggestions that football be played with less emphasis on the physical, and that some of the finer points of the game be encouraged by the appointment of a 'trayning maister'. Such views smacked of continental effeteness, while his suggestion that football be organized into teams with a referee ('indifferent person') fell on barren ground in a society still more aristocratic than middle-class.

The uncontrolled violence of football was not looked on with kindly light by the authorities, the moralists or the men of property, and much of the early history of football is written from the condemnation of its enemies and their attempts to suppress it. Firmly in this category was Thomas Elyot, who in 1531 pleaded that 'Footeballe, wherein is nothinge but beastlie furie and extreme violence . . . be put in perpetuall silence'. At Oxford fifty years later ministers and ordinary scholars were threatened with serious punishment if they brought discredit to the university and their vocation through 'plainge at football and maintaining of quarrelles'. A major complaint then that was barely to change over the centuries was that football was played by the common people. A chronicler in the reign of Henry VI, towards the end of the fifteenth century, referred to the 'foot-ball-game' which he found 'abominable enough, and, on my judgment at least, more common, undignified, and worthless than any other kind of game, rarely ending but with some loss, accident or disadvantage to the players themselves.'

The state saw little to recommend in a game that had no military purpose, and which, moreover, had great potential to disrupt law and order. Edward II of England, before leaving for a famous defeat in Scotland in 1314, sought to maintain peace at home by proclaiming that since there had been 'great uproar in the City, through certain tumults arising from great footballs in the fields of the public, from which many evils perchance may arise . . .' that such games cease forthwith upon pain of imprisonment. His successor, in 1349 and again in 1365, specifically banned football along with a host of other 'dishonest and unthrifty or idle games' which interfered with the proper practice of archery, pellets and bolts. In 1388 Richard II banned tennis and other 'importune games' along with football, and Henry IV at the start of the new century tried to enforce similar acts. It seems clear that not only was football played regularly, but it did so in defiance of the authorities who were powerless to squash its popularity. For an England at war with France, concern for archery was understandable, and in France Philippe V and Charles V passed similar legislation, but there is at least one recorded instance of a champion archer who was also a champion footballer.

The monarchs of Scotland were equally zealous in trying to crush the game, and throughout the fifteenth century James I and his successors passed laws against football and golf. He himself, in the poem often attributed to him, 'Christ's Kirk on the Green', referred sadly to the popularity of the game, and in the first parliament at Perth in 1424 passed an act declaring 'That na man play at the fute-ball.' In 1457 James II, and in 1471 James III, decreed that there be reviews of weaponry four times each year, with golf as well as football 'utterly cryed down and not to be used.' James IV prohibited golf and football and 'other sik unprofitable sportes', which did not stop him, so the story goes, playing the game in disguise, while James V included a football among his expenses. Little wonder then that the attempts to suppress the game were unsuccessful. The City of Glasgow was paying twelve shillings out of the civil purse to buy 'futt balls' for the 'Fastern's E'en' ' (Shrove Tuesday) revelry, and six footballs were supplied in this way until 1590 when such expenses were given over to private initiative. When some of the military heat was removed from Scotland with the accession to the throne of the new United Kingdom by James VI of Scotland (and I of England) in 1603, the new monarch showed a favour to sports notably lacking until then. He was partly motivated in this by his dislike of Protestant practices, rigid in his homeland, but well established in England, albeit in gentler guise, under Elizabeth, another monarch who, like her father and others before, had tried to tell the tide of football to turn back.

In 1618 James issued his famous *Book of Sports*, in which he specifically authorized the playing of sport on Sunday after the completion of devotions. He praised it for keeping the 'meaner sort of people . . . more able for war', and offering an alternative to ale houses and other centres for sedition or dissipation. Moreover, he pointed out with an insight denied more narrow-minded prelates, that it was unwise for religion to set itself up as the enemy of the people's pleasures. Football he did not particularly like, and banned his son from playing it. Charles I reissued James's decrees on sport, and when the Puritans were removed from government with the Restoration, Charles II, it is said, actually bestowed his presence on a game between his servants and those of the Duke of Albemarle, in 1681.

Football had still not achieved social acceptance, however, and royal patronage would come later than it did to other sports. In March 1886 the Prince of Wales, later King Edward VII, attended a charity festival which included a football match at Kennington Oval played between Gentlemen and Players, and in 1894 he became patron of the FA. It was not until well into the twentieth century, however, that a reigning monarch deigned to appear at a football match. This was for the FA Cup Final of 1914, played between Burnley and Liverpool. The game was by then the passion of the people, and the year in which the Cup was played before George V was that in which the subjects of His Britannic Majesty were needed for what was to become the slaughter of the First World War.

In Ireland the first mention of football came with the Statutes of Galway in 1527, when parliamentary decree banned hurling and any other ball game that interfered with archery, with the exception of 'football with the grate ball.' Thereafter references to football came mainly in the literary works of poets like MacCurta in the seventeenth century and Concanen and Redmond Murphy in the eighteenth. Wrestling the man with the ball (and without the ball) was an important part of the game, which was usually played in winter when there were no crops to be ruined. Before the disastrous famine of the mid-nineteenth century two distinct types of football had developed, one restricted to a field and the other rambling all over the countryside.

Primitive football as described by its opponents makes fearsome reading today. The notorious Philip Stubbes seemed to relish his descriptions of the game which caused broken necks, legs and backs, noses that 'gush out with blood' and eyes that at times 'start out.' In earlier days players were killed by falling on each others' daggers or swords, and there has never been a period when a death of some sort or other was not attributed to football. Judgements on the game, of course, were left to the literate, but it has always had its supporters as well as its detractors among the class generally called 'respectable'. Richard Mulcaster, in his advocacy of football as a healthy pastime, defended it against accusations of violence and anarchy by claiming, and so testifying to its great popularity, that it could not have grown to the greatness it had if it had not been a great help to health and strength. Whatever the balance between improved health and broken limbs and lives, however, football posed other problems.

The laws of God and property

In the days before the Calvinists of Puritan or Presbyterian flavour took over, football was often played on Sundays and Holy Days, these being the only days of rest. The rulers of God's servants had doubts about the merits of football. As early as 1364 the Synod of Ely forbade the clergy to play games, and in 1519 a curate was expelled from his vocation for an unwarranted enthusiasm for football: it seems that the said curate of the church of St Mary in Hawridge was so keen to play football that he often rushed through his devotions in order to get on with the game. David Lyndsay of the Mount, writing with the popular democratic sympathies peculiar to Scottish poets of the royal court, described in *Ane Satyre of the Thrie Estatis*, first performed in 1540, a priest who was addicted to football, and of his romantic hero squire Meldrum he boasts:

> 'He wan the pryse abune thame all,
> Baith at the buttis (archery) and the futeball.'

For those with moral messages about God and football the evidence was there to use as you chose: one man caught in a fire was the only one to be consumed by the flames, unable to escape like the others because he was suffering from an injury sustained playing football; then again there is the case in 1722 of a church hit by a hurricane on the Sabbath, bringing down the steeple, and which might have had dreadful consequences for the worshippers, except that they were all outside having a game of football.

Sabbath breaking and pleasure were two of the great moral evils against which the Puritans set their righteous zeal, and it was in this regard that Philip Stubbes, player in his younger days but grown wiser with age, delivered the most savage attack of all times on football. This was in *The Anatomie of Abuses* of 1583, where he placed football with the reading of 'mery bookes' as drawing people away from 'godliness and vertue' and leading to 'wikednes and sin.' Football he specifically denounced as a 'freendly kinde of fighte', and far from being a recreation or a 'felowly sporte or pastime' he castigated it as a 'bloody and murthering practice', out of which grew 'envie, malice, rancour, cholor, hatred, displeasure, enmitie, and what not else: and sometimes fighting, brawling, contention, quarrel picking, murther, homicide, and a great effusion of blood, as experience dayly teacheth.' Clearly not a game for the Sabbath . . . or perhaps any other day. But the Puritans, however powerful, were never more than a minority, and their attempts to extirpate popery by the reduction of superstition and elimination of saints days meant a decrease in the number of days given over to leisure. It was for this, rather than their attacks on popery, that made them unpopular, particularly when the sabbath, the one day of rest, was deemed to be a day devoted to God.

It would appear that even in Scotland strictures against sabbath breaking were not always taken too seriously. In 1656 the Scottish Parliament was still trying to beat the sabbath-breakers by passing a law for the 'better observance of the Lord's Day' and forbidding all boisterous games. Sometimes the English were blamed as being a bad influence in this regard, but it was in Scotland that a more subtle approach to tackling the evil could be detected, at least in the case of the Rev. Michael Potter. In 1700, on seeing that a match was about to take place on the sabbath, the reverend asked to join the players and then, the players no doubt still stunned at the request, was allowed to precede the game with a prayer. In the manner of Scottish ministers he then prayed on until everyone had gone home.

Property owners had more practical reasons to dislike the practice, and took measures to protect their shops, houses, gardens or whatever else found itself in the path of the bladder being pursued by panting masses. From about the middle of the eighteenth century the growth in the middle classes could be measured in some degree by the increasing sensitivities of those inconvenienced by football and other vigorous pastimes. There was an increase in the number of complaints about the loss of trade to add to the more usual concerns about the threat to property. Football played in an agrarian society was an irregular affair, and its violence could be tolerated by its infrequency, and as a necessary safety valve. Towns were growing significantly in this time, and the perennial complaints by pedestrians were occasionally met by laws that helped push the game out of the streets and into the countryside.

In the countryside the enclosure movement threatened traditional areas where football was played, but the threat was not accepted passively. In May 1647 the Dorset Standing Committee warned of sedition being planned under the guise of 'football matches and cudgel playing and the like.' In the border country a football match was often the preliminary to a raid. More practically, football could be used to interfere with the advance of capitalism. In 1638 protesters against draining ditches at the Isle of Ely did so by arranging a football match of several hundred men. Gathered for the kick-off they then set about destroying the ditches. In 1699 a notice advertising a football match was seen by the authorities, already plagued by the disruption of their work, as a further attempt at destruction 'under Colour and pretence of Foot Ball Playing.' Protest against the enclosing of Holland Fen in Lincolnshire in 1768 was done by using football as a cover to tear down the offending hindrances, and in the riot that ensued women were taken prisoner along with the men. In July 1765 the *Northampton Mercury*, presumably in innocence, advertised a game at West Haddon and in its next number had to report how the 'tumultuous Mob' who gathered for that game caused considerable damage, including the 'Fences designed for the Inclosure of that Field.' Football was also used in the food riots that were an endemic problem in the eighteenth century, being able to call on, as it did, hundreds of able bodied men.

The broad popular appeal of football did not mean that it was the pastime of the poor alone. French kings played *soule*, and while James VI and Charles II had about them the taint of popery, there was good sense in a *Book of Sports* that not only pointed to the usefulness of games in military preparation (making 'bodies more able for war') and as a safety valve (preventing idleness, drunkenness and 'discontented speech'), but pointed to the poor tactics of trying to convert catholics with a religion that denied 'honest mirth'. In 1621 Robert Burton's much reprinted *Anatomy of Melancholy* supported the leisure pursuits of the common people. He criticised the government's opposition to the people's pleasures and recommended that they be 'winked at', as there were worse evils into which they might fall. And even among the Puritans, Oliver Cromwell was a footballer of note in his days as a student at Sidney Sussex College, Cambridge. He is even said to have admitted that he was more afraid of being tripped by John Wheelwright, a fellow undergraduate and later clergyman in the colonies, than of 'meeting an army in the field.'

Another fervent admirer of the game with impeccable social pretensions was Walter Scott, who not only sang its praises in verse, but according to his biographer and son-in-law, Lockhart, would sooner have seen his son 'carry the banner of Bellenden gallantly at a football match in Carterhaugh, than he would have heard that the boy had attained the highest honours of the first university in Europe.' The match at Carterhaugh in the border country, played before 2000 spectators on 5 December 1815, between Scott's team distinguished by a 'slip of fir' and that of the earl of Home wearing a 'sprig of heather', is one of the most famous ever recorded. Before it began spectators were handed out broadsheets containing poems by James Hogg, the Ettrick Shepherd, and Scott himself, the latter providing for sports journalists writing later in the century the lines to head their column:

> Then strip lads, and to it, though sharp be the weather,
> And if, by mischance, you should happen to fall,
> There are worse things in life than a tumble on heather,
> And life is itself but a game at football

In France, it would appear, football was still popular with the men of God: even at the height of the Terror in the French Revolution. One of Hubert Robert's paintings depicts a scene in the Saint Lazaire prison, in 1794, where several inmates are playing a game of football watched by about 200 spectators. It was noted that the artist, who was himself a prisoner, frequently joined in the games.

The civilizing process

By the beginning of the nineteenth century Blake's 'green and pleasant land' was being scarred by the 'dark satanic mills' of early capitalism. Village football was one of its minor victims, and the resistance of footballers to its interference in their pleasures was a mere hindrance as capitalism continued on its inexorable way. The state might be able to re-order the holidays in the Christian calendar, but it could not re-order the seasons: capitalism could. With the coming of industrialization football became an essentially urban game, and the passions that had always ruled it were controlled by a new time and work discipline. When the game came under the rule of law after 1863 it was men of property who used it to their own political advantage. Then, along with the moralists and the state, instead of condemning the people's game, they channelled it to their own advantage by using it to inculcate moral values that justified the right of those in power to stay there.

Writing in 1801, Joseph Strutt, in his *Sports and Pastimes of the People of England*, declared in regard to football that: 'The game was formerly much in vogue among the common people, though of late years it seems to have fallen into disrepute and is but little practised.' Other writers in the early nineteenth century, particularly William Hone writing between 1838 and 1842, commented on the decline of football. These comments have at times been taken as the starting point for the assertion that in the first half of the nineteenth century football as a popular pastime died out, and was saved only by the public schools. Somehow this seems unlikely.

Morris Marples has shown that despite what Magoun claimed about football having lost its popularity with the Puritans, this was far from the case for the eighteenth century. Later researchers like Brailsford and Malcolmson have shown how football was as popular as ever then. They show that football had become more generally accepted, and the less frequent references to it were simply because it was less controversial. Throughout the eighteenth century the game was becoming better organized, with matches representing different parishes, villages, towns and even counties. Challenges were issued, games were advertised in the press (and not just as an excuse for riot), and the game described by Strutt, in the size of the field, the number of players and the placement of the goals, is remarkably similar to the modern game. The folk game still prospered, an occasion for young men to display their masculinity, a means of expressing communal solidarity, an excuse to settle old debts (tradition covering a multitude of what would otherwise be deemed crimes), and an event to be remembered until the following year. One story recalled by Malcolmson would concede nothing to today's fans discussing the intricacies of the previous Saturday's game. In this case the witness describing the match fifty years after the event 'seemed to remember every close and field that the ball went into, and various feats of skill and activity, disasters and hurts that occurred.' The match had been played at the turn of the century.

Marples, in his chapter on 'The decline of mass football', suggests that football entered a sort of sporting Dark Age with the decline in folk football at the start of the Victorian age. Malcomson in turn accepts that popular recreations were being undermined with the breakdown of traditional society, and cites the second quarter of the nineteenth century as the low point of recreational life. He quotes sources pointing to the decline of football, but does not accept that the game was dying out. Indeed he gives many examples of where the opposite seems to be the case: as late as 1840, 1857, 1864 and 1867 various towns in Surrey were still trying to stamp out street football, and in the story of a conflict between Sunday School and football in the mid-1840s it seems that football was still holding its own. In this case a concerned minister confided to his diary how his initial success (after 1826) in winning boys and young men away from idle pursuits was under threat from those under his charge who arrived late because they had been playing football: with their thoughts fixed on how long it would be before they got back to the game, they could barely concentrate on Christ and his good works.

Where the sources and the social realities are in closer agreement is that the face of Great Britain was being radically changed in the first decades of the nineteenth century. The desolation wrought by the early stages of the industrial revolution was dramatic, and the cramped conditions, long hours and debilitating work did not leave much time for leisure pursuits. But the moral face of Britain was also undergoing a face-lift. The new policing system introduced by Robert Peel helped bring order to the streets of the rapidly expanding towns, and the Highway Act of 1834 finally made street football a criminal act. The Royal Society for the Prevention of Cruelty to Animals was formed in 1824, the Temperance Movement was founded five years later, and in 1831 the Lord's Day Observance Society was established. The reforming zeal of goodly citizens that helped wipe out blood sports was also directed against the more brutal aspects of football, as well as the drinking and gambling that often accompanied it. Many of the new middle-classes played football, and for those who wanted to pursue their new professions and continue to play football at the same time it was necessary to create a more civilized game: one that eliminated its worst excesses and allowed them a better chance to play it without having to appear before their clients with a black eye or a broken arm. But while they might have reshaped the game, they did not re-invent it.

The first element in civilizing the game was in codifying it, and this stemmed directly from the public schools. In the second half of the eighteenth century football in many forms was played at public schools, but it was a sport low in the hierarchy of pastimes, and was left for the boys themselves to organize. The middle-class teachers in these schools were faced by boys who considered themselves aristocratic, and the insolence of youth and social class led to frequent disruptions: at Rugby in 1797 it needed the army to quell a riot, and at Winchester in 1818 the military with fixed bayonets was called in.

Such a situation could not go on for ever, and as more middle-class boys filled the classrooms, systems of discipline were introduced, while sport was used to encourage notions of teamwork and discipline. The masters played a major role in this development, which also allowed them to establish a more favourable rapport with the boys. When Tom Hughes wrote *Tom Brown's Schooldays* in 1857 he was describing Rugby School as he liked to remember it in the 1830s. The influence of this glorification of sport for building manly character on future educators was immense. The primacy of games set the education of middle-class British boys apart from their German or French equivalents, where in the one case gymnastics took pride of place and in the other games were despised. When the Baron de Coubertin set about trying to rouse his fellow Frenchmen from the sloth which he believed had accounted for the disasters of the Franco-Prussian war, no influence was more profound than his adolescent admiration for the English public schools and their games.

Football was well established in the public schools by the middle of the century, but none of them played against each other; as a result each had developed its own rules. These were generally governed by the conditions under which the game was played, whether it was in cloisters or in fields, on grass or on hard surfaces. Between the extremes of Eton on the one hand, where handling was not allowed and the ball was kicked through a goal, and Rugby on the other, where running with the ball was allowed, as well as hacking and 'throttling', and where the ball had to be kicked over a crossbar to score a goal, there were many varieties. At Winchester there were no goals at all, and points were awarded when the ball was kicked over the goal-line; at Charterhouse no handling was allowed; teams were kept to twenty a side and the main feature of the game was dribbling the ball on the stone surface of the cloisters.

The first combined rules were drawn up by Old Salopians and Old Etonians in 1846, but Harrow seems to have been one of the main forces in shaping the rules of what became the association game. As early as 1814 they played a game with eleven a side, 'bases' that resembled goals, and a minimum of handling. Many Old Harrovians went to Cambridge, and it was there in 1848 that another set of rules was drawn up. They have not survived, although they are generally recognized as being close to those known as the Cambridge Rules and published in 1863. In 1862 J.C. Thring, one of the architects of the 1846 rules, drew up the rules of what he called 'the simplest game.' Letters to the editors and articles in sporting newspapers discussed the merits of the various proposals.

It was amidst this fervour for rule-making and attempts to standardize them that Ebenezer Cobb Morley called a meeting of representatives from clubs in the London area for the purpose of 'forming an Association with the object of establishing a definite code of rules for the regulation of the game.' The meeting, held in the Freemason's Tavern in London's Great Queen Street on 26 October 1863, was to be a historic occasion, for it was here that the Football Association was founded, to do for sport what the British parliament did for democracy. Morley was not himself a public school boy, but there were many old boys among the dozen London clubs represented at the six meetings that gave birth to the laws of the Football Association. The public schools themselves were not represented, as they wanted to preserve their independence and their own rules. Charterhouse, however, sent an observer. Dissenting from the decisions of the new body was the Blackheath club (mainly old boys from Rugby), whose departure at the final meeting was to prove to be so significant in the code of football founded eight years later.

At the first meeting the Association was formed with each of the representatives paying one guinea to be members, and over six meetings that lasted into December, Morley's draft rules were discussed and eventually agreed upon. No sooner was this done than it was arranged to have them printed in a booklet by John Lillywhite, who was given the sole copyright and right to sell them, at 1/- and 1/6. Commerce and privileged access, it would seem, were there at the birth. So too was the urge to get on with the game, and rather than wait for the match planned for early in the new year, Barnes, the team founded by Morley, and Richmond met each other at Barnes on 19 December 1863. The game ended in a 0–0 draw. There were few people to see that first game, which was nevertheless given a small notice in *The Field*. Morley himself was appointed the first secretary of the Football Association (1863–1866) and second president (1867 to 1874). He lived to see an estimated 200,000 spectators gate-crash the first Wembley Cup Final in 1923, and died the following year, aged 93.

At the time of its founding the Football Association (FA) was just one of many associations playing by their own rules. A dribbling code of football was particularly popular in Sheffield, where the first football club north of London was founded in 1857. Like Harrow and Cambridge, the Sheffield club banned hacking and running with the ball, but allowed limited handling. The Forest club, which played on the edge of Epping Forest, was founded in 1859 and composed mainly of Harrow old boys. It was the first club to devote itself exclusively to the dribbling game, and when it was disbanded in 1864 it reformed as Wanderers Football Club, the most famous in the early years of the FA. Notts County also played a dribbling game. Founded in 1862, they can claim to be the oldest soccer team still playing in major competition.

The main rival to the rules of the London FA were the Sheffield rules; despite their differences representative games between London and

Sheffield were played in 1866 and annually from 1871. When the two came to a compromise agreement in 1877, the London FA stood as virtually the sole authority for the game in England, as an increasing number of local associations affiliated to it. In 1867 the FA had a mere ten members; four years later this had risen to 50. The 1000 mark was reached in 1888, 10,000 in 1905. In 1880 the FA took up residence in its first permanent office, and six years later employed its first salaried secretary. By then the London FA had dropped its regional qualifier. Known thereafter as the Football Association, it was the ruling body of football in the land, eventually throughout the world. The acronym FA became a recognized symbol to millions regardless of the language they spoke.

The new rules and competitions

In the initial discussions over the rules the main disputes were over running with the ball and hacking/kicking. The 'dribblers' carried the day by a large majority, and when hacking was banned the representatives of Blackheath went off breathing scorn at such an unmanly game. But when those who had so vigorously championed the right to hack and carry the ball formed their own rugby code in 1871, they did not allow the hacking whose removal they had dismissed as a pansy reform in 1863. The first rules of association football allowed handling (the 'fair catch') under certain conditions, but no throwing of the ball or running with it; in 1866 handling was forbidden altogether, but in 1871 this privilege was reserved for the 'eleventh' man on the team, and only in his own half of the field (later restricted to the penalty area).

This 'eleventh' man became the goalkeeper, and attitudes to him were perhaps the greatest single source of conflict when British teams played continental teams in the twentieth century. British players would happily try to bundle goalkeeper and ball into the net to score in what was deemed a perfectly legitimate way; on the continent the goalkeeper was considered sacrosanct, permitted to flounce and flaunt with the ball without a forward being allowed as much as to breathe on him. In the 1870s it was considered a popular skill in football to floor the goalkeeper *before* he touched the ball, but this was changed in the 1890s so that he could be charged only when in possession of the ball and with both feet on the ground. Such mollycoddling was commented on sadly by William Pickford in 1906. He recognized that some change in the rule was necessary, particularly since a goalkeeper had actually been killed by charging, but he still thought that the FA 'went just a little too far at the moment' in protecting him.

If attitudes to the goalkeeper introduced a culture clash between Britain and the continent, the off-side rule introduced a bone of contention from the start and in all countries where the game was played. In the original rules any player was deemed off-side who received the ball from behind, thus striking at the 'loathsome' practice of 'sneaking', 'loafing' or 'loitering' near the opponent's goal. The Sheffield association had a liberal off-side law, with only one opponent in front of the man receiving the ball from behind needed to play him on-side. In 1866 the FA weakened on this law by allowing a player to be on-side if he had three of the opposing team nearer their own goal line. This left the way open for future conciliation of the Sheffield association. When they played each other it was with local agreement on their differences regarding the off-side rule, but in 1877 the Sheffield association gave in.

This might have allowed the two major associations to come to an agreement, but the problem of the off-side law is one that has remained with the game ever since. The major problem in off-side is one of vision and perspective: how to tell whether or not the attacking player receiving the ball from behind is in line or not with an opposing defender, or, what is even more difficult to determine, whether a player in an off-side position, but not receiving the ball, is interfering with play.

The FA compromise remained unchanged until 1925, when the number of players between receiver and the goal was reduced from three to two. Further changes in the off-side law have been suggested, even abolishing it altogether, but this would be to change the nature of the game entirely. There is nothing wrong with the law itself. The problem is purely one of perspective, and for this reason, today as much as in the 1870s, the off-side rule is guaranteed to be the most controversial of the referee's decisions.

The method of scoring by kicking *under* a certain height, first a tape and then a crossbar (1875) determined the peculiar nature of scoring in soccer. The size of the goal was set at a mere eight feet high by eight yards wide, and this, with the particular privileges given a goalkeeper to handle the ball within a certain area around his goal, made scoring difficult. This is another of the distinctive features of soccer, and has contributed to the low-scoring nature of the game. But there are few spectacles more thrilling than that of a goalkeeper repelling every shot that is fired at him, with the ball occasionally bouncing from posts or crossbar. For those not brought up with the game, the excitement not only of draws, but non-goal scoring draws, is somewhat baffling. However, it is not the low scoring that is the problem; rather it is the way it encourages defensive play. Soccer is the only football code in which a team can play a purely defensive game and hold out for a draw or a win from a goal on the break.

In the soccer of the 1860s off-side was no problem as players tended to rush or dribble in one great pack towards the goal, the forward pass never used. Then the Scots developed the passing game, with players in fixed positions and dribbling reduced. The ball was then doing more work than the players, and teamwork rather than individual displays took over. At the same time the game became less rough. It also became more defensive, as forwards were reduced to five or six, while two full-backs played behind three or four half-backs. Instead of direct attacks on goal, play was built up more slowly; the forward pass became an essential skill, the wings were used more frequently and wingers developed the skill of crossing the ball into the middle for a better placed forward, in preference to making a bee-line for the goal to score themselves.

One of the great oddities of soccer to outsiders is 'heading' the ball, and even in the early days this was seen as something of an anomaly. Writing in the 1880s, Montague Shearman could admire the skill involved, but still thought it 'savours more of clowning than of manly play, and many would be glad to see some limit placed upon the exercise.' In fact it became one of the game's great attractions, and a skill brought to a particular pitch by British players.

When Shearman was writing the game was still controlled by a referee and two umpires, picked from either team. If the two umpires agreed on an offence the referee blew his whistle or raised his flag; if one umpire signalled an offence and the referee agreed he brought the game to a halt, otherwise the umpire calling for an offence was left to wave his flag in vain. This was no doubt an improvement on the days when the players themselves, as in park games throughout the world today, decided when an offence was committed, but was hardly suited for the professional game. In 1891 the referee became the sole judge, with neutral linesmen to assist by calling the ball in or out of play, waving for off-side, and occasionally consulted for their view on a difficult decision.

Various refinements would be introduced over the years, in regard to the throw-in, free kicks, penalty kicks, the corner kick, the off-side rule and the role of referees as noted above, and the tactics of the game would change dramatically. But the rules drawn up by that group of men in the decade or so after 1863 are essentially those of the game that is played and watched by tens of millions of people in virtually every country in the world today.

Competition

The games played under the auspices of the FA over the first few years were somewhat desultory affairs, but in 1871 this changed with the introduction of the Challenge Cup, a knock out competition of all the teams in the FA leading to a Cup Final when all but two teams had been eliminated. Not only did this establish the authority of the FA throughout England, it gave birth to the most famous competition in the history of sport, imitated in most lands where soccer was taken up.

The man behind the Cup was one of the great pioneers of the game, Charles William Alcock. Born in Sunderland in 1842, he left the Wear to go to Harrow, and after graduating in 1859 was, with his brother J.F. and other Old Harrovians, behind the founding of one of the first football clubs devoted entirely to dribbling, the Forest Football Club. When they folded in 1864 he founded and largely ran the Wanderers, the most famous team of the early years, made up of university and former public school men.

Alcock was behind the first 'international' in 1870, and from 1869 published the *Football Annual*. Thereafter he wrote widely about the game. As a cricket enthusiast as well as a football fanatic, he reflected the social class of the pioneers, and as a player he was behind the introduction to England of the passing game (as opposed to the mad rush game). He captained the England team in 1875. But it was the introduction of the Cup that was his greatest creation and contribution to the game.

Fifteen teams competed for the first competition, held in season 1871–72 for a trophy valued at £20. It was won by the Wanderers, with Alcock as their captain, and they would dominate the other old boy clubs who were their main competitors in the early years. Until 1885 crowds for the final never reached 10,000, but even before then the romance of the competition had begun to flower. Part of this is in the nature of soccer, where a resolute and inspired team of 'rabbits' can upset much more powerful opponents having an off day. It is also in the nature of the competition, with its sudden death encounters and the luck of the draw for the home fixture: only the final and semi-final are played on neutral grounds. The day of glory for the 'rabbits' seldom goes beyond that one day, but some have come close to the ultimate prize of the final in London. Today that prize, contested at Wembley, has achieved an almost religious aura which surrounds few other sporting events.

Conquering the UK

The FA Cup was open to any member club, and this included teams from Scotland. Queen's Park twice appeared in the final, in 1884 when they were beaten 2–1 by Blackburn Rovers, mainly through different interpretations of the rules as played in Scotland and England, and the following year when they were convincingly beaten 2–0 by the same team. Glasgow Rangers reached the semi-final in 1886, where they were beaten 3–1 by Aston Villa, and the following year the Scottish Football Association (SFA) banned Scottish teams from taking part in foreign competitions.

Unlike England, where the Cup Final became the main event of the year, in Scotland national attention focused on the annual encounter with

England. The first international football match was held in 1870, when two teams, one calling itself England and the other calling itself Scotland, played in London. That was an unofficial match, and the Scottish team was made up of players some of whose claims to Scottish allegiance were as slight as the spelling of their name. Several such games were played before the first official match between the two countries in 1872. Since then these games were played every year (barring war) until 1990, the longest surviving annual international in the history of sport.

In Scotland, where football had been played as vigorously and condemned as fulsomely as in England, the same opposition between dribblers and carriers was evident, with the carrying game more popular. When its first official club, Queen's Park, was formed in 1867, they were prepared to play a bit of both, but when they applied to join the FA in 1870 they had to give up any connection with the game that would be known as rugby. They donated one guinea towards the purchase of the FA Challenge Cup, at a time when their own annual income was scarcely much more than that, and in the first competition, having graciously been exempted from previous rounds, they drew with Wanderers in the semi-final. Unfortunately, they had to withdraw as they could not afford to stay on for a replay. Wanderers went on to win the first final. Queen's Park dominated Scottish football until the advent of professionalism, and it was the gentlemen amateurs of Queen's Park who were behind the founding of the Scottish Football Association in 1873. It was also their players who comprised the entire Scottish team that faced up to the English opposition in the first official international.

The game, played before 4000 spectators at the West of Scotland Cricket ground in Glasgow on 30 November 1872, ended in a scoreless draw, but *Bell's Life in London* enthused about the 'splendid display of football in the really scientific sense of the word.' The success of Scotland in this game was the major impulsion towards the formation of a separate Scottish Football Association the following March. In that same year, 1873, it inaugurated its own SFA Cup competition. In terms of 'scientific' football the Scots would dominate for years to come.

The role of Scotland in the establishing, but more particularly in the promotion, of association football was paramount. Scots were present at the founding of the FA, and later in the foundation of the Football League; knock-out competitions and leagues would become inevitably associated with the growth of soccer wherever it was played. In the promotion of the game abroad Scots were present in numbers out of proportion to their population. Above all, and to the chagrin of Scots for well over a hundred years, they have provided an inexhaustible reservoir of football talent for English clubs.

Ireland and Wales, by virtue of their much smaller populations, but also by the quirk of fate that saw the workers in these countries take an unusual interest in Rugby Union, have been left in the shadow of England and Scotland. The Welsh FA was founded in 1876, following the first international match, when a Welsh team was defeated 4–0 before 17,000 spectators in Glasgow. The first Welsh Cup was won by Wrexham, formed in 1873 and the longest surviving of the teams still in major competition. They beat Druids 1–0 in that first Cup Final in 1878. A Welsh league was founded in 1890, but until recently it never became professional. Football in Wales grew mainly in the north, but in 1893 a South Wales and Monmouthshire FA was founded. Despite the prodigies of William Meredith, an all-time great who played between 1893 and 1924, retiring when he had almost reached his fiftieth birthday, football as a national game was slow in coming. This changed after 1910, when E. Robbins became secretary of the Welsh FA, and between the two world wars Wales, who had been able to record regular victories only against Ireland, had many successes in the home internationals.

Wales has suffered from the dominance of England, and the best Welsh teams have competed in the English competitions, with moderate success in the English League from the 1920s, but special joy came in the FA Cup in 1927 when Cardiff City beat Arsenal 1–0 to take it outside England for the only time in its existence. The Welsh national team, at the World Cup in 1958 and especially in recent years, has performed minor miracles against stronger opposition, but Welsh nationalists seeking solace against the numerical superiority of their overweening neighbour, at least until recent years, have had to turn to rugby.

The Irish FA was founded in 1880, at a time when rugby was the most popular football game: indeed the first official Association game was not played there until 1878, when Queen's Park and Glasgow Caledonian FC came over from Scotland to play an exhibition game. Shortly after this the newly formed Ulster FC played Lenzie FC, another visitor from Scotland, and in 1880 the Irish FA Cup was introduced. The first club was Cliftonville, formed in 1879, but throughout the 1880s Scottish clubs and Scottish players dominated Irish football. The first League was formed in 1890–91, and Linfield, founded in 1886, set up a fierce local derby with Glentoran. In 1891, however, Belfast Celtic were founded in conscious imitation of their Glasgow counterparts, and politics inevitably entered into the game: Linfield and Belfast Celtic became the sounding boards for the two warring religious communities at the same time as they became the strongest clubs in the competition.

Politics equally inevitably affected the game at the official level, and in 1921 the Dublin-based FA of Ireland broke away to form its own administration, taking some catholic Ulster clubs with it. In 1923 the Dublin-based FA of Ireland was formally recognized and the Belfast-based

IFA continued to control football in Northern Ireland. Ulster had always been the stronghold of football in Ireland, but its successes on the international scene, none against 'foreign' opposition before 1951, were minimal. In 1958, however, and again in 1982, Northern Ireland did well in the World Cup. In George Best it produced one of the great ball players of all time.

Although Eire was spiritually committed to the Gaelic game of football, the English-tainted association game thrived, and in 1949 Eire inflicted the first defeat at home on England by a foreign team, when they won 0–2 at Goodison Park, Liverpool. Since most of the Eire team were playing for teams in the English league this is not usually considered as a defeat by a foreign team. That would have to wait another few years. In recent times changes in the rules regarding nationality, and the bold move of adopting arch-Englishman Jackie Charlton as coach and honorary Irishman, have seen a Republic of Ireland team of many colours and accents, but with a catholic faith at its core, achieve some astonishing successes.

From 1883–84 until recent years these four countries, (but not Eire) each independent and run by their own association, competed in what was known as the Home International competition, the oldest international competition in the history of sport. Each year the four nations of the United Kingdom played each other once on a league basis, alternating home and away fixtures. The independence of each of the countries comprising the United Kingdom has caused great confusion among non-soccer specialists from abroad writing about the game. But it has raised even greater difficulties for the international administrators of the game who, once they have accepted that the FA is only one of four members of the home countries of the United Kingdom, then raise the legitimate grievance that a single political authority should be represented by only one football team. They are correct in claiming that the United Kingdom is a single political unity, and therefore should be represented by only one association; but even in these days when commercialism and the rigid realism that go with it rule the roost, the historic origins and contributions of the four British associations have seen a victory of romance and tradition over cold-hearted logic.

Another historical legacy of the British ascendancy, and one that comes under even more severe criticism, is the role of the International Board, the guardian of the rules of the game. In 1882 it was proposed by the FA that the four national associations of the United Kingdom form a Board to bring uniformity to the rules as played by the four associations. Scotland, proud of its independence, was at first unwilling to take part, but the threat of games with England being cut off helped to change their mind. As a result the International Football Association Board came into being, made up of two representatives of each of the four home countries, to control the rules of the game. In 1882 Britain was virtually the only country playing the game, but even when international control of the game passed to FIFA, a body to which the four British associations were only intermittently members, it was the British International Board that ruled over the laws of the game. The only concession made to the 'foreigners' was that FIFA was allowed to send two representatives to the Board, to give them two votes against the existing eight.

The British provided the rules and gave the example of how to organize the game. They also provided the ethos of sportsmanship that has guided the game since. Today, and not without reason, 'Fair Play' is left in English in most foreign languages. It is football, more than cricket, that has propagated that ideal, and won it more respect around the world than all the gun boats used for more hard-headed diplomacy. And the word 'football' and most of its technical terms have been adopted into other languages often in the original, usually with minor modifications.

The urban missionaries

Before football conquered the world it had to conquer the British Isles, and in this regard the missionary work of middle-class philanthropists and more spiritually inclined clerics took the game to the darkest recesses of industrial Britain. Or at least they entered ground that was already prepared, the ball giving them entrée.

From the 1860s men of the cloth realized that with a Bible in one hand and a ball in the other they could use the developing craze as an instrument of their evangelism. These Muscular Christians did not have it all their own way, and came into conflict with their colleagues who saw football as a magnet for the vices of violence, gambling and alcohol. On this issue there were conflicting voices in the churches into the twentieth century, and while society at large might be divided over the morality or immorality of soccer, there were men of the cloth who saw that without it many young souls who might otherwise have been lost, were saved. Like many missionary efforts, however, the cause was in danger of being converted by the converted, as the working classes took up the game with an enthusiasm that threatened the assumptions of the ruling body. That they did not do so was in part because of the pragmatism of the proselytisers. It was also because for many love of the game was more important than its use as a means of gaining merit points in heaven. This was the saving grace of the secular missionaries as much as of the clerics. Nowhere was this better demonstrated than in the person of A.F. Kinnaird.

Lord Arthur F. Kinnaird stands as a parable for the game at its noblest as well as the blind spots that left the ideal sullied by hypocrisy. The only son of the tenth Baron Kinnaird, he was born at Rossie Priory, Inchtone, Perthshire in Scotland in 1847. Sent to Eton he distinguished himself in the football matches there, and continued his enthusiasm for the game when he went to Cambridge in 1864. Four years later he joined the Committee of the FA, and remained with that body until his death in 1923. He was the first president of the London Association, starred for the London Wanderers before representing his country against England, first in an unofficial match in 1870, then in the official match in 1873. As late as 1883 he captained Old Etonians in the final of the FA Cup, and while in his mid-forties he was still known to turn on a sprightly exhibition in scratch matches. His robust play matched his flowing red beard and the enthusiasm that marked all his activities. The hoary old story about broken legs, to be recounted down the ages with details and names changed to suit the times, probably began with him. In his case it was his wife who is said to have expressed the fear that one of these days he was going to come home with a broken leg, only to be reassured by a friend that if he did so it would not be his own.

A merchant banker and a liberal aristocrat of the best type, he concerned himself with the welfare of the poor, accepted high office in the Young Men's Christian Association, and between 1907 and 1909 he was Lord High Commissioner of the Church of Scotland. He did not claim, like some, that there were no classes and if there were it didn't matter, but he saw in football a social democracy that brought the classes together, and thanked God 'for the great progress of this popular national game.' However misguided such a notion may be to some, it has the leaven of humanity that made Britain, however class ridden and socially obsequious, that bit more tolerable for the disadvantaged. Kinnaird became treasurer of the FA in 1877, and president in 1890. It was his generous spirit, shared by others on the FA, that saw it through its most serious crisis since its inception, when the working classes brought into the game ideals of fair play and teamwork that were not those of the ruling class.

For some the threat of the working classes came with the Chartists and the Trade Unions. For others it came with the FA Cup Final of 1883, the year when Blackburn Olympic won the FA Cup and took it north, where it would remain, with only a few exceptions, for the next four decades. Their opponents were Old Etonians, with Lord Kinnaird as their captain, and the southern aristocrats with top hats and canes faced up to the rugged northerners with their cloth caps and scarves. The previous year the Old Etonians had beaten Blackburn Rovers, a team formed from former pupils of Blackburn Grammar school and so, while not having the purer working-class credentials of Blackburn Olympic, nevertheless men more of hodden grey than silk. The same Rovers returned from London as victors in the next three years, and the Cup threatened to take up permanent residence in the north.

Football had returned to the people. For the amateurs of the south it was a defeat not taken in the best of spirit: when Blackburn Olympic received the Cup it was to 'somewhat reluctant applause', in stark contrast to the ecstatic crowds who greeted Olympic on their return for what the *Blackburn Times* called 'a signal victory of the plebeian over patrician Englishmen.' The mean-spiritedness of the defeated Etonians was excused in the *Eton College Chronicle* in part because of the hard way in which Olympic had played, but above all because of the way they had indulged in special training for the game. The college *Chronicle* muttered darkly about how strange it was that 'a football team composed of eleven mill-hands and working men should be able to sacrifice three weeks to train for one match, and to find the means to do so.' Olympic in fact were made up of weavers, a cotton spinner, a plumber, a metal-worker, an iron-moulder, a picture-framer and 'one or two with no visible means of support.' Such distinctions of labour were no doubt beyond the college reporter, but he was correct in his assumptions about the time taken off for training: player-manager Jack Hunter organized training trips to Blackpool, and he was also well known for organizing exhibition matches for profit. It was quite obvious, then, that these sturdy northerners who played the game so well did not do so merely as a pastime; they were being paid, and the horrors of professionalism faced the middle-class controllers of the game with their first major controversy since the banning of hacking and handling.

Endnotes

For the early history of the game historians have had to go over many of the same sources, much of it based on the flawed but excellently documented

Frances Peabody Magoun, Jr., *History of Football from the beginning to 1871*, Verlag Heinrich Poppinghays OHG, Bochum-Langendreer, 1938.

Of the early histories

Montague Shearman, *Athletics and Football*, in the Badminton Library series, Longmans, Green, and Co., London, 1889 (third edition),

is particularly interesting, having been written by one of the old school who was not repelled by professionalism. For someone who was, see:

N.L. Jackson, *Sporting Days and Sporting Ways*, Hurst and Blackett, London, 1932.

Marples (1953) makes extensive use of primary sources in his work, which is most valuable for the early history of the game.

Two official histories of the game's great institutions, the FA and the FA Challenge Cup, are:

Geoffrey Green, *The Official History of the FA Cup*, The Naldrett Press, London, 1949
Geoffrey Green, *A History of the Football Association, op. cit.*

The most recent official history of the FA is lavishly illustrated, but with a wealth of useful comment:

Bryon Butler, *The Official History of the Football Association*, Queen Anne Press, London, 1991.

Invaluable for football from the foundation of the FA to 1906, as much for its superb illustrations as for its comments on the contemporary game and its recent history, is the four volume

Alfred Gibson and William Pickford, *Association Football and the Men Who Made It*, The Caxton Publishing Co., London, nd (*circa* 1906).

Two standard works for the early period in which football is dealt with alongside other sport and leisure pastimes are:

Dennis Brailsford, *Sport and Society. Elizabeth to Anne*, Routledge and Kegan Paul, London, 1969.
Robert W. Malcomson, *Popular Recreation in English Society. 1700–1850*, Cambridge University Press, Cambridge, 1973

The report of Blackburn Olympic's Cup victory is taken from

Tony Pawson (ed.), *The Observer on Soccer. An anthology of the best writing*, Unwin Hyman Limited, London, 1989.

The account of *pasuckquakkohowog* is from

Sam Foulds and Paul Harris, *America's Soccer Heritage. A history of the game*, Soccer for Americans, Manhattan Beach, California, 1979.

CHAPTER TWO

For Love and Money

The amateur footballer played for nothing more than his own enjoyment: motivated neither by fame nor profit, for him the game was the thing. At school the masters might hope to prepare him through sport to spread the virtues of British good manners to those under imperial control, and poets might urge him to see beyond the season's fame and paltry prizes to the greater goal of slaughtering savages on foreign soil, but the true amateur had no ulterior aim. He played solely for himself, taken to its logical conclusion in the case of the Hon. Alfred Lyttleton playing for England against Scotland in 1877, who, when criticized for never passing the ball to his team mates, replied disdainfully that he was playing purely for his own pleasure. Not for him to stoop so low as to play for the crowd, and above all not to have them pay to see him perform. Spectators are as much an irrelevance to the purely amateur game as they are the life blood of the professional game, and the two views of the game, like the two views of the world that reflected the two nations of Disraeli's *Sybil*, came to a head in soccer in the 1880s.

The business of pleasure

The first games of football played under the new rules attracted a curious public who thought nothing of joining in the fun; but as the fun was taken more seriously, interested spectators had to be kept behind a painted line or a rope, eventually a fence. From games in the 1860s where players outnumbered spectators, the crowds in the 1870s reached a few thousand for the big FA Cup games, increasing steadily until 110,820 were squeezed into Crystal Palace for the Tottenham Hotspur vs. Sheffield United Cup Final of 1901. The big surge in the game's popularity came in the 1880s, and from then until the middle of the following century, interest continued, with a few dips, to grow.

The crowds who rolled up to watch a game from behind a rope or fence might be asked to make a donation for the privilege of watching; as the crowds increased and clubs erected fences to prevent free viewing, they were equally willing to part with sixpence to go through the gate or, later, the turnstile. At first, money left over after expenses usually went to charity, but when income at the gate began to exceed all expectations, charity took second place as committee men and volunteer workers were replaced by directors and paid employees: a good return at the gate then became as important as the afternoon's entertainment. This was an attitude that the FA regarded with some alarm, and it insisted, for instance, that all money from friendly matches go to charity. Successful clubs, however, needed money to keep improving their facilities: the pitches where the games were played as well as the stands and the terracing to house the increasing number of spectators. Then there was the rent, which landlords were wont to raise steeply when the big crowds rolled up, in turn encouraging clubs to go out and buy their own ground. The main factor drawing big crowds was the standard of play, and above all the presence of star players. Some of these players had the audacity to expect a share of the money they attracted through the gate; some clubs were happy to meet such demands, and were prepared to entice other players with a large signing-on fee, the offer of a job, and wages in the form of lavish expenses. All under the counter, of course. Most of these 'shamateur' teams came from the north, and for the former public school boys and the men of the FA who had set the ball rolling this was an unwelcome development. Those with nothing to lose but their amateur status challenged the amateur administrators in a struggle for control of the future. The players came to find that in casting off their unpaid status they were born into a new form of subjection whose chains they had to bear for decades to come.

The commercialization of football, like any other sport, became impossible to avoid once people were prepared to pay to watch it. Aston Villa were founded in 1874 by members of the Villa Cross Wesleyan Chapel in Aston, and two years later leased an enclosed ground at Wellington Road so that they could charge admission. Entry to their first game at that ground was 3d, and receipts were 5/3. They were then paying a lease of £8 for the ground, but success was such that within a few years the landlord was asking £200. So, like many other clubs faced by such demands, Villa bought their own ground. In season 1904–05 the published records of Aston Villa revealed that £17,783–7–3 was taken in gate money (less £3453–13–1 'paid away') and net profits amounted to £3,376–18–3. Only Newcastle United, with £17,065–0–5, bettered their returns that year. Most clubs charged sixpence for the terrace and a shilling for the stand.

In the years before 1914 the average net annual profit for the top teams could be as high as £3282 (Tottenham Hotspur), £2872 (Liverpool), £2551 (Burnley, including time in the second division) and £1550 (Blackburn Rovers). In Scotland, Celtic cleared £1241 on average, and Rangers, for whom figures are not available, would have cleared significantly higher profits, given their higher attendances and equally efficient running of the club. The vast bulk of the clubs' income came from what was taken at the gate; a much smaller sum came from season tickets, rents and interest. Transfer fees varied from year to year. There were virtually no returns from sponsors.

In England the biggest crowds were to be seen at the Cup Finals. Average attendance increased for every decade after 1875: from 4900 to 23,400, 66,800 and 79,300; in Scotland the equivalent figures were 8550, 13,900, 23,100 and 51,000. These, of course, were exceptional games, but the average crowds for ordinary league games show a similar increase. In England in the 1889–90 season this was 4600, in the 1913–14 season it was 23,100. In Scotland there were already crowds of over 10,000 to see the big games in the 1870s, and the first 50,000 crowd was to see Scotland play England at Celtic Park in 1895; after the 1890s Rangers and Celtic could draw bigger crowds than any two English teams, particularly when they played each other, but the average gates for Scottish games as a whole were generally lower.

Most of the spectators contributing to these expanding gates came from the working classes, and in the early days this was not always a welcome development. Some clubs tried to keep them out by raising the cost of admission, and restricted membership by increasing fees. Reporters in the middle-class papers frequently criticized the 'rough elements' who were coming to the games, condemning their raucous behaviour and expressing the hope that the rapidly expanding clubs would encourage 'the better elements' to come along and elevate the social tone by their presence. Women in particular were welcomed, as it was hoped they would have a moderating influence. They were usually allowed in free to the terracing or at half price to the stand. Better accommodation, such as seats and protection from the rain, was provided for those who could afford the higher prices, and clubs were also keen to do this since they were allowed to retain all stand takings rather than share them with the visiting team. In all grounds in Britain, however, the seating accommodation in the stands was a small fraction of the total capacity, and the bowler hats and ties in the other sections of the ground were swamped by the cloth caps and scarves of the artisans, skilled workers and more affluent members of the working class who made up the bulk of the football supporters.

The industrial system in the second half of the century began to bear some fruit in cheaper goods and higher wages. This meant more disposable income, and together with shorter working hours gave working men more time and money to spend on leisure pursuits. A week's annual unpaid leave was given in industries which had to close down to have machinery and equipment serviced and cleaned. More important in terms of regular recreation time, however, were the reductions in the working week. In the 1850s textile mills introduced early finishing on Saturday, and in the 1860s this leisure time became common in many trades.

The change in working conditions was assisted by the recognition on the part of some employers that constant use wore out their machines, as well as the men who worked them. Consequently it could be more productive to allow workers some time to recuperate. Trade unions applied pressure with the threat of strikes, and the reforming zeal that had campaigned against brutal animal sports, almost wiped out pugilism and tried to civilize wakes, fairs and bonfires along with mob football, was turned to the need for leisure and its proper use. There was a rapid rise in real wages in the late 1870s, and the national availability of leisure and surplus cash had no more marked effect than in the crowds coming to football matches. In the eighteenth century there had been large crowds at some sporting events, particularly prize fights, cricket and racing, but the potential income from such sources was reduced by their infrequency. As a result there was little impulse to enclose spectator space. Attempts were made to do so in 1826 and 1837, but they were unsuccessful. The spread of railways opened up new opportunities, and this gave a boost to race meetings and itinerant cricketing professionals. Professional athletic meetings and rowing regattas drew large crowds, but the money generated was in gambling, liquor sales and other spin-offs rather than fees to watch. It was only with soccer in the 1880s that *regular* gate money sport made its appearance on the sporting scene. And this came only when the workers could become consumers. The hope of playing for the local team or watching the local heroes in action gave those in work something to look forward to, and for those out of work, something to do. Football could now be added to alcohol and religion as one of man's great comforters: in Glasgow the more fanatical could enjoy all three at the same time.

The Industrial Revolution in sport

By the 1890s football was intertwined in the industrial revolution, being part of it and taking advantage of it at the same time. Football created a market for leather balls and boots, shirts and shorts, and the materials to build the ever multiplying football stadiums. In and around the stadiums grew spin-offs in the provision of food and drink, and in the newspapers that recorded the game for pre-match prognosis, *post mortems* on the game just played and prospects for the coming week.

Urbanization and the transport revolution grew with the game. Even before the advent of mass football railway companies had seen the possibility of sports drawing large crowds and had offered 'specials'. From the 1880s rival companies offered this service to football fans, particularly for internationals and big cup games. More important were the trams that linked up the outlying parts of the ever-expanding suburbs from the 1890s,

so that a town like Birmingham could produce three top teams, and
Glasgow five. Horse drawn 'brakes' took the first organized supporters'
clubs to games. Nottingham, Sheffield, Manchester, Liverpool, Edinburgh, Dundee and some other cities gave rise to two teams in the one city
whose rivalry dominated all other club matches in what became known as
local 'derbies'. For teams like Sunderland and Newcastle the 'derby' was
between cities. Only the big Cup games could equal these 'derby' games
for the interest and passion they evoked. Moreover, matches in competitions organized by city or county associations, and now long forgotten,
could almost bring industry to a standstill.

These games were news, and as sport took up more and more space in the
press, so football took up more and more space in the sporting sections of
the information press as well as in the specialist journals beginning to
proliferate from the 1870s. From occasional paragraphs alongside
pedestrianism, prize fighting, ratting and cycling, football dominated
sports coverage. Already in the 1880s it was clear that football sold
newspapers, and advertisers and the papers themselves reacted accordingly. In the late 1880s the *Athletic Journal* offered prizes for forecasting in
a tear off section of the newspaper the correct results in selected matches: in
Scotland the *Scottish Athletic Journal* offered free insurance worth £100 to
any person 'killed or fatally injured' at a football match, simply by signing
in ink in the space provided by the paper. These appeared alongside more
conventional advertisements: for playing equipment, announcements of
coming games, cures for the body's sporting ills, and means of sustaining
oneself during the game – 'Bovril' seems to pop up as ubiquitously as
Coca Cola advertisements in later times.

It was for the football, news and reports, however, that these papers
were bought, and Saturday evening 'specials', often in coloured paper,
brought the afternoon's scores to the public in the shortest possible time.
Speed meant sales, and before the telephone took over, telegrams and
pigeons were used to carry the scores. In pubs throughout the land this
information was received and transferred to a large board where the scores
were progressively posted. This was a task the press soon took over,
especially when in the early 1890s some clubs set up telephone facilities for
reporters inside the ground, allowing scores and reports to be passed on to
the newspaper office. In Glasgow in the early 1900s the Saturday sporting
editions came out while the games were still being played, with brief
reports, half-time scores then final scores, leading up to complete coverage
of the matches of the day by 7.30pm. Early in the century the *Football Star*
and the *Football Evening News* in London had their teams of specially
trained clerks 'glued to the telephone', who took down reports, sent them
to the composing room and from there to the linotype machines, where a
whole page of seven columns could be set up within half an hour. From

there came casting and correcting before the vital information was released from the presses to teams of young men who took off on bicycles, carts, cabs and motors to distribute the papers to trains, shops and the streets. It was a scene that would be re-enacted regularly for decades to come in all the major cities of Great Britain. Radio became popular in the 1930s, but the British Broadcasting Company (BBC) did not allow the broadcasting of any scores before 6 pm. The press was still the major disseminator of sporting information, and this role has continued into the age of television.

While football sold newspapers, newspapers acted as free publicity and public relations channels for football, a relationship that has remained until the present time, if not always harmoniously, at least always resolved in the knowledge that the one could not do without the other. Star or personality players could receive a small sum of money for adding their name to articles on football (although this was banned in Scotland for a time after the 1912–13 season) or even by endorsing some item for sale; such payments were seen at the time as a lucrative perk.

The tone of reporting was different then; all was made out to be rosy in a sport where talent was rewarded at the ruling rates and players, however underpaid in comparison to the income they created, were thought to be living in luxury. A players' revolt against their conditions of employment in 1909 received little support in the press.

Football's social transformation

By the turn of the century football had become the main outdoor leisure pursuit of the working classes and the most highly prized career for workers who might otherwise be consigned to a life down the pits, amid the clamour of the shipyard or bound to a bench in the boredom of the factory. The best teams were no longer the elegant ruffians who charged around in long trousers and still wore caps. Now they were made up of the more serious men of toil whose approach to the game was in all ways more professional. Writing in the 1880s, Montague Shearman disdainfully scorned the new men who wore shin pads, who preferred skill to the fun that was in the rough and tumble of the game, and who even went in for training.

Even as the former public schoolboys were dominating association football through the 1860s and into the 1870s, the teams that would be their nemesis were coming into being. Most of these were still made up of middle-class players, often a group of young men who got together for a casual game, sometimes in response to an advertisement in the press, requesting that they contact the paper to arrange regular games at a selected spot at a particular time. Most of these teams disappeared, some continued in obscurity, but others, like Glasgow Rangers, founded in 1872 by a .

'group of lads' from the Highlands, went on to become a power in the land. Teams formed out of cricket clubs, like the later Sheffield clubs, were obviously of middle-class origins. Many football clubs, such as Derby and Accrington, were originally cricket clubs who played soccer to keep fit through the winter months. Football in Derby had a long history associated with the Shrove Tuesday game that was the subject of so much debate in the 1840s before it was officially suppressed in 1847, but the present Derby team was originally part of the Derby County Cricket Club, which took up soccer in 1884. Preston North End were originally a rugby club, until they were taken over by William Sudell in 1881 and moulded into the most powerful team of the 1880s. Nottingham Forest came into being in 1865 when they converted from a form of hockey called 'shinney', or 'shinty'.

The success of clubs with a religious impulse can be seen in many teams still prominent today: Aston Villa (Villa Cross Wesleyan Chapel), Barnsley (Rev. T.T. Preedy, curate of St Peter's Church), Birmingham City (Holy Trinity Cricket Club before they became Small Heath Alliance, their original name), Bolton Wanderers (pupils and teachers of Christ Church Sunday School), Blackpool (local St John's Church), Everton (St Domingo Sunday School). In Scotland Queen's Park were founded by members of the Young Men's Christian Association, Hibernians and Celtic began as minor political arms of the Catholic Church. Schools like Blackburn Grammar gave rise to Blackburn Rovers, and after the 1870 Education Act in England other teams emerged from schools of more lowly status: Sunderland came from the Sunderland and District Teachers' Association and Queen's Park Rangers from Droop Street State School.

Pubs and the workplace produced teams; as Tony Mason has shown, these were the most common point of origin of football teams after churches. Pubs, sociability and sport came together in easy harmony, and it was a natural move for the fellow-drinkers to form their own teams. Patrons who encouraged discussion of the game and provided updates on the scores of matches in progress, might also sponsor a team, provide a field or offer a place where the players could change. Chelsea are said to owe their origins to a 'discussion in a Fulham pub', while Middlesbrough were founded in equally prosaic circumstances by a group of enthusiasts at a 'tripe supper'. The association of the drink trade with sport, and football in particular, is a long one. Many football club directors were in the drink trade, and wealthy brewers and the brewing industry have always invested heavily in it.

Where teams were founded at the workplace this was often by the workers themselves, but wise or paternal bosses could encourage this by providing facilities or even giving full support. Some saw in this a subtle means of social control, but in Britain the sponsorship of major teams from the workplace never reached the lengths it did on the continent and elsewhere: in Britain there were too many alternative ways of finding someone to play with. Nevertheless, some of today's best known teams were founded in this way. Manchester United were formed, as Newton Heath, by working men of the Dining Committee of the Lancashire and Yorkshire Railway, in circumstances so obscure that early references pointed to them as being founded 'around 1880' rather than the club's official date of 1878. It was not until 1902, when the club was threatened with receivership, that Newton Heath became Manchester United, and under a wealthy brewer soon became one of the best teams in the land, with a stadium as good as the best in Scotland. Crewe Alexandra owed their existence to being in a central railway centre. Coventry came from the Singer Cycle factory, and West Ham were founded by the boss of the Thames Ironworks, A.F. Hills. Arsenal retained the name of the industry which supplied their first team. Though works might sponsor teams they were not allowed to advertise this through the club's name.

The absence of strong industrial teams in Britain at a time when most players earned their living from industry is an indication of the spontaneous nature of the game's growth. It was as the representatives of their community that the teams from the industrial north and midlands of England and the central industrial belt of Scotland finally ended the old boy monopoly of playing success. When Aston Villa were formed in 1874 they were the only club in Birmingham: two years later there were 20 clubs in that part of the Midlands. When the Birmingham Association played their London counterparts in 1877 they were thrashed 11–0 at the Oval: two years later at the same place they beat the Londoners by two goals. By then the game had taken off in Lancashire, Staffordshire and the whole of the Midlands, played, as Shearman said, 'by all classes of players, but chiefly by the mechanics and artisans.'

From out of the north

A feature of the most successful English teams in the late 1870s was the number of Scotsmen in them. These 'Scotch professors' owed their reputation to the technical superiority of the Scottish national team in its games against England, and many of them came south in search of work and better pay. Bolton, Darwen and Preston included many Scottish players, and at one stage Bolton Wanderers had only one Englishman in their team, while later, in 1892, the first Liverpool team was made up entirely of Scots. This led to sneers about 'the populace of an English town becoming frenzied with delight over the victories of eleven hired Scotch players', the sarcasms being aimed as much at them being Scottish as the allegation that they were paid. For many of these players the better job opportunities were secondary to the money they got from football. Locals were learning to love a victory, and they were unconcerned who achieved it for them. Certainly it was nice to win with local talent, but if it had to come from over the hill or over the border, it was the jersey and the skill of the footwork that won the day over accents. Soccer 'mercenaries' were immediately accepted as honorary citizens of the locality, country or ethnic persuasion of the team they played for.

In the late 1870s the money was in England and the talent was in Scotland, and local worthies were prepared to entice skilled workers south to work that was secondary to their soccer ability. Newspapers in Scotland, including those denouncing professionalism, ran advertisements for players asking them to state their conditions. This at least was safer than trying to recruit players on the spot, for any agents from an English club found trying to lure away a local star did so at the risk, if not of their life, then at least of a severe thrashing. Rising income at the gate covered some of the cost of persuading a new star to play for a particular club, but local businessmen could see the benefits in helping establish a successful local team. This they might do by illicit payments or by providing the newcomer with work that did not interfere with his football. For most of these 'sponsors' enthusiasm for the game and local pride were at least as important as any business advantages that accrued.

The FA tried hard to overlook the obvious evidence that the most successful teams from the north were paying their players, but they could not ignore the complaints that poured in from genuinely amateur teams, particularly when they were eliminated from the Cup. Such complaints, however, were often buried in sub-committees or met by strenuous denials from the accused clubs that players were paid no more than necessary and limited expenses. If seriously investigated the accused club could always produce an account book specially cooked up for the purpose. In 1882 the FA passed a law against players receiving money for playing above the most meagre expenses, under penalty of exclusion of the player and the club that paid him. Little came of this. The Lancashire and Birmingham Associations, where undercover payment of players was rampant, took the issue more seriously, and forced the FA to form a sub-committee early in 1883 to investigate the issue. They found nothing. Later in that year Accrington Stanley were found guilty of paying a player and were suspended.

A major crisis blew up in January 1884 when Upton Park, a strictly amateur club from London, were beaten by Preston North End in the fourth round of the FA Cup and entered a formal protest on the ground of the Preston players being professionals. This brought the old boy clique of the FA into direct confrontation with the new industrial wealth of the north and the midlands in the form of Major William Sudell. Sudell, a cotton manufacturer and man of substance, saw nothing to be ashamed of in making money, whether it was from football or the produce of a factory. When faced by the accusation of playing professionals in his team he refused to deny it and went on to say that Preston were far from being alone in paying their players. The shamateur clubs, instead of admitting this, refused to concede their dishonesty. Preston were disqualified from the Cup for that year, and the FA was driven to more discussions and further legislation, one outcome of which was a rule banning Scots from playing in the FA Cup, though the Scots, much as they seemed to be everywhere, were far from the only players being paid.

Matters came to a head on 30 October 1884 when the FA was faced with a breakaway movement by 28 northern clubs who threatened to form a British Football Association. In the rugby code a similar challenge to the south, by Yorkshiremen, precipitated what became the split in the Rugby Union. The FA was less hide-bound. It engaged in a flurry of sub-committees, meetings, proposals and counter-proposals, before coming up with a system that mirrored the subtlety of the political ruling class. On 20 July 1885 professionalism was recognized, but under strict conditions, most of which imposed residential qualifications. These were abolished within four years.

Righteousness and reality

To the more modern mind there is something baffling in an attitude that accepts the right of some people to capitalize on their talents in one sphere, but denounces it in another. Even in leisure pursuits, actors have not been castigated for making money from acting, painters for painting or musicians for making music. Yet when an individual's talent came from athletic ability, the right to make money out of this rare skill caused near apoplexy in some. Every sport that attracted spectators was involved in this controversy, including soccer wherever it was played. In Britain, however, the issue was more heatedly debated than elsewhere, partly from the timing of the debate, coming as it did in the second half of the nineteenth century, but more so because of the peculiar nature of the class system. In football the debate paralleled the agitation of the workers for representation in parliament, where the middle-class products of the public schools were challenged by the middle-class products of the rising industrialism – crudely and unfairly caricatured as the public schools against the public houses. The class interests of the two groups, however, brought them together when faced by the threat to their privileged status from the workers. The ruling classes in football, like their equivalents in parliament, found that change was the best way, if not to remain the same, at least to stay in control.

The opponents of professionalism varied from the simple fanatics who believed they were possessed of some divine form of social grace, to those who had reasonable fears about the threat to the purity of sport when extraneous forces usurped it in their own interests. Those who carried the day were the realists who did not like professionalism, but recognized that it would not go away and so sought the lesser evil of controlling its excesses.

The ideological opponents of professionalism, those who regarded it as 'degrading for respectable men to play against professionals', were a minority in soccer: some of them refused to take part in any game that involved competition, be it for a badge, flag, pennant or cup: the play was its own reward. In association football the strongest arguments against professionalism were put forward by those who claimed that it would lead inevitably to corruption: if someone could be paid to win they could also be paid to lose. In this regard there were many examples from other sports: prize-fighting, athletics, racing and cycling, where results were not so much based on merit as who organized the best fix, usually in the interests of a betting coup. But all of these sports were essentially different from football in that they depended on the individual, not a team.

Cricket bore a better comparison with football. It was a team game and had been drawing large crowds long before football became a mass spectator sport. The football legislators, too, were familiar with the problems that faced cricket. Alcock in particular, who was secretary of the Surrey County Cricket Club among his other tasks, was influenced by the way in which professionalism in cricket had been controlled. There had been a time in the middle of the century when teams of itinerant professionals, playing against each other or against local teams, looked like establishing their own competition, but the formation of county teams and the authority of the MCC preserved the game from those who might have poisoned it with money. This control was achieved by recognizing professionals, who were allowed to compete alongside amateurs, albeit in circumstances aimed at degrading them: in their dress, the way in which they were addressed, the separate gates by which they entered the field, the role they played on the field and in social activities off it.

A more serious accusation against professionalism was that it would lead to the rule of the rich. Football, instead of being fun or a healthy exercise, would become a mere business. Profits would subvert ethics, and all means would be adopted to achieve this end, from cheating off the field to fouling and illegitimate violence on it. Professionalism, with its intensification of the competitive spirit, would lead to the demise of the weaker clubs.

In fact, professional football in Britain was probably more honest than the amateur game, where excuses for defeats resulted in so many protests that at least one writer in the 1880s wrote an exasperated letter to the press protesting about protests. Nor did professional football turn the youth of the country into a nation of watchers: on the contrary, it was more likely to inspire emulation. Only strict controls by the authorities, however, prevented a few rich clubs running off with all the trophies, as happened in some countries where restrictions were never applied.

The realists among the opponents of professionalism saw that it was better that it be brought into the open. It was Alcock, who never allowed his morality to cloud his judgement, who pointed out to the 1884 AGM of the FA that most amateurs were prepared to play against professionals, but not while they called themselves amateurs. If they had to sup with the devil, they would have to make sure that it was with a very long spoon. The men of wealth, who had no moral objection to professionalism, had strong social reasons for wanting its introduction, for it would allow them to control the people they paid. It was this marriage of aristocratic and industrial self-interest, between the men of the south and the men of the north, that carried the day. Both factions saw themselves as members of the ruling class, and saw in professionalism the means of preserving the proper relationship between master and servant, employer and employee. Nowhere was the opinion more brutally and frankly put than by John McLaughlin, honorary secretary of Glasgow Celtic when the issue was debated in Scotland some years later: 'With veiled professionalism players are masters of the clubs, and can go and debauch themselves without being called to account. Under the new system the clubs will be masters of the players . . .'

Underlying the whole debate was the British class system. Soccer, because of its overwhelming popularity with working men, could never have applied a clause simply stating that any mechanic could not be an amateur, as was done in rowing, or recognize professionalism, as the Northern Rugby Union did in 1898, and then insist that all such players be engaged in full-time employment. Nor could soccer ban players who played against professionals, as the southern RFU did in an attempt to prevent members of their Union playing with those of the NRFU. The aura of aristocratic class prejudice still hung over the game, however, in the aspirations of those who sought social elevation, and in the prejudices of those who already had it. The FA deemed that even if professionals had to be recognized, only amateurs could administer the game in an efficient and non-pecuniary way, and so banned professional players from positions on Boards and the running of the game. The first professional to play for England, against Scotland in 1886, had to play in a different shirt, and it was not until 1900 that a professional captained the England team. Matters had improved since 1872, however, when Charles Clegg, later to become a president of the FA, but then a mere lawyer from Sheffield playing for a provincial team in London, found that the 'snobs from the south' refused to pass the ball to him, let alone talk to him. Writing in his autobiography in 1932, N.L. Jackson saw nothing of class prejudice or snobbishness in such attitudes, merely the desirability of social apartheid: the need for separation was the natural reaction of two different sets of people, inhabiting different social spheres and virtually speaking different languages. What was more natural, then, than that both should wish to remain apart. . . .

The League of the Selfish

The threat to the FA's hegemony was not yet over with the recognition of professionalism, for the men from the north wanted a more business-like organization of the game. The outcome of this was the formation of the Football League, which became the ruling body for professional soccer, while the FA was left to supervise the general welfare of the game. It was an arrangement not without its problems, and there was frequent talk of 'wars' between them down the years, but none of this was particularly serious until 1990.

When professionalism was recognized in England in 1885, the FA Cup was the central feature of the playing season, with friendlies and local cup competitions making up the rest. Some clubs revealed a truly amateur approach to the game, refusing to turn up every now and then, arriving late, or perhaps sending a reserve team if a more attractive fixture turned up at the last moment. This was the right of the amateur, not to be tied to a regular schedule, but it could not work for professionals: they had to be paid whether or not they were playing, and whether or not they played before a record crowd or an empty terracing. Early elimination from the FA Challenge Cup or any of the local cup competitions left blank Saturdays, which had to be filled in, even with unattractive fixtures.

It was in Birmingham, around the figure of the genial Scot, William McGregor, that discussions were carried out to form a 'league'. Born in Braco in Perthshire in 1847, McGregor is a man who was said to have won 'the goodwill of everyone and the enmity of none'. He arrived in Birmingham in 1870 to set up a linen drapers' shop and built up a successful business. He did not allow profits to interfere with his football, however, and closed his shop on Saturday afternoons to attend games, and re-opened it at 6pm. He was a man of many interests, a member of the Liberal Party and a Methodist who preached to the poor, a teetotaller but not a moralizer. His love of football began in Scotland where as a small boy he saw it played by stonemasons in the 1850s. His enthusiasm for the game north of the border knew no bounds, particularly as played by Queen's Park. But it was with Aston Villa that he made his name, attracted to the club shortly after its foundation by the presence of brother Scots, no doubt its Wesleyan associations, and perhaps even their colours and neat turn out. Not much of a player, he excelled as a committee man, and whether in discussions in his shop or in the corridors of power, through his single-minded devotion to the idea of the League he turned out to be one of the most influential individuals in the early history of the game.

The idea of the league came from County Cricket (and not the National Baseball League starting up at this time in the United States). It was to be a regular competition in which selected teams would agree to play each other on set dates, on a home and away basis, promising to field their strongest team and to give the league fixtures preference over all others. The men engaged in these discussions were essentially of 'new wealth', small businessmen who came from a different social category from the men of the FA. With the suspicious eyes of the FA looking on they conducted their correspondence and meetings, with more apparent squabbling than agreement, and with the major catch, the Preston 'Invincibles', remaining aloof.

The letter sent out by McGregor on 2 March 1888 to five clubs, following discussions carried out over the previous months, resulted in an historic meeting on 17 April, where the idea was accepted. On 8 September 1888 the new league kicked off with twelve teams, including Preston North End, who not only won the first League 'flag' without losing a game, but completed the 'double' when they won the FA Cup without losing a goal. On 11 January 1889 the first official rules were drawn up, confirming the precedence to be given league fixtures over all others; formalizing such details as the points scoring system, where two points were awarded for a win and one for a draw (and not, as had been strongly argued, none); goal average to decide between teams level on points. There had also been disagreement about the split of gate money, McGregor having favoured sharing it between both teams once expenses had been cleared; in the end the home team kept all but the visitor's guarantee, set at £12. At least this resolved the problem of honesty in regard to the actual amount of money received. Share of gate receipts was an issue that would come up for frequent debate and compromise.

In 1893 that other institution so intimately associated with soccer leagues was established when a second division with promotion and relegation was introduced. At first this was by play-offs, but from 1898–99 promotion and relegation were decided automatically by position at the top or bottom of the league.

The new body called itself the Football League, despite McGregor's unwillingness to use a name so disliked in England 'on account of the doings of the Irish Land League', but his alternative, 'The Association Football Union' would not have pleased the rugby people. The aim of the League was to protect the interests of the clubs taking part in its competition: as McGregor openly declared: 'The League should never aspire to be a legislating body . . . by the very nature of things the League must be a selfish body.' N.L. Jackson thoroughly agreed, but in a different sense, despising the commercialism that he believed was behind it. At first the League had envisaged controlling all aspects of professional football, but eventually willingly conceded to the FA the right to control football in all its other spheres, most notably the Cup, internationals and the running of amateur football. It also ruled on certain matters concerning the rewards and disciplining of the professionals. This led to many tensions, especially in the early days, but a common interest in keeping the players in their place prevented any splits. There was periodic talk of the more powerful clubs throwing off the control of the smaller clubs, but while the idea of a Super League was there in the very formation of the league, based as it was on an elite carefully selected, neither the league nor the FA supported any such proposals. That would have to wait for another time and other standards.

When the new Football League was founded it deliberately did not call itself the *English* Football League, as it still hoped to include teams from Scotland. In the event the Scots founded their own league in 1890, a precursor to the introduction of professionalism three years later. In Scotland, where professionalism was denounced with the added spice of Calvinistic fervour, the Scottish Football Association maintained an even more dogmatic stance than in England, despite the fact that they lost so many of their players to English gold. Local vigilantes did their best to terrorize agents acting for the English, but a much more successful way of keeping the best players in Scotland was to pay them under the counter. In 1890 Glasgow Celtic enticed some players back by paying them higher wages than they paid the rest of the team. As a result they were faced by the threat of a strike from the home-based 'amateurs' which was defeated only by paying them the same as the recent imports.

There was nothing hypocritical in Celtic paying their 'amateur' players, as they were outspoken advocates of professionalism from the moment of their explosive entry on the Scottish football scene. Founded by a Marist brother priest in November 1887, playing their first game the following May and attracting to the game thousands who had not until that time shown much interest, their players and supporters were mainly Scots of Irish origins and catholic religion. The club made little secret of its foundation to feed the catholic poor, was a bit more reticent about it also being to keep them out of the clutches of protestantism, and individual members of the team and the Board openly associated themselves with causes such as Irish 'Home Rule'. But the club also had some hard headed businessmen, the most notable of whom was John McLaughlin. It was he who wanted to see the players kept in proper subjection to their employers, and it was he who was one of the leading instigators of the league in Scotland in 1890, with the clear aim that this would lead to professionalism. In this he was supported by Celtic's great rivals, Glasgow Rangers. There was nothing unusual in this: the two clubs came to be divided bitterly along sectarian lines, but in financial matters they often worked in common. It was for this reason, and the way they had come to dominate Scottish football by the turn of the century, that they were called, sarcastically, The Old Firm.

The Scottish League pledged its loyalty to the SFA, whose governing committee was made up mainly of non-League members, and relations between the two bodies suffered less strains than those of their counterparts in England. In 1893 a Second Division was introduced and both divisions increased in number through to 1914. Automatic promotion and relegation was not introduced until 1921–22. In contrast to England, there was no maximum wage imposed in Scotland, nor was there any restraint on the amount directors paid themselves. The overwhelming dominance of the two Glasgow 'giants', however, had less to do with the absence of restraints on capitalism than on the religious allegiances that they carefully nurtured. With players playing 'for the jersey' neither club needed to pay significantly more than other top teams, although Rangers' reserves were often paid more than most second division teams.

When the League was founded Rangers and Celtic were already challenging the authority of Queen's Park, who remained loftily aloof from the social changes taking place around them. The 'Spiders' refused to sully their amateur principles, and while they dominated the SFA, they refused to join the League, rightly claiming that it would lead to professionalism. Unlike the Corinthians in England, who refused to play against professionals in competitions, they eventually agreed to join the Scottish League, in season 1900–01. By then they had been caught up by the times, and their last major success in Scottish football was their victory over Celtic in the Scottish Cup of 1893. Nevertheless, their agreement to play against professional teams was a situation somewhat unusual in the weird world of amateur sports. Today they still continue to exist in the lower levels of the professional Scottish league . . . and until 1950 they were owners of the world's biggest football stadium.

Amateur rearguard

Queen's Park's faith in their future as an amateur lamb among professional wolves was matched by a commercial venture more daring than anything their professional rivals could equal, when on 3 April 1900 they decided to build the biggest football stadium in the world. The estimated cost of this venture, on the 12 acres of ground they had purchased in the suburb of Mount Florida, was £10,000. In 1910, seven years after the first game was played on the new Hampden Park, their debt was cleared. Hampden Park is still owned by Queen's Park, and stages the big international and cup games in Scotland, but the grandeur of the days when it held world and European record crowds is long past. Without the capacity of Hampden (crowds of nearly 150,000 were recorded in 1937 and 1939, but after that a limit of 134,000 was usually set) to hold much bigger crowds than its other Glasgow rivals it would no doubt have gone the way of other amateur clubs.

When Blackburn Olympic took the FA Cup north in 1883, the days of the great amateur teams were already numbered. The Corinthians, the most famous of the amateur teams, were formed by N.L. Jackson out of public school and university men in 1882. They set out to reverse the dominance of Scotland in international matches by perfecting the short passing game, but refused to play other than in games that were purely for charity, initially even in games where a trophy was at stake. They supplied one third of the players for England in the first 25 years of their existence, and twice, against Wales in 1894 and 1895, they provided the whole team. They also spread their name and that of soccer around the world in tours to Europe, South Africa and South America. In the traditional New Year's day games, when Rangers were playing Celtic, Corinthians played Queen's Park. Although they could more than hold their own with the best professional teams in the 1880s and 1890s – they frequently played and beat the FA Cup winners – and even into the twentieth century, when they eventually deigned to enter the FA Cup; after 1922 they were outclassed.

Corinthians and Queen's Park sought to combat some of the evils into which they believed the game was falling, as professionalism and the commercialism that was its inevitable accompaniment replaced the spirit of fun and sportsmanship they liked to believe characterized the amateur game. They resisted the introduction of goal nets in 1891, claiming that not only were they a restriction of the goalkeeper's liberties in the way he was 'cribbed, cabined and confined', but they were a slur on the honour of defenders who would dispute whether or not the ball had gone between the posts. (There had in fact been many disputes over this issue.) They also refused at first to recognize the penalty kick, introduced at the same time, seeing in it the calumny of cheating. At first both teams refused to take a penalty when given one, or defend one when it was given against them.

The annual Corinthians vs. Queen's Park game was suspended for thirteen years after 1907 when, after several years of simmering discontent at the way the FA was falling into line with the foul ways of professional-ism, Corinthians joined Oxford, Cambridge and the upholders of the Old Boys' traditions in a break with the FA which resulted in them founding a separate Amateur Football Association. The split was provoked by a FA directive that all county associations had to admit professional teams into their ranks. The dissident amateurs, nearly all from the south, founded a cup of their own, presented by Corinthians, to compete with the FA Amateur Cup competition that had been inaugurated in 1893. Cut off from competition with the amateur clubs still under the jurisdiction of the other British associations, the dissidents failed to prosper, and returned to the FA just before the outbreak of war in 1914. A few amateur players continued to play in professional teams in England through the 1920s and 1930s, and as late as 1946 three amateurs played in an Arsenal first eleven; admittedly an Arsenal team severely affected by the recent War.

The amateurs in Britain played in their own leagues, had their own cup competitions, and the home countries played amateur internationals against each other. Outside Britain the main competition for amateurs was in the Olympic Games. Football was played at the first three Olympics, but not officially. At Athens in 1896 there was an exhibition game, and part of the farce that was the Olympic Games in Paris in 1900 saw Upton Park representing Great Britain in another exhibition game. At the even greater farce of St Louis in 1904 there was an unofficial competition, in which Canada won a gold medal against two teams from the United States. At London in 1908, however, football entered official competition. Com-peting as Great Britain, the game's founders strolled through to win the final. They won gold again four years later in Stockholm, but this time had to fight hard to defeat Denmark, the beaten finalists in 1908. It was only at this time that the Games were established on a firm foundation, and for many years it was soccer that helped make them a financial success. For while Great Britain did not take soccer at the Games seriously, other countries did: too seriously for it to be left to mere amateurs. Technically the other soccer teams at the Antwerp Games were amateurs, and the Norwegian team that bundled Britain out in the first round certainly was, but many teams had a definition of amateurism that was not that of the British. As a result Britain took no further part in the soccer competition of the Olympic Games until 1936.

The professional game

By the turn of the century professionalism was irreversibly established in British football, and far from suffering, the standard of play in terms of skill and commitment improved: some, perhaps with the mists of imperial glory clouding their vision, would say that the football played in the first two decades of the new century was the best ever. Certainly the behaviour of the crowds showed a marked improvement on the early days: better facilities at the grounds, improved policing and a higher standard of play and refereeing accounted for much of this, but also a growing maturity. There were still ground invasions enough, but more often caused by overflows from overcrowding than malice. There were also occasional attacks on referees, and missiles were still thrown at players and officials, but more and more such incidents were being restricted to the lower grade games, the park games and amateur games. The one major riot of this time was at Hampden Park in 1909, when supporters of Rangers and Celtic were goaded into a pitch invasion after a replayed Cup Final again ended in a draw and no extra time was played. It was suspected, not without reason, that the clubs were looking for a third monster gate; many in the crowd thought they had paid enough, and wanted to see the game played to a finish. In the battles that followed nearly 100 were injured, six seriously. The Cup was withheld that year.

In England in 1910, with a population of over seven million males aged between 15 and 39, there were 300,000 to 500,000 amateur footballers, 6800 professionals. In Scotland where there were 1650 professional players in this time, the equivalent number of amateurs might have been about 150,000. In Ireland the game was well established with strong rivals in Gaelic football and rugby, and in Wales rugby was even more popular than soccer. But it was soccer that was expanding more rapidly, with a vast network of leagues spreading over the country, run by county, municipal and other local associations and other voluntary bodies. It was these amateurs, playing in parks, for their schools and for various youth teams, who made up the vast majority of those playing football. Churches ran leagues throughout the country, and particularly in Scotland the Boy's Brigade, associated with the Protestant churches, ran successful league competitions. There were also the schools' associations; in England in 1904 the English Schools Football Association was founded with 21 towns affiliated. From such competitions young lads could join various 'junior' or amateur leagues until such times as they were spotted by a scout from one of the professional teams. For most that time never came, but in no way did it diminish the energy and enthusiasm that went into games played before few or no spectators.

Among the professionals football was firmly entrenched throughout the United Kingdom, with separate leagues in England, Scotland and Ireland, and each, as well as Wales, had its own Cup competition. A Southern League in England was free from the control of the English League, and as such offered an alternative for the professional player unhappy with his lot in the club to which he had tied his living. This freedom was diminished through mutual agreement of the two Leagues, and disappeared shortly after the First World War when the Southern League joined the Football League.

The lot of the professional footballer was the envy of his working-class peers, with short hours and a wage for the best at least double that of the skilled artisan. In addition to being paid for what most workers did for nothing, professional footballers enjoyed a star status that the creators of industrial wealth could never enjoy. This status was not one that was always accorded by the wealthier social classes, and from Billy Meredith early in the century to Jimmy Hill sixty years later, their social behaviour was a matter of no little concern. Meredith, writing in 1906 when at the height of his long career, spoke of the rigours of the professional footballers' life and the sacrifices they had to make, noted the surprise on the part of fellow train travellers on a journey to London that they could sing so well and behave themselves. The days were gone, he noted proudly, when hotel proprietors 'absolutely refused to allow a football team on their premises', while in 'dress, conduct and general behaviour' the paid player was well able to take care of himself.

Footballers had more serious problems than their status in the eyes of their 'betters'. Although they had skills that were in short supply and high demand, their career was so short, as Vamplew has said, that it could hardly be called a career. Not only short, but subject to the ever present threat of it being terminated through injury or the arrival of a younger or fitter player. They also had few opportunities to continue in the game when the last hurrah had sounded. And however good life at the top was for the star footballer, there was the reality that he was bound by a contract more restrictive than that of the most exploited industrial worker.

The attitude of the FA and the League to the employment conditions of professional footballers was the subject of great dispute between the two bodies in the early years, with their point of agreement being that the footballers they governed had a particular station in life – the only point of disagreement was how low that station was. The FA never quite managed to overcome its repugnance to professionalism, but for this very reason found something distasteful in the way players were marketed as though they were cattle. Its resultant liberalism in regard to freedom of movement was opposed by the League, which saw players as a form of property, and as such to be disposed of under conditions of contract as set out by the owner. In 1897 the FA wanted to abolish the 'trafficking' in players between clubs at an agreed fee and tried to pass a law that players be free at the end of each season. The League rationalized that this would be bad for the weaker teams. When the fees for transfers escalated to £1000 with the transfer of Alf Common from Sunderland to Middlesbrough in 1905, the FA tried unsuccessfully to impose a £350 limit. Apart from the unworkability of such limits, the League pointed out that the income gained by smaller clubs through selling their best players often helped to keep them afloat.

This suited the clubs. The player was still saddled with the 'retain and transfer' system, which gave virtually complete control of the club over the player. Once signed, for a maximum fee to the player of £10, he became the property of the club, and could not be transferred except with the club's permission. So long as a club offered a player the same wages as the previous year he had no grievance in the eyes of the League or the FA. The player's only right under this system was to refuse to go to a team to which he was being transferred, but this could result in loss of wages and a bad reputation.

On the issue of wages the League was divided. The bigger clubs were happy to pay more. In the early days of the League players could do quite well in trading their ability for a cash return, but in 1900 the FA suggested that a limit of £208 be placed on all players' salaries. In addition they banned bonuses as 'detrimental to sportsmanship', despite the fact that a team winning its way through to the last rounds of the Cup was bringing in a vastly increased revenue to the club. The maximum wage of £4 per week was introduced from the 1901–02 season, but ten years later less than a tenth of the professionals in England were on the maximum. In 1910 a few improvements were made in regard to bonuses and long service benefits, but this came only after the threat of a strike at the start of the 1909–10 season.

The idea of a players' union had first been brought up in 1893 when players were faced with the threat of a maximum wage and the cessation of summer payments. A more serious attempt at forming a union was made in December 1897, this time on the right to sign contracts for more than a year, but the Union lasted barely a year and was wound up in 1901. Prior to this footballers in England had been better able to trade their services, but few were full professionals, relying on outside income to maintain a reasonable standard of living. As they became more fully professional they were met by a League that was growing in strength and determined to keep its players under their control. In the great expansion of the game in the 1890s, clubs revelled in bonanza gate takings, but they refused to share this with the players, on the grounds that they needed the extra money to build ever better accommodation for the ever-increasing crowds. In this decade many clubs became limited liability companies. Disgruntled players could play in Ireland, Scotland or the Southern League, and many did, some for vastly improved incomes and signing-on fees, some for promises that never materialized. Gradually, the League cut off these avenues to freedom of movement, with mutual agreements respecting playing contracts.

It was not until 1907 that the idea of a union was revived again, mainly under the urging of Billy Meredith, who, as well as being one of the greatest players of the age, had been the scapegoat of the Manchester City 'scandals' of 1906. This revolved around the payment of illegal bonuses to players, a common practice of the wealthier clubs, detested by the FA, which investigated them with all the zeal of their amateur idealism. The new union, first called the Association Football Players' Union (AFPU), later the Professional Footballers' Union (PFU), founded at a meeting in Manchester on 2 December 1907, was destined to lead the players into a historic confrontation with the authorities, when a threatened strike at the start of the 1909–10 season was avoided only at the last minute.

Like other union activity throughout the western world at this time, there was disagreement about whether the Union should concern itself only with matters of employment, or whether it should seek political action outside the workplace. In the case of football the question was whether the role of the Union was to look after members in distress, through accident and pension funds, or to disregard the 'loyalty clause' to the FA and take the matter up with the laws of the land rather than those of the football authorities. The players hoped that they might get some support from the authorities, since the richer clubs favoured abolishing the maximum wage, while the FA had expressed its distaste for the retain and transfer system. The League and the FA, however, drew together to defend themselves, and in football as in society, the interest of the rulers proved stronger than that of the ruled. The FA made a conciliatory gesture to the League in the summer of 1908 when it offered it an amnesty on illegal payments and other irregularities; in return the League consented 'to be honest' in order to fight with it against the demands of the players.

The issue that most raised the hackles of the ruling authorities was when the AFPU took the case of a Reading player to court, on the basis of the Workman's Compensation Act of 1906, claiming that his club was responsible for compensation for an injury he had sustained. Further cases of recourse to an authority outside the FA brought the clubs and the FA together, and did not win much public appeal for the Union. The thought of a strike was also far from palatable. Meredith had written a light-hearted article in the fine, if utopian, vision of the political socialists of this time, in which he pictured a Britain without football: of deserted terracings, empty trams and trains, no sports news and a public resentful of the 'inadequate payment and scurvy treatment' of the players. Sutcliffe of the League replied with sarcasms and lies that were part of the armoury of the keepers of Fair Play morality, claiming without any basis in fact that the players were preparing for a strike within three years time. He also had some points to make which were closer to the truth: should there be a strike there were hundreds of players craving for an opportunity to play; and the public believed players were amply rewarded with £4 a week.

The Union made two tactical blunders in April 1909: first it gave the impression that it was trying to get the England team to go on strike before their annual game against Scotland; second it appeared to make an agreement with the General Federation of Trade Unions (GFTU), a body independent of the Trades Union Council, and more concerned with conciliation than disruption. The FA could thus play on the proposed treachery on the eve of the Scotland game, and 'prove' that a strike had been contemplated because the GFTU had been called in. The FA then demanded that all players resign from the AFPU. On 1 July the AFPU affiliated with the GFTU.

Player support for the AFPU at this time is difficult to ascertain, as their membership ceased between 30 April and 1 September of each year; they could thus tell the FA that they were no longer members whether this was the case or not. The likely success of a strike was never tested, as the players agreed to disaffiliate from the GFTU and the FA made a series of promises in regard to the key issues, none of which had much substance. They also introduced concessions in regard to bonuses and long service payments and agreed to pay the players' summer wages. Moreover, the £500 benefit due to Charlie Roberts was paid. With Meredith and Colin Veitch of Newcastle United, Roberts was one of the leaders in the players' agitation. A radical rather than a socialist like Veitch, he had put his career and his benefit at risk, and went on to fight for the rights of players as Chairman of the AFPU from 1913 to 1921.

The strike was averted. A few elite players gained some benefits, but the clubs had reaffirmed their power over the players through the 'retain and transfer system', while the wage maximum was still in place. These issues would be a constant source of discontent for players for half a century. But the Union had survived the attacks on it by the FA. It even survived near bankruptcy emerging out of the Kingaby case which came to a head in 1913. Kingaby of Aston Villa had been kept unemployed at the will of the club, but the lawyer who took up the case on behalf of the player and the AFPU made a hash of it, attacking the motives of the club instead of the injustices of the retain and transfer system. The costs awarded against the Union almost ruined it. Nearly fifty years would pass before another English player's case was taken to court, and then with revolutionary consequences.

The position of professional football players in regard to strikes is always ambivalent. The elite players can easily look after themselves (Roberts, Meredith and Veitch were exceptional in their sophisticated political views), and whatever the reality of most players not being on the maximum wage, and a career which if short and uncertain, was far from nasty and brutish, the same thousands who worshipped the men they paid sixpence each week to see could spill few tears over their condition. To talk of 'work loads' in an 'industry' where the greatest worry was not being called on to 'work' is somewhat farcical. None of which diminishes the reality of a system that demeaned the players.

The professional footballer of the first decade of the twentieth century had a life style that was the envy of his working-class mates. But it was an essentially working-class life. The threat of unemployment was constant, as injury could strike at any time, and loss of form came to even the best players. At most he could expect ten to fifteen years in the game, and after that, if he was lucky or prudent, might enter into small business, as manager of a pub or owner of a small shop. The short-lived skills of the playing field were not much in demand: a few could coach, in what passed for coaching at that time; even less might find a job in journalism; most, however, who came into the game with a trade, could return to it, and hope that the humdrum life of the factory after being so long in the public eye did not drive them to drink.

Football in 1913

On the eve of the First World War Great Britain had established itself as the home of association football, with efficiently run league and cup competitions that had no equal in any other sport or any other football code. More to the point, it was to be the envy and emulation of countries in Europe and South America that were even then establishing soccer. If the rules of the game could easily be exported, the spirit of the FA and its fellows could not; this was a mixed blessing. The very stuffiness and amateurism of the FA and the narrowness of the league combined to preserve an equality of outcome, in England, that few other countries achieved. Profits were shared to some degree. The directors of English (and other British) clubs could not make a large profit out of the game; all research points to them getting involved more as a pastime than as a business, with individuals indulging in practices in football they would never tolerate in their businesses. For those who watched the game it was a cheap form of amusement: the cost of entry, the price of a paper and a pint at the pub, kept the game within the reach of the ordinary supporter, giving many of them the feeling, in spite of all economic and legal rationality, that the local team belonged to them. Women were by and large excluded. In some ways the players had to subsidize this cheap amusement, but millions dreamed of following in their footsteps. The game, too, was kept free from overt political interference. The press could not ignore it, and if it was in some ways to exploit it, the game remained bigger than the media, at least until the advent of television.

At the turn of the century it was a popular practice to predict the future, usually as a means of criticizing the present. In *Scottish Umpire* in 1884, a game was described that took place in 1901 between the United States and Scotland. The 'Yankees' had accepted the challenge, sent out on the 'amazing postage system', after defeating Australia, Canada and England. Distance was no problem, as the new electric ships cut across the Atlantic at 100 knots per hour in perfect comfort. In none of these accounts was there the slightest thought that the game might be taken up by 'foreigners'. The imperial vision of the British was in keeping with a nation that believed it was the master of football, as well as other important matters. This was soon to be put to the test, for when football emerged from the slaughter of the First World War it was in a world where belief in the mastery of the British could be maintained only through keeping firmly in place blinkers indelibly stamped 'Made in Great Britain'.

Endnotes

The period covered by this chapter has been the most assiduously worked over by historians, resulting in some of the best histories of football. Above all:

Tony Mason, *Association Football and English Society. 1863–1915*, The Harvester Press, London, 1980.

combines rigorous scholarship with the insights of someone thoroughly steeped in the game. Another first class work, in which football is analysed along with cricket, rugby and racing, and in which the author achieves the remarkable feat of making economic history a pleasure to read, is:

Wray Vamplew, *Pay Up and Play the Game. Professional Sport in Britain, 1875–1914*, Cambridge University Press, Cambridge, 1988.

Of Richard Holt's many excellent works:

Richard Holt, *Sport and the British. A Modern History*, Clarendon Press, Oxford, 1989.

Specifically on football:

Richard Holt, 'Working Class Football and the City: The Problem of Continuity', *BJSH*, Vol. 3, No. 1, May 1986, pp. 5–17.
Richard Holt, 'Football and the Urban Way of Life in Nineteenth Century Britain', in J.A. Mangan (ed.), *Pleasure, Profit, Proselytism. British Culture and Sport at Home and Abroad. 1700–1914*, Frank Cass, London, 1988.

John Hutchinson, *The Football Industry. The early years of the professional game*, Richard Drew Publishing, Edinburgh, 1982

has some excellent illustrations and a short but useful text.

There is still no work on Scottish football to match that of Mason on English football.

Queen's Park have had two histories written by lovers of the club:

Richard Robinson, *History of Queen's Park Football Club. 1867–1917*, Hay Nisbet, Glasgow, 1920.

R.A. Crampsey, *The Game for the Game's Sake. The History of Queen's Park Football Club. 1867–1967*, The Queen's Park Football Club, Glasgow, 1967.

Crampsey also wrote the official centenary history of the Scottish League:

R.A. Crampsey, *The Scottish Football League. The First 100 Years*, Scottish Football League, East Kilbride, n.d. (1990).

For Rangers and Celtic and their fusion in 'The Old Firm', see:

Bill Murray, *The Old Firm. Sectarianism, Sport and Society in Scotland*, John Donald Publishers, Edinburgh, 1984.

For statistics on Scottish football to supplement the data in Vamplew, see:

Forrest Robertson, *Mackinlay's A to Z of Scottish Football*, Macdonald Publishers, Edinburgh, 1979.

The Football League has had its official histories with the usual faults of such works: for its centenary history, however, the League commissioned Simon Inglis, who combined celebration with criticism in his unique style:

Simon Inglis, *League Football and the Men Who Made It*, Collins, London, 1988.

For a more critical view of the role of the League, Braham Dabscheck has written extensively on players' rights. Many of these are listed in his most recent work, a study of the 1909 controversy:

Braham Dabscheck, ' "A man or a puppet"? The Football Association's attempt to destroy the Association Football Players' Union', *IJHS*, Vol. 8, No. 2, September 1991, pp. 221–38.

John Harding, *For the Good of the Game. The official history of the Professional Footballers' Association*, Robson Books, London, 1991, is an excellent coverage of the subject. Harding has also written several biographies, one on Billy Meredith, the pioneer fighter for players' rights:

John Harding, *'Football Wizard'. The story of Billy Meredith*, Breedon Books, Derby, 1985.

The quotes from Meredith are from Gibson and Pickford, an essential source for this period.

CHAPTER THREE

Colonialism by Consent

At the turn of the century football was being played in English-speaking countries throughout the world: only in the United Kingdom, however, was soccer the dominant code. In all of its former colonies soccer was the poor relation to rugby or a local invention. The irony is that whereas soccer was dismissed in countries where Britain had once had some political control, it was to be embraced elsewhere in the world, spread in ships of trade and ships of war by Scots and English engineers, merchants, clerks and others in the selling, supplying, service and protection of industrial products 'Made in Britain'. When British economic expansion collapsed, soccer remained as Britain's 'most enduring export'.

By 1900 football teams had been formed in most countries in Europe, eventually to be followed by a national controlling body. Most of these teams were founded by Britons or people who had been to Britain and became infected with the game there. Occasionally the first games were a mixture of rugby and soccer, but as the two went their own way rugby lost popularity. Only in France did it survive as a serious rival to soccer. In central Europe soccer often began within a club catering for several sports before splitting to form an independent football club. Most commonly teams were founded by Anglophiles, often language or engineering students who had been to Britain, or Britons working and living abroad, at shipping ports or other key points of commercial activity, such as in the construction of railways or the installation and running of factories. At first confined to these British or cosmopolitan groups, the game would then be taken up by the local elites. In this way, in Europe and South America, the British found themselves unwitting missionaries when the pastime they brought with them to other lands was eagerly adopted by the locals, who willingly sought British advice in playing the game, organizing it and controlling it. Before 1914 the game on the continent was still largely in the hands of middle class elites of the major urban centres, an amateur game controlled by amateurs, and as such no match for the teams from Great Britain.

Expansion in Europe

Football on the continent first took root in those countries with strong connections – geographical, moral or economic – with Britain, but it was in the central European capitals of Austria, Hungary and Bohemia that the game best flourished before 1914. In northern Europe the Scandinavians took to the game early, but retained their amateur status longer than most countries; in southern Europe, on the other hand, Italy and Spain were prepared to spend vast sums of money to get star players to play for them, and in the 1930s Italy became the dominant soccer power. In Spain the Civil War from 1936 to 1939 did not encourage football, and its glory days would have to wait until the 1950s. France and Germany had thriving competitions by the 1920s, while in eastern Europe football became caught up in the ethnic struggles that led to the collapse of empires and the creation of new ones. Few of those who took up the gentlemanly game at the beginning of the century could have envisaged the frenzy with which it would be followed throughout Europe within a couple of decades. For the British, who got the ball rolling, it was all an irrelevance.

Switzerland and Denmark were the first to take up the association game. In Switzerland the British influence was immense, particularly in the regular interchange of students in the two countries, and it was British pupils in Swiss private schools who popularized a form of football in the 1860s, particularly in the French-speaking areas of Lausanne and Geneva: the Lausanne Football and Cricket Club was founded as early as 1860. Saint-Gallen were founded in 1879 in the German-speaking region, and seven years later a group of students in a Zurich café decided to form a team to be called Grasshoppers. The unusual name was thought up by Tom Griffith, an Englishman who was studying biology, and it was he who took the proceeds of the collection and went back to Britain to buy a set of blue and white halved shirts and a ball. The following year the new team won the first Swiss championship, which they went on to win on many subsequent occasions. Grasshoppers are seen as the team of the banking and industrial giants of Zurich, and this and their success have not made them the most popular team in the country. Although a small country with a small population, football took firm root in Switzerland, and despite the difficulties of terrain, its protagonists managed to construct an impressive number of grounds and stadiums, good enough to host the World Cup in 1954.

Switzerland's main impact on the world game was less in its playing strength than its export of players and coaches, particularly to the western Mediterranean areas of Italy, France and Spain. One of the most successful teams in Marseille in the early days was Stade Helvétique, a team composed entirely of Swiss. Switzerland's main claim to fame in the football world today, however, is that Zurich is the home of the world governing body, FIFA.

Denmark was closely related by geography and economic activity to

Britain. Its first and greatest club, KB (Københavns Boldklub) was founded in Copenhagen as early as 1876. On 18 May 1889 the Danish FA (Dansk Boldspil Union) was formed, and in the early days of amateurism, Denmark was one of the top nations: they reached the finals of the soccer competition at the Olympic Games in 1908 and 1912, only to be defeated on both occasions by Great Britain. Denmark did not adopt professionalism until 1978, and refused to play expatriates in its national team before 1976, but thereafter, in the 1980s a sparkling Danish national team delighted millions of TV viewers in the World and European Championship Cups with its open and attacking play. This came to a fairy tale climax at the 1992 European Championship in Sweden, when a Danish team which had failed to make the finals was hastily recalled to take the place of Yugoslavia, forced to withdraw because of its political problems. They went on to stun powerful neighbours like the Netherlands and Germany and take the title, showing that even in today's clinically professional climate the romance of soccer is not dead. At club level, however, the realities of today's multi-national game, with the best players going to the richest countries, has made it difficult for even top clubs in the smaller nations to succeed in European tournaments.

The Netherlands was the first continental nation after Denmark to set up its own FA, when the Nederlandsche Voetbal bond, (with 'K' for 'Royal' added to the title on 26 November 1929), was founded on 8 December 1889. Since the late 1960s, the Netherlands has produced teams that have enjoyed a success that such a comparatively small country has no right to expect: before then, however, its achievements were modest. The game was brought to the Netherlands by a Dutch student who had gone to school in England, Pim Mulier, who founded the first Dutch club, Haarlemse FFC in 1879. Mulier was one of those ubiquitous 'fathers of the game' whose energy and dedication would be responsible for its growth in many countries. In 1882 he founded the first Dutch sports newspaper, *Nederlandse Sport*, and continued to be involved in football through to the 1930s when the Netherlands, still amateur, as it would be until 1954, had one of the most carefully developed systems of coaching schools. Shortly after Mulier's pioneering efforts the game was given a boost with the boom in the Dutch cotton industry and workers were brought over from Lancashire to set up spinning mills at Enschede. They soon put down football roots in the eastern provinces.

Football in neighbouring Belgium, another strong trading partner of Britain's, spread from an indeterminate form of football emanating from the British colleges of Bruges, Brussels and Antwerp in the 1860s to the first association club, Cercle des Régates de Bruxelles, in 1878. Several other clubs were founded, but among those best known today, Royal Antwerp were founded in 1880 and FC Brugge in 1891. Not until 1908 were RSC (Royal Sporting Club) Anderlecht founded in the capital. The Belgian FA, the Union Belge des Sociétés de Football Association/ Belgische Voetbalbond (with 'royal' added to both titles on 10 February 1920) was founded in 1895, and a league set up that same year, one of the first outside the UK. Like Denmark, Belgium was a powerful force in the early days of amateurism, and again like Denmark, performed remarkably in the 1980s, particularly in the World Cup of 1986 in Mexico, where they came fourth, and as a result were given a royal reception from King Baudouin on their return.

Of the other countries of northern Europe, Sweden, from the 1920s until recently, dominated the Scandinavian countries. Indeed, in the period after the Second World War, under English coach George Raynor they won the Olympic Games in London in 1948, and then against professional opposition came third in the World Cup in Brazil in 1950, and were defeated finalists on home soil in 1958. A truly amateur nation throughout this time, Sweden has never taken up full professionalism, and as a result has been constantly plundered of its many outstanding players. The game is said by one account to have been brought to Sweden by Scottish riveters engaged by the Municipality of Gothenburg on a huge boiler building contract, and this port city has remained the major bastion of football in Sweden. The Swedish FA (Svenska Fotbollförbundet) was founded on 18 December 1904, two years after an unofficial body founded in Gothenberg. Norway was never to become a major soccer power, and although causing the occasional upset, most recently defeating England and the Netherlands to qualify for the 1994 World Cup, it has enjoyed regular success only against Finland. Nevertheless, its Cup competition and FA (Norges Fotballforbund) were both founded two years before Sweden's, in 1902. The Finns were at an even greater disadvantage than their neighbours in regard to terrain and climate, but nevertheless succeeded in establishing a thriving football competition, in the beginning, according to one account, thanks to 'a family of lads called Crichton' who returned from school in England and settled in Turku. Its FA (Suomen Palloliitto- Finlands Bollförbund) was founded in 1907 and its national championship a year later. A glimmer of success came in the 1912 Olympics, but for sporting success the Finns have had to look to their athletes.

Relations between Britain and France have often been marked by a mutual distrust, and little that happened in football, particularly in its international developments, helped to overcome this. It was France, despairing at British arrogance, that took the lead in the establishment of the governing body of world football, the Fédération Internationale de Football Association (FIFA), founded in Paris in 1904. Frenchmen were also behind the establishment of the World Cup in 1930 and the various European competitions that began in the 1950s. With Coubertin's role in founding the modern Olympic Games it could well be said that the French genius, in sport as in politics, has more often been to the benefit of the rest of the world than to itself. In what is perhaps a measure of her social maturity, football in France has never attracted the fanatical support it has among some of her neighbours, but France's reputation for more cerebral concerns has masked its deep commitment to sport in general and football in particular. Although the most popular sport in France from the 1920s, its footballers have not entered the national conscience to the same degree as its great cyclists and boxers: most of France's great football players have been of foreign extraction, particularly the Kopa/Fontaine strike force that shot France to world class in the 1950s, and Michel Platini who led France into the glory days of the early 1980s. And long before it became the fashion in other countries, France was prepared to use the talent in its colonies, Arab or black, to boost the domestic game.

Football in France began in the busy port towns of the Channel, where the families of British shipping and rail agencies conducted their work and set up residence. The first official football games were played by Le Havre Athletic Club, founded in 1872. Its patron was F.F. Langstaff, head of the South Western Railway Company, which linked Southampton to the continent. There it was that a reverend gentleman by the unlikely name of George Washington decreed that football should be played: it was, however, a mixture of rugby and soccer, and it was not until 1890 that the two codes were clearly separated. Football was being played in the Bois de Boulogne from the late 1870s, and in 1887 the short-lived Paris Association Football Club was founded. By the early 1890s a few clubs took on a more permanent organization, most notably the White Rovers, composed mainly of Scots (1891) and the Standard Athletic Club (1892) reserved exclusively for Britons. The first purely French team was founded in 1892, but even then most of the players of Club Français had some education in England or Scotland (the Jesuit College of Saint Joseph in Dumfries). Schools throughout France followed the lead of Club Français, and formed old boy teams when their school days were over. Rugby was more popular than soccer at this time, untainted as it was by professionalism, and it was not until 1919 that the first autonomous FA was set up, the Fédération Française de Football Association (FFFA).

Football was also slower to take off in Germany. Organized sport in Germany is older than that of any other continental European nation, going back to the militaristic/nationalistic (not to mention anti-semitic) gymnastics associations of Ludwig Jahn. The inspiration behind these *Turner* was to unite body and soul in the war of liberation against Napoleon from 1813, and was continued afterwards in the quest for German unification. This was not completed until the Franco-Prussian war of 1870–71, and although it was done more by 'blood and iron' than muscle and mind, the reputation of the *Turner* movement as a German institution meant that football had a powerful rival when British settlers, tourists and students started organizing games from the 1860s. Football often originated within one of the multi-disciplined sports clubs that were popular in central Europe. Rugby was often the preferred code at first, but soccer soon took over. After the war it surpassed even the various *Turner* organizations in popularity. However, it was not until the 1950s that Germany produced world class football teams: since then it has been the most successful football nation, along with Brazil, Argentina and Italy.

In the mid-1860s a certain Ferdinand Hueppe could be found playing football with British boys. He later became first president of the German FA (Deutscher Fussball Bund/DFB) when it was formed in 1900. Two others closely associated with the establishment of football in Germany were Konrad Koch and Walter Bensemann, both teachers. Koch introduced football to his school in Brunswick in 1874, drew up the first rules in German in 1876, and as early as 1886 was calling for a German FA. Bensemann, an Anglophile and gifted linguist, was the son of a wealthy Berlin family who was educated in Switzerland and England. He founded football clubs wherever he went, always calling them 'Kicker'. Among these was a small club founded in Frankfurt at the beginning of the century, which merged with another Frankfurt club called Viktoria in 1911 to become the Frankfurter-Fussball-Verein and nine years later Eintracht Frankfurt. His fascination for 'kickers' did not end in football teams, however, for in 1920 he founded Germany's foremost football journal *Der Kicker*.

Football in Germany first took root in the seaports and other trading centres. The first specifically soccer club was founded in Hamburg in 1887, and in 1919 a merger with SC Germania and FC Falke gave birth to the famous Hamburger SV (Sport-Verein/Sports Club). In addition to the seaports, football was particularly popular along the Elbe and Weser rivers, and in Berlin, which played the first inter-city match, against Hamburg, in 1896. As in Britain in its early days, football was played overwhelmingly by white-collar workers, but unlike Britain, where the free Saturday afternoon released workers to take up the game, in Germany it was clerks, shop assistants, technicians and engineers who were released to play the game when the free Sunday was introduced in 1891. Many industrial bosses found their way around the banning of Sunday work, while other workers had long had Sunday free. Many of them, however, were married, and preferred to stay at home with their families. The middle class emerging from the burgeoning consumer society in Germany in the 1890s, on the other hand, was often young, fit and single, and it was they who took to the game, suppressing their religious conscience to ape their social 'betters', and showing a mania for titles and medals which saw players not only sport their entire range of decorations at presentations, but in civilian life as well. Before the foundation of the DFB in 1900, and for some time after that, most games were played as a middle class version of street football, with teams picked on the spot and changed to even up the game if it became too unbalanced. By the turn of the century, nevertheless, most of the seven regions of Germany had founded their own associations, and in 1902 a national Cup was instituted. As a spectator sport, however, football did not arouse local loyalties, while on the national scene it could even be dismissed as disloyal.

In 1899 incipient Anglophobia in Germany was stirred up by the Boer War, but this did not prevent Walter Bensemann and Ivo Schricker, later to become a secretary of FIFA, bringing an English amateur team to Germany. This first visit by an England team was organized by Bensemann, but sponsored by Schricker's mother, who was persuaded by her son to put up 4000 marks to underwrite the tour. A German team paid a return visit in 1901 only to be beaten 12–0 by an amateur XI and 10–0 by a professional XI. Bensemann was expelled from the South German FA for his efforts; the Reichschancellor withdrew his name as patron of the organizing committee.

Opposition to things foreign in Germany had the added venom of the ultra-nationalist *Turner*, which favoured gymnastics against team games and hated all that was not truly German. In Bavaria, football was banned in all schools until 1913. Despite this, and the low esteem held for the game in the royal household and the military, where the *Turner* spirit prevailed, the game progressed, if slowly. The attitude of the court changed as the country lurched towards war, and in 1910 the military allowed their parade grounds to be used as playing fields for football. The old military qualities of discipline and precision that were the hallmark of gymnastics gave way to a new emphasis on teamwork and individual initiative, and the language of football, whose British origins were skipped over, took on the familiar vocabulary of military formations. In 1911 the DFB and the largest white collar union joined the paramilitary *Jungdeutschlandbund*. In the years immediately after the war the popularity of football in Germany soared.

In southern Europe the game came early to Portugal, where university students played the game as early as 1866. The first team, Lisbon FC, was founded in 1875, and in the 1890s the Portuguese themselves, particularly students who had been to Britain, formed their own teams. Soccer was played in Spain in the 1890s, encouraged by British mining engineers in the Basque provinces, where the first team, Athletic Bilbao was founded in 1898. British military personnel fostered the game in Madrid and Valencia, but in Barcelona, the thriving commercial city where French influences were stronger, it was the Swiss, Hans (or Juan or Joan) Gamper, who founded the first major team in the Catalonian capital, in 1899. FC

Barcelona was at first made up of foreigners, mainly British, but they were in turn challenged by Català, a team of locals who merged with Español a few years later. Spain's international debut had to wait until after the First World War, as football served as a platform for regional separatism rather than national unity. In Catalonia most football contacts were with the French, and through to 1918 the major competition was the Pyrenees Cup. Spain's first major impact on the world football scene had to wait until the Réal Madrid team of the 1950s, a team of international talents bought by the ever-open cheque books that were a feature of Spanish football directors. Spain's national team has suffered as a consequence, and has a mediocre record.

Italians have waved cheque books around with as much abandon as their Spanish colleagues, but they have achieved world class at both club and national level: in the 1930s under the cloud of Fascism, in the early 1990s with unsurpassed class at club level; above all, AC Milan have entered the ranks of the greatest teams of all time. In 1982 Italy won their third World Cup trophy, in Spain, and in 1990 as the host nation almost made it four. Italy has its regional differences, like Spain, but based more on economic than cultural factors and unlike Spain, success at the national level is an occasion for widespread national joy.

Football had an ancient history in Italy, and so the British influence has been muted by long indigenous traditions. The British influence could be seen in the title of the first Italian FA, founded in 1898 (Federazione Italiana del *Football*), but this was soon changed to the more Italian title, Federazione Italiana Giuoco Calcio, in 1908. It was in the industrial north that football first flourished, particularly in the Turin/Genoa/Milan triangle, often in gymnastic associations. The first organized game of football is said to have been arranged by Edoardo Bosio in 1887. Bosio was an optical goods manufacturer who made frequent trips to Britain, and decided to organize a team among his employees. According to Pierre Milza, he arranged games with the Turin aristocracy, and in 1891 the two groups came together as the Internazionale Football Club. Later scissions gave rise to the Unione Sportiva Torinese, then to the two great Turin rivals, Juventus in 1897 and Torino in 1906. The first official football team was founded in Genoa in 1893, as the Genoa Cricket and Football Club. Made up equally of Britons and locals it dominated the first championships from 1898. In Milan the basis for the future rivalry of Inter and AC Milan was set at the turn of the century. Milan Cricket and Football Club were founded in 1899, with British and Swiss dominant, but perhaps of more significance was the presence of the Italian Dr Piero Pirelli, whose interest in tyres helped ensure the financial stability of what became the famous Associazione Calcio Milan, better known as AC Milan. Their famous rival, Internazionale, were founded after a split within the club in 1908.

It was not until 1910 that something approaching a national championship was organized, and in that year Italy also played its first international,
beating France 6–0. Bologna Football Club were founded in 1909, but the
success of the southern clubs came later. Lazio Societa Sportiva were
founded in 1900, but their local rivals Roma Associazione Sportiva came 27
years later. There was a football team in Naples in 1898, and in 1904 a team
using, as was so often the case, the English spelling, Naples, appeared,
before today's Napoli were officially founded in 1926. Despite a large and
fanatical support, they were late in making their impact. Millionaire
shipowner Achille Lauro poured money into the club, but it was not until
the arrival of Maradona in 1984 that the men from the south seriously
challenged the northern dominance. Even before this, however, they were
drawing crowds averaging 70,000.

In the old-world empires

When the peace-makers at Versailles dismantled the empires of Austria–
Hungary and Turkey after the First World War, their attempts to create a
new Europe out of the ruins of the old were to fail. Political idealists were
no more successful than sporting idealists in curing the incurable: although
football was the sporting passion of central and eastern Europe, it was
unable to overcome the hatreds of generations.

The old-world capitals of Vienna, Budapest and Prague soon picked up
the pieces after 1918 and took up football where they had left off. Before
1914 they led the football world outside the United Kingdom, and into the
1930s they continued to do so. Neither Austria nor Hungary was to regain
the political power they lost following the Versailles Treaty, but both
Austria and Hungary reached the status of world champion, if only
unofficially and by popular acclaim: Austria with its 'Wunderteam' of the
early 1930s, Hungary with its state-sponsored national team of the early
1950s. From the beginning of the century they, or rather their Viennese
and Budapest selections, were the best on the continent. They played each
other in the second international outside the United Kingdom, in 1902,
Austria winning 5–0. Future games between these former partners in the
Dual Monarchy were fought with all the drama of a local derby.

Vienna was home for a large population of expatriate Britons. Football
was played there in the 1880s, but the first official game took place on 15
November 1894, between members of the Vienna Cricket and Football
Club and the gardeners of the Baron Rothschild. The 'Cricketers' became
the Wiener Amateure SV in 1911, then changed their name to the famous
FK Austria in 1925. The 'gardeners', who called themselves First Vienna
Football Club, are still known as First Vienna. In 1898 the third great

Austrian team was born when some workers in Vienna founded the 1. Arbeiter-Fussballklub (First Workers' Football Club) but changed their name a year later, when several British players joined the team, to Sportklub Rapid, better known as Rapid Vienna. In 1897 the first knock-out tournament, Der Challenge-Cup, was held, and the first league competition began in 1911. These were for Viennese teams only, and it was not until 1949 that provincial teams were invited to join the league. In 1904 the Vienna Sports Union was formed and its football section, the Oesterreichischer Fussball-Verband was accepted into FIFA in 1905. M.D. Nicholson, who arrived in Vienna in 1897 to take up his post in the office of Thomas Cook, was an early pioneer of the game in Vienna, and had a Cup named after him, but the main driving force in Austrian, and even European football, was Hugo Meisl, to whom we shall return.

Football was played in Hungary in the 1880s, within gymnastic clubs. The most notable of these, both British inspired, were the Ujpest Sport Club which was formed in 1885 and gave rise to Ujpest Dozsa, and the Budapest Gymnastic and Athletic Club, which put out a team in 1888 under the name Magyar Testgyakorlok Köre (MTK). Others followed, the most famous of which was Ferencvaros Torna (Gymnastics) Club in 1899. The first recorded match was played in May 1897 under the auspices of the Budapest Gymnastics Club (Budapesti Torna Club/BTC). Before 100 spectators two teams played on the Millinaris field, and despite the criticism from onlookers and the press for the violence of the game, it progressed undeterred. Thirteen clubs made up the first championship in 1901, and in that same year the Hungarian Football Association (Magyar Labdarugok Szovetsege) was formed.

The third great city of the Austro-Hungarian Empire, Prague, could hold its own with Vienna and Budapest as a football centre, and in its two great arch-rivals, Slavia (1892) and Sparta (1893), had teams to beat the best in continental Europe from the early days to the 1930s. Slavia Praha was one of the oldest sports clubs on the continent. It was founded by students as a cycling and gymnastic club in 1882, to become, as an official report claimed, 'one of the streams which made up the mighty flow of the struggle of the Czechs, Slovaks and other Slavonic nations for national liberation against the then Austro-Hungarian monarchy.' The club also brought ice-hockey to Czechoslovakia as well as field hockey and rugby. Soccer, however, was clearly the most popular sport. In 1896 the first of many games between a Budapest and Vienna selection was played. The Bohemian FA, controlling Moravia but not Slovakia, was founded in 1901, although its first league had to wait until 1912. On the international scene, Bohemia did not match the standards of its leading clubs, which had regular victories against teams from other countries.

Football in other parts of the outdated empires was not encouraged by the authorities, who feared that meetings to form football teams or even to discuss tactics could lead to discussion of tactics of a more explosive nature. Football in Poland had to wait until liberation from the rule of the three powers that had partitioned it in the eighteenth century. The Russian and Prussian overlords banned football for fear of it being used as a cover for nationalist activities, but in that part of Poland under Austrian rule a more relaxed attitude and a love of the game prevailed. As a result a few successful teams, like Cracow, were formed.

In the Ottoman empire the game was played mainly by the ethnic minorities, particularly Bulgarians, Greeks, Armenians and Jews, and as such was highly suspect to the Turks, who were a long time in adopting the game. British sailors brought football to Greece, and Greek students embraced it with zeal and a political commitment in Constantinople and other Balkan cities under Ottoman control. As a result their teams were suppressed. Returning home they spread the game, but could never keep it clear of politics. One result is that despite the passion of the Greeks for football they have been unsuccessful at club and national level. They have taken their enthusiasm with them to the many non-soccer countries to which they have emigrated, and contributed hugely to the development of the game. And in 1993 the Greek national team qualified for the first time for the World Cup finals.

In other parts of the Balkans a German is said to have taken the game to Belgrade in 1896. In Romania a federation was founded in 1910 and a championship played the next year. Olympic of Bucharest won the first, the second was won by United Ploesti, made up of British workers in the extensive oil fields and the textile factories. Football in Bulgaria suffered from the unstable political climate and uncertain administration. What success it had was mainly due to Bulgarian students at the universities in Constantinople. In the late 1920s Yugoslavia, its club teams representing the bitter ethnic divisions of the new state, emerged as the most successful of the Balkan countries, and exported players and coaches to other countries in a profusion equalled only by Scotland.

After the Bolshevik Revolution of 1917 the Russian game that had been beginning to flourish continued in a politically more correct manner. Rugby was the first form of football brought to Russia, introduced by a Scot called Hopper, but it was banned in 1886 as brutal and liable to incite riots. The Scots, English and Germans then took to soccer, founding teams proclaiming their national identity, and at first excluding Russians. The first recorded game involving Russians was played at a cycling meeting in St Petersburg in 1892, and the first under something approaching FA rules in 1896. The official birth of soccer is set a year later with the Amateur Sports Circle in St Petersburg. The first football league, made up entirely of foreign teams, was founded in St Petersburg in 1900, and although it was not until 1910 that a Moscow league was set up, the game was played there long before this. As the Russians took to the game the dominance of the British, and to a lesser extent Germans, became irksome. English was used for all the technical terms, but the British presence also made itself felt in the administration and control of the game. As the play of the Russians improved, the bias of the British was increasingly resented, and this was brought to a head when Chirtsov of the Russian team Sport was sent off the field and banned for a year for retaliation against what he thought was violent play by his English opponent, Sharples, who nearly strangled him. The British claimed Sharples's tackle was 'hard but quite legitimate', but the Russian paper *Sport* pictured it as a savage attack, and parodied the unpunished aggression of 'Sharples the throttler' as an encouragement to future would-be assassins like 'Jim the Stabber and Jack the Ripper.'

The prime mover in Russian football was the Orekhovo Sports Club, sponsored by the Morozov Mills, fifty miles from Moscow. Football was first encouraged there by the Charnock brothers, particularly Harry, the manager, in an attempt to distract the workers from drinking too much on Sundays, their one day off. Known as the 'Terror of Moscow' for their apparent invincibility, Moscow teams with Russian players challenged the ascendancy of the Mill team, so that even 'Red Headed Willie Charnock' ceased to be called the Peerless. After 1904 there were as many Russian teams as foreign, and games between the nationalities, especially where the Russians were expected to win, were attracting large attendances. Robert Bruce Lockhart, enthusiastic rugby player and soccer player by default, but also a British agent who later wrote of his adventures there, claimed average crowds of 12,000, of whom a third were women, to games where he played with the Morozov team. The top Russian team, Sport, went on tours of the empire and even abroad to Finland and Sweden. In 1912 Russia sent a soccer team to the Stockholm Olympics with disastrous results, being thrashed 16–0 by Germany.

Success on the playing field and the continuing social and sporting arrogance of the foreigners resulted in the Russians forming their own league: the first national championship was played in 1912, the second was cancelled as a result of a dispute (Odessa played more than their quota of foreign players), and war interrupted play in the following season. When football resumed after the Revolution it would be an entirely new ball game. By 1914 it was clearly the most popular game in Russia, and it continued to be played in the first years of the First World War, but in addition to the discrimination between nationalities there was also a rigid class distinction. The workers, who were excluded from the bourgeois leagues as artisans and mechanics, formed their own teams and leagues, and often used this as a cover for revolutionary activity. This led Lockhart to claim, with more literary licence than historical insight, that if the owners of the factories in Russia had spent more time harnessing the enthusiasm of the workers for soccer they might have won on the playing fields of Moscow what they lost in the reading room of the British Museum.

Throughout Europe by 1914, then, the game was being played, watched and organized by the local elites. Before 1914 none of them could come near the standard of the game being played in Great Britain, whose teams crossed the Channel and the Atlantic in increasing numbers. For the foreign hosts this was a great honour, but while the crusading spirit was part of the motivating force in many of the touring teams, a holiday atmosphere was easily maintained in games that were played as picnic matches. Like the British Empire, the world of British football could look down with Olympian splendour on all beneath it. Well might they enjoy their superiority, for British football, like the British Empire, was seeing its best days.

Picnics and propaganda

The first regular visits to the continent were made mainly by amateur teams, particularly those in the south of England, who had the time, money and proximity to Europe to indulge in Easter or early summer jaunts to see the sights, enjoy the scenery and give the locals football lessons. In 1890 Clapton Orient beat an Antwerp team 0–7; an Oxford University team played Slavia in their new home ground in 1897; and in 1899 the FA sent a representative team to Germany and Prague. From Scotland, Queen's Park paid the first of their visits to Denmark in 1898 and beat KB Copenhagen 0–7 and 0–3; in the following year Oxford University waltzed their way to big victories in Vienna, 0–15 and 0–13. It was Corinthians, however, who established themselves as the world's great wanderers, with trips not only to Europe, but South Africa and South America. In 1904 they scored 29 goals for one against in a three match tour of Sweden, and squeezing in another tour in that year, to Budapest and Paris without their usual comforts, they achieved the remarkable feat of beating a Paris team 4–11 after being 4–2 down with less than half an hour to go.

The amateur team that achieved the greatest reputation on the continent was Middlesex Wanderers. In 1905 the Richmond Town Wanderers were constituted by a few players from Richmond Old Boys, with the object of sending 'teams on tour on the Continent of Europe'. Originally they were made up of players registered with the Middlesex County FA, but as competition stiffened they extended their catchment area to players who had 'gained Amateur International, County or other representative honours approved by the Committee.' In 1912 they changed their name to Middlesex Wanderers, and under the driving force of the two Alaway brothers, continued to tour the world until the eve of the Second World War. By then their games were no longer the walkover they once had been, but they still managed to raise 'many thousands of pounds in the cause of charity.'

The professional teams had less interest in charity, but they could not avoid their duties as ambassadors for the game, and incidentally their country. Southampton were the first, beating Vienna 0–6 in 1900; they returned the following year to beat Budapest 0–8 and 0–13 in successive days. In May 1904 Newcastle beat Britannia 1892 of Berlin 0–10. A full English team visited central Europe in 1906 to celebrate the 60th year of the Austrian emperor's rule; they recorded easy victories in Vienna (1–6), Prague (0–4) and Budapest (0–7).

Although English teams were the most frequent visitors, it was the Scots who made the bigger impact, through coaches like Jackie Robertson of Rangers and John Madden formerly of Celtic, who introduced what was called the Scottish game: short-passing positional play, keeping the ball on the ground, that had made Scotland the dominant football power in the 1870s. This was the method taught a few years later by the Englishman Jimmy Hogan which formed the basis of the 'Danubian style' adopted by the central European countries with brilliant effect in the inter-war period. Celtic and Rangers made the first of their many tours to central Europe and Denmark in 1904, and Rangers came back with the Austrian Karl Pekarna, the first of their foreign imports. Aberdeen toured Poland in 1911 and thrashed Cracow 1–11 and 1–18; Third Lanark made a trip to Portugal in 1914 where they defeated Benfica 1–4.

The few teams that made the journey the other way were even more comprehensively defeated. A Brussels team made the first trip in 1900, and the following year Bensemann's Germans, as we have seen, were beaten by double figures in two games. In 1904 a Paris side that came to play Woolwich Arsenal lost 26–1, their solitary goal being scored by an English substitute, compliments of a complaisant Arsenal defence. (Another story has it that the goal scorer for France was given a hero's welcome at the Gare du Nord when the team returned home.) France's two teams at the London Olympic Games in 1908 did not do very much better.

In such circumstances the players and directors could come back from the continent with tales guaranteed to tickle the prejudice of Britons about the inadequacies and quaint ways of the foreigners: of the referee at a game between Racing Club de Bruxelles and a German team who seated himself in the middle of the field and tried to control the game with a cane; of a well dressed French referee who refused to enter the muddy field, and so ran up and down the touchline to maintain his sartorial decorum and the shine on his shoes (but who had the good sense to disallow four perfectly good goals by the visiting Englishmen on the grounds that it made the game more interesting); of how the most difficult job of the visiting British goalkeeper was coping with the boredom, sitting on the crossbar smoking a pipe throughout the match; and of the French official in charge of keeping the score who shut up shop when double figures were reached, claiming that it was no longer a matter of football, but statistics. In fact the Middlesex Wanderers had a rule never to score more than nine goals, and any player who went beyond that was fined by having to finance that evening's entertainment.

The easy victories of the British visitors tended to hide the fact that the victories were getting harder, and that a few British teams were getting beaten. In 1907, at a time when Celtic were probably the best team in Britain, they lost 2–1 in Copenhagen, and in 1913 Rangers were held to a draw there. Sunderland were the first English team to lose on the continent: in 1909, when they were third in the English League, they lost 2–1 to Wiener AC in Austria. One reason for the improved performance of the locals was that they matched rising enthusiasm in their own countries with the expertise of British coaches who liked what they saw on the continent and were tempted to stay there. The wages and conditions were a major incentive, but so too was a respect denied them in Britain.

John Madden of Celtic was one of the first to go. He took up the job as coach of Slavia in February 1905 when he was forty years of age, and remained there until he died in 1948. When he retired in 1938 he was given a pension, and his memory was venerated long after his death. In 1988 players and officials of the club visited his grave to lay floral tributes. Madden was one of the many sons of Irish immigrants who came to Scotland in the mid-nineteenth century. He was born in Dumbarton on the Firth of Clyde where he played for local teams before becoming a key player in the Celtic team that revolutionized Scottish football in the early 1890s. Barely literate, but self-educated enough to look after the interests of fellow players with their contracts, his was a bold step to set off for a place that a British Prime Minister more than thirty years later described as 'a far away country, populated by people of whom we know nothing.' Madden knew not a word of the language when he arrived, and on his death had learned only enough to curse the players, but he imposed his presence by the power of his personality, his tactical innovations, emphasis on fitness and his skills as a masseur. He married a Czech woman and was buried in the Olsanké cemetery in Prague.

One story of how this small and unremarkable man was offered the job is that Slavia had first sought the services of Jacky Robertson of Rangers, one of the greatest players of the age but then about to retire. Robertson, a fellow 'Son of the Rock', had been offered a job in Scotland as a journalist and so got Madden to pose with a Scottish international cap as himself. Madden's identity would soon have been revealed, but in 1909 as publicity for a tour of Britain, he was described as a Rangers player. Robertson later went to coach on the continent where he had great success with Rapid Vienna and MTK of Budapest. He returned to Scotland, however, and when he died there in 1935, Madden, who himself had been a riveter, was quoted 'from the luxury of Prague' as having said to Robertson on one of their meetings, that life on the continent certainly beat 'boiler-making in Scotland.'

Among other coaches who crossed the Channel were Jack Kirwan of the Spurs cup winning side of 1901, who went to Ajax of Amsterdam, and Jack Greenwell who worked with Hans Gamper when he settled in Barcelona on the eve of the First World War. Several players left for France at this time, encouraged by French agents who hung around the employment exchange on the look-out for talent, but it was after the war that a minor exodus of British professionals began; by the 1930s, however, it was Yugoslavs and Hungarians who were more in demand.

The best known of the British coaches who went to the continent before the War was Jimmy Hogan. Hogan had been a moderate player with Bolton Wanderers and first toured the continent with them in 1909. He returned as a coach to the Netherlands eighteen months later. In 1912 he accepted a two-month coaching appointment with Austria to prepare them for the Olympic Games of that year, so beginning the Hugo Meisl/Jimmy Hogan combination that was to have such benefits for Austrian and European football in general. Crowds of up to 5000 are said to have paid sixpence each to watch Hogan put his players through their paces, and however that may be, his reputation saved him from the worst rigours of war-time internment. After the war he stayed on the continent coaching in several countries, including Hungary. When he returned to England to coach his services were not required, but Celtic brought him north in the late 1940s to revive the club's flagging fortunes. Hogan was never forgotten by the Hungarians, any more than Madden was by the Czechs, and they invited him to be their special guest at their historic victory over England at Wembley in 1953.

Most games played on the continent were friendlies or cup competitions, often regional and frequently across national boundaries, but the games that aroused greatest interest before 1914 were those specially arranged to be played between two British clubs. Ten thousand turned up to see Everton play Spurs on 7 May 1905 in Vienna, more than double the previous record. Such games did not always turn out to be picnic games, and when Celtic played Burnley in Budapest before 20,000 spectators in May 1914, each the holder of their national cup competition, they showed the 'hot-blooded natives' that they had no monopoly on fiery temperament. The game ended in a 1–1 draw, with some players keen to finish it off in fisticuffs. It was played for a specially presented trophy and the proceeds were to go to charity. A return match was played in Burnley on 1 September 1914, which Celtic won, but they never received the expensive trophy, which disappeared. By then other matters were exercising the minds of young men in western Europe – but much later, in 1988, thanks to the efforts of a Celtic fan and the generosity of the Ferencvaros club, a special trophy was presented to Celtic to make up for the one that was lost in 1914.

While the British teams were giving the lessons, European teams were developing the game in their own way, while international encounters multiplied. In such circumstances there was a clear need for a controlling body, to supervise internationals and to help regulate affairs within particular countries. Football in South America was advancing as rapidly as in Europe at this time, and there was even talk of a World Cup being organized, but when the first international controlling body was founded in 1904 it was an essentially European affair.

The founding of FIFA

The attitude of British teams to the game on the continent was shared by the men who ran the game at home. Thus when some foreigners approached the FA about the foundation of an international federation to supervise football at the international level, they were treated with patronizing indifference. The Belgians had first raised the idea in the late 1890s, and the Dutch banker, C.A.W. Hirschman raised the matter again in 1902. The main force behind what was to become the controlling body of world football, however, was the French engineer and newspaper man, Robert Guérin. He was a member of one of the major French sporting societies, and they hosted the inaugural meeting of what became the Fédération Internationale de Football Association (FIFA). As reported in the French newspaper *Tous les Sports* in May 1904:

International Congress of Association Football

Held in Paris, at the office of the Union of French Athletics Societies

Session of 21 May 1904, opened at 2h 30m, under the chairmanship of M. Fringnet, vice-president of the USFSA.

Present; MM. Hirschman (Netherlands Football Union, Holland), Schneider (Swiss Association of Football), Sylow (Danish Football Union, Denmark), Robert Guérin and A. Espir (Union of French Athletics Societies), Muhlinghaus and Kahn (Union of Belgian Athletics Societies)

M. Fringnet welcomed the foreign delegates

CORRESPONDENCE. – Letters: from Dr Karting, announcing the replacement of M. Manning by M. Henschen; DFB from the English FA, offering its apologies and announcing the calling of a Congress in London for 1905; from the Madrid FC., apologising for not being able to send a delegate, but offering its support (M. Espir will represent Spain)

There follow details of the matters discussed by those at the historic meeting, which was continued over the next two days. The apologies sent by the most powerful football nation did not placate the founders. Writing nearly 30 years later, Guérin recalled his stupefaction at the ignorance of Wall, secretary of the FA, at what was happening on the continent, how he listened to his plans for an international federation which he hoped the FA would lead, and how he waited several months in vain for a response. Frustrated at this 'wait and see' attitude, Guérin returned once more, this time to be met with a warmer response from Lord Kinnaird, but without any positive outcome. Wall was unable to 'see the advantages of such a federation' but agreed to confer on any joint action which was 'considered desirable'.

And so it was that Guérin decided to go ahead without the FA. FIFA, soon set down firm roots and thereafter continued from strength to strength. It was founded to control the national federations, but also to arrange international competition, and even at this time the idea of a 'world cup' was thought of, a somewhat preposterous notion in 1904. It was taken up by another Frenchman, Jules Rimet, and has grown from its first competition in 1930 into the biggest competition in the history of sport, the Olympic Games being its only rival.

When it became apparent that FIFA was not going to die away the four British associations began to show more interest, and the FA invited representatives of the continental nations to a conference on the eve of the England vs Scotland game in London in 1905. Following this the FA agreed to enter FIFA, which then had trouble recognizing that the three other British associations were not represented by the FA. This contradicted FIFA's stipulation that only one body could be allowed to represent each country. Eventually they relented on the sporting divisions within the political unity of the UK, and Scotland (1910), Wales (1910) and Ireland (1911) then joined FIFA.

Despite the cool response from London, it was still anticipated that the FA would take the lead in the new body, and so while Guérin was elected first president of FIFA, he was willing to cede his place to the president of the FA after his first year in office. Guérin resigned on 4 June 1906 and was replaced by D.B. Woodfall who held the post until 24 October 1918. It was not until 1956 that another Englishman held the post, Arthur Drewry, and he was followed by Stanley Rous in 1961. In 1974 the British influence on FIFA came to a crashing end when Rous was 'deposed' by the Brazilian, João Havelange. Until then, and despite the infuriating attitude of the British, the founders of the game retained a great respect among those to whom they were so condescendingly indifferent. Although French and German (and later Spanish) were the official languages of FIFA, in cases of dispute it was the English version that was to be used. This applied even during the many years when there were few English-speaking countries in FIFA. The rules of the game, too, were controlled by the International Board, dominated by the British associations.

Of the founding members of FIFA, France and Sweden did not even have a federation of their own in 1904, while Spain was represented by Madrid FC. And the country that founded the Federation was one of the first to be expelled. The problem arose from France's perennial conflict between Church and State, replicated in sport with a clerical association at bitter odds with a secular association that enjoyed the support of the state. The sports association represented on FIFA was the anti-clerical USFSA, its rival the catholic FGSPF. The anti-clerical body was as fanatical in its attitude to amateurism as it was in regard to clericalism, and so when the English Amateur FA asked to join FIFA when it split from the professionals in 1907, the French representatives supported them, unsuccessfully. At the 1908 Congress in Vienna, despite playing on anti-British prejudice in regard to its dictatorial attitude and linguistic imperialism, the French delegates threatened to form a rival body, but were unable to persuade the Swiss, Italians and Hungarians to follow them. FIFA could not tolerate this and the French delegates had to resign. This left the way for the rival FGSPF, which had amalgamated with several regional and other bodies into a French Interfederal Committee (CFI) in 1907, to apply for membership. In 1910 they were accepted into FIFA.

FIFA had survived its first major power struggle; the teams of the USFSA suffered from not being allowed to play teams not associated with FIFA and were told that the only way to overcome this was by joining its detested rival. Leader of the CFI was Charles Simon, who would give his name to the first French Cup after he died at the front in the First World War, but the other major beneficiary of the quarrel was Jules Rimet.

Rimet was born into a moderately wealthy family in 1873, in the village of Theuley in the north of France. His parents suffered from the agricultural crisis following the Franco-Prussian war, and eventually moved to Paris, where Jules joined them when he was eleven. Rimet was the eternal bureaucrat, bland and inoffensive, ambitious and discreet, prepared to make a dramatic gesture of principle so long as he would not be held to it. In his youth he was attached to the social catholic movement of Marc Sagnier, *Le Sillon*, but failing in politics he took up football instead.

As a catholic he sided with the FGSPF and the CFI, and reaped the benefits of their success with FIFA. He was a founding member of Red Star (1897), one of the most famous clubs in French football, particularly strong in the 1920s, and it was as president of Red Star that he first came into contact with FIFA. This was when he campaigned against the actions of the French delegates to FIFA, took Red Star out of the USFSA and encouraged other teams to do the same. After 1910 he resigned as president of Red Star, without losing interest in them, and thereafter devoted his time to unifying the warring French federations into one body. When the Fédération Française de Football Association (FFFA, later FFF) was founded in 1919, he became its first president, a position he held until 1949. He became president of FIFA in 1921, although he spoke no language but French, and held this position until 1954, when he had the honour of presenting the World Cup, then named after him, to the victorious German team. He died in 1956, aged 84.

The major splits ahead for FIFA would be in regard to the British associations, but from 1904 its story is one of continuous growth. By 1914 it had 24 members, four of whom came from outside Europe: South Africa (1909–10), Argentina (1912), Chile (1912) and the USA (1913). On the eve of the Second World War there were 51 members, and between 1950 and 1984 membership more than doubled from 73 to 150. In the draw for the 1994 World Cup there were 143 entries, and as the old Soviet Union and other empires collapse the number of members continues to grow. Today there is barely a nation in the world that does not want to be part of FIFA. With more members than the United Nations, FIFA has not been exempt from the problems of international bodies committed to high ideals, but it had a power that none could resist: the French delegates were the first to discover this, later there would be others. When the British associations left FIFA in the 1920s (twice) it was they who suffered most.

War and peace

Before the First World War some of the continental teams were already showing the approach to the game that would transform them from victims to masters. In Italy, Vittoria Pozzo, won over to the game from the terracings of Manchester United, returned to his own country determined to teach it how to play the game in a scientific manner. In Austria the combined talents of Hugo Meisl and Jimmy Hogan would shape the Austrian club teams and national teams into world beaters. These pointers to the future, however, were dimmed as the lights went out all over Europe in 1914. But they would come on again, and Hogan, Meisl, Pozzo and a host of British (and Hungarian) coaches would lead European football out of the paternal grasp of Britain.

The First World War brought a ghastly unreality to much of the rhetoric that had accompanied the virtues of sport before 1914. Some souls, living in another world when they thought up the idea and soon to visit it when they tried it out, actually did kick balls into the enemy territory urging their men to follow them. The ball kicked out of a rain-sodden trench in Maroc by the London Territorial Regiment to launch the battle of Loos was retained as a historic trophy. Other football memorials relate to the opening of the Somme offensive on 1 July 1916: four balls were dribbled into the enemy ranks, and two were subsequently recovered and made into objects of propaganda and put on display as mementoes of the occasion. For some the actions of Captain Nevill of the East Surrey Regiment, who died with the ball at his feet, helped restore the good name of soccer in Britain, sullied for some by the refusal of the FA and the League to abandon their competitions after the outbreak of hostilities. Both competitions were abandoned after the 1914–15 season. In Scotland the Cup competition was abandoned for the duration, but the league continued, albeit with conditions restricting training to ensure that players did not neglect essential war work. No-one could claim that the Scottish war effort suffered for this, and individuals from teams of potentially (but baseless) suspect patriotism, such as Celtic, and super patriots like Queen's Park, supplied heroes and martyrs, while the whole Hearts team enlisted *en masse*. They were not the only ones, since in England football grounds were used for recruiting – usually with miserable results, as those at the grounds had come to see a football match and take their minds off the war. Nevertheless, this gave another excuse for the football haters to abuse working men and their heroes along the lines of the cartoon: The Ideal (soldier in uniform); The Idol (football player); and The Idle (spectators at a game). The passions of the first year of war withered, and as the early enthusiasm died out means of maintaining morale had to be found: football was one and balls were sent by their thousands to the front. As in the days of Edward II the game's threat to national honour proved to be illusory.

Football served an essential purpose in this time, and most of the players and spectators were also engaged in war work. But more to the point, the vast number of willing conscripts came from working-class football teams, from the ranks of the unseen and the unheard who played for their own amusement each week. In uniform abroad they played the game with the same sense of fun and lack of ulterior motive, incidentally bringing the game to many Belgian and particularly French provincials who had never seen the game before: or seen it played properly. Some were to die playing it, not having cleared the field of unexploded shells before they began. It is said that games were played between the Allies and the Germans during the first Christmas armistice but they were soon banned. In one trench where a group of Celtic supporters celebrated news of their team winning the 1915 championship with an impromptu concert, Germans in the nearest enemy trench, with fond memories of the dynamic centre-forward seen on previous Celtic tours, called out in English 'Good old Jimmy Quinn'.

In France there was no chance of continuing the football season, as the north, the stronghold of the best teams, was so quickly overrun. The cessation of organized football, however, was only temporary, and new competitions were soon introduced, with special rules to allow British and Belgian soldiers to play for teams near where they were posted. One of the new competitions was the Coupe des Alliés. Newspapers, such as *Sporting* and *La Vie au Grand Air*, previously more favourable to rugby, gave the game hitherto unheard of publicity, and sent thousands of footballs to the front: *L'Auto* sent 2500 in one season, and *Sporting* 3000. French football was strengthened as a result of the war, and out of it came its first national Cup, its first unified federation, and a new international competition.

Although football was not a major sport in France at the beginning of the war, some of its star players were used in propaganda pieces; men such as Chayriguès, the goalkeeper, defending his country as he defended his goal, and whose name was given greater billing than the two teams when it was announced that he would be home 'on leave' and able to play. Gabriel Hanot, who had played football as a student in Germany, was captured and after three attempts managed to escape; an injury shortened his playing career, but he went on to even greater fame as a selector, journalist and founder of the European Cup. Lucien Gamblin, another pre-war favourite at full-back, also had his virtues as a defender in football translated into him being a defender at the front. The name of Charles Simon was commemorated in the first national cup competition, based on the FA Cup, and played twice before the armistice. Simon was president of the Catholic FGSPF and of the CFI, the most powerful football group in France, and was killed near Arras on 15 June 1915. Two of his close associates seized this opportunity to perpetuate his name: Dr Michaux donated the cup to be played for in his name, and Henri Delaunay, his energetic secretary, took over as the new power broker. He became the secretary of the first French FA when it was formed in 1919, and with Rimet set up a formidable if at times stormy partnership in the stewardship of French football and the development of the world game. Delaunay gave his name to the European Nations' Cup when it was founded in 1954.

War interrupted football in Germany, but in Austria it continued to be played. The three Axis powers also sent teams to compete against each other, while Austria and Hungary played as many as four internationals a year against each other throughout the war. Germany and Austria also maintained friendly relations with the Swiss football authorities, and this propaganda among neutrals evoked a response in France that teams should be sent to Spain, Portugal and Latin America in the cause of the Allies. In

Spain opinion was split, with Catalans fighting for France to secure sympathy for their cause, while Barcelona FC was accused of having pro-German sympathies. To offset this, as Gabriel Colome has shown, they played a series of matches with teams that were called the 'Allies'.

In 1913 Germany had criticized the control of the International Board by the British associations, and tried to take away its control over the laws of the game. But in the nationalist phobias that swept both Britain and Germany on the outbreak of war, leading to the change of suspect names – of towns, villages and even breeds of dogs – the Britannia football club of Berlin, and that grand old man of German football, Ferdinand Hueppe, resisted the germanization of the club's name. Footballs were sent to the front in Germany as elsewhere, and football was the main recreation of those caught up in the enforced leisure of the prison camps. In the Ruhleben Camp in Berlin, Steve Bloomer, one of England's all-time greats, was the most talented of a group of footballers who were in Germany at the outbreak of war: others included Jack Cameron of Everton and Spurs, who had been player coach to the Dresden football club at the outbreak of hostilities, and former first division players, Wolstenholme, Hartley, Pentland and Brierley.

Also in Germany when the war broke out were teachers, tourists, engineers, students and sportsmen of various persuasions. About 4000 of them were interned in the Ruhleben racing course, which for the four years of hostilities served as the enforced residence of the British aliens. Before long they had recreated a microcosm of British society in their new surroundings, with debating societies, drama clubs, university classes and a wide variety of sports. Football was far and away the most popular activity: as one former internee said, 'all other sports paled before Association Football.' League and Cup competitions were organized, and as many as a thousand watched some games, which the Camp magazine reported in full. The authorities were said to have been won over to the game, even providing equipment. Not all aliens were interned: in Austria, Jimmy Hogan was smuggled from Vienna to take up a coaching position in Budapest, while George Blakey, representative for a Lincolnshire agricultural implements firm, who had helped establish the game in Vienna, was left free to go where he wanted throughout the war.

With the cessation of hostilities football flourished. The rhetoric about the joys of sport as preparation for military glory was seen for what it was, but the nonsense surrounding sport as a creator of national strength was not yet ready for the dustbin of mad ideals. In a German book of 1927, Rudolf von Kircher's *Fair Play. Sport Spiel und Geist in England* seriously suggested that British methods of playing sport should be studied to see how Germany had lost the war. One would have thought that the folly of provoking the United States was much more important. The value of sport for fitness, discipline and teamwork was not lost on the dictators, however, and Germany under Hitler would use sport in a masterly way in preparation for his next onslaught on Europe.

In the meantime, while football took Europe by storm, in the rest of the English-speaking world outside the United Kingdom it was by-passed by other forms of football. At the close of hostilities soccer surged ahead in continental Europe, becoming the most popular sport in virtually every country, with professionalism being widely adopted in the 1920s and 1930s. In the former British colonies, however, and indeed in those most directly under British cultural influence, soccer remained a minority sport. The USA, Canada and Australia founded their own brand of football, and parts of Australia, all of New Zealand and white South Africa took up rugby. The West Indies preferred cricket, while in the Indian sub-continent hockey became the passport to international fame.

Recalcitrant colonials

In the United States, soccer was never taken seriously, falling a long way behind the national passion for baseball, basketball, American football and ice hockey. And yet when Americans celebrated the centenary of their native football code in 1969, the game that marked its beginnings was closer to soccer than any other code. This was the Princeton/Rutgers game of 6 November 1869, played with 25 a side, a round ball and no running with it. After this brief affair with the round ball, the Americans then proceeded to continue in their own peculiar progress, making themselves an island in the sporting world, rejecting both soccer and rugby to found 'gridiron' football. Of the top Ivy League colleges, Harvard, after two matches with McGill from Canada in 1874, one under their own carrying rules and one under the rugby rules favoured by McGill, were won over to the McGill game. They then persuaded first Yale, then Princeton and the other big colleges to do the same. By the 1880s Walter Camp was devising the changes in the rules that resulted in the creation of America's own game, which was then played in the uniquely American circumstances of college football. In Great Britain when the former public school boys saw the game they codified being taken over by working class players, they kept their distance from it, and in the universities, colleges and schools it remained purely amateur.

In the 1870s baseball was already becoming the passion of the people in the States, the game that could be played on sand lots and with rudimentary equipment, and the game whereby recent emigrants could establish themselves as good Americans. In 1891 the Canadian-born American Dr James A. Naismith invented the entirely new game of basketball, which spread from the YMCA and YWCA to the States as a whole before becoming the one American sport to spread throughout the world. For blacks in particular it was to fulfil the role of disadvantaged minorities held by soccer in most other countries, an escape from poverty and a source of pride. Soccer suffered from the stigma of being a foreign game, and never caught on other than in isolated pockets. Frequently there were predictions that soccer would become a major sport in the States, but while they were never fulfilled, the success of the US in international soccer was greater than is generally recognized, particularly in the 1920s and 1930s.

Canada developed its own variation of American football, dismissed soccer, and adopted with a passion ice hockey, known to North Americans simply as 'hockey'. Unlike the States, at the time of the various codifications of football, Canada still had strong British migrant communities, and the English-speaking areas at times were caught in terms of national identity between the brother on the border and the motherland across the sea. It is perhaps symptomatic that the football code that won most popularity, although called Canadian, is effectively American 'gridiron'. Behind the growth of soccer in Canada the role of immigrant Scots – and a handful of Ulster Irish – is particularly striking. Canada had its 'father of football' in David Forsyth, born in Perthshire, Scotland in 1852, but brought to Canada with his parents a year later. An all-round sportsman, distinguished educationist and visionary, he was a founding member of the Western FA (1880) which played an important part in Canadian soccer until 1940. Forsyth took a Canadian team to tour Britain in 1888, and remained active in the administration of the game until his death in 1936.

Soccer spread as the railways linked up the far flung wildernesses, trading centres and eventually the Pacific and Atlantic coastlines, with Vancouver, Winnipeg and Toronto the main soccer centres. In the sparsely populated province of Saskatchewan it was the most popular sport for a while. Attempts to establish regular internationals with the United States failed in the mid-1880s and mid-1920s, and the follow-up to the successful 1888 tour of Great Britain, in 1891 with a team reinforced by players from Fall River and Pawtucket in the States, was a failure. For the people of Galt, if not for the whole of Canada, came the glory of Olympic gold in 1904, when the 1903 league winners beat the University of Toronto to go to St Louis as sole representatives of Canada in the soccer. There they met the two other competitors, Christian Brothers College and St Rose, whom they beat 7–0 and 4–0.

As in the States, soccer was to remain the game of the ethnics, Britons before the Second World War and 'continentals' thereafter, and while the game enjoyed popularity as a participant sport, as a spectator sport it could attract big crowds only when there were international visitors: as big an indicator as any of the failure of the game at the local level. In 1986 Canada qualified for the World Cup finals in Mexico, but failed to score in its three games in the preliminaries.

Australia's ties with the 'motherland' when forms of football were becoming popular in the 1850s were much stronger than in Canada, and although it was faced by a similar 'tyranny of distance' the main urban centres were scattered around the coastline, blessed with a perfect climate for sport. Like the USA, Australia developed its own code of football. Credited with its first game in 1859, rules that clearly delineated Australian Rules Football were drawn up in 1866: absence of an off-side law, scoring between two goal posts with no crossbar, an oval ball with restrictions on tackling and running, and emphasis on high kicking and spectacular marking. The Australian game, then, was established at much the same time as soccer, and it caught on rapidly in Victoria, a middle-class game that was being picked up by the masses so that from crowds of about 1500 in the late 1860s, they increased to 10,000 in the next decade then 20,000 the next, until in 1890 a club match attracted 33,000. Between the wars, when Victoria's population was less than three million, crowds of 100,000 attended the Grand Final in Melbourne.

From Victoria the game spread to South Australia, Tasmania and then Western Australia, but not New South Wales or Queensland. There provincial jealousies looked unkindly on imports from the southern states, and a warmer climate, superb beaches and open waters delayed the growth of football. When it came it was rugby that was the chosen code: Union through until the split of 1907, when Rugby League developed as the premier football code in Queensland and New South Wales, a professional rival to the Union game, which retained its popularity mainly through the universities. The northern states could not match the Victorian game for spectator interest, but despite changing the name of the game from Victorian Rules to Australian Rules early in this century, and more recently relocating teams to Sydney and Brisbane to create a national league, the Victorian game is still a minority sport in two major states. Soccer is the second most popular football code in every state, but despite the pioneering efforts of the inevitable Scots and other Brits in the early days, and the comparative success in the 1974 World Cup and the publicity that followed it, soccer has still to overcome the prejudice of being either a 'pommie' or a 'wog' game.

Australian Rules has some resemblances to Gaelic football, but owes nothing to it, despite the claims of those who have mistaken externals and a raucous Irish immigration as a coincidence too close to be dismissed. Gaelic football was codified only in 1885, but despite the efforts of the ideologues of the Gaelic Athletic Association who wanted no Irish sports to be contaminated by things English, geographical proximity left the Irish too seriously exposed to the contagion of soccer for it to be replaced by the native game.

In New Zealand and white South Africa, Rugby Union was embraced with fanatical enthusiasm. In the case of New Zealand, however, rugby was adopted by the indigenous blacks as well as the newcomers, and it was only in games against South Africa that the native blacks were told they could not play for the national team, the 'All-Blacks' (the national team colours are black jersey, shorts and stockings). Soccer clubs formed in Dunedin, one of the most Scottish towns outside Scotland, in 1880, and in the north island shortly after this. A national organization, the New Zealand FA was founded in 1891, and immediately sought affiliation with the FA in London. In many ways more British than the British, with all the middle-class assumptions this implies, cricket and rugby have been the national sports; Great Britain, South Africa and Australia the main opponents in the international sports world. In 1970 New Zealand introduced professionalism and a national soccer league, and in 1982 made it to the World Cup in Spain, where it was far from disgraced, but since then success has been restricted to the Oceania region.

Today, as it has been for much of this century, soccer is by far the most popular game in South Africa: but only with Africans, coloureds and Indians. With whites soccer ranks behind rugby, tennis, bowls, cricket and hockey. Yet even among whites, South Africa has supplied more players for the top British clubs than any other country outside the United Kingdom, at least until the recent realization that British football could benefit from foreign players taking part in its leagues. The small town of Boksburg alone supplied nine players to top British football in the years between the wars, Charlton Athletic in the 1950s had several South Africans, and picked up a whole forward line for less than £1000. One of these was Eddie Firmani, who went on to play in Italy and even for Italy when he took out Italian nationality. At that time, too, Glasgow Rangers enjoyed the services, among other South Africans, of the incomparable Johnny Hubbard and the ineffable Don Kichenbrand. And it was a South African, Bill Perry, who scored the winning goal in the famous 'Matthews' FA Cup Final of 1953.

Football was played in South Africa in the 1860s around the port towns where British sailors came ashore, and one of the first recorded riots of modern times, at least according to major Horace Porter, later a long standing member on the council of the FA, was when at the end of a game watched by a few hundred Zulus the ball was given to the spectators who saw in it some totem and proceeded to tear it and themselves to pieces. In 1882 the Natal FA was founded, making it with the New South Wales FA in Australia the first to be founded outside the United Kingdom. In 1892 the South African FA was founded and became affiliated with the FA in London. The Corinthians came in 1897, three stayed behind to settle there and they and other British immigrants and the military brought over for the Boer War set the game up on a healthy footing. In 1906 a South African team was invited to Argentina and went on to tour several other Latin

American countries, winning 11 of its 12 games. A British professional team toured in 1910, and in 1924 the first South African team toured Great Britain. By that time many of the whites were turning to rugby. Before the war soccer had been played extensively by working-class whites, and the Indians took to it with such vigour that an Indian team was able to tour the Indian sub-continent in 1921, playing before 100,000 spectators, and received a return visit in 1933. By that time soccer had been taken up by the blacks, so that with the exception of the Cape, where rugby enjoyed some popularity with the coloureds, soccer was far ahead in popularity, played on dusty paddocks before fanatical crowds.

Soccer was the one sport in South Africa where serious attempts were made to bridge the racial divide, and one of the first to take action against apartheid, which was becoming official policy in the 1950s. In 1952 the three non-white groups came together in a 'non-racial' soccer league, the South African Soccer Association, and in 1959 created a professional league. This threat to the racist policies of the government, particularly when the South African Football Association (white) was suspended by FIFA in 1962, was met by intimidation: most grounds were controlled by the municipality and the whites bribed blacks to come into what they called a 'multi-cultural' league, an umbrella league of non-mixed teams that it was hoped would give some respectability to apartheid. In their anxiety to retain international sporting contacts, the white controllers even offered to send an alternative white and black team to the World Cup, blacks to England in 1966 and whites to Mexico in 1970. Such magnanimity was received in disbelief elsewhere, and the non-white controlled SASA rejected it. Attempts to give respectability to apartheid succeeded, for a while at least, in pulling the wool over the eyes of a FIFA investigating committee led by Stanley Rous. When Rous left the situation changed: suspended in 1962, South Africa was expelled from FIFA in 1976.

Timing and social snobbery are two of the factors in determining the failure of soccer among English-speaking whites outside Britain. By the 1860s the United States had turned its back on the country it had fought a war to get rid of, developing its own sport along with its own values. In Canada, South Africa, Australia and New Zealand the British were still the major source of immigrants in the second half of the nineteenth century, with Boers in South Africa and French in Canada helping to emphasize their Britishness.

In these countries relationships with the old country were complicated by close ties of blood, the desire to establish a national identity, and the need for military protection. New people in new lands were in a position to create new games, and the wide expanses of most of these countries allowed a greater variety of options. The very simplicity of soccer in its basic requirements was irrelevant in societies which were more middle-class, and in the process of becoming even more so, than in the 'old country': the adoption of professionalism in soccer from 1885, with its working-class implications, further emphasized this. The US had nothing to prove except to itself, whereas in varying degrees Canadians, South Africans, Australians and New Zealanders had to prove to the motherland their independence and even superiority: sport was one means of doing this, particularly through rugby and cricket. Once a particular code is established it is difficult to dislodge, and in the cases of American football, Australian Rules and Gaelic football these locally invented codes had the stamp of national approval. The acceptance of rugby is more difficult to understand, in that it was the game of the imperial elite, and yet was accepted in Wales and Ireland, where English imperialism is a dirty word, as well as South Africa, New Zealand and parts of Australia.

By the turn of the century soccer had become a foreign game in the English-speaking colonies: the game of the immigrants, working-class and British at first, then 'continental', to use the more polite term less likely to be used by locals, especially after the Second World War.

As for Britain's colonies in Asia and Africa, the soccer explosion would come when the colonial masters left, and can best be left to a later chapter. Enough to say for the moment that on the Indian sub-continent cricket maintained the colonial sporting relationship, while the Hindus and Muslims established themselves as the undisputed world champions in hockey for many years. Nevertheless, soccer enjoyed great popularity in parts of India, particularly Bengal, and through to the 1950s India looked like emerging as the strongest Asian soccer nation. By then the post-colonial soccer explosion was under way, with Africans outstripping Asians in reaching international status, while in Asia India was left behind by other countries. Perhaps the most peculiar anomaly in regard to Britain, colonialism and the spread of soccer is in the West Indies. There the comparative failure of soccer can be ascribed to the joy with which local blacks took to cricket and overcame racial prejudice and poverty to thrash the inventors of that game.

Endnotes

In addition to works cited in the Introduction, see:

Willi Meisl, *Soccer Revolution*, Phoenix Sports Books, London, 1955/Panther, 1957,

an indispensable source for football in central Europe and attitudes to British football by a friendly foreigner.

Luciano Serra, *Storia del calcio*, however, is a better history.

A book of particular interest, though rarely mentioned in bibliographies, is
W. Capel-Kirby and Frederick W. Carter, *The Mighty Kick. Romance, History
and Humour of Football*, Jarrolds, London, 1933.

Unlike most English language books on soccer, it devotes much space to the game
outside Britain.

Vingtième siècle. Revue d'histoire, No. 26, Avril-Juin 1990

was devoted entirely to articles on football.

Most countries have their own histories, usually official and often essentially
statistical. Of the major countries, in addition to previously cited works, on Italy
there is the regularly updated history by the journalist:

Antonio Guirelli, *Storia del calcio in Italia. Con tutti i resultati, le squadre e i
record*, Giulio Einaudi, Torino, 1990.

For a history of Italian football seen through the eyes of one of its more irreverent
sports journals, *Guerin sportivo*:

Paolo Facchinetti (ed.), *Dal football al calcio*, Conti, Bologna, 1989.

For the origins of football in Italy see the article by Pierre Milza in *Vingtième siècle*,
'Le football italien. Une histoire à l'échelle du siècle', pp. 49–58.
Stefano Pivato, 'Le origini del football italiano fra identità nazionale e identità
religiosa', in 'Le Football et l'Europe' (EUI, Florence).
Stefano Pivato, 'Soccer, Religion, Authority: notes on the early evolution of
Association Football in Italy', *IJHS*, Vol 8, No 3, December 1991, pp. 426–28.

On France:

Alfred Wahl, *Les Archives du football. Sport et société en France (1880–1980)*,
Collection Archives, Gallimard, Paris, 1989

is an excellent collection of documents linked by extensive comments by Wahl.

Pierre de Launay, Jacques de Ryswick, Jean Cornu, *100 ans de football en France*,

is a centenary history, beautifully illustrated, with text by three leading journalists.

On Germany:

Siegfried Gehrmann, *Fussball – Vereine – Politik. Zur Sportgeschichte des Reviers
1900–1940*, R. Hobbing, Essen, 1988

is the most serious. Parts of this and other works by Gehrmann have appeared in
English, some of which are indicated below.

Carl Koppehel, *Geschichte des Deutschen Fussball-sports*, DFB, Frankfurt-am-
Main, 1954

is an official history of the German FA.
    For the early history of football in Germany:

Christiane Eisenberg, 'Football in Germany: Beginnings, 1890–1914', *IJHS*, Vol
8, No 2, September 1991, pp.205–220

On the Soviet Union:

Jim Riordan, *Sport in Soviet Society. Development of sport and physical education in Russia and the USSR*, Cambridge University Press, London, 1977, paperback edition 1980

devotes ample space to soccer. Much of this is reproduced in his chapter on soccer in

Soviet Sport. Background to the Olympics, Basil Blackwell, Oxford, 1980.

Prior to the 1958 World Cup, former Soviet star and journalist, Andrei Starostin wrote an interesting pamphlet,

Soviet Football. 60 years of the game, 'Soviet News', booklet no. 18, London, 1957.

The story of British amateur teams taking the game on goodwill missions around the world is told in:

R.B. Alaway, *Football all round the World*, Newservice, London, 1948.

Alan Tomlinson and Garry Whannel (eds), *Off the Ball. The Football World Cup*, Pluto Press, London, 1986

has two articles on the early spread of football: Tony Mason, 'Some Englishmen and Scotsmen Abroad: the Spread of World Football'; Alan Tomlinson, 'Going Global: the FIFA Story'.

For a survey of the origins of the various football codes see

Mason, *Football*, (1974)

For the founding of FIFA, see the official publication

FIFA. 1904–1984, FIFA, Zurich, 1984.

On Rimet see:

Guillaume Hanoteau, *Le Red Star. Mémoires d'un club légendaire*, Editions Seghers, Paris, 1983.

The history of football in the First World War has still to be written: in the meantime there is the short article on reactions to its first year in:

Colin Veitch, 'Play up! Play up! and Win the War! Football, the Nation and the First World War 1914–15', in *The Journal of Contemporary History*, Vol 20, 1985, pp. 363–78. Despite the title this article deals only with England.

For the extensive literature on the Ruhleben camp, see:

J. Davidson Ketchum, *Ruhleben. A Prison Camp Society*, University of Toronto Press, Toronto, 1965.

The boom in soccer in the United States in the late 1970s was reflected in a plethora of articles and books on the subject. One book, as useful as anything else for the unique American approach to the game, and the hyperbole of the late 1970s, is:

Harvey Frommer, *The Great American Soccer Book. A total assemblage of everything needed to play, understand, appreciate and enjoy the world's greatest sport*, Atheneum, New York, 1980.

Specifically on the failure of soccer in the States is:

Andrei S. Markovits, 'The other "American exceptionalism". Why is there no soccer in the United States?', *IJHS*, Vol 7, No 2, September 1990, pp. 230–64.

For Canada:

Colin Jose and William F. Rannie, *The Story of Soccer in Canada*, W.F. Rannie publisher, Lincoln, Ontario, 1982; John M. Dewar, *Saskatchewan Soccer. A History*, Saskatchewan Soccer Association, no date (ca. 1990).

On Australia:

Philip Mosely, 'A Social History of Soccer in New South Wales. 1880–1957', Department of History, University of Sydney, March 1987. (Doctoral dissertation).

On New Zealand:

Tony Hilton, *An Association with Soccer. The NZFA celebrates its first 100 years*, NZFA, Auckland, 1991.

For South Africa:

Robert Archer and Antoine Bouillon, *The South African Game. Sport and Racism*, Zed Press, London, 1982.

A tendentious book, but detailed and scholarly.

For the information on John Madden and correspondence from the Czechoslovakian FA on the early history of Slavia, I am indebted to Tom O'Neill, who sent me many pages of information and documents arising from his family relationship with Madden. For contemporary press extracts on the Celtic tours of the continent I am once more indebted to Pat Woods. For Bensemann and comments on early German football history I am equally indebted to Ulrich Matheja. For putting me in touch with the Ruhleben material, my thanks to La Trobe colleague John Jenkin.

CHAPTER FOUR

Europe Goes its own Way

Soccer in Europe and South America swept all before it, and by the 1930s was the dominant sport on both continents. As the old continent started to recover from the shocks of war and revolution, the decade the French call the 'Crazy Years' was marked at some levels by fun and frivolity, as the cinema and dancing dominated indoor leisure interests, and football the outdoors. If the new wireless was still in its infancy, telephones linked nations with a new clarity, automobile transport assisted trains in shifting people from place to place, and after the passing of the eight-hour law in most European countries from 1919, more workers had the leisure to take advantage of the new technology. So, too, would certain individuals with political ambitions, and sport was written into the programmes of the new totalitarian regimes, football somewhat reluctantly: its virtues were not in its macho qualities and it was too tainted with its British origins and notions of fair play.

Take off in Europe

The crowds who turned up to watch football matches in the first years after the war were enormous in comparison with those before it, and they continued to increase for several years. In the new Weimar Republic international contacts were renewed when 40,000 spectators turned up in 1920 to see a Berlin team play a Budapest select in the Grunewald stadium. In Vienna crowds of up to three times the pre-war attendances of 15,000 came to watch local matches, while internationals against Hungary leaped from 20,000 in 1920 to 45,000 and 65,000 in the following two years, never falling below 45,000 over the next decade. In a Budapest racked with communist revolution and right-wing reaction, crowds of 30,000 still turned up in the midst of the upheavals to watch the football. The newly created Czechoslovak FA (Ceskoslovenska Associace Footballova) was accepted into FIFA in May 1923, but the seeds of future problems could be seen in its division into four federations for each of its German, Czech, Hungarian and Jewish communities. In France, too, the crowds flocked to the football: from attendances of 3000 to 4000 for big games before 1914, cup games and internationals were drawing regular crowds of 30,000 to 35,000. When France hosted the Olympic Games in 1924, 60,000 turned up to see the final in the new Colombes stadium, although neither of the finalists was France, and 30,000 came to see Italy play Spain. Soccer was already the Olympic Games's major spectator attraction, and the financial interests of the organizers preserved it from exclusion by those who from their aristocratic perspective would otherwise like to have seen it removed. The financial success of the Antwerp Olympics was secured only because of the soccer final, where the hosts played before a packed crowd with thousands left outside.

Inevitably and increasingly, these crowds came to be made up mainly of working men, as were the teams, and the payment of players became a major issue. Class divisions and class antagonisms were far from absent on the continent, but football, while predominantly working-class by the 1930s, remained a game played by all classes, and rugby and cricket never became the social escape routes for those who wanted to be preserved from having to mix with the vulgar classes in sport and leisure. One result of this is that while under-cover payments and shamateurism was a troublesome issue, it never approached the moral obsessiveness that had marked the debate in Britain.

In the Netherlands, according to Dr C. Miermans (*Voetbal in Nederland*), football underwent a significant social change in the 1920s. Between 1894 and 1906, of a sample of 104 footballers, 99 came from the 'upper' classes, 4 from the 'middle', and one from the 'popular' classes. Rounding out his figures to percentages, these changed to 77, 13 and 3 for the period before 1919 and then underwent a dramatic change in the decade to 1929: 30, 18, 52.

The social transformation of football in Germany can be seen in the example of Schalke 04, one of the many clubs from the industrial region of the Ruhr, whose teams were drawn from the workers and grew from strength to strength as a result. The middle-class teams of the powerful Westdeutsch Spielverband (WSV), the biggest body supporting football in Germany and a sub-association of the German FA (DFB), feared this progress, so much so that in 1923 they abandoned the promotion and relegation system whereby clubs could work their way from the minor C Class through B and A to County and then District League. The administrators who abolished this avenue of advancement for the new working-class clubs claimed they were doing so to check the disputes and violence that the fierce competition was giving rise to. As Siegfried Gehrmann has shown, this is not how it was seen by members of the Schalke 04 club, which went on to win six German championships between 1934 and 1942.

Unlike most German football teams Schalke did not emerge from schools or sports clubs, but began as a boys' street team, growing in strength as they attracted miners, factory workers and skilled craftsmen from the heavily industrialized region of Gelsenkirchen. Their social stain meant more than their skill when they first applied for admission to the WSV, however: they were doubly despised as 'proles' for their social origins and as 'Poles' (*Polacken*) for the ethnic origins in East Prussia of many of their players. They eventually gained admission in 1915. Schalke are also a prime example of workers preferring to join a 'bourgeois' league to the more politically committed communist, socialist and catholic sports clubs vying for the workers' soul at this time. Schalke were a community club of the working-class, but they preferred to enjoy their football in a politics-free zone.

In terms of club membership, the growth of football in Germany surpassed even England. When the DFB was founded at the turn of the century there were 66 clubs and 1215 members; in 1921 there were about 1300 clubs and 300,000 members, while just over ten years later, in 1932 these figures had exploded to 8602 and 1,025,326. In 1954, in the geographically reduced West Germany, there were still more official players and clubs than in England; 12,845 and 1,607,724. The DFB was about to adopt professionalism when the Nazis took over in 1933 and eliminated commercial along with other impurities in sport. Full-time professionalism would have to wait until the foundation of the Bundesliga in 1963.

In France, less industrialized than either the Netherlands or Germany, the working-class composition of the teams was less marked in the early 1920s, and in the Red Star team that played in the 1923 Cup Final there was only one worker, a mechanic. In the 1920s businessmen became increasingly involved in the game, and took a controlling interest in many clubs. France adopted professionalism in 1932, a reflection of the working-class involvement.

In Vienna, Prague and Budapest, the middle-class interest in the game was still paramount in the years after the war. When Celtic visited the region to play Sparta in 1922, before crowds of over 30,000, it was noted that 'the people who attend are all of the business class.' These capitals had been comparatively untouched by the war, and in the coffee houses that served as the great outdoor social exchanges, opera and football were discussed with equal enthusiasm by connoisseurs who could appreciate a well sung aria as much as a classically executed goal. Some of this is recalled in the writing of Friedrich Torberg, water-polo player and football fanatic, and author of one of the early sports novels, *Die Mannschaft* (1935). Torberg was born in Vienna in 1908, but spent most of his youth in Prague. In Vienna he became a habitué of the Café Herrenhof, where many of the literary luminaries gathered, but just when he was making his own name in this illustrious circle his world was brought to an end. As a Jew he was forced to emigrate to the States in the late 1930s, to Hollywood at first, then New York. Life in that alien land was made bearable by recreating the Café Herrenhof in his New York apartment, where he offered open house to other émigrés, especially if they could discuss European football and above all his beloved FK Austria.

The media and the football explosion

The football explosion was reflected in the publications devoted to it. At the beginning of the century cycling was the main sporting interest, and it inspired the early sports journals. The first sporting daily, *Le Vélo*, came out in France from 1 December 1892, and in Italy *La Gazzetta dello Sport* made its first appearance in Milan in 1896. The only paper to equal it, *L'Auto*, first came out in 1900, but despite its name was mainly concerned with cycling. *L'Auto* came out as a daily from 1903 and survives today as *L'Equipe*, the name change necessitated by *L'Auto*'s collaborationist role in the Second World War; as such it is the longest running sports daily in the world. *La Gazzetta dello Sport* became a daily only in 1913. By the late 1920s in Italy, and the 1930s in France, football had taken over from cycling as the most popular sport.

Sports magazines were popular in Germany in the 1890s, and as early as 1891 the *Deutsche Ballspiel-Zeitung* was founded as a bi-monthly paper devoted to ball sports. Its rival, *Fahrrad, Ballsport-und Eislauf Zeitung*, as its title indicates, was also interested in cycling and ice-skating. In the early 1900s Berlin had two prominent sports papers, *Neue Sportwoche* and *Der Rasensport*. As in Italy, the leading papers did not come from the capital, however, and in 1910 appeared *Sport in Mitteldeutschland* and *Spiel und Sport im Ostland*, 'provincial' sports papers that devoted much space to football. It was not until the following year, and in Munich, that *Fussball*, the first paper concentrating on football came out. This much-loved paper was surpassed in 1923, however, when the Berlin based *Die Fussball-Woche* appeared, rising to fame under the editorship of Ernst Werner and the merger of *Der Rasensport*. The war years did not diminish the interest in football, and among the papers that appeared shortly after its conclusion was the famous *Der Kicker*, founded by Walter Bensemann in July 1920. *Kicker*, *La Gazzetta dello Sport* and *L'Equipe* are the big three of the present day European sporting journals. All are heavily committed to coverage of football.

In the 1920s magazine-type journals were popular. Already *Guerin sportivo* had come out in a satirical cartoon style in 1912, inspired by the French *L'Echo des sports*. *Goal* came out in Italy from 1925 and in France the first magazine devoted entirely to football was the weekly *Football*, from 1929. By the 1930s technology allowed magazines to feature relatively cheap and clear photographic reproduction, and sport was an obvious subject for such spectacular productions, In Italy *Lo Sport Illustrato* was one of the best of these and in the boom in the Italian sports press in the early 1930s *Il Calcio Illustrato* specialized in football. In France *Match* and *Miroir des sports* made their appearance in this time, and in Germany *Der Kicker* advertised itself as an 'illustrated football weekly'.

By the 1920s the daily press was increasingly devoting space to football, with Sunday supplements previewing the games to come, and sections on Monday devoted to the previous day's games. *L'Auto* had shown with the Tour de France that sponsoring a popular sporting event was good for business, and other newspapers soon followed suit, giving their name to Cup or special football competitions. Great Britain had comparatively few specialist sporting papers, particularly on football, because the daily press covered it so fully in its sports pages. In France Gaston Bénac transformed *Paris-soir* into the biggest selling evening paper. This was due largely to an increased coverage of sport, but also in the way it was presented. Bénac dramatized sport, specialized in stories about the 'stars' and exaggerated or even invented crises, all with big headlines, vivid illustrations, drawings and photographs. He worked on the principle that a good football match could sell papers as well as a good murder. At the World Cup in Italy in 1934 most editors were evidently aware of this: 275 journalists representing newspapers from 29 countries were sent to cover the event.

The spread of football could also be seen in the plethora of books on the subject. Many of these were instruction manuals. In 1934 FIFA was able to list nearly 100 books devoted to football: in addition to the 24 in English there were twenty in Dutch, eighteen in French, eleven in Danish, ten in Italian, nine in German, seven in Norwegian, five in Spanish, four in Hungarian and three in Swedish. Few of these were works of great literary merit, but this is not to say that football was looked down on by intellectuals on the continent: such snobbery was a more British trait.

In Britain, apart from a few writers like J.B. Priestley and George Blake, football was generally ignored as a serious social issue. This was not the case on the continent. In France, Henri de Montherlant, Jean Giraudoux and George Duhamel not only played the game, but wrote about it, and later Albert Camus, goalkeeper in his native Algiers, would claim to have learned more about life from football (and the theatre) than any other source. Some of his happiest conversations with Jean-Paul Sartre in the 1950s were said to have been while the two of them watched Racing Club de Paris play. Arthur Koestler was a football fan, even if it did not come into his work, but when he reminisced with his old friend, Friedrich Torberg, it was with memories of their shared interest in football. Before astonished younger members at a conference in the Austrian College in Alpsburg in the 1950s they reconstituted from memory the great teams of

FK Austria in the inter-war period and then burst into song with the war chants of the Rapid Vienna supporters. The ill-fated president of Czechoslovakia, Eduard Benes, betrayed by the democracies in 1938, joined Slavia as a footballer in 1898 at the age of 14; a few years later the Bohr brothers, both professors at Copenhagen University, played for Denmark, Nils later going on to win the Nobel Prize for atomic physics in 1922.

By the 1930s radio was no longer a luxury, and within a few years the technically advanced nations had a wireless set in virtually every household. Despite the fears that listening to broadcasts of matches would encourage people to stay at home, radio was a boon to the game. When the Austrian *Wunderteam* went to England in December 1932, groups of Belgians and Dutch made a special trip to see the game, while unemployed workers from Vienna made their way across the continent on foot, only to be blocked by the Channel and the customs authorities. For the less adventurous radio could fill the gap, their needs catered for by enterprising cafe and restaurant owners. In Vienna, Budapest and Berlin, as well as in towns and villages throughout the land, dancing and drinking parties were held, where at regular intervals an interpreter listening to the match commentary gave reports on the game. At the Heldenplatz in the centre of Vienna thousands gathered to hear the match broadcast over loudspeakers.

Italy tried to sell the broadcasting rights for the 1934 World Cup, but only the Netherlands took up the offer. Nevertheless, various other deals resulted in 15 nations hearing the broadcast of the first world championship to be held in Europe. In that same year another star made his appearance on the Italian sports scene: the radio commentator Nicolo Carosio. Born in Palermo in 1907, of a Sicilian father and an English mother, he reigned over Italian radio for thirty years, and was still commentating at the time of his death in 1984. It was his coverage of the England vs. Italy game at Highbury in 1934 that won him his fame, as innumerable Italians, at home or in the thousands of public squares where loudspeakers were erected, listened to the drama being staged in London. Encouraged by the patriotic passion of the commentator they urged the Italian team to equalize as it fought back from three goals down early in the first half, to reduce the margin to one goal shortly into the second half. Meazza, who scored the two goals, and Ferraris IV who earned the nickname 'the lion of Highbury' for his performance, were welcomed back to Italy as heroes. And so too was Carosio.

By the 1930s the time of the international football supporter had arrived, with newspapers offering train and hotel packages to take fans to important games; most of them were middle-class, the cost of sporting tourism being beyond most workers. At the World Cup in Uruguay in 1930 more than 20,000 Argentines crossed the Río de la Plata to see their country play the hosts in the final, and in Europe the World Cup in Italy in 1934 was the signal for fans from many countries to converge on the grounds staging the games. Those who made the biggest impression, especially with the noise they made, were the Dutch, an estimated 7000 of whom, letting everyone know that 'We are on our way to Rome!' saw their team eliminated in the first round by Switzerland. The Swiss, with less distance to travel, brought 10,000 supporters for that game. For the Italy vs. Austria semi-final there were 10,000 Austrians. Czech supporters arrived for the final in two special trains and three coaches, while gifts were sent by air for the players which included special Czech food, silver rings and amulets which the players were urged to sew on to their jerseys. They also received more than 1700 telegrams.

The World Cup was something special, but even in club matches the travelling fan was there: coach loads of Belgians travelled to see their expatriate star, Raymond Braine play for Slavia in their big games. Most supporters, however, came to support their team and wear its colours, and governments and private entrepreneurs were there to cater for their wishes. A pale shadow of what was to come, soccer had nevertheless arrived as a media event.

Professionals and professionalism

Football in the 1920s and 1930s was becoming increasingly sophisticated. In Glasgow Celtic's European tour of May 1922 they failed to win a game, losing to Sparta (2–1) and Slavia (3–2) in Prague and drawing with a select German team in Berlin (1–1). Despite comments on the 'semi-barbarous Slovaks', baked and bare grounds and a ball as light as 'a toy balloon', they had some praise for the Sparta team and had to admit that despite the roughness and poor refereeing, 'the foreigners have come on at the game lately'. In 1923 Hakoah of Vienna visited Upton Park and beat West Ham 0–5. The crowd who came to see that year's beaten cup-finalists run rings around the foreigners, marvelled at the absence of 'kick and rush', and the *Daily Mail* had to admit that the Hammers, albeit with several reserves, were thoroughly outplayed. The postwar world of continental football was becoming professional in every sense of the word: a commitment to perfection and playing to the highest standards. Some even became technically professional: Hungary and Austria in 1924; Czechoslovakia in 1925; and Spain in 1928 when it established its first national league. Italy under Fascism refused to recognize the difference between professionalism and amateurism, which was handy for Olympic competition, while its players had no complaints about the rewards they received. France became professional 1932, and in Switzerland the national league began in 1931 and in 1933–34 it became professional. Germany, as we have seen, would have become professional but for the Nazis. In most other European countries professionalism came after the Second World War.

Long before professionalism was adopted, the best players were being paid, as they had been in England and Scotland before it was legalized. On the continent there was less reticence about treating gifted players as stars and paying them accordingly. In Hungary Dr Arpad Brull treated football as his millionaire hobby, so that his amateur footballers were among the best paid in Europe. Even with Pirelli (AC Milan) and the Agnelli family (Juventus) in Italy, Peugeot (Sochaux) in France or the giant Philips Electrical Company in the Netherlands (PSV Eindhoven), it was the football that came first. And where state or private sponsorship did not reward the players, the crowds coming to watch were enough to pay their wages. As Jean Giraudoux commented in 1929: 'In many football teams the stars receive a bonus in money for every winning kick. The only way in which they are amateurs is when they play poorly.'

In the late 1920s the competition between clubs and nations at international level was institutionalized into regular competitions. Prior to this there had been many regional competitions played on a regular basis. The Scandinavian nations played a regular championship from 1924, with each of Denmark, Finland, Norway and Sweden playing each other four times over a four-year period. A Baltic Cup began in 1929, between Lithuania, Latvia and Estonia, which at least allowed these small nations to get the feel of victory in European competition. Released from the Russian empire by the First World War, they were returned to the sterner grasp of the Soviets in 1940, and the Baltic Cup, along with many other things, came to an end. Freed once more from the grip of the Russian bear in 1991, the Baltic countries immediately sought affiliation with FIFA and entered the World Cup. In Europe's perennial trouble spot, a Balkan Cup was instituted on 11 May 1929, to be played over a ten-day period each year on a league basis in one of the competing countries: Bulgaria, Greece, Romania and Yugoslavia. Despite the explosive potential of such a league, it survived until 1936. It was resurrected in 1946, when Albania replaced Greece, hosted the competition and won it. It was transformed into a meaningless competition and then revived as a Cup in 1975.

The most prestigious competitions at this time, however, other than the Olympic Games and later the World Cup, were the two central European competitions, one for clubs the other for nations: both were inaugurated in 1927. The first of these was the Mitteleuropäischer-Cup, or Mitropa Cup, instituted on 31 March 1927 and played annually on a knock-out home and away basis. The first competition was played by two clubs from each of Austria, Czechoslovakia, Hungary and Yugoslavia. In 1929 Yugoslavia, losing most of its best players to France, withdrew and was replaced by Italian teams. Later Switzerland and Romania entered their champion clubs. The competition was suspended during the war, unofficially resumed in 1951, and officially in 1955, but by then it was about to be submerged in the other European competitions that were starting up.

At the same time as the Mitropa Cup for club teams got under way, an international competition for national teams was begun, contested between Austria, Czechoslovakia, Hungary, Italy and Switzerland. It was played over two or three years, as a league, each team playing home and away. Politics disrupted the fourth competition, with Switzerland the only team to complete its fixtures, but finishing bottom of the table. Austria disappeared from the sporting map with two games to play, Czechoslovakia with one. Italy was preparing for its World Cup triumphs in Paris. As a result only four of its fixtures were fulfilled. The competition was revived after the war, and then delayed by new sets of political problems: the first was played over five years and won by Hungary in 1953, the second between 1955 and 1960, and won by Czechoslovakia. The competition was then renamed the Dr Gëro Cup, after the Austrian luminary who had narrowly survived the *Anschluss* and its repercussions, but it could not survive the competition of the European Nations' Cup.

Austria, Hungary, Czechoslovakia, and Italy, at national and club level, dominated these competitions. Two individuals dominated football in this time: Hugo Meisl and Vittorio Pozzo, both multi-lingual anglophiles who were the despair of their well-to-do families for the way they took up the trivial pursuit of soccer instead of making money.

Meisl was born into a wealthy Jewish family in Vienna in 1881. He was a small and skilful footballer who became a member of the Vienna Cricketers, but it was as an international referee that he made his reputation. Such was his all-consuming passion for football that his father sent him to Trieste for three years to get involved in something more useful. There he continued to play the game and learned Italian, among half a dozen other languages, and returned to Austria for his military service. The joys of banking could not resist the pull of football, and as his younger brother Willi, a sports journalist, later said, he threw away a fortune and a career in banking because of this. Meisl was the main force in Austrian football, in its administration and in organizing visits by foreign teams, especially from Britain. He was instrumental in bringing Jimmy Hogan to Vienna in 1912 for the Olympic Games in Stockholm, and later, when Hogan sought a coaching job in Germany and asked Meisl for a recommendation, Meisl signed him up himself. After a spell with MTK of Budapest and other European teams, Hogan rejoined Meisl to create the incomparable *Wunderteam* of the early 1930s. By that time Meisl was actually earning money from football. In 1927 he was made general secretary and team manager of the Austrian FA. That same year he saw two of his ideas come to fruition when the two central European cup competitions began. In 1936 he may have contributed to Austria's victory over England in Vienna: on the morning of that game Meisl took the English team on a long tour of the extensive delights of the capital. On foot! He died in 1937.

Meisl and Pozzo first met at the Stockholm Olympics in 1912, where Pozzo was in charge of the Italian team. Born near Turin in 1886, Pozzo's sporting interests were in athletics before he took up football. To promote his studies he was sent to Zurich, then England, and it was there that he became obsessed with the games he saw at Old Trafford, Manchester, particularly the performances of Charlie Roberts, United's attacking centre-half. Roberts was approached by the young Italian and happily shared with him his theories about the game. By this time Pozzo's family were trying to get him back to Italy, and when they failed, cut off his allowance. Undeterred he eked out a living teaching languages, but was eventually lured back to Turin for his sister's wedding. He became secretary of the Italian FA, and took the Olympic team to Stockholm where they were eliminated by lowly Finland. Pozzo was never a Fascist, but its authoritarianism suited him. After a brief period as manager of the 1924 Olympic team, and then as a prime mover for the creation of a national league, in 1929 he was appointed *commisario tecnico* of the national team. He held this position with brilliant results until 1949, when his *metodo*, based on the attacking centre-half, was replaced by the defensive system that the Italians were to make notorious in the 1960s.

Meisl and Pozzo were the presiding geniuses of European football in the 1930s. Both of them owed much to the game in Britain, and never denied this, but at the time both were at their peak the British influence was very much on the wane. No longer were their coaches and players in the same demand: Yugoslavs and Hungarians had in large measure replaced them, while at the administrative level two successful World Cups and the thriving central European competitions showed that the isolation of the inventors of the game was of little relevance to the continent.

Great Britain versus FIFA

In Britain much of the progress on the continent was passing unnoticed. The British associations left FIFA shortly after the end of the First World War, rejoined it again in 1924, but left again in 1928, not to rejoin until after the Second World War. Politics and amateurism were two of the basic issues, but behind that there was a fundamental difference in the approach to the game among most of the countries comprising FIFA and those of the home associations. Traffic in footballing ideas was all one way before the Second World War, and the few voices suggesting that the Europeans had something to teach the masters were lost in the abyss of British apathy and indifference.

A major criticism by the British of the Europeans was in regard to the political intrusions in the continental game. And yet it was the British FAs' wish to inject a specifically political note that led to the first split with FIFA. This was on 29 December 1919 when it was proposed by the UK associations, supported by France, Belgium and Luxembourg, that they have no contacts with the defeated belligerents in the recent war, and that they leave FIFA to form their own Federation of National Football Associations. The British associations wanted even neutrals to have no sporting truck with Germany, Austria or Hungary. A similar ban was successful in the Olympics of 1920 and 1924, but it did not work in football.

The attitude of the British associations was a reflection of the spirit of the outraged amateur at the caddish behaviour of the enemy. Nowhere was this more outrageously expressed than in the words of the Queen's Park historian, Richard Robinson, writing in 1920, his mind still fevered with the thought of the treacherous Hun. He was thinking back to the attempt by Walter Bensemann (unnamed) in 1902 to arrange a fixture in Scotland:

> It would have been a sore thought to look back in the after years, and
> remember, that the classic slopes of Hampden had been desecrated by
> the foot of a Hun, in an encounter which might be, and probably was,
> a spying expedition. The vileness of the race was not then known, or
> even suspected. We are truly a confiding and simple nation.

This was the same Bensemann who founded *Der Kicker* while Robinson was concluding his history and who as a devoted anglophile, it might be remembered, brought the first British footballers to Germany in 1899. He was also a Jew. Shortly after the celebration of his sixtieth birthday in January 1933 he was forced to leave Germany for Switzerland and died there in 1934.

The patriotic outrage in Britain was also vented on Glasgow Celtic when they played in Berlin in 1922, but they were no strangers to drawing the wrath of nationalists who did not see them as properly Scottish. They were welcomed by *Kicker* as 'the first peace swallows' and by the British troops stationed there. They also contributed a substantial sum to charity for poor relief in the city, and as manager Maley pointed out, trade relations had been re-opened, and it was time for reconciliation. Britain's continental allies, France and Belgium, who suffered most from Germany in the war, were at one level all for destroying the menace on their border, but in football politics they were reluctant to follow the British lead. Switzerland was the first to play against Germany, as it would be after the Second World War. Other neutral nations, encouraged by Hugo Meisl, were unwilling to cut off their sporting contacts to spite nations who had not been their enemies. Italy, who had joined the Allies later in the war, expressed its opposition to the boycott. The champions of sport for sport's sake left FIFA on 23 April 1920 and expelled FIFA's two members from the International Board. For two years they banned their members from competing with FIFA teams. When the British associations rejoined FIFA on 14 June 1924 it was again for political reasons, this time closer to home: Ireland.

The Irish Free State (Eire) was created in 1922 after terrible bloodshed, but this did not solve the question of the political sovereignty of the island. In the course of this dispute the southern states broke from the IFA, run from Belfast, to create their own Football Association of Ireland. This was in June 1921 and it was followed by the creation of their own League two months later. There followed disputes over the right to use the title 'Ireland', Eire objecting to 'Northern Ireland' calling itself Ireland when it controlled only six counties; moreover, some teams in Ulster, of Catholic inspiration, wanted to play in the FAI. The IFA, for its part, wanted the Dublin-run Association to call itself the Football Association of the Irish Free State. The problem, to become familiar enough after 1945 when other nations claimed sole right to a national title, was brought to FIFA when the FA of Eire asked for affiliation with FIFA and separate representation on the International Board. Recognition one way or the other was loaded with implications. In this case the FAI was accepted into FIFA in August 1923; this was recognized by the International Board, which denied the FIA a role on its Board. Teams in Ulster, with the powerful Belfast Celtic particularly in mind, were forbidden from playing in the Eire League. Moves to have an international team picked by a joint IFA/FAI committee were rejected by Belfast, and so in football (but not rugby) as in life, much Irish talent has been wasted by division.

The main issue bedevilling relations between the UK and FIFA on its return was that of amateurism, particularly payment for broken time, but it was also, as the official history of the FA admits, 'partly because of the suspicion that [FIFA] was aiming to become the final authority of the game.' The FA was peeved that in the organization of soccer for the Olympic Games FIFA had made the 'inflammatory' statement that it was 'the final authority on the game.' However, it was the issue of amateurism that provoked the split.

On this issue the British, who had been through it all more than three decades previously, had reason to feel a bit testy. Moreover they were still controlled by those who had accepted professionalism more or less as a necessary evil. They wanted a definition of amateurism that restricted payments to *necessary* travel and hotel expenses. Players could pay a coach or trainer, but all other training expenses had to be paid by themselves. They were forbidden to play for any football prize 'in a football context'.

They were not to be paid or compensated for time lost at work, which effectively restricted teams playing soccer in the Olympic Games to the rich. And it was obvious that the brilliant young Uruguayans who took off the top medal in the 1924 and 1928 Olympic Games were not in that category. Apart from the time taken to sail from their homeland to Europe it was well known that they had been practising together for months. For the British associations, niggardly in the expenses granted to their own professionals, and who looked on serious training as some form of blasphemy, this was too much, and they left FIFA on 17 February 1928. This time the break was not so complete, and sporting contacts continued at club and even international level.

Football under the dictators

Shamateurism was only one of the things the British FAs found rotten in the footballing states of Europe: another was the intrusion of the State. The period between the wars has been called the age of the dictators, and among the old fashioned autocrats and dictators dressed in more modern guise came those whose control was more 'total', demanding not just the obedience of their subjects, but their active participation. In this sport was to play a key role, and football became an integral part of totalitarian rule.

In Britain the government's main connection with football was to tax it; but as we have seen the British associations were not above injecting politics into sport. In domestic matters the British government and the football associations usually managed to keep a respectful distance, but in international affairs it was impossible to keep politics at bay.

The British ambassador in Finland admitted the political use of football when he told a visiting England team that they could do more for international goodwill in one afternoon than he could do in a year. Similar stories could be told from other embassies, and the defeat of England by Spain in 1929 prompted a statement by the ambassador on the need for British teams to do their best on the continent. And always there were the sensitivities of the expatriates to think of, for whom life for a long time after could be nasty or sweet depending on how well the tourists had performed.

The Foreign Office was not above pressuring the FAs into doing what it wanted, and with control over passports it could determine which games outside the United Kingdom or those involving teams visiting the United Kingdom, should be played. It refused to grant visas to a workers' team that wanted to take part in the great Moscow Spartakiad in 1927, and in sports other than football the issue of race or communism could make it break out in a moral sweat: in 1911 the black boxer Jack Johnson was barred entry to fight 'Bombardier Billy Wells', and in 1930 a Soviet team was banned entry to Britain. On the other hand, no obstacles were put in the way of the visits by teams from Fascist Italy and Nazi Germany in the 1930s.

When some British teams tried to sign foreign players in the early 1930s they found the Minister of Labour a stumbling block. Belgium's greatest ever player, Raymond Braine, who starred in the 1928 Olympics and captained the 1938 Rest of Europe team in their match against England, was signed by Clapton Orient, but was not allowed to take up the position. He went to Sparta of Prague instead, and like Madden he was better remembered there than in his home country: in his case national recognition was clouded by his doubtful relations with the Nazis when Belgium was under their heel. In 1931 an entry permit was refused Rudi Hiden, the star Austrian goalkeeper whom Arsenal wanted to sign. Braine and Hiden, whose talents were rare, were rejected on the grounds that they threatened the employment opportunities of native subjects. All of this, however, is as nought when compared with the involvement of the State in many countries on the continent, with Fascist Italy the prime example.

The Fascists were swept to power in Italy in 1922. Mussolini's regime invented the word 'totalitarian', with state organized control not just of politics and the workplace, but of leisure activities: elite preparation for the stars, and the *dopolavoro*, or after-work programme for the masses. Unlike some dictators, Mussolini was genuinely interested in sport, but mainly those like skiing and riding that had some military significance. Football was too British for the new Italy, and teams that had retained their English names were told to change them: AC Milan became Milano, and Genoa 93 became Genova 93; Internazionale became Ambrosiano, the original name smacking too much of the equally offensive cosmopolitanism or bolshevism. The Fascist sports authorities tried to create a uniquely Italian game, *volata*, a mixture of soccer and handball, but it never won favour. Football was the game being played in the streets of the cities, the dusty tracks in the countryside, and watched in the growing stadiums around the country: organized into the *dopolavoro* movement it was one of the positive features of Fascism.

Sport was a distraction and a means of indoctrination; a healthy pursuit and a preparation for the military: it was also an important organ of propaganda, inspiring nationalism at home by winning glory abroad. This meant the Olympic Games and after 1930 the World Cup in football. Italian football, so far behind the central powers in 1914, began its short march to world class in the 1920s. Millionaire industrialists promoted particular teams, the Pirelli firm had an interest in AC Milan before 1914, and the Agnelli family, owners of the Fiat car company, purchased a major holding in Juventus of Turin in 1923. For clubs such as these money was no object, and the search for foreign mercenaries that has been a feature of

Italian football led to South America in particular where Italians and the descendants of Italians were starring in the local football. Some would not just play for Italian clubs, but for the national team, even where in some cases they had already played for Argentina. Private individuals and the State found plenty of money for football, its promotion and the building of impressive new stadia. At the same time the art of bribery and corruption as a means of dealing with the opposition, the *trasformismo* that had become almost a way of governing since the first days of unification in the 1860s, was developed to a higher degree, in soccer as in society.

Pozzo took over as supremo in 1929, enjoying all the authority of a regime whose adolescent ideology suited the infantile way he treated his players, cutting them off from normal social contacts for weeks before important games so that he could impress his will on them. Italian teams did well in games against the club teams of other nations, but the national team was based on a core of Juventus players. In 1932 Pozzo found in Argentina the key player for his success: Luisito Monti, a player whose skill as an attacking centre-half was unquestioned, as was his reputation – with the sole exception of Pozzo – as one of the most cynically violent players to take the field. Brutality was only one of the characteristics of the Italian national team of the 1930s, as it was combined with the artistry of the central Europeans to produce a blend that was spoiled only by suspect temperament.

Italy was the host nation for the World Cup in 1934, and after some ugly exhibitions, strange refereeing decisions and egged on by fanatical crowds, they won the trophy. Overseeing it all was Mussolini, the 'Caesar of the Carnival', happy to win at any cost: it was, after all, the way in which he had come to power. At the third World Cup in Paris, in 1938, with less pressure on the referee, away from home support, and playing with more skill and less intimidation, the Italian players showed that they could win without resort to fascist tactics.

Football was also used by Mussolini as a direct arm of politics. In April 1937 he cancelled the Italian football team's visit to France as part of the celebrations for the Paris Exhibition of 1937. His excuse, based on the abuse of Italian players by French anti-fascists, was that they would be in danger. In fact he quite simply wanted to embarrass Léon Blum's Popular Front government. Already the Italians had pulled out of the Tour de France the previous year. After a flurry of activity in which Rimet resigned (temporarily) as president of the French National Sports Committee and a basketball team due to leave for Italy nearly had its trip cancelled, England sent over Charlton to take Italy's place. In June, however, Bologna represented Italy in the Paris Exhibition tournament, a knock-out competition for club teams, and defeated Chelsea in the final. The Fascist press and Fascist leaders gloried in this great victory by Fascist Italy, which proved that 'whenever any Italian citizen has to fight, whether in the heart of the motherland or beyond its frontiers, he can always bring the Italian flag to triumph.' Not all the players in Italian colours shared such nationalistic posturing, and three of the Argentine imports, Guaita, Scopelli and Stagnaro were arrested crossing the frontier in an attempt to escape conscription for the war in Abyssinia. The press, however, related their offence to financial irregularities.

In late 1936, the Portuguese dictator, Salazar, also had a cheap shot at the Popular Front government in France by refusing to allow his national team to play there. Nor was the French government immune from football politics. It encouraged football as part of its 'little entente' policies, maintaining friendly relations with the smaller countries surrounding Germany to provide some sort of buffer. When the visiting king of Yugoslavia was assassinated by a disgruntled Croatian in Marseille in October 1934 the government quickly arranged for a football match to be organized between France and Yugoslavia. France's friendship with Romania encouraged that country to make the long trip to Uruguay for the 1930 World Cup. France, Romania, Belgium and Yugoslavia all went on the same ship. But this was far from the direct influence operated by the dictatorships, and in 1939 the French government came under fire for not sending an official representation to an international against Poland. Other nations, *Paris-Soir* pointed out, would not have insulted such a valuable ally in this way.

Some dictators enjoyed their sport and so could be something of a boon to the game. King Carol of Romania was a sports fan before he became king: founder of the Federation of Romanian Sports Federations and its first secretary, he was particularly keen on football and so was happy to accept French encouragement to send a team to Uruguay for the 1930 World Cup. He lifted all suspensions on delinquent footballers, picked the team himself and applied pressure to those employers, the British oil companies in particular, who were reluctant to release their workers to play.

The two sides of dictatorial decree can also be seen in Mussolini, who was as likely to use threats as rewards to reach the chosen end. When Italy came to England to launch the infamous 'battle of Highbury' in 1934 they were said to have come with promises of bonuses as high as £150, cars and – strange inducement for a military regime – exemption from military service. In the World Cup of 1934 the Italian players were said to have been galvanized into action by threats of immediate call-up for the army if they did not win.

In the Soviet Union, that other great totalitarian power, soccer was the most popular sport, among players and spectators, but apart from a few visits to neighbouring countries, participation with a few socialist brothers that were used mainly for sectarian political purposes, and a well publicized visit to France in 1936, Stalin was keeping Soviet sport in wraps until such times as it was ready to appear before the world: this would come with dramatic effect in soccer straight after the war, and elsewhere with the Olympics from 1952.

Nazism came to Germany in January 1933, and sport was one of the first elements in society to come under *Gleichschaltung*, or absorption into a single system. The Nazi ideology on sport fitted easily into the most extreme nationalism of the *Turner* movement, but while this was suitable for training a nation to go out and kill on its behalf, it did little to enamour it in the eyes of other nations. In this regard soccer, tennis, and boxing to a mixed degree, but above all the Olympic Games, played a key role in Germany's successful conduct of international affairs. In the Weimar Republic football flourished alongside other sports, and provided the Nazis with playing fields, stadiums and indoor facilities that they were subsequently to proclaim loudly as their own work.

Hitler, unlike Mussolini, was no sportsman, showing an interest only in boxing. Like Mussolini, however, from whom he borrowed so much, including the After Work Programme (*Kraft durch Freude*), he saw that the prestige arising from international sporting competition was too great to be ignored. In this regard his great triumph was the Olympic Games of 1936, rejected at first on ideological grounds as a 'mongrel, Jewish' conspiracy, but converted by Goebbels into the nation's greatest window to the world and source of national pride. The one jarring note in this festival of sport and politics was not so much the victories of the black athletes as Germany's loss to Norway in the quarter-final of the football.

In December 1935 Germany came to White Hart Lane, home of Tottenham Hotspur, to play England in a game which proved more than anything else that the British authorities were less repelled by Nazism than by antifascist protests. Germany lost that game 3–0, but the result was not important: their players and supporters, ten thousand of them let off the leash for the game, all behaved themselves. When the German team visited Scotland shortly after the Olympic Games the results were also seen as less important than the after-dinner speeches, where the racial ties of the two countries was one of the favourite topics. The Scottish press minimized any political disruption, and two individuals waving anti-Nazi placards were arrested. In the 1938 World Cup, where Germany, despite the absorption of the Austrian players, was knocked out early, sports-loving people praised the Germans for taking action against a player sent off for kicking an opponent without waiting for the decision of the disciplinary board.

In May 1939 England toured Italy, Yugoslavia and Romania. In the game with Italy all was sweetness and light as the Italians welcomed

England as 'Masters of Association Football', while they were merely the 'Holders of the World Cup'. Italy managed a 2–2 draw thanks to the complaisance of German referee Dr Bauwens, who not only overlooked a 'hand of God' goal by Piola, but the follow-through that almost knocked out English defender George Male. The worst exhibition at that game, however, was the sight of the England team giving the Fascist salute to the four corners of the ground.

Hitler, the Jews and the old boys

When Hitler annexed Austria in March 1938 the Danubian style of life, in football as in other aspects of culture, came to an end. Austrian football was absorbed into Greater Germany, and Rapid Vienna had the ambiguous honour of winning national championships in 1938 (cup) and 1941. Many Austrians welcomed the arrival of the Nazis – they had been living under a dictatorship before Hitler arrived, and in 1934 the government had brutally smashed much of the work of the Social Democrats in Vienna – but when the Germans appeared as just another imperial power, pride in German unity disappeared under the reality of a Prussian conquest. At football matches between Austrian and German teams there were near riots on the field, while the crowds, as Paul Hofman tells us (*The Viennese, Splendour, Twilight and Exile*), roared their abuse at the visitors: 'Piefke [Prussian/square-head] go home!', was one of the more polite insults thrown at them. FK Austria, associated with the liberal-bourgeoisie, and hence Jews, were told to change their name to something more German. They became FK Österreich, but within a few months reverted to their old name.

It was the Jews who were the most obvious victims, of course. Shortly after the *Anschluss* the Jewish team Hakoah, winners of the first Vienna league in 1925, relegated at the end of the 1936–37 season, but top of their division in March 1938, were dissolved and their record consigned to oblivion. Walter Nausch, former captain of the *Wunderteam* and of FK Austria, was offered a post as manager of one of the new administrative divisions, but only on condition that he divorced his Jewish wife. He refused and went to Switzerland instead, where he became player-manager of Grasshoppers then Young Fellows of Zurich.

The most celebrated sporting victim of the *Anschluss* was Sindelar, claimed in most English language accounts of his life to have been Jewish. Sindelar was the greatest player of the inter-war period. This 'Mozart of football', called *Der Papierene*, or the man of paper, for the way he floated about with the ball at his feet as though he was being wafted with the wind, mesmerised opponents, creating openings for the other forwards or walking the ball into the net himself. Born in Vienna in February 1903, son of a bricklayer who died at the front in 1917, he played for only two club teams: as a youth for the local team of the working-class suburb of Favoriten where he grew up, FK Hertha, and from 1923 for FK Austria. He played 44 games for the national team, where he was the brains behind the *Wunderteam*. His last international match was in 1937, and his last club match on 26 December 1938. A month later he was dead, found gassed in the room above his cafe on the morning of 24 January 1939, apparently from suicide. A 40-year-old woman, Camilla Castognola, was found with him and taken to hospital where she died shortly afterwards.

In most English books Sindelar's suicide is said to have been because he was denounced as a Jew by one of his team mates, and at least one account has him dying in a concentration camp during the war. Where all the accounts agree is that he was Jewish or part Jewish, and was denounced as such. In fact he was 'Aryan', and his being a Jew seems to be an invention of the English language press. His death came many months after the *Anschluss*, and the Nazis, as they had done in Germany, wasted no time in cleansing their sport of all unclean elements. Moreover, the Nazi Sportführer, von Tschammer und Osten, sent a telegram of condolence to his old club, and this was published in an effusive obituary in *Der Kicker*. This Nazi vetted report was anxious to discard notions of suicide and claimed accidental death. Their main concern was that the political opinions of the sporting hero be kept quiet: Sindelar detested the new regime, and although the café he owned had been bought from a Jew, he had paid a fair price for it. Some mystery remains, and Torberg, in his poem 'On the death of a football player' does suggest that there was a political motive, without any suggestion, however, of Sindelar being Jewish.

Whatever doubts remain on the cause of his death, there were none on the hold he had on the public's consciousness. Up to 20,000 came to his funeral, in a ceremony previously reserved only for statesmen. The mourners were led by one of his colleagues wearing Sindelar's Austria uniform and holding a ball. On his grave was a half-length portrait of him in the same colours. For years to come fresh flowers were to be found there.

The role of Jews in the spread of football on the continent cannot be overestimated. Apart from pioneers like Hugo Meisl and Walter Bensemann, there were promoters like the leading French manager, Bernard Lévy of Racing Club de Paris: he was to die at the front in 1940. Jewish businessmen founded Ajax of Amsterdam in 1900, where the Jewish connection has survived through to the present. Among the players a third of the Hungarian national team and most of MTK (known as Hungaria from 1930 to 1950) were Jewish. Bela Guttmann, one of the most successful managers of the postwar period, particularly with Benfica in Portugal in the 1960s, played in pre-war Budapest for MTK; they were closed down along with other Jewish clubs in Hungary in 1940. In Vienna there were several jewish clubs, rich and poor, the most famous of which was Hakoah, a typically all-round sports club whose members excelled in wrestling, water polo and swimming, but above all in soccer. Hakoah's athletes lived up to their name ('Strength') as they deliberately set out to upset anti-semitic stereotypes, with a physical style that resulted in many free-for-alls.

There were so many Jewish teams in Vienna that they frequently played against each other: games between Hakoah and Austria were billed as Jews against Israelites, with supporters yelling insults that would otherwise have been seen as anti-semitic. On the other hand, nationalism could rise above religious culture, as in the case where Hakoah represented Vienna against the Jewish team from Budapest, Vivo Budapest: Viennese supporters yelling: 'Come on Hakoah! Get stuck into these Jews!' And when a Hakoah victory saved their team from relegation, one supporter of the relieved team, more given to the expression 'Jewish pig!', applauded Hakoah with a mumbled; 'Well done, Herr Jew.'

In the years before 1939 Jews had bitter battles to fight, sadly against a sea of indifference at the best, hostility at the worst. In sport no more than in life were the Jews accorded much sympathy, and the rulers of British football were happy to send football teams on goodwill missions to Nazi Germany. One of the most degrading sporting spectacles of these years was that of the England team giving the Nazi salute before the international match in Berlin in May 1938. In his memoirs written nearly 40 years later (*Football World*, 1978), Stanley Rous, secretary of the FA at the time, claimed that the players were left to make their own decision, that all agreed and 'saw it as a bit of fun'. This was flatly refuted by Eddie Hapgood, England's captain who said the players were furious (*Football Ambassador*, 1945, 1951). Neither the 3–6 victory nor the actions of Aston Villa, touring Germany at the same time and who refused to salute, could wipe out the ignominy of that occasion. Rous, of comparatively humble social origins, was more besotted by football than infected by the right-wing politics that were the mark of other 'old boy' luminaries in most amateur sports organizations, but he was not entirely without political bias or ignorance.

Speaking with more prejudice than historical accuracy, Rous claimed that the England vs. Germany game of 1935 was an innocent sporting exercise, and that the objections of the Trades Union Congress were because General Franco had received the support of Germany and Italy to enable him to get the better of the Republicans 'and their Russian allies'. In the time Rous was speaking of, the Spanish Civil War was still more than seven months in the future.

Another old boy, Ivan Sharpe, who played for Great Britain in the Olympic Games of 1912, and later became a distinguished journalist, could not understand what all the fuss was about. Referring to the Nazi salute he said it was 'just a friendly gesture' . But perhaps the crassest of old boy confusion about a sport free from politics and yet which could still act as a builder of national character and bring peace to the world, came from F.N.S. Creek. In his younger days, Creek played amateur football for Cambridge, Corinthians and England, then became a master in a private school and commentator on football, before going on to become a member of the FA executive. In 1937 he wrote a book, *Association Football*, in which he stated his belief that soccer was destined in international affairs to play an even greater role in the future than it had done in the past. Football, he claimed, spread friendliness and goodwill wherever it went on its 'mission of peace', reconciling nations through sport. Specifically, he pointed to the German team and its supporters in 1935, a visit which did more good for Nazi Germany 'than any number of speeches.' (Which is presumably why the TUC was objecting.) The shallowness of Creek's judgment was matched by his insular ignorance in his reference to 'the *so-called* World Soccer Championship held in Italy'! (italics added).

In much of the so-called deconstructionist literature and history so fashionable today, appeasement has gained a new popularity. The old boys had no need of such theories; even as the realities of the Nazi record were unfolded at the Nürnberg Trials, Montgomery Belgion could write in *Epitaph on Nürnberg* that he found the trials 'unsportsmanlike', and as someone brought up in the principles of 'English sportsmanship and fair play', he had no wish to hit another fellow when he was down.

Britain and Europe: not so splendid isolation

Apart from shamateurism and politics, Britain was divided from the continent by a culture gap deeper than the Channel. The British played a fast, physical game, admiring courage and tenacity over artistry and skill, and were scornful of the 'Latin' player's reaction to a heavy shoulder charge and his theatrical displays in response to imagined injustice. They were also frustrated at such petty practices as ankle tapping, shirt pulling, obstruction and elbowing. The bruising British game was more suitable to soft, muddy pitches than it was to the sun-baked surfaces of warmer climates, but it also reflected the long legacy of football as a 'manly' game. Back in 1863 when the rules were being formulated one of the advocates of hacking claimed that if this was removed it would do away with the 'courage and pluck' of the game, and raised an easy laugh by going on to say that if this came about he would 'bring over a lot of Frenchmen who would beat you with a week's practice'.

This British bash was less admired on the continent, particularly southern and central Europe, where a more cultured, individual game was highly prized, and to be called a 'trier' was regarded as an insult. Harsh tackling was condemned, loss of temper condoned; revenge for injured pride was met with immediate retaliation by punching or kicking, while in Britain vengeance was administered at the appropriate opportunity by the culprit and ball being 'bundled out of the park'. Continental goalkeepers were thought to be showy rather than safe, and threatened to collapse if a forward so much as breathed on them. Continental crowds were delighted by tricks with the ball, the master playing with his opponent as the matador the bull; the sympathies of British crowds were more likely to be with the bull.

One aspect of the British game the continentals could admire without reservation was the referee. He was the embodiment of British justice; his decision might be wrong, but it was not made out of malice or worse. As a result he was seldom attacked by players or spectators. On the continent this was not always the case.

From the first tours to the continent, British teams came to expect that spectator passions would interfere with the game. Referees and players were frequently attacked; in the early days, reflecting the social class of the offender, often with umbrellas. One of the worst years was 1929, when a touring Newcastle team was faced by a violent crowd in Milan and were saved from serious injury only by the police with drawn revolvers coming on to the park. When they tried to leave the ground their coach was immobilized and a cordon of police was needed to keep fans away while it was being fixed. Even their hotel was stormed by fans. In Hungary on that same tour they had to face a hail of missiles thrown by fans who thought (justifiably) they were drunk and not trying. Indeed the Hungarian officials wanted to withhold match expenses because of the frivolous attitude of the visitors.

Much has been made of the 1923 Cup Final at Wembley where a crowd had to be cleared back from the pitch so that the game could proceed. It was then played without serious interruption, despite the crowd being packed to within a couple of feet of the touchline. Pictorial evidence from continental games would indicate that many games there, too, were played before overflow crowds who lined the touchline without interfering with play. Nevertheless, many football matches on the continent between the wars seem to have been tumultuous affairs. The supercilious attitude of British touring teams and their hard tackling provoked trouble enough, but throughout the 1920s and 1930s there were continual reports of violence and bad sportsmanship in matches where no British team was involved.

At the Antwerp Olympics in 1920, Czechoslovakia walked off in the final against Belgium because of what they claimed (with some justice) was bad refereeing; in 1932 the Mitropa Cup semi-final between Juventus and Slavia was abandoned and the cup given to the winner of the other semi-final, Bologna, after a game marked by violence on the field and on the terracing. It was said in central Europe, and only half in jest, that the increasing emphasis on national prestige led to fights on the field, brawls in the stadium and matches being abandoned, so that it wasn't a real Mitropa Cup match unless it was decided in the embassies. The Italian satirical sports journal *Guerin sportivo* featured cartoons in which football matches resembled battles, with tanks and guns and barbed wire. Many grounds in fact, had to be fenced off from the spectators, to protect players and officials. In the late 1930s there were increasing reports of trouble at matches, but by then the political tensions that were always more apparent on the continent were reaching crisis proportions.

In Britain the ethnic, religious or national tensions behind the riots on the continent were dismissed as a foreign disease, a phrase that would be returned with justifiable glee half a century later. Yet even in this time in Britain all was not rosy. In Belfast political tensions led to Belfast Celtic refusing to play in the Ulster League for a few seasons after the creation of the Irish Free State, and in Glasgow, Rangers and Celtic echoed the Irish tensions. But this was as much a safety valve as an active ingredient in the Irish/British problem. In the home internationals the Scot found nothing more delicious than beating the English in their annual encounters at Hampden (from 1906) or Wembley (from 1923).

Given the political state of Europe, particularly in the ethnic disputes that were a major cause of the Great War and which were far from solved in the attempt to create new nations respecting minority grievances after it, it would have been surprising if European football had been free from trouble. It had been the boast, or rather the hope, of the founding fathers of the FA that football would bring the classes together, that sport would always bring out the best in people. In the 1920s and 1930s there were similar hopes voiced on the continent about the ability of football to calm the native passions in sporting rivalry. For the most part they were to be disappointed.

Even in this period the example of the British was one that most football leaders on the continent admired. Lucien Gamblin, former international and respected reporter on *L'Auto*, complained about the way British teams did not take foreign opposition seriously, but for the sportsmanship of the players and the behaviour of British fans he had the highest regard. On the extreme right of the political spectrum Lucien Dubech, author and sports journalist, had as much respect for the courage and character of British athletes as he had contempt for some 'latins', while Pierre Marie, socialist activist and sportsman, shared his opinion about the sporting behaviour of the British. Unlike many British footballers who travelled to the continent, David Jack of Bolton Wanderers and Arsenal liked most of what he saw there in the early 1930s, but he had to admit that while there was occasional reason for criticism of crowds in Britain 'on the whole, they set a standard that Continental enthusiasts would do well to copy.' Hugo Meisl at this same time, half-heartedly defending Britain against accusations that it was decadent in sport, could more warmly praise Britain for its sportsmanship – as would his brother, severe critic of most aspects of British football play, twenty years later. And Luciano Serra, in the history of football that he brought out in 1964 (*Storia del Calcio*) described the England/Austria game of December 1932 as a 'great spectacle set within the framework of a crowd that applauded both teams with a chivalry unknown in Austria and Italy.'

If the British were top of the good behaviour league, their playing supremacy was coming under serious challenge, while in attitudes to such matters as coaching and facilities they were decidedly old-fashioned. Early in 1933 a Hungarian sports writer on *Pesti Naplo* placed Austria as best of Europe's 'Super' teams, with Scotland, England and Italy next. Among lesser teams came Hungary, followed by Switzerland, Czechoslovakia, Spain, Holland, Germany, France, Belgium, Sweden and Denmark. Any such judgments are guaranteed to draw the wrath of those who know better, and while British commentators might have been scandalized by Austria being given a higher ranking than Scotland and England, others would have claimed that the British teams were being overgenerously treated. The problem was that there was no official competition at this time to test the relative merits of British and continental teams.

In the 1930s Scotland's record on the continent was better than that of England, but both nations were beaten on several occasions. England's first defeat by a team outside the United Kingdom was a 4–3 loss to Spain in May 1929: coming at the end of a tiring tour in which they had beaten France and Belgium, the players wilted in the heat – the game had deliberately been brought forward so that it was played in the middle of the day – after leading 3–1. The ambassador had warned them about the seriousness with which the result would be taken, and he also pointed out that Spain had recently inflicted a 5–1 defeat against Portugal in Seville and a 8–1 thrashing of France in Saragossa. The defeat was more easily brushed aside when Spain came to England in December 1931 and were trounced 7–1. On this occasion the pitch suited the English and an early charge on goalkeeper Zamora unsettled the Spanish hero who was already suffering from the refusal of the coach to allow his wife to travel with him. Instead of his usual brilliant performance he had a miserable day.

The home games were the only ones the British public took seriously, and so they could dismiss the victories over England on the continent by France in 1931, Hungary and Czechoslovakia in 1934, Austria and Belgium in 1936 and Switzerland in 1938. On home soil it was a different matter, but even here there should have been cause for concern. A year after England's thrashing of Spain they were lucky to beat Austria 4–3 in London. Even the local press had to marvel at the skill of the visitors. Two years later Italy, the reigning World Champions, were beaten at Highbury and this time the press had few words of praise for the visitors. It was a brutal match which England won 3–2 against ten men, with the dressing room looking like an ambulance room at the end. The Italians were desperate to win and the English made up the majority of the walking wounded, but what is usually overlooked is that Monti, the number one thug in the Italian team, was met by his own treatment in the first minute, and was a passenger before he eventually left the field. If the Italians had been able to control their tempers it is likely that even with ten men and a pitch more suited to England, they would have won. In 1937 England's home record looked shaky against a Czechoslovak team that scored four goals, only to meet a young Stanley Matthews on rare goal-scoring form, his hat trick helping England to a 5–4 victory. To celebrate the 75th anniversary of the FA a team representing Europe was invited in 1938 to play England and lost 3–0: manager Pozzo did his best with a team of nationalities with whom, he complained, he did not have the three weeks he thought necessary to lock them away and prepare them for the game.

When Pozzo complained about the lack of time to prepare his team for the game against England he would have been laughed at by his hosts, for an England team manager would have been lucky to get three days. Like the attitude to 'manliness', the British suspicion of coaching has a long history, steeped in the 'amateur' ethos, and the prophets of coaching in the 1930s were treated with as much indifference as Richard Mulcaster back in the sixteenth century.

There were a few men in Britain whose vision saw beyond the fog of the Channel. James Catton and Ivan Sharpe, editors of the *Athletic News*, had emphasized the need for coaching, but the closest the British got to adopting any of the ideas of the continentals was through Herbert Chapman, a mediocre centre forward in his playing days who became manager of Huddersfield in September 1920 and took them from near chaos to unprecedented success before leaving for Arsenal in 1925. Chapman repeated his success with Arsenal, in a lowly position in the League when he joined them, soon not only the most successful in Cup and League, but the glamour club of the decade and the most sought after club on the continent. He was prepared to spend big money on players, and even, had he been permitted, to bring them over from Europe. Chapman treated his players as adults, discussed tactics with them and saw the future of the game as not necessarily resting in the British Isles.

In a series of articles written for the *Sunday Express* and published in 1934 shortly after his sudden death, Chapman set out his progressive ideas on the need for making use of floodlights for competitive matches, numbering players' jerseys and giving the manager more say in the running of the team. What he considered his most revolutionary idea was that a squad of twenty of England's best players meet regularly under a selector, coach and trainer to prepare for international matches. As a realist he declared that 'I have no hope of this international building policy being adopted.'

Chapman, a good friend of Meisl and Pozzo, is best known for his negative tactics, introducing the 'third back' to counter the change in the off-side rule of 1925: following the advice of experienced players, he brought back the roving centre half to play a policing role in the middle of the defence. In addition, the two inside forwards were brought back to play behind the two wingers and the centre forward, linking defence to attack in a W or M formation. However you looked at it, a forward line of five, or six when the centre half came forward to attack, had been reduced to three, or five when the inside forwards attacked. Chapman was certainly a defensive minded coach, but it is difficult to see how the previous off-side rule, often used to bring the game to a standstill, as McCracken and Hudspeth of Newcastle United did to perfection, was any better.

It is always easier to defend than attack, to spoil than to create. Part of the romance of soccer is the way weak teams have used this to bring about upsets. The pity is when a star-studded team like Arsenal in the 1930s adopts such tactics. Chapman was a prophet of the deadly *verrou* tactics of the Swiss and the *catenaccio* of the Italians from the 1950s. The only manager to match Chapman in his day was Bill Struth of Glasgow Rangers. Rangers played Arsenal regularly, usually beat them, and in terms of facilities and glamour attracted the same adulation and hatred: from the late 1940s Rangers were best known for their 'Iron Curtain' defence. Struth and Chapman, too, were less interested in the game than in the power it could bring. Writing in 1946, towards the end of a career in journalism, Trevor Wignall claimed that Chapman 'somewhat arrogant and decidedly loud-talking', had no interest in the game as 'a sacred trust', but was essentially a showman whose main interest was packed grounds regardless of the spectacle provided on the park. And Chapman was happy to boast that his proudest moment had nothing to do with football, but rather with his son completing a law degree.

It was not for such reasons that his ideas on coaching were ignored. Those who had invented the game thought they had nothing to learn from those who had grown up under their tutelage. The British FAs were not for turning, and certainly not from upstart foreigners. Those in Britain with a sincere lack of interest in what was happening on the continent were doing no more than following the lead of those who should have known better, but the consequences of a football fan for whom the names Hugo Meisl and Vittorio Pozzo meant nothing were scarcely as tragic as those of a Prime Minister in 1938 who hardly knew where Czechoslovakia was and thought he could talk to Hitler as though he was discussing a cricket match.

Cut off mentally from the continent, the prodigies that were being introduced into the game from the other side of the world did not even enter into discussion. Since the British FAs spurned the Olympics after 1920 the brilliance of the Uruguayans in 1924 and 1928 passed unnoticed; not being a member of FIFA the World Cup was ignored, and so too the play of the first victors, again Uruguay (using much the same team as had won in the Amsterdam Olympics); or that of the Brazilians in 1938. Certainly the Uruguayans tarnished their reputation with a brutal and disorderly performance in Paris in 1936, and Peru brought attention to themselves for the wrong reasons in the 1936 Olympics, while Brazil did little to enhance the reputation of the South Americans in the 'battle of Bordeaux' in the 1938 World Cup. Bloodier battles were ahead for Europe, but when the nations of the world regrouped for the more orderly battles of the football sphere, the brilliance of the South Americans was not to be denied. Spared the destruction of the Second World War they entered the world scene soon after it with a variety and artistry that further emphasized the apparently inexhaustible richness of the game.

Endnotes

In the special edition of *Vingtième siècle* see:

Georges Vigarello, 'Les premiers Coupes du Monde, ou l'installation du sport moderne', pp.5–10;
Pierre Milza, 'Le football italien. Une histoire à l'échelle du siècle', pp. 49–58.

Of the many articles by Pierre Lanfranchi, see:

Pierre Lanfranchi, 'Les 'footballeurs-étudiants' yougoslaves en Languedoc (1925–1935)', *Sport histoire*, No 3, 1989, pp. 43–59.
Pierre Lanfranchi, 'Rugby contro calcio. La genesi delle due pratiche sportive nella francia meridionale', *Ricerce Storiche*, anno XIX, no.2, Maggio-Agosto 1989, pp. 339–351.
Pierre Lanfranchi, 'Bologna: the team that shook the world! A football team in Fascist Italy', *IJHS*, Vol 8, No 3, December 1991, pp. 336–346.
Pierre Lanfranchi, 'England's most durable export? Recent trends in research on football development in continental Europe', paper delivered to 'Sporting Traditions VIII', Canberra, July 1991.

On Fascist Italy see also:

Felice Fabrizio, *Sport e fascismo. La politica sportiva del regime. 1924–1936*, Guaraldi editore, Firenze, 1976.

On Nicolo Carosio:

Gianni Isola, 'Nicolo Carosio. La voce del calcio', in 'Le héros sportif' (EUI, Florence).

On Schalke 04:

Siegfried Gehrmann, 'Football in an Industrial Region: the example of Schalke 04 Football Club', *IJHS*, Vol 6, No 3, December 1989, pp. 335–355.

On the German visit to London in 1935:

Brian Stoddart, 'Sport, cultural politics and international relations: England versus Germany, 1935', in Norbert Elias and Joachim Rühl (eds.), *Sport History*, Schors-Verlag, Niedernhausen, 1985, pp. 385–412.

For the Germany vs. England match of 1938, in addition to the works referred to in the text, see:

Peter J. Beck, 'England vs. Germany, 1938', in *History Today*, Vol 32, June 1982, pp. 29–34.

On Hakoah:

John Bunzl (ed.), *Hoppauf Hakoah. Jüdischer Sport in Österreich. Von den Anfängen bis in die Gegenwart*, Vienna, 1987.

For English football between the wars:

Nicholas Fishwick, *English Football and Society: 1910–1950*, Manchester University Press, Manchester, 1989.

The late Stephen Jones has written many articles and books on sport and leisure between the wars: see in particular:

Stephen Jones, 'The Economic Aspects of Association Football in England, 1918–1939', *BJSH*, Vol 1, No 3, December 1984, pp. 286–299.

Ivan Sharpe's invaluable recollections are in:

Forty Years in Football, Hutchinson's Library of Sport and Pastimes, London, 1952.

Herbert Chapman's collected articles are in:

Herbert Chapman on Football, Garrick Publishing Company, London, 1934.

On Chapman,

Stephen Studd, *Herbert Chapman. Football Emperor: a study in the origins of modern soccer*, Peter Owen Ltd, London, 1981.

See also:

Trevor Wignall, *Almost Yesterday*, Hutchinson, London, ca 1946.

Of football biographies with comments on the European scene:

David Jack, *Soccer*, Putnam, London, 1934;
Charles Buchan, *A Lifetime in Football*, Phoenix House, London, 1955.

For material on Friedrich Torberg I am indebted to Heidi Zogbaum, who introduced me to him and extracted for me most of his comments on football. The best example of this is in his chapter 'Lieben Sie Sport?', in *Die Erben der Tante Jolesch*, Deutscher Taschenbuch Verlag, Munich, 1981. For material on Sindelar from the German and Austrian press, and for information on Austrian football at the time of the *Anschluss* I am indebted to Ulrich Matheja.

CHAPTER FIVE

Football Becomes the World Game

At the Maracana Stadium, Rio de Janeiro, on 16 July 1950, a world record crowd of 199,854 watched Brazil play Uruguay in the final of the fourth World Cup. The result, an upset 2–1 victory against the host nation, left the city where it was played and the millions who had been listening to the game on radio mourning Brazil's defeat. It was the second time South America had hosted the tournament but, unlike 1930 when only four teams made the trip from Europe to Uruguay, many of Europe's top footballing nations went to Brazil in 1950, eager to capture the world crown. There were defections as usual: Argentina was one of them, while Czechoslovakia and France found trivial reasons not to come; Belgium, Denmark and Austria chose not to enter, while Hungary and the Soviets stayed behind their Iron Curtain: Germany was still banned from sporting contacts for its role in the recent war. But Italy was present, despite having lost the flower of its football talent when the champion Torino team perished in the Superga air crash in Turin the previous year. The British associations were available for the first time, offered two spots for their regional competition. This magnanimous gesture by FIFA, however, was dismissed by a haughty Scotland who said they would come only as champions of Great Britain. England won the Home International championship in 1950 and so went alone. They returned even lonelier, defeated by the USA and Spain, and so failed to qualify for the final play-off. There could be no denying that the game that had begun in the British Isles now belonged to the world at large. That the final was played between two Latin American teams was no accident of geography, but a reflection of the new balance of power in the football world.

The World Cup in Brazil opened the same day as the Korean War broke out, but in Brazil and other soccer mad countries the war had to take second billing. In Britain, however, the World Cup was virtually ignored, even although England were competing, and when the England team was eliminated officials, players and even the press went home, not interested in seeing the world's best teams in action in the finals. The competition was a great success, despite the distances that had to be covered to play the games, distances that were measured in hours by plane rather than miles or kilometres. And despite the folly that had the competition run in leagues instead of a knock-out formula, it was sheer chance that the final game was also the decider, with Brazil leading Uruguay by a point, and so needing only a draw to win the Jules Rimet Cup. Henri Delaunay, co-founder with Rimet of the competition, resigned from the 1950 organizing committee in protest at how it was run. None of this troubled Brazil as they prepared not only for the final game, but for the celebrations that would follow. The Brazilians firmly believed they had won the game before it began, said as much in official pronouncements, and were poised for the greatest carnival of all time. Uruguay played the party poopers, however, and the carnival was cancelled. The Uruguayans made their lap of honour holding the Brazilian flag by its four corners in homage to the host nation, but most of their hosts had left, and they received the newly named trophy almost surreptitiously in a stadium so recently and so noisily packed with delirious Brazilians.

Rio was like a dead city: the firecrackers were put away, along with the fancy dress, the musicians packed up and countless speeches remained unused. For Flavio Costa, director of the Brazilian team and candidate for the municipal council, his hopes were trampled in the dust along with his effigy and thousands of his electoral pamphlets. For the European observers seeing football in South America for the first time, the grip of the game was something they could scarcely believe. It would shortly become legendary.

Football comes to South America

The growth of football in Latin America passed virtually unnoticed in Europe before the 1920s, although British, Italian and South African teams went on tours there early in the century. In Argentina and Uruguay soccer was probably more advanced than in Europe at this time, and it was in South America, in 1916, that the first major international soccer competition outside the United Kingdom was formed: the South American Cup. Argentina and Chile joined FIFA as early as 1912, but it was at the Olympics that the Latin Americans first gave notice to the Europeans that a new force had entered football. This came with the brilliant victories of the Uruguay national team in 1924 and 1928, the latter in a replayed final against Argentina. In 1925 three South American club teams toured Europe with spectacular success, Paulistano from Brazil, Boca Juniors from Argentina, and Nacional of Uruguay who stayed for five months and, like the other South American tourists, lost on few occasions. The first World Cup was held in Uruguay, but despite this it was not until 1950 that the growth of soccer in Latin America attracted the interest of Europe as a whole. This attitude often angered the South Americans in much the same way as British disdain and indifference to the continentals annoyed them.

Association football arrived in Latin America in much the same way as it came to Europe, in the kit bags of British sailors, the leisure pursuits of British businessmen, and the peculiarities of British expatriates whose enthusiasm for play was taken up by the local social elites, inadvertently infecting the poorer classes with the joy of the game and then fighting to stave off the proletarian upsurge that threatened to swamp their privileged and political ascendancy.

It was among the large British communities of Argentina and Uruguay that the game first took root, played in the 1860s on an occasional basis, and by the turn of the century organized into the first leagues to be formed outside the United Kingdom. These two countries played the first of their many internationals against each other in 1901 and in subsequent years they were involved in so many competitions with each other that by the mid-1930s they had played each other one hundred times, with honours slightly in favour of Argentina. Their first game in the Cup named after its donor, the Scottish sporting philanthropist and tea baron, Thomas Lipton, was played in 1905. In 1906 another trophy was offered for annual competition by Richard Newton, and in 1908 and 1911 the respective Ministries for Education of Argentina and Uruguay put up trophies also for annual competition. To add to fixtures which could now result in the two countries playing each other up to five times in one year came the Association Cup in 1912.

Although intended as annual competitions, there were years in which these trophies were not contested: the two Ministry of Education Trophies ceased in the 1920s and there were many occasions in that decade when play in the various cup competitions was interrupted. By then, in any case, a more important international competition, one that was intended to take in all of South America, had been founded: the Copa Sudamericana. Argentina had organized a competition with Uruguay and Chile in 1910, but it was not until six years later that it was decided to hold similar competitions on an annual basis. Argentina were hosts to a championship which included Uruguay, the eventual winners, and Chile and Brazil. It was during this meeting that the brainchild of the Uruguayan, Hector R. Gómez, was taken up, and the Confederación Sudamericana de Fútbol, better known as CONMEBOL, was formed, the first sporting confederation on a continent-wide basis. The European equivalent (UEFA) would not be formed until nearly forty years later.

The first major task of CONMEBOL was to institute the South American Cup and organize it on a regular basis. Each year it was to be played in the capital of a different host nation, on a league system, over a set period. Paraguay joined in 1921, Peru in 1924 and Bolivia in 1925. Thereafter politics (Paraguay and Bolivia were at war with each other from 1932 to 1935) and the disputes over professionalism in the early 1930s meant that the seven major nations did not play in the same competition until 1936–37. (An unofficial competition for professional teams was held in Lima, Peru in 1935.) Ecuador, which joined CONMEBOL in 1927, first took part in 1939, and Colombia entered in 1945, five years after joining CONMEBOL.

The inevitable political problems in such a competition were exacerbated by problems of violence on the field, but even more so by a lack of enthusiasm on the part of some nations, most notably Brazil. When the Copa Libertadores, the continental club championship, was introduced in 1960, interest in it almost died. It survived sporadically, but in recent years seems set for a more successful outcome, played on a two-yearly basis. The problems of violence on the field continue.

The most successful team in the Copa Sudamericana has been Argentina. The first games of association football in South America were played in the Argentine province of Buenos Aires, where there was a thriving British community. In the 1860s sailors and workers on the Rio de la Plata played a form of football, and in 1867 the first soccer club was formed – the Buenos Aires FC, from the Buenos Aires Cricket Club, founded five years earlier. In the 1880s British railway workers became involved in the game, formed unofficial leagues and founded two of Argentina's oldest clubs: Quilmes FC (1887) and Rosario Central FC (1889). The driving force in Argentine football, however, still remembered today, was the 'visionary Scot', Alexander Watson Hutton, who founded the English High School in 1884, with football an important part of the curriculum. It was he who formed the Argentine Association Football League in 1891, and the first FA in 1893. Hutton, whose name is commemorated in the library of the AFA, was its first president, and English was the official language until 1906.

British teams dominated the first twenty years of the league, in particular Lomas Athletic, the team of the prestigious British boarding school, Lomas de Zamora. Their nearest rivals were Alumni, the team from Hutton's English-speaking Buenos Aires High School. Belgrano were the only team to break their hold, in 1904 and 1908. Lomas and Alumni are seldom heard of today, but the British influence is retained in the names of teams like River Plate, Rosario Central and Newell's Old Boys. The latter were founded by the schoolteacher Isaac Newell, as Club Newell's Old Boys de Rosario.

The British dominance of Argentina did not last long into the twentieth century, but has its memorial in the interest in rugby unusual in South America. As a major meat and cereal exporter Argentina had an expanding economy, attracting thousands of immigrants, particularly from Italy, and by 1930 Buenos Aires had a population of three million, a third of whom were of European origin. Most of these were Italian, and football teams that were started by English speakers were taken over by Italians, even if the name was left in the original. CA (Club Atlètico) River Plate were founded in 1901, and within four years the big five of Argentine football were founded: Racing Club in 1903, of basically French origins, and who would dominate competition for six years from 1913; CA Boca Juniors in 1905, founded by an Irishman, Patrick McCarthy, but who would grow to success and popularity as an Italian club; CA Independiente were founded in that same year by the Argentine employees of a store called The City of London, who wanted to form their own 'independent' team; last and least of the big five, also founded in 1905, were CA San Lorenzo. In 1908 the working-class team Huracàn were founded.

The governing body was faced by many tensions as the ascendancy of the British was challenged by other ethnic groups, and by the problems of professionalism, which was finally adopted in 1931. The declining British influence could also be seen in the change in name of the governing body, which in 1934 became the Asociaciòn del Fùtbol Argentino, the first time the Spanish word for 'football' was used in the title. In that year River Plate and Boca Juniors emerged as the two great rivals: the former, called Los Millonarios for their free spending in the 1920s, the latter who produced some of the most brilliant players of all time. It is possible that Argentina lost something in administrative stability with the fading of the British influence, but there can be little doubt about what it gained in footballing brilliance with its stars of Italian origins: from Monti in the 1920s to Maradona (only partially Italian) in the 1980s, the one combining artistry with brutality, the other genius with petulance. Between them came a succession of stars; Orsi in the 1930s, Moreno, Labruna and Pedernera who formed the core of River Plate's 'Machine' (La Máquina) in the 1940s; the incomparable Di Stefano in the 1950s, Sivori in the 1960s . . . and we are merely skimming some of the cream of the Italian influence on Argentine football. For Argentina the Italian connection has been a far from happy one, as its best players were constantly enticed over to Europe for the bigger money, particularly to play for Italian clubs and even for Italy, at the expense of Argentine football. The adoption of professionalism in 1931 was in large measure an effort to foil the raids by the Italians.

Uruguay, with its population of a mere two million in the 1920s can justly claim to be the most outstanding football country in the history of the game. Not only did it hold its own with neighbouring giant Argentina in the early decades of the century, but it dominated the Olympics in the 1920s, won the World Cup in 1930 and 1950, was the first winner of the South American Cup in 1916 and on many occasions thereafter, and until the 1970s continued to hold its own against the best in the world. Football was first played in Uruguay by British residents and workers in the 1870s and the first club, Albion, was formed by an English teacher, William Poole, at the University of Montevideo in 1891. In 1900 the Asociaciòn

Uruguaya de Fùtbol was founded by four clubs; Peñarol, Albion and Central Uruguay Railway, all British, and the Deutscher Fussballklub. In 1899 a club of native Uruguayans was formed with the merger of Montevideo FC and Defensa, and it was this team, Nacional that, with Peñarol, was to divide Uruguayan football into two camps. The other teams in the league, all based in Montevideo, did little more than make up the numbers.

Peñarol, called Central Uruguay Railway Cricket Club until 1913, were founded by some Britons in 1891, and it was they who organized the first championship. The club was taken over by the Italians when the British sold out their railway interests at the start of the First World War, and they renamed it after the suburb in Montevideo where they played: Pignarolo, or Peñarol in Spanish. Nacional took as their colours the blue, white and red of the revolutionary tricolour adopted by General José Artigas, the hero of Uruguayan independence. The Uruguayan federation was formed in 1900, and although Uruguay became a world power in football it is perhaps an exaggeration to say, as their World Cup manager did in 1966: 'Other countries have their history. Uruguay has its football.'

Chile shared with Argentina and Uruguay a population that was overwhelmingly of European extraction, and a long coastline and important seaports that attracted British ships and commerce. The first association was founded in 1895, but regional and other disputes in a nation squeezed between the Andes and the sea and more than 4000 kilometres long from its northern to its southern border, delayed the formation of a national league until 1933, when professionalism was introduced. Chile was the second South American country to join FIFA, in 1912, but following disputes with rival leagues they were suspended in 1925 before being readmitted when the two major rivals came together in the Federación de Football de Chile in 1926. Everton, of obviously British influence, are one of Chile's more successful teams, while Wanderers of Valparaiso were inspired by the famous English amateurs; of Chilean and not Irish inspiration, however, are the less successful O'Higgins FC, named after Bernardo O'Higgins, the Chilean patriot of the early nineteenth century, who also gave his name to a cup competition between Chile and Brazil: the most famous Chilean team is Colo Colo, founded in 1925 when five players left the Magallanes FC, founded in 1902, to form their 'wildcat' team.

At club and national level Chile have not been able to match their two great footballing neighbours. It was not until 1991 that they won a major club competition, when Colo Colo won the Copa Libertadores. In 1962 Chile hosted the World Cup and came third, their best performance in international competition. Against a backdrop of perennial poverty and devastation caused by the earthquake of 1961, two new stadiums were built, one of which was the national stadium at Santiago. In 1973 this stadium was the venue for some of the torture and other brutality that followed Pinochet's ousting of Allende, and when the Soviet Union was drawn to play Chile there in the preliminaries for the 1974 World Cup they refused, offended in their humanitarian sensitivities at the thought of playing in a country that did not respect civil rights.

Brazil has produced the best and most loved football teams the world has seen, particularly with their triumphs between 1958 and 1970 when they won the World Cup three times. They are the only country to have gone through to the finals of every World Cup, and although Italy and Germany, with three championships each, have won it as often as they have, only Brazil has captured the free flowing spirit of a game that was meant to be enjoyed. But while they have captured the imagination of the world, in South America itself they have not been so popular, frequently spurning competition with their neighbours. Brazil, with a population and land mass as great as that of the rest of the continent, also has a unique racial mix, with Portuguese rather than Spanish the national language.

Football as a national game developed slowly in Brazil. In addition to the problems of vast distances separating its one hundred million and more inhabitants, the social barriers of race and wealth were difficult to overcome. The Brazilian FA was part of the omni-sports body, the Confederação Brasiliera de Desportos (CBD), which was founded in 1914 (as the Federação Brasileira de Sports) and became affiliated with FIFA in 1917, provisionally, before being accepted in 1923. At the beginning of the century rowing was the most popular sport, and soccer clubs developed within them, at times breaking away to form a separate club, or at least remaining within the club as its dominant activity. Some of these clubs boasted luxurious facilities, but these were not always available to the soccer players, who might be accepted for their earning power at the gate but were excluded from the social activities of the wealthy elites. With the decline of the quintessential amateur sport of rowing, and without the social alternatives of cricket or rugby, football in Brazil was accepted, as in few other countries, by society as a whole. This came in the 1930s, and not without some acrimonious splits over the issue of professionalism. The most aristocratic clubs, like Paulistano, refused to have anything to do with open payment to players, others wanted to get rid of the sham of *amadorismo marrom*, but the deciding issue was the loss of top players to Argentina and Uruguay, where professionalism had been recognized, and even Europe. Brazil recognized professionalism in 1933, but the splits this caused were not healed until the end of the decade. Radio was then linking most of Brazil, and football became the one issue on which all Brazilians could be united.

The first league in Brazil was founded in São Paulo in 1901, the second in

Rio in 1905, and by 1919 when a club was formed at Rio Branca in the remote province of Acre in 1919 the last soccer frontier had been conquered. By this time soccer had been taken up by the press in a big way, with as much as an entire page taken up by the description of one game. However, it was not until the 1970s that a true national championship was established, and even then it was in three stages, with elimination as in cup games. In recent years the administration of soccer in Brazil, never easy, has become something of a nightmare. From the beginning the São Paulo and the Rio leagues dominated all the others. Nevertheless, in the creation of a nation from the six major regions in a country as large as Europe, and as diverse in ecology as in ethnic and racial mix, football has played a significant role.

The origins of organized football in Brazil are usually credited to Charles Miller, born in São Paulo in 1875 of English parents. Much of his childhood and youth was spent in England where he played for South-ampton, and when he came back to Brazil in 1894 he packed his soccer kit and two footballs. In the absence of an existing competition he formed a team at the São Paulo Railway Company where he worked, encouraged the English Gas Company and London Bank to do the same, then persuaded the São Paulo Athletic Club to add football as well as cricket to its sporting pursuits. In 1898 Mackenzie College, although English-speaking, became the first actual Brazilian team, and in 1901 the São Paulo championship was established.

The great rivals to the paulistas are the cariocas from Rio. As in São Paulo, sports clubs at the turn of the century were upper-class social institutions combining various sports, particularly rowing. It was from two such clubs that the greatest of club rivalries in football developed: Fluminense and Flamengo, popularly known as Flu-Fla, and holders of the world record attendance for a club match when they played before 177,656 spectators in 1963. Flamengo came from the Clube de Regatas do Flamengo, formed in 1895, but founded as a break-away football team in 1911. The following year they entered the Rio league. Fluminense were founded in 1902 by Oscar Cox and some British immigrants, and they were behind the founding of the first Rio Championship in 1905, which they dominated until they came up against their great rival, Flamengo. Fluminense, nicknamed the 'face powder' team for their aristocratic pretensions, have retained their socially exclusive stamp to the present day, with some of the most luxurious facilities on the continent, and with fees to match. Flamengo on the other hand, broke all social barriers in their search for the best players in the 1930s and became known as the 'people's club'. With their vibrant attacking game they became the most popular team in Brazil.

Of the other major carioca teams, Vasco da Gama are the team of the

Portuguese immigrants and their descendants, with their origins in the Lusitania Esportes Clube, founded in 1898 by wealthy Portuguese merchants and bankers; Botafogo were formed in 1904 out of a rowing club in the then wealthy district of that name, and although now attracting more supporters from the industrial zone, they continue to attract the new rich. América were the club of the old social elites who had come to live in the city. At the other end of the wealth scale Bangu were formed when some British technicians in a textile factory in the suburb of that name persuaded the management to form a football team, which other workers in the factory soon joined. In the São Paulo league two of today's best known teams came from similarly simple social origins. In the early years São Paulo AC and CA Paulistano were the main rivals, but this changed with the success of Corinthians (usually left in the English) and SE (Sociedade Esportiva) Palmeiras. Corinthians were founded in 1910 by a group of workers, a team of poor origins unabashed at calling themselves after the wealthy amateurs who had just toured the country. SE Palmeiras, founded in 1914 as Palestra Italia, became the main rivals to Corinthians in the paulista championship from 1920 through to the arrival on the scene of Santos and Pelé in the late 1950s. Elsewhere in Brazil the appeal of class and ethnicity was reflected in the formation of football teams: Grêmio in Porto Alegre and Cruzeiro in Belo Horizonte played the aristocratic role of Fluminense and Paulistano. In São Paulo, Portuguese were the team of the Portuguese community and Juventus the team of the Italian community.

In the beginning football was the game of the elite, whether British, Portuguese, German or Brazilian, and that was how they wanted it to remain, a transplanted European culture and language cut off from the native soil. As in Britain and Europe, however, the elite were unable to keep the game to themselves, and as teams were formed among those they liked to think of as inferior, so too did this widening social base provide the best players: in Brazil this meant among the blacks and mulattoes. No institution has done more than Brazil's national football team to contribute to the myth of racial democracy in Brazil. Racial attitudes were as much dominated by social class as colour, however, and the colour of a man's skin was not an automatic barrier. Thus Brazil never went the way of the United States or South Africa in the creation of separate sporting competitions for different 'races'. The facts of Brazilian life, where slavery was abolished only as late as 1888, were that most blacks and mulattoes were very poor, and so some of Brazil's top football teams through to the 1960s were almost exclusively white: Fluminense, Grêmio, and Sport (from Recife). This ambiguity was encapsulated in the case of Brazil's first football hero, the mulatto Artur Friedenreich, regarded by many who saw him and others who followed as the best player ever. Friedenreich was born of a German father and a black mother, but was accepted into the elite only because of his upbringing as a European and his desire to be seen as such. He played for the aristocratic Paulistano club and was on one occasion mortally offended when selected to play for the blacks against the whites in a friendly match. He played between 1909 and 1934, in which time he is reputed to have scored 1329 goals.

Before Friedenreich, another black player, Manteiga, was signed by FC América, as a result of which Fluminense gained a new influx of members and players from those at América who could not bear the insult. The racial barrier was first seriously breached by Vasco da Gama, who in 1923 won the Rio league with several non-whites and went on to repeat their success the following year. This prompted the more socially conscious clubs of Rio to form their own competitions and play among themselves for a while. Vasco had broken away from Lusitania Esporte Clube in 1914, and in 1916 entered the third division of the Rio league. Their success in 1923 and 1924 inaugurated a new era, as other clubs opted for sporting glory rather than social exclusiveness. In the 1930s Flamengo outdid even Vasco and América in signing black players, and Bonsuccesso fielded a team of eleven blacks. Brazil were to become the most racially diverse of all national football teams, but their strength has always been in their non-white players. It was they who brought to the game its joyous samba style and the mysteries of *macumba* rites, combining a rhythm and inspirational spontaneity that no other players could match.

The adoption of professionalism confirmed the role of the black player. In 1933 Santos and São Paulo declared themselves professional, and by 1936 the last of the amateurs gave in to the irreversible social and racial realities. Like the men of the FA, however, they did not lose control, and while star players could be paid much larger sums of money than professionals in Britain, most players were on very small salaries. The stars were regarded with paternalistic superiority where they did not suffer from outright social contempt, a situation akin to that of professional cricketers in England, or golf and tennis pros elsewhere in the 1930s, but in degree much worse: many of them were illiterate and even undernourished when they arrived at the big clubs, who fed them, clothed them and even tried to teach them 'manners' – and expected due gratitude and servility in return.

The new status accorded black stars followed a familiar pattern to that of sports in other countries, especially the United States: so long as they were prepared to play the game and know their place they were accepted. Leonidas da Silva, one of the greats of the 1930s, refused to deny his working class origins and his skin colour and was penalized for it in racial abuse. Fausto dos Santos, one of the great players of all time, played as hard in the night clubs as he did on the field, exhibited his individual brilliance at the expense of the team, and was punished for it: above all he clashed with Krieschner, the racist Hungarian coach of Flamengo who wanted to instil some European discipline into the free born talent he found so difficult to deal with. Fausto died prematurely of tuberculosis in 1939, and the clubs he had played for paid nothing towards the funeral expenses. Even the great Pelé had to overcome racist taunts before he became a national institution, used by the generals and as a result criticized in more radical quarters in the 1970s as an uncle Tom. He also became the highest paid soccer player of his day, wealth denied the vast majority of his fellow professionals in South America.

The three other major soccer powers in South America were Paraguay, Bolivia and Peru (discussed in more detail below). Bolivia, set high in the mountains surrounded by Brazil, Paraguay, Argentina, Chile and Peru, has the doubtful distinction of having the world's highest major city, La Paz, whose rarefied atmosphere might have given it home advantage, but it did not encourage many teams to want to go there. Bolivia had other problems, not all related to terrain. Its small European elite lorded it over a population of about 95% mestizos and Amerindians, and after independence from Spain in 1825 revolutions became a standard way of removing governments. None of this stopped football from making some progress, and in 1925 the first FA was founded and the FBF (Federación Boliviana de Fùtbol) was accepted into FIFA the following year. Bolivia has never made a name for itself in the world of football, but it has given it some strange names. Its most outstanding team, The Strongest, founded in 1908, is redolent of British influence and Latin machismo; their main rival, Bolivar, are more conventionally named after the country's liberator, but in addition to teams called Military College and Military Sport, they have the more peaceful Always Ready. All of these teams have won the much-interrupted national championship.

Paraguay has overcome many problems to make its not inconsiderable impact on the football scene, particularly at club level through Olimpia, who have twice won the Copa Libertadores. Landlocked like Bolivia, and plagued by border wars in the 1930s, its population is overwhelmingly made up of mestizos. A Dutchman, Willem Praat is credited with introducing the game, when he arrived as a physical education teacher at a school in Asunción, the capital. Paraguay's FA was founded in 1906, the same year as its first league, based in Asunción, and in 1921 it joined FIFA and CONMEBOL. Professionalism was adopted in 1935, but since many other South American countries did the same about this time the nation was unable to hold on to its best players.

Colombia has the third largest population in South America, but until recently one of the poorest records in football. It put itself on the football map in the late 1940s with a rebel league that became a refuge for disgruntled Argentine, Uruguayan and a few British players. Since then drugs and bribery have been linked to football and the threats to referees, including at least one assassination, forced FIFA to intervene. The 1986 World Cup venue was withdrawn from Colombia when it became apparent that the mess in the domestic league was likely to be repeated as hosts to an international competition. Colombia has made a spectacular impact on the world scene with a 0–5 thrashing of Argentina in Buenos Aires to qualify for USA 1994, with promise to do even better than in Italy in 1990.

Ecuador has not made a great impact, but the traditional rivalry of Quito the capital, and Guayaquíl, the port town and industrial centre, has been played out on the soccer field. Venezuela has the unique distinction of being the only South American country where soccer is not the main sport. Like its other northern neighbours, it has fallen under the influence of the United States, and baseball is the ruling passion. Like the other small countries in the north of South America, sporting relations are often with Central American and Caribbean countries. Indeed, in soccer Guyana and Surinam are part of that Confederation known as CONCACAF, rather than CONMEBOL. (The former French colony of Guiana affiliated with the French Football Federation.)

CONCACAF

The organization of the many countries of Central America and the islands of the Caribbean into a soccer confederation goes back to the 1924 Olympics, during which it was agreed that these countries would hold regular sporting encounters. As a result meets were arranged in 1930, 1935 and 1938 with soccer part of the programme. A separate soccer body (Confederación Centroamericana y del Caribe de Fútbol/CCCF) was founded at the 1938 games, and in 1941 a competition for soccer alone was contested, open to professionals as well as amateurs. In 1939 Mexico, Cuba and the United States formed the North American Football Confederation (NAFC), and it was the merger of the CCCF and the NAFC, including Canada (under pressure from FIFA), that resulted in the foundation of the Confederaciòn Norte-Centroamericana y del Caribe de Fùtbol, better known as CONCACAF, in 1961. CONCACAF runs a nations and a club championship, but seldom with all countries or clubs competing: from 1972–73 the main interest in the CONCACAF nations championship has been as a qualifier for the World Cup.

The American influence in this region has been overwhelming, and one of its effects has been in the spread of baseball and basketball. As in Taiwan, the Philippines and Japan, the spread of American games was part deliberate, part incidental. In countries like Nicaragua, Panama and even the francophone Dominican Republic, the inhabitants are baseball mad.

In some of the West Indian islands cricket is still king, but cable television and the wealth to be made out of basketball in the US threaten to change this. In Cuba soccer was very popular in the 1930s and 1940s, but since then, and even since Castro's revolution of 1959 and his attempts to wipe out Yankeeism, baseball is the number one sport. Boxing, as it is in most poor countries, is also very popular. Nevertheless, in the sporting boom that followed the First World War, soccer played its part, with Costa Rica, one of the more stable political regimes, the most successful.

Soccer has reflected the region's volatile and violent political history, but the so-called 'Soccer War' of 1969 between Honduras and El Salvador is a misnomer. Much as these two countries take their soccer seriously, football was at the most a precipitating factor in that war, whose causes lay deeper in social and economic discontents. The FAs of both these countries were founded in 1935, and both of them were at the World Cup in Spain in 1982, where El Salvador, in the midst of a savage civil war at home, fared poorly, while Honduras managed to draw with Spain and Northern Ireland. Remarkably, even here the British influence in football can be found in the naming of two cup competitions: the Great Britain Cup in Costa Rica and the Winston Churchill Cup in Honduras.

Strongest of the CONCACAF countries is Mexico, twice (1970 and 1986) host for the World Cup, and because of its dominance in the region the fourth most frequent qualifier for the finals, behind Brazil, Germany and Italy. In the Estadio Azteca and the Estadio de la Ciudad Universitaria, both in Mexico City, it has the largest soccer stadiums in the Americas outside Brazil. Soccer came to Mexico with its modernization in the late nineteenth century, spread by British, Spanish and French technicians. A national league was founded in 1903, its first FA in 1927, and in 1929 it joined FIFA. Mexico has suffered as a soccer island cut off from the major countries of South America and the lack of interest of its northern neighbours, although this has been reduced with the advent of jet travel. As host to the 1986 World Cup Mexico made it through to the quarter finals, only to be eliminated on penalties by Germany. Out of these games emerged its greatest hero, the brilliant goal scorer Hugo Sanchez, inevitably lured to the more lucrative fields of Europe, where he starred with Réal Madrid in Spain.

The many small countries of the central American region have tended to have closest playing relations with those who spoke the same language, the Dutch, French and British affiliating with the FA of the colonial overlord. In this regard the Dutch have been the most active and in Surinam were to give the Netherlands and the world of the late 1980s such stars as Ruud Gullit and Frank Rijkaard, children of immigrants who left for the Netherlands in the 1950s to retain Dutch nationality.

Football in Lima

In a continent so large and inhabited by such a variety of ethnic communities and social groups there is little that can be said to be typical. In the growth of football, however, there were many elements in common, and they in turn have echoes of the development of the game in Great Britain, albeit with a racial edge to add to social snobbery. This can be illustrated in the growth of football in Peru, a small country with none of the pretensions to power of its much bigger neighbours, but where the hopes of the poor and the pretensions of the rich came together in the cultural melting point of the national game.

The origins of football in Lima, Peru's capital, have been outlined in a fascinating article by Steve Stein, and offer a model case of football development on the South American continent. The key factor in the growth of football in Lima, as elsewhere, was in the social effects of industrialization and urbanization. Between 1900 and 1931 the population of the capital increased by 125 per cent, while the working class grew by 200 per cent in this time, much of it in immigration from the rural areas.

Football arrived in 1892, an elite and foreign import. The word 'football' has been kept in the original English, along with other technical terms for the game, to the present day. At first football shared the sporting scene with cricket, boat racing, fencing and polo. It was adopted by the two main clubs in 1893: Lima Cricket and Football Club, made up of foreigners, and Union Cricket, where well-to-do Peruvians shared the privileges of the foreigners. The first working-class team emerged in the port city of Callao where British sailors played with the locals, and in 1901 Peru's most famous club was formed out of purely working-class players and 'administrators': Club Sport Alianza, later Alianza Lima. The originators of the club were the young men who looked after the horses of Augusto B. Leguía, future president of Peru; later they attracted players of various working-class occupations in the poor district of La Victoria.

A year later, in 1902, Club Atlética Chalaca was founded in Callao, and by 1910 there were several working-class clubs, all formed more or less spontaneously. As Stein points out, the first priority of these teams was their *barrio*, putting their local district before the city and priding themselves in their spirit of 'picardía', where the street urchin virtues of manoeuvring and dodging were prized more than winning. As the game developed after 1910 they played for the approval of the ever increasing crowds who came to watch them, but for the players the rewards were still in being valued, feeling accepted or even revered. By the 1920s this extended to hero worship by young and old (and also the females), and the beginnings of materialism came in the form of prizes such as certificates, trophies and medals. Players also received payment in the form of 'tips'.

By this time the game was well organized, and from a record crowd of 7000 in 1918, a national stadium was built in 1922 to hold 25,000, a gift of the British community to honour the centenary of Peru's liberation from Spain. The Peruvian Football League was founded in 1912 by members of the Peruvian social elite and British community, notably Eduardo Fry and H.G. Redsaw, while the ubiquitous Thomas Dewar provided a plaque for the competition. Admission was charged for these games. The league prospered until 1921 when it was faced by a schism and collapsed. A new federation was founded in August 1922 and two years later it joined FIFA.

Stein raises the question as to why the strong working-class clubs were unable to develop a strong sense of economic solidarity, given the pride they showed in their football teams. In fact the star players of Lima were being faced by the same temptations as star players elsewhere in the world, and despite some remarkable resistance, it seems they went the way of all flesh when the temptations of material gain and greater national glory were waved before them.

Many employers, seeing the interest in soccer by their employees, provided balls, kits and playing areas, took an interest in their progress and often reaped the benefits in a happier work force. Some players thought this worked the other way, and believed they were taking advantage of the boss. When the working-class teams played against each other, too, energies were dissipated in battles that some players of the time likened to the wars with Chile. Star player Miguel Rostaing claimed to play with a knife in his hand ready to beat off spectators, and that the stevedores and fishermen of the port town of Callao inspired fear in the citizens of Lima when they invaded the capital armed with dynamite to throw at the players and knives to cut up the goalkeeper.

More real were the fears held by the teams of the social elites who found themselves being beaten by teams made up of workers, many of whom were black. For the beleaguered elite of the *gente decente de buena familia* the main hope was in the university team, Universitario de Deportes. Supported by the rich, University's games with Alianza were built up by the press as class warfare to encourage more people to come and watch. A new dimension was added to the local tensions when the growth of football led Peru to consider entering international competition. Now the middle-class controllers of the game were faced by the dilemma of playing a socially acceptable team that might be beaten or a team of social undesirables who could do well. This came to a head in the late 1920s, when Peru decided to enter the South American Cup in 1927 and 1929, and the World Cup in 1930.

In preparation for these competitions normal league games were cancelled, which did not please the Alianza and other working-class players who enjoyed the supplementary income they received for playing football, but worse was to come when those selected for possible national honours realized in the course of practice matches that preference would be given to players with correct social credentials. As a result Alianza withdrew and went back to their *barrio*, playing before their own people in their own competition as they had done in the early days. For this they were banned by the Federation, whose team went on to Argentina and the games in the South American Cup, where they were humiliated. More humiliation was to follow, as the Federation approached Alianza, who had to offer a limp apology before they were reinstated. It was compromise all round, but in the final analysis it was the racial and working-class pride of Alianza that was defeated. The rewards, both material and in the prestige that came with playing in a national competition, were too great a temptation to resist, but in addition the club was forced to accept as its president a high-ranking officer in Lima's municipal government. This was to tame the Aliancistas and make them more respectable. But were they tamed and was it a sell out? Among the many mysteries of football teams throughout the world is the aura of class, colour or religion that stamps some teams from their origins and refuses to leave them, even when they have become giant conglomerates, a pride that millionaire owners often find easier to accommodate than discard, and even at the cost of their own pride or profits. Through to the 1970s Alianza and Universitario remained the best known clubs. Sporting Cristal were founded when the brewery of the same name bought Sporting Tabaco in 1955; they won the league in 1956 and on a few occasions thereafter, but never won the favour of the public.

South America and the World Cup

World soccer before 1930 meant the Olympic Games. No soccer teams from Latin America participated in the London, Stockholm or Antwerp Olympics, and in Paris in 1924 only one: Uruguay. But what a sensation they turned out to be as they swept aside Yugoslavia (7–0), the United States (3–0) and France (5–1) in the early rounds, then beat the Netherlands in the semi-final where they conceded their first goal in a 2–1 victory. In the final they consolidated their superiority by defeating Switzerland 3–0. European eyes were further opened in 1925 with the triumphal tours of Boca, Paulistano and Nacional. Others would follow.

For the 1928 Olympics in Amsterdam, then, the astonishing success of the Latin Americans was less of a surprise. This time they had three representatives: Mexico who established a regular pattern by being easily eliminated (7–1 against Spain), and Uruguay and Argentina who went through to play each other in the final. Argentina's victories were overwhelming: 11–2 against the United States, 6–3 against Belgium and

6–0 against Egypt. Uruguay had more difficulty, but they had to face sterner opposition: the Netherlands (2–0), Germany (4–1) and Italy (3–2). After a 1–1 draw in the final, Uruguay won the replay 2–1 in exhibitions of football that thrilled the appreciative crowds. The Argentine press consoled its readers with a reminder that the competition had been a 'triumph for rioplatense football'. This was no exaggeration: in the two urban conglomerations of Montevideo and Buenos Aires on either side of the estuary of the River Plate was the greatest concentration of football talent in the world.

At the meeting of FIFA during the Paris Olympics Jules Rimet continued with his crusade for a World Cup competition, energetically assisted by Henri Delaunay, and each year the two continued their campaign. They finally won acceptance for their idea at Amsterdam in 1928, when it was decided that such a competition should be held in 1930. On 19 May 1929 Uruguay were granted the right to host the first world championship in soccer open to amateur and professional alike. The choice was popular, such was the admiration for Uruguayan football, while for the Uruguayans it was an honour to be celebrated in conjunction with that of the centenary of their constitution. Immediately they set to work to build the Estadio Centenario for the occasion.

Once the initial enthusiasm had died down, however, most of the European countries started to have second thoughts. The Uruguayan association had promised to pay all travel and hotel expenses, but that still left some problems. To reach that distant outpost of football would require a long sea journey and absence from Europe of two months. For the professional teams there was the problem of paying wages, for the amateurs, who were the majority, there was the problem of getting time off work. The professionals of Hungary, Austria and Czechoslovakia said they would not be making the trip. The Uruguayans were furious at what they took to be a snub by the Europeans and threatened to break away from FIFA. They had reason to be angry: by 19 May only three countries had expressed their willingness to compete: Belgium, fully amateur and itself celebrating the centenary of its independence from the Netherlands, had agreed immediately, while state intervention in Romania and Yugoslavia ensured participation. King Carol of Romania told the British oil companies that they had to release players selected for the team, while king Alexander had only recently (1929) declared himself dictator and needed some lustre for the federal state of 'south Slavs' which was now called Yugoslavia. France still wavered, but the embarrassment would have been too great for the president of FIFA and his compatriot and co-campaigner for the competition to bear, and so France left with the other European countries on the *Conte Verde* on 26 June. In its team were Thépot, the goalkeeper, who had been given time off by the Customs

Department, Capelle, whose military service had been suspended, and Pinel, who worked for the Foreign Office, and was given a special assignment to work at the consular office in Montevideo.

As the date set for the opening match approached, between France and Chile on 13 July, the Centenary Stadium was still not completed, but its main stands had been named, each in honour of victories past and still to come: Colombes in honour of Paris, 1924, Amsterdam in honour of 1928, and Montevideo in anticipation of 1930. This fine feeling on the part of the Uruguayans for their recent history was matched by that for their more distant past: 10 July was the centenary date of the Constitution, 11 July of the national flag, and 18 July was a national holiday. The anniversary of the fall of the Bastille, 14 July, was also celebrated.

Because of withdrawals only thirteen teams took part, in four uneven leagues, the four winners of which went through to a knock-out competition. Of the Latin American teams, Mexico lost their three group games and Bolivia their two. Peru also lost both their games, but by narrower margins: 3–1 to Romania in a kicking match and 1–0 to Uruguay. Paraguay, expected to do well in view of their performances in the South American championship, beat Belgium 1–0, but lost 3–0 to a strong United States team, the core of which were five muscular Scots and one muscular Englishman, all of whom had been professionals in Britain. Since the US team beat Belgium 3–0 they went through to the knock-out stage. Brazil were still a long way short of their potential, and after beating Bolivia 4–0, lost 2–1 to Yugoslavia, Europe's sole survivor to the finals. Chile, who were in the most difficult group, beat Mexico 3–0 and France 1–0, but lost 3–1 to Argentina in a game which developed into a pitched battle when Monti deliberately kicked Chile's Torres who retaliated in kind. Both goalkeepers joined the ensuing fray, which had to be broken up by the police.

This was neither the first nor the last time that Argentina (or Monti) would be involved in controversy – nor the last in which two teams would be embroiled in no-holds-barred brawling. In their game against France Argentina won against the run of play, and partly thanks to the Brazilian referee blowing his whistle for time six minutes too early, just as Pinel looked like scoring the equalizer for France. In the confusion that followed the players left the field to officials and spectators, one Argentine player fainted, then the referee admitted his mistake and called the players back on the field – some were already having a shower. The French had lost their élan, however, and the Argentines held their lead. The Uruguayan crowd, who had supported France throughout the game, then carried the French players from the field, eliciting an outraged protest from Argentina that a European eleven should be so fêted by South Americans. They threatened to withdraw from the competition, but were not very serious about it.

Argentina went on to thrash the US team 6–1, while Uruguay disposed of Yugoslavia by the same score. This brought together the two old rivals and the meeting of national passions that sections of the press set out to inflame: the Argentines not failing to remind their readers that Uruguayan independence had been gained partly at the expense of Argentina, the Uruguayan press attacking the Argentine government.

On the eve of the final boatloads of Argentines crossed the Rio de la Plata for the game, and thousands more in the capital complained that there were not enough boats. Those who could not make it packed the street outside the offices of *La Prensa* for news of the game, others paraded with placards and chanting 'Death to Uruguay'. Those who made the journey, in scenes somewhat similar to those of English fans crossing the Channel five decades later, were searched and had potential weapons removed: they underwent a similar inspection before entering the ground. The Belgian referee, John Langenus, the finest in Europe, asked for a police escort to take him to his boat as soon as the game was finished, as it was due to leave soon after. This later gave rise to stories that he had to be protected from the crowd. In fact his main problem at the start of the game was whether it would be played with an Argentine or a Uruguayan ball. A toss of the coin decided and Uruguay went on to win 4–2 before 90,000 spectators. The Argentine players had received threats on their life before the game, and whether or not this affected them, all but four of them were condemned as 'chicken-hearts' for their performance: above all – irony of ironies! – Monti. Sixty years later one of the youngest players, Pancho Varallo, recalled with disgust how Monti had descended to helping opponents after he knocked them down, and dismissed him as a pansy. In Montevideo delirious Uruguayans enjoyed a national holiday. In Buenos Aires rioters stoned the Uruguayan consulate. Shortly afterwards the Argentine government was overthrown, although this was doubtless mere coincidence.

Uruguay did not go to Europe in 1934, partly in retaliation for what they regarded as a snub in 1930, partly because they were in dispute with Argentina, and partly because, like other South American teams at this time, they were in the throes of a dispute over professionalism and faced by a players' strike. Argentina went, unwillingly and with a deliberately weakened team, in protest at the theft of their players by Italy: three of them, Monti, Orsi and Guaita, were now playing in an Italian jersey. They lost 3–2 to Sweden, and since it was a straight knock-out competition this was the only game they played. Brazil, also weakened by a split over professionalism, also made the trip for only one game, losing 3–1 to Spain. Mexico fared even worse, as their one game was a preliminary, played in Rome against the United States, which they lost 4–2: a long way to come to play your neighbour, especially when you lose. The US team did not survive the first round, beaten 7–1 by Italy in Rome.

The South American contingent for the 1938 World Cup in France was made up only of Brazil and Cuba, who qualified because of Mexico's withdrawal. Uruguay were still in the huff and suffering from the crisis of professionalism, Argentina were miffed that France had been chosen for the venue, and delayed and procrastinated before finally pulling out. The wrath of the Argentine football supporters was now turned against their own federation, which required police protection to keep potential rioters at bay. The omens of their absence were less sinister than those of Austria and Spain, the one now part of the greater Third Reich, the other in the death agonies of its civil war.

The Europeans, with short memories, complained of the shilly-shallying of the South Americans, and the failure of Uruguay and Argentina to compete brought Lucien Gamblin to comment on the

> 'incomprehensible attitude of the Americans from the extreme south: Chile, but above all Uruguay and Argentina, whose beating about the bush and eventual abstention resulted in a flood of ink and showed up in a bad light those whom FIFA honoured with its confidence ten years ago'.

He did not add that the Europeans failed to match their confidence with their actual participation in 1930, and that France went only at the last minute. Then just before the World Cup of 1938 was getting under way 'a new South American affair' presented itself when a Basque team touring South America was banned by FIFA and some South American countries threatened to ignore the ban. Brazil, then in France, pledged their allegiance to FIFA.

Since the 1934 World Cup the South Americans had not added any lustre to their reputation in Europe. There had been no soccer at the 1932 Olympics in Los Angeles, the only time since 1908 it has not been included, but in Berlin in 1936, Peru were the sole South American team. They beat Finland 7–3, and then were engaged in controversy when some of their spectators invaded the field in a game against Austria, which went into extra time with the score at 2–2. When the pitch was cleared Peru scored two more goals, the Austrians blamed this on the pitch invasion, and when the International Olympic Committee ruled that the game be replayed, Peru refused to turn up and went home with the rest of their Olympic representation. In the meantime, the German and Austrian consular offices in Lima were stoned.

Earlier in 1936, in March, a Montevideo select had played a Paris select, in what was universally described as a deplorable exhibition by the Uruguayans: bad temper, open intimidation, refusal to obey the referee, who was manhandled and left the field, an interval prolonged to 25 minutes and after which eleven Uruguayans took the field, despite one of them having been ordered off. With the crowd of 30,000 calling for their money back, the game somehow proceeded, with a substitute referee, a French team that refused to be provoked and spectators who in the end kept their cool. One newspaper sadly reported that this team had little in common with the great teams of 1924 and 1928. The Uruguayan ambassador expressed his regrets, as he had hoped the tour would cement relations between the two countries, and officials at the dinner tried to make light of it by inviting the referee to the main table, assuring him he would be safe there.

All of this was overlooked in 1938, and the Brazilians, their amateur and professional administrations reunited the previous year, were greeted warmly, the Cubans no less so. Part of the enthusiasm shown for the Brazilians was to make up for the absence of Uruguay and Argentina, but it was also because they were known to be a vastly improved team, with four blacks among their stars, most notably Leonidas da Silva, Tim and da Guia. These simple adopted names set the fashion for such later gems as Didi and Vava, who were stars, and others, like Alcibiades, Nero and Hercules, whose names were their claim to fame: from Greek history came Socrates, a star of the recent past, white and a doctor of medicine. Most famous of all, of course, was Edson Arantes do Nascimento, better known as Pelé.

The Brazilians arrived early, to 'acclimatize', and disappeared into the Black Forest for training. They were seldom out of the news for their balletic artistry and their generally ebullient approach to the game. There was also evidence of the intense interest in the game back in Brazil: its newspaper and radio contingent paid 600 francs for each three minutes to cover the 6000 mile relay of their games; the players spent a small fortune on calls back home and the gifts they took back with them. From Brazil came a telegram with five hundred signatures and one of even greater interest with one signature, from the president of the Brazilian Sports Federation promising the players a house and share of the receipts from the final if they won the Cup.

Cuba surprised everyone when they drew with Romania (3–3) and then won the replay (2–1), only to be brought back to earth with a 8–0 thrashing from Sweden. Brazil gave some indication of the footballing brilliance that was to startle the world from the 1950s onwards, as they advanced to the semi-finals and won third place in the play off against Sweden with a 4–2 win. John Langenus, who refereed that game, thought they would have been the best team in the world if they had matched their 'marvellous game' with some form of tactics. To get to the semi-finals Brazil played their first round game in Strasbourg, overcoming the muddy conditions they feared in a 6–5 victory over a Polish team playing above itself under the inspiration of Wilimowski. That game was won in extra-time, the score being 4–4 after ninety minutes. Brazil's next game went to a replay, after a viciously contested encounter with Czechoslovakia, the spirit for which was set in the opening stages when Zézé, for reasons best known to himself, kicked Nejedly and left the Hungarian referee with no option but to send him off. Two more players were expelled for fighting, one from each side, and a broken leg to Nejedly and a broken arm to goalkeeper Planicka headed the list of more or less serious injuries inflicted in the course of the 'Battle of Bordeaux'.

Brazil won the replay, with a virtual replacement team, and a spirit of perfect correctness. The Czechs, with less reserve strength to draw on, also played with a very different team. But however good Brazil's reserves, they did not warrant the breathtaking confidence of their manager who 'rested' Tim and Leonidas in the semi-final against Italy so that they would be fresh for the final. There was also a suspicion of racism in this dropping of the two black stars, but whatever the reason it proved costly, as Italy won 2–1. Brazil would engage in one more major battle – at Berne in 1954 – before settling down to win three World Cups with a brilliance and sheer joie de vivre that still sparkle in the memory.

Sport, football and the generals

The intrusion of politics into sport in South America followed a similar pattern to that of Europe: at first the game was dismissed as beneath the dignity of the high office of state, was occasionally patronized when it was the preserve of the wealthier classes, and then when it became the people's game it was used for the prestige and popular support it could bring. In South America, the intrusion of politics meant the intrusion of the military regimes that alternated with occasional parliaments, more or less democratic.

In Brazil the first association of the political elite with football came in 1905, when President Rodrigues Alves attended a game in Rio between Fluminense and Paulistano. Although both these teams were of the social elite it was considered that the president had diminished his prestige by attending such a game. The ruling oligarchy ignored the sport for two decades after that, then in 1925 president Artur Bernardes made a point of congratulating the Paulistano team on their return from their successful tour of Europe. Two years later, when the game was entering its popular phase, with black players starring in many teams, president Washington Luis, a paulista, was present at the final game between the São Paulo and the Rio champions, when the paulistas, believing the referee was favouring the cariocas, walked off the field. The president then asserted his authority, and presumably sportsmanship, by sending an emissary to tell the paulistas to get back to the game. He was told by the black captain, however, to mind his own business.

In 1930 Getulio Vargas came to power to rule for fifteen years with a version of authoritarian populism. Like the totalitarians in Europe at this time he appealed to the masses, but more so than in Europe he did so through football, and this set the pattern for subsequent regimes. Massive amounts were spent on the construction of huge stadiums, politicians associated themselves with successful footballers and encouraged star players to be present at important political functions. The widespread use of radio in the 1930s helped bring the game to the farthest reaches of the vast nation, and by the late 1930s the three popular heroes in Brazil were said to be Vargas himself, the popular singer Orlando Silva and the star footballer, Leonidas da Silva.

When the military regime that put an end to a tenuous flowering of Brazilian democracy took over in 1964 they made no secret of their support for the game, and tried to cloak their repressive policies in a love of football. One of their main aims was to achieve national solidarity by integrating the provincial and the urban in a new modern state. This problem was particularly acute in view of the massive immigration from the outlying parts of the country: in 1940, 69 per cent of Brazilians lived in the country; by the 1960s, 69 per cent lived in the cities. Football was one of the ways in which the provincial immigrants could come to terms with their new urban life. In the country, although Brazil already had an impressive collection of top class stadiums when the generals took over, the jewel of which was the Maracana, they continued to build more, so that by the early 1970s new stadiums with capacities of over 100,000 were erected in places as far apart as Belem on the north coast and Porto Alegre in the south; Belo Horizonte in the Minas Gerais and towns of various sizes in the Mato Grosso also had their large municipal stadiums. These showpiece stadiums helped distract from the absence of basic facilities. In 1970 a football lottery was introduced, in part to recoup potential taxes lost to the black market, but also to make Brazilians familiar with other parts of the nation.

Above all the regime used Pelé. Son of a semi-pro, born in Três Coraçes, Minas Gerais in 1940, Pelé was brought up in Bauru where he played with others much older than himself until his obvious genius brought him to Palmeiras. He did not last long there, leaving in anger at the way the club treated its black players. He joined Santos, of the port city of São Paulo, and at sixteen starred for Brazil in the Rio Branco Cup, and at seventeen in the World Cup. Thereafter he became the most famous Brazilian in the country's history, a national institution. He was also the continent's best paid athlete, as sponsors such as the Brazilian Coffee Institute ensured that he would not be bribed to leave for Europe. He virtually ended the racism that had lingered on among the Brazilian football authorities as late as 1958, when they were embarrassed about having too many blacks in the team. Pelé, too, was the first black not to be portrayed as a Sambo.

For the generals who took over in 1964, Pelé became a resource to be shamelessly exploited in their own interests. He was encouraged to speak on behalf of their dictatorship, claiming that Brazil was not ready for democracy, and in a country with more soccer pitches than schools pointed to himself as an example of how the poor and blacks could do well. National solidarity implied racial cohesion, and when Pelé married a white woman in 1965 this was proclaimed as an exemplary act for a national hero. Pelé's handsome face with its infectious grin could not be avoided as he smiled out of television sets or his triumphant body leaped out of billboards, advertising commercial products or the benefits of the regime. In 1972 Pelé claimed that there was no dictatorship in Brazil, a land of happiness in which a free people were governed by their leaders in a spirit of toleration and patriotism.

When Brazil won the World Cup in 1970 under the slogan: 'In sport as in life, integration brings victory', the generals claimed this as a victory for the regime. The players were given a tax free bonus of $US18,000 and were flown direct to the President's palace in Brasilia for an official reception. For the rest of the nation a day's holiday was declared and the palace was opened up to the people. Sport is a two-edged weapon, however, and in the 'failure' of Brazil in 1974 the role of the generals was not overlooked. The team had been ordered to forsake its open-ended spontaneous game in favour of disciplined teamwork, and finished fourth, beaten 1–0 by Poland for third place. Indeed, while the victory of 1970 could not seriously be attributed to the generals, the 'defeat' of 1974 could. Regimes only hinder when they interfere, and from 1970 they did so in a clumsy way, expelling players for their political opinions, or parading them to mumble the national anthem before important games. By the end of the 1970s football was at a low ebb and the regime was more unpopular than ever.

In Argentina in 1978 Brazil finished third in the World Cup, beating Italy 2–1 in the semi-final play-off. Argentina won that tournament, securing a place in the final at the expense of Brazil in the most suspicious of circumstances: Argentina beat Peru 6–0 in the last game of the round-robin preliminaries to pip Brazil on goal difference. Long before the accusations of bribery, however, the Mundial 1978 was tainted: indeed, it was the first World Cup to be seriously threatened with a boycott, as leftists throughout the world protested against holding it in a country run by the generals who had seized power in 1976: in Argentina itself guerilla groups said they would not upset the Mundial because it was a 'feast of the people'. The regime of Videla, like Hitler and the 1936 Olympics, inherited the 1978 Mundial from its predecessor. Like Hitler, the military wasted no time in making the most of their opportunity to show how they could organize a world-class event, and spent vast sums of money to impress visitors: on the installation of colour TV facilities, the improvement of existing stadiums and airports, and the building of new hotels.

Argentina won the Cup, but despite some brilliant players they failed to wipe out the reputation for violent play with which they had entered the competition, and there was a persistent smell of corruption hanging over their landslide victory against Peru. In violent play and suspicion of corruption Argentina were far from being alone, but the Argentine football team had too much in common with its regime not to have the two linked. Argentina emerged from the 1978 World Cup, like its football team, unchanged: its commitment to terror, its failure to control the economy and its disastrous involvement in the Falklands/Malvinas War finally brought the regime down. When the Argentines arrived in the Falklands in 1982 the World Cup in Spain was about to begin: one of their first priorities was to set up television so that the invading/liberating army could watch it. But neither football nor war could deflect public attention for more than a limited period from the chronic inefficiency of the regime, which fell shortly afterwards.

The staging of the World Cup in Argentina gave the opportunity for groups on the left to expose the regime before a worldwide public that would not otherwise have been interested; other reporters came and told it as they saw it, usually with as little political depth and as much blinkered vision as had marked most of the reports on the Nazi Olympics of 1936. The choices were there to make according to your pre-existing views on political violence. For Argentines, the victory of Kempes and company gave momentary pleasure but no commitment to the regime, and as Joseph Arbena comments, in the end 'the administration of the Mundial had been another sad chapter in the longer story of corruption and terror.' Argentina won the World Cup again in 1986 in Mexico, thanks mainly to a display of individual brilliance, devastating passing and total commitment to a team effort on the part of Maradona that must surely have surpassed Pelé, Di Stefano or Friedenreich at their best. Yet it is doubtful if the European sporting world, even if it overlooked Maradona's 'hand of God' goal, was converted to a new admiration of Argentina: there were too many ugly incidents in the past to be forgotten, as well as a prejudice on the part of many Europeans towards Latin Americans, Brazil notwithstanding, that has many similarities with the prejudice and arrogance of the British that the continentals found so annoying.

'Superlatins'

In the 1950s when the Latin American teams were in the news, but still something of a novelty, most of the stories that were reported in the European press were of a fanaticism that made European (especially northern European) football rivalries look like picnics in comparison. They dwelt on the moats and high spectator fencing to safeguard players and referee alike, and reported incidents of shooting involving referees, players and even on one occasion, and more sensibly, the ball. In 1952 Ivan Sharpe described the fireworks exploding from darkened terraces at floodlit games in Rio as something out of Dante's Inferno, and told of spectators at Peru who fired blanks from guns to put players off their kick, and who lit newspapers to drop on rival fans: this precursor to the coloured flares popular today was to have tragic repercussions just over a decade later.

Jacques de Ryswick, who reported the 1950 World Cup from Brazil, returned to South America in 1954 for *L'Equipe* to cover the elimination matches for the next World Cup. The first game he saw was in Asunción, between Paraguay and Brazil. No sooner had the fraternal preliminaries been completed and the game set in motion, he wrote, than players were swapping wild kicks and punches, interspersed by spitting, while the spectators bombarded the pitch with a variety of fruit and bottles. In Montevideo he came across the fierce local partisanship when his taxi driver told him that the only reason he took him to the Peñarol club was because he was a foreigner; as a Nacional supporter he would not otherwise go near it. In the Uruguayan capital he heard criticism of European football that could well have been an Italian talking of the British: the European game, he was told, was too disciplined, mechanical, lacking in initiative, as though it came straight from a manual on the game. Back in Brazil for the return match against Paraguay he saw Brazil qualify for Switzerland before a crowd of 180,000, waving their white handkerchiefs and calling in unison: 'Vamos Suiça . . . We're going to Switzerland'. Outside the ground they took off their shirts and set fire to them in a triumphal torch parade. In Mexico he saw the same fanatical enthusiasm, but tongue in cheek was unwilling to give credence to stories of marksmen with pistols who practised so that they could shoot the ball when it got dangerously close to the home goal. All in all he returned with images which he described as 'superlatin'.

The pronouncements of British observers were often less light-hearted. In 1953, a few months before England went on a tour of Uruguay, Argentina and Chile, Charles Buchan ran an editorial in his *Football Monthly* calling for the tour to be put off. England had nothing to gain from it, he claimed, and it would be better to devote 'our attentions to the sport-loving countries of the British Commonwealth.' In a dramatic centre spread photograph of spectators trying to invade the field and being repulsed by water hoses, he asked if England players should risk this kind of scene, and added his concern that if this could happen at an ordinary club match in Argentina 'what might happen when the tension of an international clash increases the pressure on the Latin blood?' When the tour was completed, however, he had to admit that Argentina was the best foreign team he had ever seen, and in comparison to England they played like artists against artisans: the Uruguay victory over England (2–1) he also classified as one of the best games he had seen and commented on how clever they were in possession and moving into space. In a turnaround from his earlier opinion he admitted that they had 'taught us how to play' and recommended that England now change its ways.

The media and cultural bias

Before the First World War, many teams from Europe (and South Africa in 1906) had crossed the Atlantic: Corinthians twice, in 1910 and 1914; Southampton and Nottingham Forest in 1904, and others in the pre-war period. Southern league club Swindon toured in 1912 with great success, and came back with stories of such hospitality and high living that Exeter were encouraged to go there in 1914. They had different stories to tell on their return, but clearly the South Americans regarded the standard of play of this minor club as an insult. Torino were in Argentina when the First World War broke out, and in 1922 Ferencvaros showed the South Americans a new brand of football. By then the game in South America had leapt even further ahead, and only the best British or European teams could hope to put up a good performance there. Chelsea managed this in 1929, playing 14 games, winning nine, and claiming that they would have won more but for the refereeing.

The Chelsea tour of 1929 highlighted much of the controversy that was to bedevil visits by European teams to South America, overwhelmed on the one hand by the warmth of their welcome, on the other despairing at the win-at-all-costs mentality that cared little for fair play. At the end of the tour the Chelsea director sent a letter of complaint to the FA. Poor refereeing was top of his list of complaints, along with the behaviour of spectators and dreadful dressing-room accommodation. There were minor complaints about the size and weight of the ball – when one game was played with the heavier British ball, five were lost when they were kicked into the crowd and stabbed beyond repair – and more serious ones about Monti and his treacherous violence, and of another player who tried to kick his way through a glass panel to get at the English team. There were obviously different interpretations of the rules, particularly charging the goalkeeper, but it was equally obvious that in cases where referees had not been bribed they were intimidated by the home support. And not just the supporters. One story the Chelsea party brought back was of a game between Boca and Independiente in which the referee had to pull out a razor to defend himself against the players. Despite all this, the tourists admired the high technical artistry of the players, spoiled only by the 'Latin temperament' and 'childish petulance'. They emphasized the courtesy of their hosts and the honesty in many press reports criticizing the behaviour of players and crowds, particularly in Buenos Aires where the worst troubles took place. The crowds in Montevideo were praised; the players described as 'splendid sportsmen' with wonderful ball control and marvellous speed. In Rio, Chelsea played under lights with a white ball, which for the tourists was a novel experience, and their only complaint about the game was that it started half an hour late – standard practice in South America. The Brazilians won that game, prompting a note from a British diplomat that visiting teams must do better, as this result was interpreted as no mere football victory, but a triumph of the entire nation. Touring football teams were giving British consular offices throughout the world a hard time in 1929.

Just over twenty years later, the domestic game in South America was brought before the British public when a few of its big stars departed for Bogotá in Colombia to join a rebel league that was attracting foreign professionals with large signing-on fees. Because Colombia had broken away from FIFA all the money went to the player. Football enjoyed a surge of popularity in Colombia in the 1940s, and a new professional league, the Liga Mayor de Futbol Colombiano (DiMayor) was founded in 1948 with ten clubs, increased to fourteen the following year. The two main rivals in this league were Deportiva Millonarios, founded in 1946 when two wealthy individuals took over the Deportiva Municipal club and started to splash out on money for new players, and Santa Fé, who were equally willing to buy up dissident talent from around the football world. In 1948 Argentine football was at a standstill, as players, fed up with their poor pay and being treated like mere puppets, tried to organize a union. Unable to force any concessions from the owners of the clubs, players left *en masse*, some to Italy, some to Chile and other South American countries, but most to Colombia. There they were joined by many Uruguayan players, also on strike in their own country, as well as some from Peru and Paraguay.

The Argentine dissidents included those from one of the greatest teams of all times, the River Plate team known as La Maquina, but this was ignored in Britain, where the press was aware only of the half dozen British players who went to join the 'Division Mayor' in Bogotá. For British players suffering under the maximum wage and the retain and transfer system, the offer of money they could only dream of in Britain was a big temptation. From Scotland went Airdrie's Bobby Flavell, but the big prize among the British departures was Neil Franklin, still at the peak of a brilliant career, a captain of England who had asked not to be considered for international honours that year, and in dispute with his club, Stoke City, over conditions of employment. With him went George Mountford and Charlie Mitten, both internationalists.

When Neil Franklin wrote his account of his Colombian adventure in 1956 (*Soccer At Home and Abroad*) he had little good to say about the affair, and his book is a *mea culpa*, a warning to other players not to stray from the kindly embrace of the FA. Franklin complained of the way the Argentines in the Santa Fé team resented him and Mountford, afraid that if more players arrived from Britain they would be shown up – all they were interested in was ball playing and exhibitionism rather than hard work. He ranked the best teams on the level of average English Third Division. The players lacked discipline, their tempers were always at exploding point, and in one game he and Mountford were the only two players not involved in a brawl. It seems nothing went right for him, from his nightmare flight to Colombia, where he was met like royalty before being driven through appalling poverty on the way to his hotel, to his final disillusionment and return to an uncertain fate at the hands of the FA: the weather was a continuous English winter, prices were astronomical and many promises about accommodation did not materialize; poverty abounded amidst great wealth; the entrance fee to grounds very high; the crowds were excitable and biased, with nothing friendly about them and needing a high net to keep them off the pitch. The political atmosphere was charged with dynamite, and Franklin claimed that football was promoted to help ease the political tensions, bull fighting having failed.

Franklin no doubt had his problems, but this account by a refugee from the British wage and retain and transfer system has a hollow ring to it. Franklin proudly tells how he advised dozens of British players not to follow him, dismisses the 'silly talk about slave markets' and baldly states that 'the present day footballer can hardly grumble about his conditions.' And while he admitted that most clubs in Britain had fans who threw things and ran on to the field, they were a small section: even in Scotland the troubles between Rangers and Celtic were caused by a mere 'handful of spectators'. Coming so soon after the Old Firm 'bottle parties' of 1949, one might question Franklin's general knowledge, even more his judgment in his inability to recognize the maturing talents of a young Alfredo Di Stefano, or the established brilliance of Nestor Rossi and Adolfo Pedernera among other genuine stars he played with and against.

Violence and Latin American football

The most frequently voiced complaint in Europe about South American football has been the violence both on the field and among the spectators. As in other countries, this was common in the early days, but it took a nasty turn in the 1920s and 1930s. The most infamous incident took place in 1924, when a Uruguayan supporter was shot by an Argentine. The culprit, a certain Pepito, a fanatical supporter of Boca Juniors, fired into a crowd of Uruguayans demonstrating in front of the hotel where the Argentine players were staying. He was protected by the Argentines and remained unpunished for his crime. Shortly after this, in a game in Buenos Aires, Uruguayan supporters invaded the field and as a result barbed wire fencing ten metres high was erected around the grounds. (Ariel Scher and Hector Palomino, *Fútbol: pasión de multitudes y de élites*.) In 1946 a Brazil team playing in Argentina was attacked at the end of the game. The atmosphere had been prepared when an Argentine player was paraded before the spectators with his leg in plaster as a result of a break sustained in a recent international in Brazil. This has echoes of the violence in Belfast two years later that nearly ended the career of Jimmy Jones of Belfast Celtic. Jones was set on by Linfield supporters at the end of the game in retaliation for him (accidentally) breaking the leg of Linfield's Bob Bryson, the extent of the injury being broadcast to the crowd at half-time. Thus inspired, the Linfield thugs broke Jones's leg. In Buenos Aires, the police joined in the attacks on the Brazil team; in Belfast, Celtic went into voluntary liquidation in disgust at the incident.

Osvaldo Bayer places the violence in Argentine football after the overthrow of the more liberal regime in 1930, and tells how attacks on referees became the rule. It took the importation of British referees like Isaac Caswell, 'a maestro of sporting justice', to restore some order. By the late 1940s there were many British referees in South America. Most of them settled down and enjoyed the life and a salary which was much higher than they could dream of in Britain. Some, such as Arthur Ellis, were offered large sums just to come out for one or a few games. When John Meade told Charles Buchan of his experiences after three years as a referee in South America, he claimed that the scare stories were exaggerated. He was impressed by the banners, colours, chanting and waving of the fans, and how they were contained by a twelve foot fence with a further two feet of barbed wire on top of that. But it would appear that one of his biggest problems, one he had in common with other British referees (in addition to insisting that games start on time), was keeping photographers and radio reporters from invading the field to photograph players and interview them to record their feelings at their moment of triumph or despair. Merv Griffiths, the cheery Welsh schoolmaster who handled games around the world, compared his astonishment at the behaviour of the English crowd at the 'beef war' game between Argentina and England at Wembley in 1951, which the Argentines came so close to winning, to the 'exemplary' behaviour of the Argentine players and the excellent quality of their football. (The defeated Argentine team were given a victor's welcome by the Perón regime on their return.)

Sifting the truth and adjusting the cultural bias in the written word is a difficult task. Gordon Jeffery writing in *World Soccer* in November 1963 claimed that he had become inured to talk of crises in South American football, of bribes and corruption, and pointed out that a foreigner could easily get a distorted picture of Scottish and English football by selective reading of the British press. In that same journal in March 1981, the memoirs of Belgian referee John Langenus claimed that in South America people were just as fair and unfair in regard to sport as they were anywhere else. Leo Horn, the Dutch referee who officiated at an International Tournament held in Brazil in 1964, however, was so disgusted at some of the violence he witnessed that he advocated that Europe, with all its problems of violence, would do better to keep to its own teams and leave the South Americans to theirs.

In the 1960s television asserted itself as the major purveyor of potentially distorted visions, the more so as it thrives on violence and spectacle and was by then present in every home in the western world. Among the lasting impressions of the 1966 World Cup in England is that of Argentine captain Rattin slowly making his way from the field of play after a ten minute argument with German referee Kreitlein over his expulsion. Ironically, his offence was disputing the referee's decision: ironic because of the violent play that had gone unpunished before, and which had been a feature not just of the Argentine team, but others in a competition marked by some appalling tackling. Rattin was seen more as a victim than a villain in Argentina, and when England manager, Alf Ramsey dismissed the Argentines as 'animals' his outburst was taken by the South Americans as a collective insult. This was just one more incident in what Bayer called the long love/hate relationship between the two countries: hatred for the colonial past, but love for the nation that 'taught us how to play this marvellous collective sport'.

Shortly after the 1966 World Cup, the image of Argentine football in Europe reached a new low, with the performances of their representatives in the World Club Championship, a two-leg competition between the champion clubs of Europe and South America that had begun in 1960. Glasgow Celtic played Racing Club of Buenos Aires in 1967, to be confronted by players who deliberately provoked the opposition into retaliation so that they would be ordered off the field. Estudiantes adopted this as a deliberate tactic, and it was they who represented South American football in the World Championship between 1968 and 1970: Manchester United, Milan and Ajax of Holland were the victims. Thereafter, the European champions found reasons not to play their South American

equivalents, and occasionally another team went in their place. In the end
the competition survived only because Toyota agreed to sponsor it, and
since 1980 it has been played in Japan each year. It has to be said, however,
that Estudiantes were hated in Argentina itself for their style of football,
and were condemned among others by Rattin.

Football in Latin America cannot escape the social and political climate
in which it is played. South America has never had to suffer the violence
that racked Europe in two World Wars and which is tearing the old
Yugoslavia apart today. But its wealth has been ill-divided, and few nations
have achieved lasting political stability. Football in Latin America has
reflected all the problems of that vast continent. For people living often in
desperate personal situations, or the liberal middle-classes seeking political
justice, football helped ease their frustration. Support for their team can
rise above family loyalties, and it was not all in jest that one *hincha* pointed
out that you could change your wife, but you can never change your
football team. Thus while Latin Americans fought ferociously with each
other on the playing field, they could all rejoice when victories were
recorded against the Europeans. That would come frequently enough after
1950 and football in Latin America has been one of its greatest causes for
rejoicing.

In 1954, Maurice Pefferkorn compared the play of the Latin Americans
to that of the Austrian *Wunderteam*. He commented on their love of the
game, their acrobatics and theatricality, reaching new heights of individual
artistry, which even the best European teams could not attain. Despite a
few differences in various South American teams, he thought it reasonable
to talk of a South American school of football. Like other European
commentators after 1950 he looked on the visitors from South America
with a new interest and curiosity. They came with their lightweight boots
and no shin pads, and condemned heavy tackling as an insult to the nobility
of the game. But, the more cynical asked, could they play away from their
baked pitches and lightweight balls? Above all, could they score?

In Switzerland in 1954, and in Sweden in 1958, they showed that they
could. Uruguay, who went straight into the 1954 finals as holders of the
Cup, scored four goals against England and seven against Scotland, but
only two against Czechoslovakia to go through to the semi-final, where
they held Hungary to a 2–2 draw before losing 4–2 in extra time in a game
judged by many as the best game ever played. Brazil, who had beaten
Sweden 7–1 and Spain 6–1 in the 1950 World Cup, beat Mexico 5–0, then
drew 1–1 with Yugoslavia before being eliminated by Hungary 4–2. That
game was badly handled by Arthur Ellis, and its superb qualities were
eclipsed by the body clashes, bad temper and expulsions that turned out
merely to be a warm-up for the big event when the Brazilians invaded the
Hungarian dressing-room to continue the battle there.

1958 belonged to Brazil, as Didi, almost left behind nominally because he was said to be too old, but really because he was married to a white women, Garrincha, the 'little bird' who had overcome deformed legs as a child to thrill with his inconsistent genius, and Pelé, at seventeen on the threshold of the first of his four World Cup appearances, swept their way to a 5–2 victory against Sweden in a final that left the spectators and the millions watching on television with an admiration that would not be diminished in the years to come.

Uruguay were offered a place in the play-offs in 1958 when the political opponents of Israel refused to play against them, but dismissed this as a 'gift'. They were represented by one of their best-ever players, Schiaffino, but he was playing in an Italian shirt. Also playing in Italian shirts were the Argentines who had excelled in the previous year's South American Cup in Lima: Maschio, Angelillo and Sivori, plucked away by the lure of Italian lire. Argentina, thus weakened, played poorly and were welcomed back in Buenos Aires by rubbish and the insults from fans who thought they had been humiliated. Brian Glanville claimed that the deadly result of this was to turn Argentina away from its traditions of spectacle and artistry to destruction and negativity. Mexico also played in 1958, but picked up only one point, against Wales. Paraguay forced Yugoslavia to a 1–1 draw and had an easy 3–2 victory over Scotland, but failed to qualify for the quarter finals.

England, Scotland, Ireland and Wales all took part in the World Cup in Sweden, but apart from Ireland who excelled themselves, and Wales who put up a plucky performance, the writing was on the wall for those who had given the original lessons. Not only in international matches, but also in the rapidly expanding European club competitions, the British clubs were coming to the inescapable conclusion that not only had it been some time since they had anything to teach their one time pupils, they now had a lot to learn.

Endnotes

In a bibliographical article on the academic study of sport in Latin America, published in 1985, Eric Wagner noted that it was still at its 'barest beginnings':

Eric A. Wagner, 'Sport', in Harold E. Hinds, Jr and Charles M. Tatum (eds.), *Handbook of Latin American Popular Culture*, Greenwood Press, Westport, Connecticut/London, 1985.

A few years later the advance in the academic study of sport can be judged by:

Joseph L. Arbena, comp., *An Annotated Bibliography of Latin American Sport: Pre-conquest to the Present*, Greenwood Press, Westport, Connecticut, 1989.

Joseph L. Arbena (ed.), *Sport and Society in Latin America: Diffusion, Dependency and the Rise of Mass Culture*, Greenwood Press, Westport, Connecticut, 1988.

This collection of essays has several on football, including the work by Steve Stein used extensively in the text:

Steve Stein, 'The case of soccer in early twentieth-century Lima', pp. 63–84.
Janet Lever, 'Sport in a fractured society: Brazil under military rule', pp. 85–96.
Matthew Shirts, 'Socrates, Corinthians, and questions of democracy and citizenship', pp. 97–112.

There are many works on soccer in Spanish or Portuguese, reflecting the hold the game has on most of the continent, so that we need no longer expect, as happened in two major books on race relations in Brazil (1964 and 1971), to find soccer omitted, gaps which have appeared in 'social' studies elsewhere before the significance of sport was recognized. Of the works in Spanish I have only been able to consult in detail:

Osvaldo Bayer, *Futbol Argentino. Pasión y gloria de nuestro deporte mas popular*, Editorial Sudamericana, Buenos Aires, 1990,

which was also made into a superb film.
Most works in English on Latin American football are by Americans:

Robert M. Levine, 'The burden of success: *Futebol* and Brazilian Society through the 1970s', *Journal of Popular Culture*, Vol 14, No 3 (Winter 1980) pp. 453–464.
Robert M. Levine, 'Sport and Society: the Case of Brazilian *Futebol*', *Luso-Brazilian Review*, Winter, 1980, pp. 233–252.
Ilan Rachum, '*Futebol*: The Growth of a Brazilian National Institution', *New Scholar*, Vol 7, Nos 1/2 (1978), pp. 183–200.
Peter Flynn, 'Sambas, soccer and nationalism', *New Society*, 19 August 1971, pp. 327–330.

Joseph L. Arbena, 'Generals and *Goles*: Assessing the Connection between the Military and Soccer in Argentina', *IJHS*, Vol 7, No 1, May 1990, pp. 120–130.

This article should also be consulted for the wide range of literature in Spanish on South American football, Argentina in particular.
For a study of soccer in Brazil by a non-soccer sociologist, see:

Janet Lever, *Soccer Madness*, University of Chicago Press, Chicago, 1983.

Geralyn Pye, 'Political football: sports, power and machismo, in Luisa Valenzuela's *The Lizard's Tale* (forthcoming)

is a fascinating analysis of the power of soccer in Argentina particularly at the time of the 1978 Mundial.
Disappointing is:

Eduardo P. Archetti, 'Argentinian football: a ritual of violence?' *IJHS*, Vol 9, No. 2, August 1992, pp. 209–235.

The French sources, where not from contemporary newspapers, are from:

Jacques de Ryswick, *100,000 heures de football*, La Table Ronde, Paris, 1962.

On the World Cup from 1930 to 1958 see:

Brian Glanville and Jerry Weinstein, *World Cup*, SBC, London, 1960.

There are innumerable books on Pelé, but probably the most interesting is the two volume compilation of press extracts that make up:

The Pelé Albums. Selections from public and private collections celebrating the soccer career of Pelé. With an introduction and commentaries by Pelé, Weldon Publishing, Sydney, 1990.

CHAPTER SIX

Teaching the Masters

Hampden Park, Glasgow, 18 May 1960. The 1960 European Cup Final had just ended, but 127,000 delirious Scots refused to leave their places, cheering rapturously as they appealed to the players who had presented them with the most exquisite exhibition of football they had ever seen to reappear and take a bow. These were hardened Scots, football connoisseurs, but not given to such outbursts of emotion, and their enthusiasm was for two teams, neither of which was Scottish. The one was Réal Madrid, resplendent in their all white strips; their beaten but far from disgraced opponents in the 7–3 game were Eintracht Frankfurt. The Spanish champions starred players from other countries; most notably Ferenc Puskas, the one-time 'galloping major' now stripped of his military title as a defector from the Hungarian uprising of 1956, who scored four goals, and Alfredo Di Stefano, the Argentine who strutted imperiously through the game as though he had invented it, and who scored the other three. On one wing was the Brazilian Darcy Silveiro dos Santos, better known as Canario, and on the other the incomparable Spaniard, Francisco 'Paco' Gento, whose breathtaking speed with the ball was equalled only by his ability to control it. This was Réal's fifth victory in the European Cup; indeed until then they were the only team to have won it.

When Hungary outclassed England 3–6 on 25 November 1953, they smashed whatever pretensions England had to any world supremacy; this was rubbed in at the return match in Budapest where they were trounced 7–1 and in the 1954 and 1958 World Cup tournaments. Réal Madrid's performance at Hampden Park in 1960 abolished whatever hopes might have lingered on in die-hard British hearts that even if they had lost their Empire, they were still masters of football. The roles had been reversed, and now it was time for the teachers to catch up on their one time pupils.

Britain had possibly lost its mastery by the 1930s, but the absence of serious competition between the British teams and those of FIFA leaves that question unresolved. Above all, there was no television to bring the truth home. This had changed by the 1950s. Television came to the whole of Great Britain in time for the England vs. Hungary game, and through Eurovision for a direct telecast of all major European games from the 1954 World Cup on. And, of course, while 127,000 watched the 1960 European Cup final in the flesh, millions more saw it on the small screen (and thanks to video have been able to see many repeats since). Through television the local product was thus shown in a less favourable light, and gave credence to what the more acute commentators had been saying for years, that the British game was behind the times. Now the British had to come to terms with a new organization of the game, introducing in a serious way such diversions as coaching and training, treating their players as though they played an important part in the game, and entering the competitions that the continentals had inaugurated. The continentals were not only teaching the masters how to play the game, but how to organize it.

The second European civil war

Unlike the First World War, football in Great Britain was suspended by the four associations shortly after the declaration of war against Germany on 3 September 1939. In Europe, football continued in some form or another in the countries of most of the belligerents, at least for the first few years. In Germany the regional championships continued until the 1943–44 season, while in the Austrian League, absorbed into Greater Germany in 1938, official competition was abandoned only with the arrival of the Soviets in 1945. In the meantime, FK Austria had won the German Cup in 1943. Czechoslovakia was divided into two leagues, patterned on the betrayal of 1938 and the invasion of 1939, with a German-speaking league in the Sudetenland and a Slovakian League that operated from 1940 to 1944. Competition in Poland was obliterated in the first weeks of the war, but the Nazis allowed some Poles, such as the great star Wilimowski to become an Aryan and play for German teams. (They also had to turn a blind eye to the embarrassing number of star players of Polish origin playing in German teams like Schalke 04.) The Croatians were granted political autonomy and their own football league, which operated from 1941 to 1944. Italy played until 1943, when the country turned against Mussolini and his Nazi ally. Germany's other ally, Hungary, managed to play football throughout the war.

While the war went well for the Nazis they were in a position to play regularly against neutral countries like Sweden, Switzerland and Spain, and satellite countries like Bulgaria, Croatia, Hungary, Romania and Slovakia. Twenty-nine such games were played before the siege of Stalingrad; thereafter there were none.

Among the early victims of Nazi invasion, competition in Belgium and the Netherlands resumed after only a season's break and continued at the domestic level until another break in 1945. France was split into three parts; one annexed to Germany and controlled from Berlin; an 'occupied zone' with Paris at its centre; and the unoccupied or 'free' zone, run by French puppets from Vichy. After the capitulation the former tennis star,

Jean Borotra, the 'bounding Basque', followed by Colonel Pascot, a Rugby Union fanatic, controlled sport, and tried to take it back to its amateur purity. With football, cycling and boxing this had to be done gently, but with a stroke Pascot eliminated Rugby League, the detested rival to his own code. Vichy played two football internationals, against Switzerland and Spain in March 1942, and maintained sporting relations with its colonies. In November of that year the Nazis took over in the 'free zone', although the puppet regime remained in place.

Of the stars of the pre-war period in France, Etienne Mattler was imprisoned and tortured by the Nazis for his role in the Resistance. At football matches towards the end of the war his name was chanted by crowds released from the fear of informers. Another star of pre-war years was accorded a different fate. Alec Villaplane, who captained France in the 1930 World Cup, was shot as a collaborator; he had been imprisoned for criminal activity before the war, but was released by Vichy in return for working for them. His dark past was brought out in the minor character of Gonzales in Albert Camus's *La Peste*.

In Britain official competition was suspended shortly after the declaration of war, regional competitions were introduced, and professionals in the army could find themselves playing in clubs anywhere in Britain, perhaps with fellow professionals, perhaps with a willing enthusiast conscripted from the spectators to make up the numbers. It was England's misfortune to have at this time some of its best ever players in the prime of their careers: Swift, Carter, Matthews, Mannion, Lawton and Finney, to be joined later in the war by Wright and Mortensen. In the home internationals which were played regularly throughout the war these players inflicted many heavy defeats on Scotland.

British football relations with France had always been friendly, and in the 'phoney war' period many British soldiers played for French teams. France played Portugal in January 1940, and in the following month the British Army played three games against the French Army. No sooner had the Germans been cleared from France than sporting links between the two countries were put back in place: a remarkable French team came to Wembley on 26 May 1945 and surprised the crowd with their skill in a 2–2 draw. This was the first time England had failed to win at home, but the match was not considered official.

In 1947 football was put at the service of the war-torn continent when the Scottish Football Association (SFA), as a gesture to mark the return of the British associations to FIFA in 1946, organized an exhibition match in which a combined Great Britain team played the Rest of Europe at Hampden Park. This game, one of the few occasions outside the Olympics when the British associations played together, raised £30,000 for FIFA and so put it on a solid financial foundation after the losses of the war years. The 6–1 win to Great Britain was seen as no surprise.

The men from the East

Shortly after the close of hostilities in the Second World War came the Soviets, the mysterious Moscow Dinamo, who toured Great Britain and Sweden in November 1945. Any team visiting Great Britain would have been welcomed by a public deprived of real football through the war years, but Dinamo were a special case, coming with fire on their boots rather than the snow of legend. However, if they came with the aura of Stalingrad, they left with a foretaste of the Iron Curtain. Dinamo lost none of their four games, which were played before sell-out crowds with thousands left outside. Against Chelsea they drew 3–3, thrashed Cardiff City 10–1 with a performance that the Welsh were happy to admit was the finest they had ever seen, beat Arsenal 4–3 in a game made farcical by a fog that obliterated the players and a Soviet referee whose decisions suggested that his life depended on them. In their final game they drew 2–2 with Rangers in Glasgow. The first Russian book on soccer was written to celebrate the tour, simply entitled *19–9*: the goals for and against, but omitting the 0–5 victory over Norrköping on the way back.

The men from Moscow came with a list of conditions, in fact fourteen points: about whom they should play (one team had to be Arsenal); when they should play (expecting the sacrosanct league fixtures to be changed to accommodate this); who should referee (the one they brought with them, reasonably enough, was to get at least one game); where they should eat (at the Soviet Embassy); and other matters concerning the composition of the teams and other matters of detail. In fact, most of their requests were reasonable enough, showing not so much impossible demands as a lack of faith in the sporting intent of their hosts. The British might have been the paragons of Fair Play, but they were capitalists after all.

Once the British crowds got over their amusement at the fancy long shorts worn by Dinamo, complete with embroidered 'D', they appreciated their brilliant ball control, fast short passing and well drilled positional play. On two occasions they brought on a substitute (one of the concessions made by the British) without taking a player off, but apart from the Arsenal game they were well received. George Allison, in his book written shortly after he ceased to be Arsenal's manager in 1947, tells of his unpleasant memories of the tour. Dinamo had demanded that they play Arsenal and then, despite their own team including several 'guests' (in fact they had two) protested when Allison wanted to play some players from other teams to make up for the ravages of war: the Arsenal stadium had been out of use and 42 of its 44 players had enlisted in 1939, some never to play again. When this was worked out Allison had to suffer a three hour interrogation that had little to do with football, but his mortification was complete when he read in the Soviet children's journal *Pioneer* what had been said about him and the tour by the radio commentator who had accompanied the team:

> In England, fatherland of football, we were met according to the English fashion: rather drily, without flags, music or flowers. Officials of the British Football Federation coldly shook our hands and then threw us to the newspapermen to be torn to pieces. Reporters showered the players with questions. But we also have our customs. We do not like to talk in vain and so we decided to keep quiet for the time being. The players were taken to the Guard's Barracks to be housed, but we discovered mould on the walls, cobwebs and hard bolsters instead of pillows. We did not like this and we went to the Soviet Embassy, where we spent the night.

From there the report went on to criticize the rough play of Arsenal, and the conditions under which the game had been played, claiming that the only reason it had gone on was because the fog suited Arsenal, being a common occurrence, and there was too much money to be lost if it didn't: in seats that had been paid for and bets that had been placed. Allison himself was said to have wagered a small fortune on Arsenal and fainted when they lost.

This piece is a reminder of the cultural (as much as political) gulf that separated the two countries. The British would eventually accept such niceties as the exchange of flowers at the start of a game, and the beauty of football played without hard body contact, but suspicions surrounding the regime which sponsored Dinamo could only have been deepened, despite the professed aim of the tour. The Soviet captain arrived in London claiming that they were ambassadors of sport and that in this way they could 'strengthen our wartime friendship even better than the politicians.' George Orwell was prompted by this to write one of his less brilliant essays on how sport was an 'unfailing cause of ill will.'

The Soviet teams were to disappear behind the Iron Curtain until the early 1950s, and many of their players fell victim to Stalin in one of his periodic purges. Among the most notable victims of this purge were the Dinamo players and the four famous Starostyn brothers, heroes of the 1930s but now banished to labour camps for eight to ten years because they had been 'abroad and told friends about Soviet life.' Andrei Starostyn later wrote an autobiography in which his years 'beyond the Arctic Circle' were barely alluded to, and in a short history of Soviet football he wrote in 1957 the few years after 1945 are omitted altogether.

Football in the Soviet Union

Sport in the Soviet Union was an integral part of Soviet philosophy, with an ideology of making it equally available to all, downplaying the competitive element and emphasizing the beauty of sport for sport's sake. It was thus to be free of financial considerations, amateur and innocent of any commercialism. It was an ideal that would have warmed the heart of Tom Hughes himself. In practice sport became intimately linked with the defence of the country, particularly in the 1920s when the new regime was most vulnerable to foreign invasion: health, hygiene and defence of the motherland were proclaimed in posters urging citizens to keep their rifles and their teeth clean.

Football was already the most popular game in Russia before 1914, and as some stability reappeared after the catastrophes that accompanied the Bolshevik Revolution, foreign intervention, civil war and famine, it quickly re-established itself over most of the Soviet Union as the most popular sport. The teams that existed through from Tsarist times were organized into workers' clubs covering a wide range of sports and given more suitably proletarian names, glorifying heavy industry, the police and the army: Spartak (members of the producers' co-operatives) was a favourite name, while there were industrial gems like Torpedo (the clubs of the automobile workers) and Locomotiv (the clubs of the railway workers), or more sinister titles like the Central Army Club and Wings of the Soviet. Moscow Spartak versus Dinamo in particular developed into a local derby to match those fought out elsewhere in the football world. Less well known than the prowess of these teams on the sports field, was the association of Dinamo with the secret police, whatever name it came under, from the Cheka to the KGB, a secret kept even from most Soviet citizens until recent times. The regime had more success in changing the names of the teams, however, than it did in changing the ethos of the game. When a system of 'factors' was imposed, whereby behaviour, or discipline, was deemed more important than scoring goals, it failed completely; the players rebelled against this and it was thrown out. In 1931 the first of the regular football competitions was held, between Moscow, Leningrad, Kharkov and Kiev. In 1935 provincial teams became involved and the following year the first USSR championship was held, not by teams representing cities, but by clubs from within the cities. The USSR Football Cup was also first held in that year and these two contests became traditional features of the Soviet sports calendar.

As in Brazil, football was used as one arm in the struggle to make a nation of a heterogeneous population spread over a vast land mass. For the Soviets the task was of a much greater magnitude, as they more or less had to start from scratch, and they did not have success on the international scene to match Brazil. Nevertheless, the Moscow imperialists enjoyed some success in spreading the joy of communism through sport, although in the more remote provinces of central Asia, where religious atavism still prevailed, local mullahs could depict the ball brought by the Russians as the head of the devil, thus mixing the medium and the message to make it rebound against the modernizers.

In Moscow itself the two powerful rivals, Dinamo and Spartak, reflected the tensions between the state and the people. Spartak had the bigger support and the better players, including the Starostyn brothers, and twice won the 'double' in the late 1930s. Elsewhere in the Soviet Union, Dinamo teams were more successful. Dinamo were founded in 1923 by Felix Dzerzhinsky. As the sporting arm of the counter-revolutionary forces responsible only to Stalin, the Dinamo teams had access to the best sporting facilities in the Union. Beria, a fanatical and even terrifying supporter of Moscow Dinamo, was himself executed shortly after the death of Stalin when he attempted a coup, presumably to save the regime falling into more humanitarian ways. We are told in a book by Aleksandr Gorbunov, *Penalty Kicks*, that came out in Finland in 1991 as one of the first examples of sporting glasnost, that Beria played for Tbilisi in the 1920s before embarking on the brutal purges of the 1930s that had more than a touch of personal rancour about them. Little wonder then that Martyn Merezov, later an editor of *Futbol* magazine, but in the 1920s a referee who once sent Beria off the field for rough play, had nightmares that only disappeared when Beria himself was executed in 1953. Indeed, again according to Gorbunov, it was Beria, with his unfailing memory, who sent Nicolai Starostyn to Siberia for twelve years, vindictively reminding him of how he had once made a fool of him in a game against Tbilisi.

Games outside the Soviet Union were first played against teams of the two Workers' Sports Internationals: the Red Sports International under the orders of Moscow and those of the Socialist Workers Sports International, its bitter enemy, with headquarters in Switzerland. For the Soviet teams politics came first, and they took every opportunity to embarrass the socialists: it was a visit by a Soviet football team to Germany in July 1927 that led to the final split between the two bodies. In addition to encouraging Communist demonstrations against the socialists, the Soviet visitors demanded different food and special accommodation, left official functions early and were not immune to asking for special coaches to be added to their train. Thereafter the two great international bodies in search of the workers' soul went their separate ways.

Football was the main sport in which the Soviet Union engaged in competition against foreigners. On 20 September 1922 the Zamoskvoretsky Sports Club defeated a Finnish Workers' Union team 7–1, and the following year a Russian football team visited Scandinavia, Estonia and

Germany. In 1934 the first game against professional opposition came when a Moscow select played Zidenice, then heading the Czech league, but lost 3–2. A more significant foray into the capitalist world came in 1936, when a combined Moscow team played the very bourgeois Racing Club of Paris.

Although they were defeated by France's elite team, local communist papers were exultant about the performance of the Moscow select, deigning even to ask their bourgeois colleagues what they thought of the Soviet performance. This match introduced the Soviets to the 'WM' system of play, which the French had picked up from England. In mid-1937 the Basque team touring the Soviet Union won all of its games until it came up against Moscow Spartak, who had been using the 'WM' system. This is said to have marked a new era in the technical development of Soviet football. As Moscow Dinamo were to show, they did not adopt it slavishly, and it was a distinctively Soviet form of football that was put before the British public in 1945.

The Soviet Union entered the Olympic Games for the first time in 1952, where they were eliminated by Yugoslavia in the semi-final of the football. It was one of the most remarkable games in the history of the tournament: the Soviets were losing 5–1 with sixteen minutes to go, but scored four times to take the game into extra-time. No more goals were scored, and Yugoslavia won the replay. This was no ordinary defeat. The Yugoslavs represented the reformist traitors who had slipped out of Stalin's grasp in 1948: as a result the team was disbanded and several players banished. They were not the first sporting victims of the Stalin/Tito clash. This doubtful honour probably went to the hitherto thriving French journal *Sports*, which as a loyal Stalinist organ refused to report the France vs. Yugoslavia World Cup qualifier in 1949. As a result it lost many of its readers and went out of existence.

Yugoslavia went on to lose in the 1952 Olympic final to Hungary, the Soviet team went home to an interrogation about being agents of Tito. The coach, Boris Arkadyev, was sacked for political incompetence and of the players, Konstantin Beskov, the much lauded 'canoneer' of the 1945 Dinamo tour and later awarded the Order of Lenin in 1985 for services to sport, was suspended for a year for 'irresponsible play and cowardly conduct in a match.' In fact, the Soviet team had been in special training under the name of the central army sports club, ZDKA, who, despite being a cover for the national team, were expelled from the Soviet league. The blow was softened by Vasilii, Stalin's son, who was a football fanatic. As a high officer in the Soviet Air Force he had some of the disgraced players drafted to form a new Air Force team, which did not last long beyond the death of Stalin. At the Melbourne Olympics in 1956 the Soviets beat Yugoslavia by the only goal, to win the gold medal.

Soccer at the Olympics from 1952 was taken over by the new state amateurs from countries where social classes had been eliminated, and so where the question of amateurism and professionalism did not exist. Since the success of the World Cup, especially after 1938, soccer at the Olympics lost much of its interest to most footballing nations. Not to the Communists, however, and it was at the Helsinki Olympics that the all-conquering Hungarians, by beating Yugoslavia 2–0, won their first laurels leading up to their triumph against England in 1953 and the rest of the world in 1954.

The state amateurs

Before England finally fell to foreigners on their own territory they had had many close calls, concealed by the 0–10 thrashing of Portugal in 1947, the 0–4 victory against Italy in Turin in 1948, when England were invited to help celebrate the fiftieth anniversary of the Italian FA; or the pulsating 2–3 win against Austria in Vienna in 1952.

In 1951 Argentina, at war with Britain over beef exports, still came to help celebrate the Festival of Britain and also came close to defeating England, holding on to a 1–0 lead only to concede two goals in the last eleven minutes. Against Yugoslavia England drew 2–2 at Highbury, and then at that same stadium on 3 October 1951 they were within seconds of losing their home record to a French team: the score stood at 2–2 with only a minute to go when René Grumellon, with only the English keeper Williams to beat, hit more turf than leather, and the English home record remained intact. In the following month at Wembley Austria delighted the connoisseurs with their close passing in a 2–2 draw, and just a few weeks before the final showdown in 1953 a Rest of Europe team (minus the Hungarians) helping the FA celebrate its ninetieth anniversary were unlucky not to defeat England, who tied the game at 4–4 in the last minute with a gift penalty. Perhaps just as well, as the éclat with which England's home record was blown apart in November 1953 was a more fitting revelation.

The Hungarian 'Golden Team' that entranced Europe from 1950 to 1956 was one of the best ever. In that time it played 46 international matches, lost only one and scored 210 goals. Organized by Gustav Sebes, the national team was built around the club team Honved (Defence of the Nation), formerly Kispest, a suburb of Budapest. It was the brainchild of the Minister for Sport, Farkas, as fanatical a football fan as he was a committed Communist. The team was nominally amateur but with the country's best players in government sinecures they could practise with as much intensity as any professional team. The players enjoyed a freedom not open to many for, as the man himself knew well, there was only one Puskas while party hacks were ten a penny. And football was no mere ornament to the regime, but an essential part; Hungary's triumphs in football helped distract Hungarians from the misery that surrounded them.

To achieve this success normal club games were often suspended to allow the national team to practise against weak opposition. Moreover, to strengthen Honved other clubs often had to surrender their best players. After a 2–5 loss to Czechoslovakia in the spring of 1949, it was decided to maintain a national squad of 20 to 22 players, which seldom varied so that players did not have to fear being dropped for temporary lack of form. In this way, tactics were perfected, but all hinged around the brilliance of players like Puskas, major in the Hungarian army, Sandor Kocsis, Zoltan Czibor and Nandor Hidegkuti, masters of every technique and thinking as one. Abroad, the players won acclaim and perks like duty-free purchases ignored by Hungarian customs officials; and at home they were revered as idols. On their return with a gold medal from Helsinki in 1952 they were greeted at the station by delirious Hungarians who made a simple ten-minute walk to their homes into a six-hour triumphal procession. When the historic game against England was played in 1953, the streets of Budapest were deserted as Hungarians sat clustered around their radio sets.

The regime milked the triumph for all it was worth. Stamps already in circulation celebrating the completion of the Nepstadion (People's Stadium, built with the help of volunteers, Puskas even lending a hand) in 1953 were overprinted with the date, venue and 3–6 score. Newsreels showed Puskas promising 'future glories', while two 'Kossuth prize-winning Stakhanovites' conveyed the affection of the people to the team for their 'unforgettable achievement' and 'heroic deed'. The families of the team were shown at home listening to the game, proudest of all being Hidegkuti's mother, who, as the commentator was at pains to point out, was 'a Stakhanovite forewoman at the Ujlak Brickworks.'

Sadly the same enthusiasm that greeted victory could turn savage in defeat. When the team lost the World Cup final in 1954 players had to leave the train early on their return from Switzerland to avoid the hostility of the crowd, some of whom were calling for the death of Sebes.

Hungary went to Switzerland in 1954, like Brazil in 1950 the runaway favourites to win the World Cup. Instead they lost 3–2 in the final to Germany, whom they had beaten 8–3 in a preliminary round. They were beaten by the odd organization (neither the first nor the last time) of the competition, and by the tactics of the German coach who took advantage of the seeded knock-out system. Knowing that he could lose by any score and still qualify for the finals, he put out a team with many reserves, which not only lost 8–3, but virtually eliminated Puskas from the competition with a savage tackle. Puskas played in the final although still suffering from the injury he received in that game. Hungary were beaten, it has to be said, by some wretched luck as they stormed the German goal in the closing stages and had a goal by Puskas ruled offside by the referee. Germany won 3–2 after being down 0–2 in the first ten minutes.

The victory of Germany so soon after the *Götterdämmerung* of 1945 was a remarkable effort: a recovery in the sports field to match that in the economic. It would appear, however, that there was still room for improvement in the public relations department, with some officials crowing in a manner that had too many echoes of the regime so recently and thankfully removed. At an official dinner in Paris on 5 October 1952 after West Germany had been beaten 3–1 by France, the president of the German FA, Dr Bauwens, stunned his French hosts when he commented on how much at home the team and players felt – this a mere few years after the Occupation. Germany's progress after 1954 was all downhill: several members of the team fell victim to jaundice a short time afterwards, leading to whispering in some quarters that their 1954 triumph had been aided by artificial stimulants. However that may be, and kicking Puskas out of the competition was surely more effective than drugs, it reinforced football opinion that while Germany were the World Champions, Hungary were the best team in the world.

The Hungarian team had to return from Switzerland in secret, the government had to cancel the issue of stamps it had prepared proclaiming Hungary World Champions, but before long Hungary and Honved took up where they had left off. It all came to an end in October 1956, when dreams of a Hungary free from Soviet domination in daily life were crushed by the tanks of the Warsaw Pact countries. When news broke in the west of the insurrections in the streets of Budapest on 27 October, Puskas was reported to have been killed in the fighting, and there were suggestions that there be a respectful silence at the following Saturday's games. Anti-Communism inspired much of the writing on the subject, and was no doubt behind the fanciful stories reported in Britain, one of which claimed that he had wanted to play for Celtic. There is little evidence to suggest that Puskas had wanted to defect. In fact, he had been offered lavish sums of money and contracts by Italian clubs, which though tempting, he rejected: for British football he maintained a sovereign indifference.

Two days after the uprising Puskas approached Imre Nagy, the temporary leader, for permission for Honved to leave for their game against Atlético Bilbao in a European Cup game. On 2 November the team left through Austria, and two days later the forces of the Warsaw Pact countries invaded Hungary. The players were split as to whether to return, fought among themselves over the issue and were concerned about their families. Eventually, most of them went back. In the meantime, they had to play the second leg of their European Cup game, which was switched to the Heysel Stadium in Brussels, where agents from Italy and Spain waited with open cheque books. Before they bowed out Honved turned the jeers of an anti-communist crowd into applause for a magnificent football display which saw a team weakened by the loss of a goalkeeper and a badly injured Czibor in his place pull back from a three-goal deficit on aggregate to come within an ace of drawing level.

The agents trying to sign the Hungarians had to abide by FIFA regulations that stipulated that the refugees would have to wander the wilderness for two years before they could return to the fold. In the meantime, the remaining Honved players played exhibition games to raise money, including a lucrative tour of South America. When they broke up, the Spaniards were there to pick up the most brilliant pieces: Kocsis and Czibor, a devout catholic, went to Barcelona, Puskas, banned from playing in Germany because of an article he had written on their 'execution squad' tactics in the 1954 World Cup, went to Réal Madrid on 12 May 1958 for a mere £9000. The team of the Spanish capital, under the inspiration of millionaire fan, president and former player, Santiago Bernabéu and the political patronage of General Franco, were set to blaze a brilliant path across Europe.

State capitalists

Franco emerged from the disastrous Civil War of 1936–39 the victor, then refused to join Hitler in his war because the Führer would not give him what he wanted in North Africa. He then concentrated on clamping a catholic and Castilian hold over his exhausted subjects, and encouraging and exploiting the interest in football, which by the 1930s was taking over from bull-fighting as the national sport. One of his prizes was Ricardo Zamora, star goalkeeper of the 1920s and 1930s, and the first footballer to win the public acclaim until then reserved for matadors. He was reported to have been killed by the republicans in the early months of the war, but in fact had merely been arrested with others who had written for right-wing newspapers. While in captivity he organized football matches with other prisoners and the help of sympathetic guards, so was never in serious danger. As the sporting world prepared to mourn his loss, he reappeared in France and gave a widely reported interview for *Paris-soir*. In March 1937 the left-wing French journal *Sport* quoted him as denying that he was a fascist, and reported the comments of his friend Blanco, that he had been led astray by the bourgeoisie and their adulation of him, that in fact he had no politics: Zamora, Blanco added, had the 'mind of a child' and was first and foremost a sportsman. Which suited the Franco regime perfectly. In 1939 Zamora became manager of Atlético Madrid.

Much of Franco's support for football came through his association with Réal Madrid, the team of the capital that became a focus for Castilian centralization and cultural imperialism. Known simply as *el Madrid* to locals, Réal Madrid were founded as Madrid FC in 1902, taking over from a team called the Madrid Football Club which had been founded by students in 1898. They were granted the 'royal' prefix in 1920 by king Alphonso XIII. The premier Spanish clubs at this time, however, were Barcelona and, above all, Bilbao, from the capitals of the two wealthiest industrial regions in Spain.

Long before Franco, these champions of the provincial nationalists had been a thorn in the side of the Madrid government: Barcelona of the Catalans, Bilbao of the Basques. Bilbao pointedly called themselves Athletic Bilbao, and when their Basque offshoots set up a team in Madrid they too used the English name, Athletic Madrid. In June 1925 Barcelona had their ground closed for six months by the dictator Primo de Rivera for irreverent whistling by their fans while a royal march was being played at half-time in their ground, Les Corts. During the Civil War play continued despite the massacres, while Barcelona and a Basque team left on overseas tours. In April 1937 Barcelona were invited to tour Mexico and went on to play in New York. At the end of the tour they had the difficult choice of whether to return to the conflict, which was turning bad for the Catalonians, or accept offers to play in North America. Three officials and four players returned, nine went to Mexico, three chose exile in France: none went back to the zone controlled by Franco. A Basque selection went on a virtual world tour, that took in Europe, including two and a half months in the Soviet Union, and then North and South America. Both teams were denounced in the Francoist press as 'wandering Judases' and 'peripatetic traitors'. Of the Basque players who stayed abroad, Zubieta was signed by San Lorenzo of Argentina, and pushed up their club membership from 15,000 to 35,000.

When play resumed after the Civil War, Athletic Bilbao and Barcelona, despite their losses, continued to dominate, while Athletic Madrid were merged with the air-force club Aviaciòn to become Atlética Aviaciòn. (In 1947 they regained their more distinctive title, but as Atlético, rather than Athletic, Madrid.) In footballing terms the great victor of the war was Santiago Bernabéu. He was in Madrid when the war broke out; he had to hide in an embassy, a hospital and other refuges before he escaped to France. From there he went back to Spain to join Franco, and was granted a military medal at the end of the war. In 1943 he took over as president of Réal, with the help (moral if not financial) of his friend Franco, and set out to crush the provincial challenge. In the process he produced arguably the greatest club team of all time, housed in one of the greatest stadiums.

Santiago Bernabéu had virtually a life-long association with Réal Madrid before he became president in 1943. Born in 1895, he joined the club as a player when only 14 years old, became captain and played until injury forced him out in 1926. He trained as a lawyer without allowing this to interfere with his roles as scout, secretary, manager and director, but it is by the massive stadium that today bears his name that he is best remembered.

Like many Spanish sports grounds, the Chamartín Stadium that had been home to Réal Madrid was destroyed in the Civil War, the pitch ruined and anything that would burn, particularly the wooden stand, used for fuel. Bernabéu set about buying up the land around the old stadium and there he built the new stadium at an enormous cost – much reduced, however, by the virtual slave wages paid workers at that time. By December 1947 it was ready for a game against Belenenses of Portugal; by 1954 it was able to hold 120,000 spectators, but it was its 'refined lines . . . rather than its scale' together with its location in Madrid's equivalent to the Champs Elysées that made it what Simon Inglis called a 'landmark edifice' unequalled by any other in Europe. Nevertheless, it was the Nou Camp Stadium of Barcelona that Inglis claimed to be one of the world's most famous sporting arenas. Despite its huge capacity the ground was frequently packed as Barcelona's success from the 1950s saw their membership pass 100,000 by the 1980s – twice as many as Réal Madrid. Today they are the best supported club in Europe.

It was Bernabéu who was largely responsible for the playing success of Réal Madrid, as Bilbao were pushed into the background and Barcelona took over as Réal's main rivals. With the help of Franco, Bernabéu secured the services of Di Stefano in 1953 after a contract dispute in which River Plate, his original club, and Los Millonarios of Colombia, who had poached him, both claimed rights over his signature. To secure Di Stefano's transfer Barcelona and Réal Madrid dealt with different FAs, with both claiming legal rights. The unlikely solution was that the two clubs share him on a year to year basis. Political harassment, however, forced Barcelona to give up their share of his playing time, and poor performances by Di Stefano himself induced Barcelona to sell their share for what turned out to be a pittance. Bernabéu's next masterstroke was to take a (small) risk on signing an overweight Puskas in 1958. Di Stefano repaid the transfer fee many times over; Puskas trimmed his figure from portly to stocky, and together they made up the greatest pair of players in the history of the game. Many people who knew nothing of the miseries Franco inflicted on his country, knew only that it was the nation that gave the world, albeit in black and white and with restricted camera angles, one of the brightest jewels in the sporting crown.

Franco's manipulation of the sporting success of Spanish clubs on the international scene did not fool the Spaniards. For them, just as Réal Madrid became Franco's team, so FC Barcelona and Athletic Bilbao become the rallying points for Catalonian and Basque separatism. Under Franco's ruthless control all opposition was crushed or forced underground. The supporters of the many Basque and Catalan clubs were banned from speaking their own languages and displaying their own colours, but it was through these very sporting clubs that the spirit of cultural and political opposition were kept alive. Athletic Bilbao were to be called simply Atlético (and Sporting Gijón had to change their name to Deportivo); Barcelona became 'Club de Futbol' instead of 'Futbol Club' and had to play in red and blue instead of red and yellow. But these teams by other names (and colours) still reeked of their old loyalties. Réal Sociedad continued to play only Basque players. After Franco's death Bilbao reverted to 'Athletic', but Madrid retained the Spanish 'Atlético'.

Franco was himself a football enthusiast, and he used it to take the minds of his people off their dismal living conditions. Football was already becoming a religion, but it was too expensive for most people to attend the big games. As the burden of poverty was slowly eased in the 1950s, so the crowds increased. Franco, as Duncan Shaw has shown, deliberately cultivated this interest for its opium effect. He had no qualms about killing his opponents, but the encouragement of social apathy and passive acceptance was a much more civilized way of retaining control. Spain had seven dailies devoted to football, and Franco also used television to keep the minds of would-be malcontents on the right track: on May Day he would run a continuous feast of Brazilian football on the small screen. This was what the satirist Evaristo Acevedo called the 'footballization' of the masses. Football took the place of bread and bulls and, in the press, of politics. There, as Carlos Santander has shown, journals like *El Diario*, *Vasca* and other regional papers devoted anything from double to six times more space to football than to politics.

For most of the decade after 1954 Spanish club teams, strengthened by foreign stars, had exceptional success in European competition, but the national team performed poorly. One reason for this was the number of foreigners in local competition, although some of them, like Puskas, became Spanish citizens. When the Hungarian-born Czech Ladislao Kubala played for Spain it was the third country he had represented. A more serious hindrance to Spain's international success was the unwillingness of Catalans and Basques to associate themselves with what they saw as a Castilian national team. They were more likely to support the opposition, a feeling that has lingered through until today. In 1964, however, Franco had the pleasure of seeing Spain win the European Nations Cup, beating the Soviet Union in a final played in Madrid before

120,000 spectators. The conservative *ABC* newspaper could boast in its sports pages how Spain, having triumphed over the evils of Communism and its fellow travellers from the 1930s was also triumphing in the fields of economic, social and institutional development. Franco had not always been so ideologically astute; in 1960 Spain withdrew from a European Nations Cup qualifier due to be played in Madrid rather than issue visas to the Soviet visitors.

Franco continued to his last days as he had begun, when from his death bed, in 1975, he ordered the execution of five Basque terrorists. The two main Basque teams, Bilbao and Réal Sociedad de San Sebastián, protested against the executions by wearing black armbands at their next game. They told the police who tried to prevent this that they were commemorating the death of some obscure hero. Racing de Santander did not get away with this ploy, and police raided their dressing room and forced them to remove their armbands. They were later fined 100,000 pesetas.

Today Barcelona are well established as a middle-class club, buying success and with it inevitably muffling their political opinions. On the death of Franco they prepared the way for the future by sending a note of condolence to the office of the recently deceased dictator, and another to Don Carlos, pledging the loyalty of the club and looking forward to a 'peaceful and democratic partnership as represented in the person of His Royal Highness.' The bitter rivalry of Barcelona and Réal Madrid continues, but the worst political tensions have been removed from these games. Basque and Catalan can still support the team of their cultural persuasion, but Réal have lost the burden of being 'Franco's team'.

Star teams and super leagues

Spain and Italy are the two great 'latin' football countries in Europe. Italy had a team, in the late 1940s, that might have reached the heights of Réal Madrid, but any such hopes were smashed when the plane returning from a friendly in Lisbon crashed into the basilica in the hillside of the Turin suburb of Superga on 4 May 1949. In one fatal moment was wiped out the entire Torino team in one of the worst tragedies in sporting history. All Italy mourned. After suggestions that Torino be granted the championship they were well on the way to winning, they played on with a makeshift team of young players and hasty transfers. In respect, their opponents also put out youth teams, and so Torino won the League. But the great team was gone, and with it hopes for Italy's return to the international success of the 1930s.

Less than ten years later, on 6 February 1958, another team of matchless potential was destroyed in a plane crash, in Munich. The team was

Manchester United; the tragedy came when the plane bringing them back from a European Cup match against Red Star in Belgrade failed to take off on its third attempt. So ended the careers of many of the 'Busby Babes', the team groomed from the nurseries of Manchester United by coach Matt Busby. There would be other tragedies involving football teams: in Chile in April 1961 a plane bringing the players of Green Cross to a game in Santiago crashed with all on board perishing; in Bolivia in September 1969 a plane carrying the players of The Strongest crashed in the Andes, killing all on board; in 1988 the Alianza Lima team perished in an air crash with suspicions of a terrorist bomb causing it; in 1989 14 Dutch-based Surinamese players died in a plane crash during an end-of-season tour of Surinam; then on the morning of 28 April 1993 African sport was dealt a terrible blow when most of the Zambian national team, 18 players, but not their European-based professionals, and five officials, perished when the government plane taking them to Senegal, plunged into the sea off Libreville, Gabon, shortly after a refuelling stop. There have been others, though none involving teams as famous as these. The age of the aeroplane had arrived, however, and with television it brought football and the World Cup to an ever increasing public, and to Europe a whole new series of competitions.

The first 'Super league' football competition was the Football League of England. It wasn't, of course, called such when it was founded in 1888, but its motives were similar to those so beloved of super league advocates today: competition restricted to the best teams so that their earning power would be kept to themselves. For better and for worse, as we have seen, the earning power of the top clubs was restricted and the elite clubs had to face the constant challenge of teams being promoted from lower divisions. Greed and complacency were thus kept in check at the same time. In the meantime, the independent development of football in the other countries of the UK was such that the occasional calls for a British League fell on stony ground. When the ground was more fertile, from the 1960s, there were wider fields to be exploited and the fourfold division of the United Kingdom gave the weaker footballing nations of the union a chance to enter the burgeoning European competitions.

In Europe the first 'Super' league was the Mitropa, or Central European, Cup, founded by Hugo Meisl in 1927. Like the Football League it was the natural extension of the top teams' preference, particularly in the Danubian countries, for playing against each other across borders, rather than with the weak teams in their own competitions. There were calls to extend the Mitropa to a genuine European Cup or League in the 1930s, but not with much hope that the British associations might be willing to take part.

In Britain, Herbert Chapman spoke in favour of the idea being mooted on the continent concerning the formation of a West Europe Cup competition, a knock-out competition involving the champion teams of England, Scotland, Germany, France, Belgium and Spain. He predicted, in 1933, that it would be launched within a year or two and would represent a big advance on 'the holiday tours that England and Scotland have undertaken in the past.' He warned that if Britain did not fall in with such a scheme they would be left behind in the development of the game.

In December 1934 Gabriel Hanot also raised the idea. Hanot had been a leading footballer in his day: as a student he played in Germany, and between 1913 and 1919 was capped for France twelve times. He later became a selector of the national team, and was active in promoting professionalism in France, but it was as a journalist that he was best known. As editor of *Le Miroir des sports* he proposed that each of the major leagues in Europe should invite two foreign teams to enter their competition, on an exchange basis, as a lead-up to a European League. His idea was enthusiastically taken up by the wealthy president of Racing-Club de Paris, Jean-Bernard Lévy. Lévy, a commercially oriented progressive who was behind the introduction of professionalism in France, could see the difficulties in such a competition: while Olympique Lille might be only too happy to share the gate money with Tottenham Hotspur, the reverse was unlikely to be the case. He thus proposed a knock-out cup competition, pointing out that with the advances in air travel, distance was no longer a problem, and just as in France the success of the French Cup had led to that of the French League, so might a European Cup. His European Cup envisaged one club from each of sixteen nations, but he saw the major problem being how to involve the English clubs. In the meantime he expressed the willingness of his own club to take part, and offered its ground as the venue for the final of a competition which he hoped would bring sporting success and 'considerable revenue'. As he and other European football aficionados knew, the Chapmans in British football were exceptional. Moreover, the central European clubs were happy enough with their Mitropa Cup.

The war dealt a serious blow to the Mitropa Cup, which limped along for nearly a couple of decades. In 1949 a Latin Cup was introduced, to be competed for by the top teams in France, Italy, Spain and Portugal. This was before television had to be considered, and some of these games became prolonged affairs as they were played to a finish. The 1950 Cup, played in Portugal, was won by the champions of the host nation, Benfica, in a final against the Girondins from Bordeaux which lasted 266 minutes! The first game went to extra time after a 3–3 draw with no further scoring. The following Sunday, 18 June, scores were tied at 1–1 at the end of normal time and no goals were scored in extra time. The game was then continued until the French goalkeeper was charged over the line with the ball in the 146th minute, thus bringing to an end the marathon match.

For the British trainer of Benfica, Ted Smith, it was the best game he had ever seen, but for two of Great Britain's leading soccer figures, Stanley Rous and Arthur Drewry, both to become presidents of FIFA, and enlightened men among some of the troglodytes who walked the corridors of the FA and the SFA, the very existence of the Latin Cup came as a surprise. The journalist Jacques de Ryswick, who met them in Lisbon at the end of the 1950 Latin Cup, as the three made their separate ways to the World Cup in Brazil, could not help commenting on their astonishment on making this discovery, adding his sarcasms about the 'wonders of splendid isolation'.

In club competition Scottish and English teams had acquitted themselves on the continent in a similar manner to the national teams before the Second World War, winning the admiration of the continentals, losing the odd game but more often winning. European clubs seldom visited Britain before 1939, while British clubs very seldom played against each other. There was no British Cup, barely even talk of one, and games between clubs of the four home associations were usually restricted to pre-season friendlies, prestige encounters like the more or less regular games between the two glamour clubs, Arsenal and Glasgow Rangers and competitions to celebrate special exhibitions, such as the Empire Exhibition in 1938, the Festival of Britain in 1951, and the Coronation Cup in 1953 (all won by Glasgow Celtic). This changed drastically from the mid-1950s when the long nourished hopes for serious European competitions took shape, in three distinct forms: a knock-out competition for league champions, one for Cup winners, and another for those who had a 'near-miss'. All these competitions were under the jurisdiction of the first European soccer federation, founded in 1954, the Union Européenne des Football Associations (UEFA/Union of European Football Associations) and none of them owed much to the British.

The new European competitions

The European Cup, probably the most challenging football competition in the world, surpassed, if at all, only by the World Cup itself, was, like the World Cup and FIFA, of French inspiration. Its main promoter was Gabriel Hanot, still active as a football journalist, but now with *L'Equipe*, the successor to *L'Auto*, originator of the Tour de France, the 24 Hour Le Mans and many other sporting initiatives. Now, with its offshoot *France Football*, the doyen of sports dailies was to add a new laurel to its crown of sporting sponsorships. The catalyst for the competition came with the crude crowing of the English tabloids when Wolves beat Honved 3–2 in the mud of Molyneux on 13 December 1954, declaring them to be the

Champions of the World. Never since Scottish Cup holders Renton beat English Cup holders West Bromwich Albion in 1888 had there been such hyperbole. The lads from Dunbartonshire also beat the English champions, Preston North End, in a charity match, and so thought they were justified styling themselves 'Renton FC: Champions of the World'. Given the minuscule world of football in their time they had more justice in their claim than that made for Wolves several decades later.

The new European confederation showed little interest in the idea of a the European competition at first, but Hanot and *L'Equipe* went ahead in any case. On 2 April 1955, on the eve of a France/Sweden game, a meeting was called in Paris of representatives from 18 of Europe's biggest clubs. (Three could not turn up: Hibernian from Scotland, Spartak Prague and Moscow Dinamo.) Interest was such that UEFA could not ignore it and so it took on the organization of what was initially called the European Champion Clubs Cup, contested by sixteen clubs in 1955–56.

The first competition was an invitational tournament, but thereafter it was played between the league champions of each of the nations belonging to UEFA on a knock-out system, based on two matches home and away, except for the final which would be held at a pre-determined venue. Apart from the first year, the format has scarcely varied, except for the introduction of a premium on away goals introduced in 1967 and penalty shoot-outs instead of the toss of a coin to decide tied matches from 1970, an exciting farce replacing a simple farce. The English Football League, as stuffy as the FA and even more arrogant in regard to Europe, would not allow Chelsea to take part in the first competition, but the Scottish League did permit Hibernian to represent Scotland. Matt Busby told the directors of Manchester United to ignore the League when they were invited to the second year of competition. Réal Madrid dominated the first five years of the competition, Benfica from Portugal won the next two and then Italian clubs AC Milan (1963) and Inter-Milan (1964, 1965). Réal Madrid won again in 1966, but the following year the first British club won when the home-grown talent of Glasgow Celtic outclassed the millionaires of Inter-Milan in Lisbon. In doing so they struck a blow not only for grass-roots soccer, but for attacking football which was being throttled by the *catenaccio* of Herrera's Inter. Manchester United won the cup the following year. The Dutch, through Feyenoord and above all Ajax, brought the 'total football' revolution to win four times in a row from 1970, to be replaced by a three-year spell of victories by Bayern Munich. English teams then dominated until banned after the Heysel disaster in 1985. In 1986 the competition was won in execrable fashion, with a penalty shoot-out which gave the trophy to Steaua Bucharest in Seville. This deplorable way of winning a final became an actual tactic when Red Star Belgrade boasted of playing for a draw to beat Marseille on penalties in

1991. Dull finals were by then the order of the day: Porto's triumph against Bayern Munich by 2–0 in 1987 was saved by the result and the class of the two late goals, but the following year PSV Eindhoven were awarded the trophy on penalties against Portugal's Benfica. In 1989 and 1990 AC Milan, well on the way to buying up the top talent in the world, disposed of Steaua Bucharest (4–0) and Benfica (1–0). The Champions' Cup returned to Spain in 1992 when Barcelona finally won the one trophy that had up until then eluded them. In 1993 the country that had started the competition won its first championship, when Marseille defeated AC Milan, only to have the fruits of victory soured by accusations of corruption that surfaced shortly afterwards, and led to serious punishment.

The idea of a competition for the winners of the various European cup competitions was first put forward by UEFA in 1958, but did not get an enthusiastic response at first. Knock-out cup competitions were never as popular in south and central Europe as elsewhere. In 1960, however, the Mitropa Cup was not contested, and the European Cup Winners' Cup virtually took over from this. The Mitropa Cup committee organized the first competition, which took place in 1960–61, and the following year UEFA took over the competition, which had 23 entries. Since it is made up of cup winners whose success might have been achieved by the luck of the draw and a sudden death knock-out win, this competition has at least begun with the romance of some Davids trying their arm against the Goliaths. The home and away nature of the subsequent competition reduces the chance of upsets, but the big names have had a few scares. Welsh club Cardiff City, regular winners of the Welsh Cup, won their way through to the semi-final in 1967–68, eliminating Torpedo Moscow on the way before falling narrowly to Hamburger SV; and Bangor, also from Wales, scared Napoli when they took them to a third game in 1962–63, where they were eliminated only by the odd goal in three.

The third European competition grew out of the Inter-City Fairs Cup, a competition not between clubs, but between cities that regularly held industrial or trade fairs. The idea was first raised by a vice president of FIFA, E.B. Thommen of Switzerland, in 1950, but had to wait for the formation of UEFA, which organized the first competition, to begin in 1954 and contested by twelve cities from ten countries. Spread over two years, the first final was not played until 1957, between London and Barcelona: the London team was made up of players from various London clubs, Barcelona only of players from CF Barcelona. After the second Fairs City Cup final, played in 1960, the competition was held annually. Clubs rather than teams representing a city took over, and from 1971–72 UEFA donated a new trophy which was then run by UEFA instead of a special committee, and became known as the UEFA Cup. Spanish clubs dominated the early years of the competition, then English teams won it for six seasons in a row between 1968 and 1973. It is played between the top teams from the various European leagues who were neither champions nor cup winners, each country being allowed places according to a calculation of the country's success in previous competitions: thus some countries can supply four teams, some three, others two and one. Teams proceed as in the other competitions on the aggregate score of home and away games right through to the final, which unlike the other competitions, is also played on a two-leg home and away basis.

In the meantime, a European championship for nations was being played on a regular basis. This was the European Football Championship, or Nations Cup, played over two years following the World Cup. It was an early idea of UEFA's, who named its trophy after Henri Delaunay, the first secretary of UEFA, but also a founder of FIFA and a driving force behind the organization of French football since its inception. Begun in 1958 on an elimination basis, the four semi-finalists played the final rounds in France, where only 18,000 turned up at the Parc des Princes to see the USSR defeat Yugoslavia 2–1 in the final. The competition was weakened by the absence of many leading countries. After the first competition the final rounds were played in one country every four years, although unlike the World Cup it was not until 1980 that the host country was granted an automatic place in the finals. Played in the shadow not only of the World Cup, but of the European Cup, it did not fire the imagination before the 1970s, and although this period was dominated by powerhouse football forces like West Germany and Italy, in the 1980s small nations like Denmark and Belgium showed how they could hold their own. The competition was won by the brilliant football of France in 1984 and the Netherlands in 1988. Then came Denmark in 1992, to show that even in football at the highest level there is still some romance. The Danes put on a gutsy performance that saw them triumph over injuries and much better-fancied opposition to eliminate the Netherlands in the semi-final and Germany in the final.

With the greed of the rich clubs growing with their wealth, the pressures for a full-scale European League have become impossible to restrain. As an introduction to this the regulations for the European Cup were altered for the 1991–92 competition, with the eventual finalists being chosen from two small leagues instead of home and away knock-out games. This is in many ways the logical development of football competitions, which will one day boast a World League, combining the best teams and the most lucrative fixtures. These were the motives that inspired McGregor back in the 1880s, Meisl in the 1920s and Hanot, Lévy and Chapman in the 1930s. But most of these men put their love of the game above their financial interests. One can't help having doubts about the millionaires of the 1990s.

Brash new world

In the 1940s, Italian clubs had been unable to lure English stars like Wilf Mannion and Tom Finney with lucrative contracts, and had to be satisfied with lesser lights like Paddy Sloan of Arsenal and Tommy Jones of Spurs. This began to change when the superb Welshman John Charles left for Juventus in 1957. Like Eddie Firmani, the South African of mixed English and Italian background, and Englishman Gerry Hitchens, he was prepared to accept the negative play in Italy and enjoy life in a new culture; others like Scotsman Denis Law and Englishman Jimmy Greaves found the discipline that went with the big salaries too much. For most British players the continent was still a foreign country: the thought of having to give up pie and beans or fish and chips for pasta and garlic was not an attractive one. No more was that of having to exchange a social life revolving around a glass of wine in a café for the traditional banter around a pint in a pub. The lifestyle of the British professional footballer was generally on a par with his wages.

The gulf between the continent and the UK was still immense. When George Raynor first went to Italy in 1954 to discuss the possibility of accepting a coaching job with Juventus, he was taken into the Fiat factory owned by the Agnelli family, owners of Juventus. With his head still reeling over the salary and other perks he had been offered, Raynor was asked if he would like a new car, said he would, and was immediately invited to choose one of those coming off the assembly line. Next day the car was delivered in the colour he had requested, all papers in order, maps to get to Sweden and back, and money for expenses in the glove box. A short time after Raynor was being lured to Italy Eddy Firmani left Charlton Athletic to begin a long and successful career there. In his book *Football among the Millionaires*, Firmani comments, without any apparent sarcasms, on the kindness of the Charlton board who allowed him to keep his football boots when he left. So it was: for Raynor a new Fiat, for Firmani the right to keep his well-worn boots. A parable of the times, and for British football a glimpse of the future.

It was a future that was not without its dark spots, but it was one in which the age-old British prejudice against coaching was discarded. George Raynor was in his prime when he offered his services to Coventry City in 1955, after a series of brilliant successes in Sweden, but he barely lasted the season. Born in Barnsley in 1907, Raynor progressed from Church football to play in every division of the English League as well as the Midland League, the Central League and the Lancashire Combination. During the Second World War he was stationed at Aldershot, where some of Britain's best footballers were also posted, but his first taste of coaching came when he was sent to Iraq, where, despite riots and players being killed and wounded by gunfire, he established Iraqi football on a fairly firm basis. On his return to Britain he hoped to get a job using his new found talents as a coach.

To no avail. So he took Stanley Rous's advice and accepted a position in Sweden in 1946. With the full co-operation of the Swedish football association and all the clubs, Raynor introduced a national system of coaching which he supervised, aimed at winning the Olympic Games in 1948. The price of that success, with Italian agents on the players' trail before they had left London, was the loss of his stars, the famous 'Grenoli' trio of Gunnar Gren, Gunnar Nordahl and Nils Liedholm (Raynor himself had been offered £1000 and a car if he got certain of the Swedish stars to sign for a particular Italian team). Undeterred, he re-built a team which he took to Brazil in 1950 and came third, allowing Raynor the right to claim, since Uruguay and Brazil took the first two places, that Sweden were the best football team in Europe. This time he was unable to recoup the losses to Italy that followed his success in Rio, and failing to repeat his success in Helsinki in 1952 and Switzerland in 1954, he allowed himself to be lured to Italy for the 1954–55 season. There the money did not make up for the change in climate, moral as much as meteorological, and homesickness brought him back to take over as manager of Coventry City. Attitudes were still in the old mould, however, and Raynor soon discovered that the mental signs outside British football stadiums, 'No coaches need apply' were still in place. So back he went to Sweden to prepare the Swedish national team for the 1958 World Cup, aided by the lifting of the ban on expatriates. The Swedes performed above themselves before ecstatic home crowds, losing only in the final to the brilliant Brazilians. The following year they went on to beat England 2–3 in London, their first home defeat by a continental side since the Hungarians in 1953.

It was after the 1958 World Cup that England and Scotland began to take football outside Britain more seriously, and this involved a more modern, or continental, approach to the game: a vision that could see beyond the local pub. Some managers coached, but generally the two functions came to be separated, with training no longer the mindless slog of lapping, the ball hidden away till Saturday. Now coaches took the players through drills and sophisticated skills and set plays. This left the manager to concentrate on more strictly managerial tasks such as finding new players, placating present ones and keeping sweet with the press.

From 1961, when the maximum wage was abolished and the retain and transfer system dismantled, players had to be treated with more respect or they would pick up their boots and go; higher wages and increased perks encouraged players to employ agents, and one time working-class lads had to learn how to invest wisely and act in the manner as befitted a potential

TV or advertising investment. Managers could appeal to team loyalty and teamwork off the field to keep players with the club, but that was wearing thin. The new sector of the middle-class was learning the meaning of market forces, individualism and the advantages of voting Conservative. There had been a time when a player given £5 for a radio interview shared it with his mates: as the rewards escalated with television some players tried to retain the notion of a 'pool', but the stars who would be expected to appear in such interviews often refused: they wanted it all for themselves. This was the attitude which at club level led to the idea of super leagues.

With its more serious approach to coaching in the 1960s Britain soon caught up with most of the continent on the playing field, with English teams winning more than their share of the European competitions before 1985. At the same time, the attitudes of the players changed in tune with the times, with the homespun and modest football hero coming to enjoy and expect the celebratory status that had always been accorded big football stars in countries like Italy.

A final bastion of the protestant morality that had acted as a restraint on the exploitation of football as a capitalist commodity before 1961 was removed with the acceptance and then embrace of Sunday football. In a country where sabbatarianism was widely upheld and many children's swings in public parks were locked away on Sundays even in the 1960s, the FA's ban on playing football on the sabbath was not particularly resented. Many Britons, including football followers, saw the playing of games on Sunday as a continental abomination. The continentals for their part saw sabbatarianism as just one more British idiosyncrasy, to be likened to its licensing hours and queuing. Sunday games were played during the War, and briefly during the energy crisis of 1973–74, but it was not until the 1980s that they became a normal part of the fixture lists. The continuing decline in crowds, the dominance of television and galloping commercialism broke down the last resistance, and British games are now regularly scattered to suit television viewers, while Sunday is set aside for a main match. The day of rest had become a day of sport, as it always had been on the continent.

In the early 1960s fanaticism was still seen as a continental trait from which the more sober Britons were immune. John Charles warned in the book he wrote (*The Gentle Giant*) on his return to Leeds United in 1962 that the two things the British player in Italy would have to learn to live with were the fans and the press. Charles found the Italian fans more knowledgeable and more demanding, after all they were paying high prices to see highly paid sportsmen, and he soon learned to live with the abuse dished out to players who made the slightest mistake. On the other hand, a brilliant performance or a winning goal could result in fans clubbing together to collect large sums of money to add to the player's bonus. Raynor was less impressed by this volatility, and pointed out that while he could get free meat deliveries and other gifts when his team was doing well, this ceased when things went against them. Adoring fans could turn into wild men who scratched his car and slashed its tyres. This side of the Italian sporting fanaticism could be turned on the players: when Italy lost to England in Turin in 1948 there were demonstrations calling for the death of Pozzo, and when Italy returned from England in 1966 after a humiliating exit from the World Cup at the hands of North Korea, there were fans to meet them at the airport with rotten fruit and vegetables.

The Italian sporting press reflected this wild enthusiasm, with minute coverage of the game and a well established gutter press. Before the 1960s the British press and national broadcasting institutions could have been accused of stuffiness, but seldom sensationalism or fraud. This began to change with the introduction of 'cheque-book journalism', and as the competition of commercial television began to push British football down new pathways. The first time television broadcast a major sporting event was at the Berlin Olympics in 1936, but there was little in the flickering images relayed to a small audience in specially built halls to indicate a threat to live sport. In Britain the FA Cup Final of 1938 appeared on an estimated 10,000 private television sets, but it was not until Eurovision and the World Cup in Switzerland that televised sport could be seen in every household in western Europe. A year later, in 1955, commercial television was introduced in Britain, and for years thereafter the BBC and Independent Television (ITV) operated a more or less cosy gentlemen's agreement about what games would be shown. In the 1960s football still called the shots, the income to the clubs was minimal, and only the big cup games and internationals were shown live.

This began to change from the late 1960s with specially packaged highlights and more emphasis on off-the-field activities. 'Personalities' were becoming a vital part of the new 'package', and they expected to be paid a 'personality' fee. So, too, were the 'experts' increasingly invited to give their opinions. In many ways this is no more than terracing banter appearing on the TV screen, but it was divorced from the fans, while the game itself was becoming just one part of a larger 'package'.

With television sets dominating the furniture arrangements in most households in the 1960s, and televised news becoming the main source of current affairs, the press had to adjust its coverage of events to suit the changing tastes of its readers. Quality papers went for in depth 'investigations', but the tabloids went more for sensationalism. In 1969 the then Australian Rupert Murdoch took over *The Sun*, and a new age was inaugurated as most of what he touched, and there was much of it, was transformed into trash. Football in such papers was often reduced to the same level as bare bosoms and crass headlines.

It would be another decade, and a few more technological miracles later, before press and television took sport further down the road of commercial claptrap, but already in the 1960s television had entered daily life in a way unknown to press and radio. It brought the problems of the day dramatically into the living room; it feasted on spectacle and violence, and in turn encouraged this. The British football fan, like the protest marchers, became a focus of TV attention and in turn played to the cameras. With their 'betters' in the media and club management showing the way, they developed their own interpretation of the new ethos in outbursts of hooliganism that it was believed had once been the sole preserve of 'continentals'.

Endnotes

Jack Rollin, *Soccer at War, 1939–1945*, Willow Books, London, 1985.
George F. Allison, *Allison Calling*, Staples Press, London, 1948

F. Puskas, *Captain of Hungary*, Cassell, London, 1955

is a typically anodyne ghosted biography. For less anodyne comments I am most grateful to Ferenc Puskas for an interview he accorded me, with Roy Hay, in Melbourne, in May 1991. I am also grateful for comments by Les Murray of SBS Television, Australia, who in addition gave me access to the SBS film library.
    For Spain under Franco:

Carlos Fernandez Santander, *El Futbol durante la Guerra Civil y el Franquismo*, Editorial San Martin, S.L., Madrid, n.d. (1991).

In English:

Duncan Shaw, 'Football under Franco', in *History Today*, August 1985.

Roger Macdonald, *Britain versus Europe*, Pelham Books, London, 1968

is a history of the European Cup. There have been numerous histories of this competition: see especially

John Motson and John Rowlinson, *The European Cup, 1955–1980*, Queen Anne Press, London, 1980;
Brian Glanville, *Champions of Europe. The History, Romance and Intrigue of the European Cup*, Guinness Publishing, London, 1991.

    Most of the player biographies referred to in the text are indicated by their year of publication: three books central to the 1961 dispute are:

James Guthrie, *Soccer Rebel*, Readers' Union, Devon, 1976
Jimmy Hill, *Striking for Soccer*, SBC, London, 1963
George Eastham, *Determined to Win*, SBC, London, 1964.

    The dispute is fully covered in the previously cited history of the Players' Union:

John Harding, *For the Good of the Game*.

Raynor's story is told in:

George Raynor, *Football Ambassador at Large*, SBC, London, 1960.

For the League and the FA, see the official histories by Inglis and Green.
For Inglis's comments on football stadiums:

Simon Inglis, *The Football Grounds of Europe*, Willow Books, London, 1990.

Of the many books on English soccer since 1945, the best is:

Stephen Wagg, *The Football World. A Contemporary Social History*, The
Harvester Press, Brighton, 1984.

See also:

Peter Jeffs, *The Golden Age of Football*, Breedon Books, Derby, 1991.

On women's soccer, see

John Williams and Jackie Woodhouse, 'Can play, will play? Women and football
in Britain', in John Williams and Stephen Wagg (eds.), *British Football and Social
Change. Getting into Europe*, Leicester University Press, Leicester, 1991.

Much of this is based on

D. Williamson, *Belles of the Ball*, R. and D. Associates, Devon, 1991.

CHAPTER SEVEN

The Changing Face of the People's Game

From the mid-1960s, Britain was faced by a hooligan problem which refused to disappear over the next two decades. At the Heysel Stadium, Brussels, on 29 May 1985 this reached an appalling climax when 39 people, most of them Juventus supporters, were killed when a wall collapsed on them following a panic set off when they were charged by rival Liverpool fans. The grisly toll of deaths at football grounds involving British fans reached even more horrific proportions four years later, when 95 Liverpool supporters were crushed to death shortly after the start of a semi-final game against Nottingham Forest at the neutral Hillsborough stadium, Sheffield, on 15 April 1989. The only factor in common between these two tragedies was that they coincidentally involved Liverpool supporters, but so linked was football in many people's minds with hooliganism that the Hillsborough disaster was at times spoken of as though it was caused by the victims. Some newspapers spoke in terms of 'British Soccer's Toll of Shame', and totted up deaths at previous tragedies implying that they were all part of the same disease from which the game was suffering. And in those countries where football is soccer and still something of a mystery, the game itself was invested with a mystical power to incite diabolical excesses in the behaviour of otherwise ordinary people.

Deaths in the stadium

There were four major disasters at British football grounds before Hillsborough. The world's first sporting tragedy was at an international match between Scotland and England at Ibrox Park, Glasgow, on 5 April 1902. This was in the days before Hampden took all the big games, and Rangers and Celtic were in vigorous competition to house internationals and major cup ties at their grounds. Among the improvements inaugurated by Rangers to attract the plum fixture was a previously untried wooden terracing to accommodate standing spectators: more customers could be crushed together more closely, but there were no seats to prevent surges, and worse, no solid earth to take the pressure of suddenly increased weight. The club was assured that the new terracing had been tested for any weaknesses, but there were a few warnings, as much out of sour grapes from Celtic sources as from genuine fears of a tragedy, that the new terracing was unsafe. Shortly into the first half spectators crowded forward to watch a passage of play and the wooden floor gave way. Some clung desperately to the edges, but others fell, 25 to their death; over 500 were injured. In the interests of safety the game was continued, but the players, who had been called off the field and saw the dead and dying as they left and re-entered the field, had no stomach for it and merely went through the motions. A now meaningless game ended in a draw.

The second Ibrox disaster could not have been said to come out of the blue. On the contrary, there had been previous warnings about the dangerous nature of Stairway 13. In 1961 two people were killed and 44 injured; in 1967 eleven people were badly enough crushed to have to be taken to hospital, and in 1969 30 people were injured on the same spot. The stairway was steep, and instead of funnelling out from a narrow entry at the top to a broader exit at the bottom, was completely parallel. Ironically one reason why there had been only two deaths at the 1961 tragedy was that the wooden fences had collapsed under the pressure of bodies. The wooden fences were then replaced by steel barriers, which instead of giving way in 1971 merely added to the pressure. Sixty-six died. If the club had refused to listen to outside advice in the decade before 1971 it took quick action thereafter, and when Rangers embarked on the stadium changes that would make Ibrox Park one of the finest in Europe, work began by demolishing the fatal stairway.

The Bolton disaster came during a Bolton/Stoke City sixth round Cup-tie in the heady days of monster football crowds just after the Second World War. This disaster was blamed on the thousands of gate-crashers who forced their entry into the ground, but its actual cause was the collapsing of a crush barrier. There had been gate-crashers at many previous games, and this was not the first time crowds had been allowed into games in dangerous numbers. The first Cup Final at Wembley in 1923 saw tens of thousands of non-paying spectators and a crowd estimated at nearly 200,000 when only just over half that number had paid to get in. In games in Scotland on the eve of the Second World War, crowds regularly spilled over into the running track, and thousands were allowed into the grounds with little hope of seeing the game. Police faced with the problem of letting disappointed spectators out usually kept the gates shut for fear of the thousands still outside forcing their way in. Throughout the 1940s and 1950s entering the playing area was a regular escape route for overcrowding or to get away from the fist fights that sporadically broke out among spectators. As at Ibrox in 1902 the game at Bolton was continued in the interests of safety, but unlike that game most of the players were unaware of the extent of the tragedy until they read about it in the papers.

There was no question of continuing the game at the Bradford disaster in 1985, the last in the season, attended by a well-above-average attendance of 11,000 to take part in celebrating Bradford's promotion to the Second Division. The fire, which broke out towards the end of the first half, was blamed on a lighted cigarette being dropped through the stand on to a pile of rubbish, in particular newspapers some of which had been lying around since the 1960s. It took less than five minutes for the 77-year-old wooden stand to be reduced to a charred remnant, and those who perished were those who tried to escape but found their exit blocked by locked gates. Some tried to relate the fire to a smoke bomb let off by a 'hooligan', but the official report opted for a lighted match or a cigarette, and came down hard on the club for its failure to meet basic safety standards.

While the Bradford disaster came at the end of a season that had been marked by frequent crowd troubles, the Hillsborough disaster came towards the end of a season of comparative calm. Eventually it was the police who were blamed for the deaths of the 95 Liverpool supporters who were crushed against a spectator fence six minutes after the start of the Cup semi-final tie between Liverpool and Nottingham Forest. The police claimed that they had opened the gates to allow entry to late-arriving Liverpool fans to ease the panic that was building up outside the ground from fans anxious not to miss the game which had already begun. The reason for the deaths was that thousands were funnelled into an enclosure from which there was no escape, crushing young men and a few women against a spectator fence. The game was abandoned.

To the extent to which fences to separate fans and to keep spectators from invading the field of play are necessary, then hooliganism was responsible. The fence at Hillsborough, however, was a fence that could have held at bay a herd of elephants. Or animals, which is how many in the private boxes and wealthier seating areas regarded the fans. It was a fence without easily opened gates, without safety release mechanisms, without any thought for what might happen to fans caught up in the pressure build ups that were as common in football grounds in the 1980s as they had been in previous decades, and which had previously been eased by access to the playing area.

Easy escape from packed terracings had undoubtedly saved hundreds, maybe thousands of lives in the days of massive crowds and no spectator fencing. This also allowed over-enthusiastic fans to invade the field for more trivial purposes, like celebrating a goal, then stopping the game when their team was being beaten, or taunting the opposition fans, in challenge for a defeat or derision for a victory. As such some means had to be found to stop spectators interfering with the game. But the fence erected at Hillsborough was more than a policing device: it was a mark of contempt by those in authority for the fans who were tolerated only for their money at the turnstile and their vocal support behind the goal. The mistake made by the police at Sheffield was a tragic error of judgment; the erection of the death fence at Hillsborough was a statement of the class divisions that had always been part of British football, as of British society, but which had been exacerbated over the previous years. As the sociologist Ian Taylor put it, it was a 'predictable outcome to the remorseless and unthinking application of law and order rhetoric to the problems of crowd control.'

In the major disasters afflicting British football the deaths were usually due at best to lack of foresight on the part of the management of the clubs, at the worst to a callous indifference to the comfort and safety of their supporters. From the 1960s, however, clearly observable groups of 'hooligans' have been a plague on the game: they have terrorized thousands of innocent citizens in and around the stadia and in the trains and other transport taking them to the match, and they have driven thousands more out of the game. But until the Heysel disaster they could not be held responsible for the deaths from disasters in football stadiums.

The tragedy of the Heysel Stadium, Brussels, came even before the start of the Juventus vs. Liverpool European Cup Final. The game went ahead, as irrelevant as the triumphant brandishing of the trophy by Juventus players at the end was an irreverence. The disaster had its origins in the lack of foresight of the Belgian authorities. They put Italian fans in a part of the ground allocated to those of Liverpool when the sale of bogus tickets to Italian supporters meant that more turned up than were supposed to; Liverpool supporters were squeezed into two sections instead of three. Only a flimsy fence separated them, and a Liverpool fan being beaten up by a Juventus supporter is said to have started the charge. The police, when faced by a disaster instead of a mere riot, behaved deplorably. So, too, the Liverpool supporters who continued their private battles. Nor did UEFA escape blame: it was they who allocated the prestige encounter to a stadium where the facilities were substandard, and it was a collapsing wall that killed the victims, not the fists and boots of their assailants.

All that said, the Liverpool supporters cannot be exonerated from blame: it was they who started the stampede that ended in disaster. The burden of guilt taken on almost immediately by the English public at large was as sincere as the anger of those Europeans who had seen their towns put on a war footing when faced by the invasion of English football supporters over the previous years. So it was not just Liverpool that was on trial and being judged that night: it was English football at large, and it was all English clubs who paid the price when they were banned indefinitely from European competitions.

There were areas of opinion where the reaction was as predictable as it was tainted: from the enemies of the game and some politicians with beams in their eyes, particularly a Prime Minister whose jingoism and insults to

the disadvantaged in her own country scarcely gave her the right to set
herself up in judgment on other types of hooliganism. Or anything to do
with soccer, revealing her ignorance with calls for the game to be returned
to the days when football had been a family game. Football in Britain and
even on the continent and Latin America has never been a family game;
fathers often went with sons, but mothers and daughters were seldom seen
and more often discouraged from attending.

There was a justifiable outrage on the part of the ordinary Briton, and a
collective feeling of shame, even among those with a love of the game.
Simon Inglis, in his enormously entertaining and informative *The Football
Grounds of Europe*, departs from his more characteristic whimsical style
when he comes to his description of the Heysel Stadium. Having dismissed
the design of the stadium and the 'lamentable' state of its terracing and
fencing as causes of the disaster, he put forward the 'fundamental' reason
for the 39 deaths:

> They died because a group of young Englishmen, intoxicated by
> alcohol and xenophobia, attacked people whose only crime, apart
> from perhaps supporting the opposing team, was to have purchased
> tickets in an adjoining section of terracing, officially reserved for
> neutral fans. How careless of them. Did they not see the Union Jacks
> and swastikas of their assailants from Blocks X and Y, and realize that
> these people saw Block Z as their rightful *Lebensraum*?

From the Nazi image of the Liverpool fans, Inglis goes on to point out
that the Heysel had housed many top class matches since its erection in
1930 as the national stadium, and many of these in the years just before the
fateful Liverpool/Juventus game. The new ingredient at that game,
presumably, were the English hooligans. True, but they did not set out
actually to kill their opponents, and as Inglis's work itself shows, there
were countless occasions at grounds throughout the world when disasters
were avoided only by accident. However that may be, the role of the
violent fan had come to dominate football, and among violent fans the role
of the British, more particularly the English fan, stood out. Britain was
back in the football forefront, but the message of its new missionaries was
quite the opposite to that of those who had first taken the game around the
world.

The English disease

Geoffrey Green still seemed rather shocked when he recalled in his 1953
history of the game the memory of an Italian supporter he had seen at the
Italy vs England international at Turin in 1948:

> . . . He carried an Italian standard about twelve feet high. All the hair

had been shaved off his head and across his new and shining bald pate was daubed in red paint the battle-cry: 'Force Italia' (*sic*) – 'Up Italy'. Imagine even a hot blooded Englishman going to those lengths . . .

In 1968 Brian Glanville, like Green a writer of great sophistication and broad vision, and like him a university graduate and amateur footballer, commented wearily on the conduct of the game outside Britain. He justified the British associations' cold shouldering of FIFA in the early days and suggested that the price of watching stars such as Pelé, Di Stefano and Yashin had been too high when considered alongside the continent's 'endless, brutal record of riots, invasion of the field by spectators, free fights among players, the three hundred deaths at a match in Peru in 1963 [in fact 1964], the forty-four deaths at a Second Division match in Turkey four years later.' (*Soccer. A Panorama*)

In the years between these two judgments the British press had smugly continued to praise the good sense of the average Briton. In September 1959 the *Leicester Mercury* thought it unthinkable that the time would come when English football grounds would need cages or wire netting to protect the players from spectators as was necessary with the volatile crowds on the continent and South America. When, as a result of crowd troubles the first protective fences in Britain went up at the Everton ground in 1963, *The Daily Sketch* ridiculed such panic measures and told those who wanted moats, cages and barbed wire to 'weep in their beer, for the British football fan is showing he can correct the stormy situation of recent weeks in the good old British manner – by common sense.' The continent was still where the British press preferred to direct its moral indignation, and on 9 October 1965 troubles in Italy found *The Times* calling for British clubs to keep clear of the continent until they had 'put their house in order.'

British football teams had fallen behind the rest of the football world by the 1970s. On the football field they had begun to catch up without regaining their former mastery; on the terracings of Great Britain and Europe they were to show that they could go to lengths that make the Italian described by Geoffrey Green look like a choirboy. And because of the previous attitudes held by Britain the continentals would have been less than human if they had not thrown back at the British the insults that had once been thrown at them.

Green and Glanville were not without justification for their comments on the game outside Britain; where they were wrong was in assuming that the excesses they pointed to could never afflict the game at home. Before the 1960s, the professional game in Britain was remarkably free from trouble from the terracing. Not completely, of course. The Celtic/Rangers games in Scotland, and their Irish equivalent in Linfield/Belfast Celtic games, were charged with political and religious implications and these matches were frequently accompanied by crowd troubles. In the early days of the game, and up to the first decade of this century, crowd troubles were frequent. They flared up again in the post-war period, but from then until the Second World War and for a decade and more afterwards millions of people watched the games being played throughout the land with a remarkable absence of disturbance.

Away from the professional games troubles were endemic, both on the field and off. Biographies of amateur players of the 1920s and 1930s tell hair-raising stories of games where it would appear that players and referees were lucky to escape with their lives if the home team lost. The records tell of clubs being warned and grounds closed because of fights. Even at the professional games fights between individual spectators were common, and there were sporadic attempts by a few spectators to interfere in the game. Drunkenness was common and damage to property a natural hazard. But they were what the essentially working-class crowds would have regarded as normal, and while they kept it to themselves there was little cause for concern: it did not affect the middle classes and while it did not affect them it was not 'news'.

From the late 1950s, however, the incidence of spectator troubles, and not just the reporting of them, appears to have increased significantly. It did so at the same time as the game was becoming more of a national preoccupation: that is to say it was being accepted by a middle class in process of change as it absorbed more of the increasingly affluent and higher educated working-class. By the 1950s football was generally recognized as the national game in England. (In Scotland it had always been so.) This could be seen in the quality newspapers, where *The Times* started to take soccer seriously with the appointment of Geoffrey Green, while *The Observer*, appearing on Sunday, only started to give significant space to football in the 1960s. When England were nominated as hosts for the 1966 World Cup attention was paid to the game as never before, and its blackspots became a matter of national concern. From about 1965, the British football hooligan started to catch up with his continental counter-part and then set about re-defining the concept.

The most thorough and fruitful investigations of hooliganism have been carried out by the Leicester University group of sociologists now working with the help of grants from the Football Trust through the Sir Norman Chester Centre. Working from a sound historical basis and writing with a blessed absence of jargon, it is they who pinpoint England's hosting of the World Cup in 1966 as a key point in attitudes to hooliganism, with an anxious media worried about the bad behaviour of English fans being broadcast to the world. This highlighted a problem which had at least until the late 1950s been played down; as the British authorities contemplated the apparent increase in troubles at football grounds, these were in turn amplified by giving the hooligans unprecedented publicity. Reporters and camera operators were sent to English games for the first time to record the problems in the crowd rather than the game itself (Denzil Batchelor was sent to Glasgow in 1949 to record Old Firm disturbances for *Picture Post*). At the roots of this hooliganism, the Leicester group suggest, was a 'rough' section of the working-class, who dominated parts of the football grounds where once they had been under the moderating influence of better behaved fans until they deserted the game to take advantage of the wider options available in a more affluent Britain. One of these options was to spend more time with their wives or girl friends, for football, never welcoming to female spectators apart from the very early days, became even less so as its male, working-class chauvinism was accentuated.

Young men have always gathered together, often in gangs, and frequently have sought outlets for their restless aggression in violence, usually against other gangs. More and more throughout the 1960s football matches became the focus for such aggression. There had always been fights at football matches in Britain, but before the 1960s few fans went with the express purpose of looking for fights. This was part of the wider youth culture where wilder and more expressive outpourings of dissent were thrust in the faces of adults by young people who no longer believed it was their lot in life to do what their elders told them.

Young people had more to spend and more to spend it on, as the consumer society encouraged them to dress up and flaunt themselves. Mere scarves and a rosette with the team's colours now gave way to whole armies of youthful supporters decked out in complete club colours. Spontaneous chants and roars became rituals of singing and abuse, and good natured banter gave way to expressions of vocal hatred. All of this was picked up by the TV cameras, which in turn encouraged those in search of momentary fame to act or dress in a manner outrageous enough to catch the eye of the cameraman.

On the field of play the attitudes of the players changed. No longer was the scoring of a goal greeted with a handshake and a pat on the back: players' reactions became increasingly wild. It had taken the British players a couple of decades to catch up on their continental counterparts: at the World Cup in 1954, Juan Hohberg of Uruguay was so violently congratulated by his team mates in their game against Hungary that he was knocked unconscious, and in 1963 players of Boca Juniors were completely stripped of their gear by wildly celebrating fans when their victory over Estudiantes won them the Argentine league.

The changing face of football in the 1960s was only one aspect of a decade of mixed values: no longer were young folks prepared to be controlled by the well worn 'kick in the backside' cure-all of an older generation, and no longer were minority groups so willing to remain silent, as blacks in the United States, women in the western world, homosexuals in their closets and the exploited in colonial empires sought their due place in society. TV commercials urged children to be greedy and adults to spend big, while on the other hand, concern for the environment challenged the mindlessness of profits at any cost and progress at any price. As Vietnam was devastated, the peace movement set out to replace war with sex and drugs and rock and roll. Television linked the world in a global village in which football, like music, sex and violence could be appreciated across national boundaries.

British football hooligans knew little of the global village. Theirs was a narrow world, and often a nasty one. For some there was little alternative: young folks living in an urban desert and with little prospect of improvement in their lives can scarcely be condemned for an exaggerated concern for their local football team. Unlike their predecessors in the 1930s, they lived in a world in which wealth and greed were flaunted before them. By the early 1970s the problem of football hooligans, of young men who went to football in search of violence, had become a way of life for a minority of mainly 'rough' working-class males. They came together to do battle on the terracing and around the ground with visiting supporters. Like loosely organized gangs who operated in other days and outside football grounds, the values of mateship and courage were highly admired. Many of them were, or became, simple thugs.

The hooligans in Britain differed from their counterparts on the continent and those of a previous era in two significant ways. First, they were organized and came to games intent on violence, and in this regard the game itself was secondary. Second, their aggression was vented mainly on the opposing fans, and seldom referees and players. Thus the spectacle on the field was secondary to facing up to and abusing fans across the 'no man's land' part of the terracing keeping them apart. For the more serious hooligans one of the main goals was to seize the 'end' of the opposing supporters: that is to say to attack or infiltrate the area usually behind the goal occupied by the opposition supporters and eject them from their 'turf'. Some such pursuits took on advance planning of a military nature, and by the late 1970s the various 'fighting firms' or 'service crews' were making a name for themselves: some, known as 'casuals' came from more affluent backgrounds and avoided police detection by hiding their regalia, travelling first-class to away matches and wearing designer clothing. Once installed in the enemy's territory they would then lash out and call for reinforcements.

By the late 1970s, racist and right-wing groups such as the National Front were attaching themselves to the hooligans, cashing in on the abuse of black players who were then beginning to appear regularly in English teams. Chelsea, West Ham and Leeds United, who were among the first teams to field black players, achieved an unenviable reputation for racism, to the horror of their more respectable fans, but few top teams were immune. Union Jacks appeared with Nazi swastikas, but it is unlikely that most hooligan groups had an ideology that went beyond football and their own primitive urges.

Solutions to the hooligan problem rained in on the authorities with the full force of political prejudice. To the Right the problem was one of permissiveness and all that was required was a return to the birch, national service, capital punishment or putting the animals in cages; to the Left it was a problem of unemployment and diminished choices caused by uncaring capitalists and politicians, and the solution was in the reorganization of society. In the meantime, the clubs and local authorities had to face up to the weekly or twice-weekly problem of gearing up for the arrival of away fans. Outside the ground this became a highly organized police operation, with supporters being met as they came off the trains and being held behind at the end so that they could be escorted back to the station. Inside the ground the fences went up, at Chelsea with the proposed added refinement of electrification – to the chagrin of the Chelsea chairman the local authorities denied the club the right to electrocute its fans. Police numbers increased from a mere one per thousand fans, as at the time of the Bolton disaster, to as many as 75 per thousand for the more notorious fixtures forty years later. Dotted around the ground and in cordons between rival fans, they became the impartial object of abuse by both sets of supporters. Eventually television monitors were installed and attempts made to ban all away fans. This latter proposal was taken up enthusiastically by the Thatcher government after Hillsborough, with a scheme for electronic membership cards to be made compulsory for all supporters. This ill-advised scheme, which won the support of few people associated with the game, was finally dropped as a consequence of the Taylor Report into the Hillsborough disaster.

One measure that worked well in Scotland after the pitched battle that followed the Celtic/Rangers Cup Final of 1980 met with much special pleading and was only considered in England after Heysel: the banning of alcohol. Many of the game's sponsors were breweries and the clubs themselves enjoyed significant income from the sale of beer and spirits, so resistance was strong. Whatever the effect on violent fans, the banning of alcohol made the stadiums of Scotland a bit more pleasant to be in as the rivers of urine ceased to trickle down the terracings.

The most commonly floated panacea, despite its failure at Coventry City, or even the Parc des Princes in Paris where Leeds fans ran amok in 1975 after some outrageous decisions by the referee in their game against Bayern Munich in 1975, is all-seated stadiums. Again, the clubs are faced with large bills to introduce such proposals, but in some cases take consolation in the hope that the poorer of their supporters might be priced out of the ground.

Certainly, it is the travelling fans who are behind most violence, whether in deliberately causing damage on their opponent's 'turf', or provoking a defensive reaction by the home supporters. From the earliest days, the British supporter was distinguished by his willingness to travel long distances and regularly to see his team play away from home. From the 1950s time, money and efficient transport made it even easier for the football fan to travel to away games. Special trains and coaches helped to develop a sense of solidarity and alcohol fed the worst passions. Local pride could easily be provoked by visitors from the north travelling south, or *vice versa*, or even travelling from one side of the city to the other. Some of the most spectacular confrontations, however, came from Scottish fans travelling into England, as they had done for decades. Latterly they came not so much with a robust sense of patriotism as with a carefully nurtured hatred of the English. One victim of the tartan hordes was the oldest annual international sporting fixture, the Scotland/England international: in 1985 it was played in Glasgow instead of London, and since it was last played in 1989 it has been discarded, the people of London no longer considering it worth the trouble it caused.

English fans were less interested in travelling north, and the few who did so to attend the 1989 international displayed a certain foolish courage, the test of which was denied only by the police. The English generally reserved their nationalism for visits to the continent, and with the rise of European football, and with basking in the Spanish sun taking over from paddling in the sea at Blackpool or Brighton, so football fans from Britain set out in their thousands to foreign parts to show the continentals the true meaning of ignorance.

Celtic fans left behind a good impression and enough stories to fill a book when they went to Lisbon in 1967 to win the European Cup, and performed even more admirably when they lost to Feyenoord of Holland in Milan in the final of that competition three years later. Rangers blotted their copy book in 1972 when their supporters took on Franco's police for trying to prevent them celebrating their Cup-winner's Cup victory over Moscow Dinamo in Barcelona. Thereafter Scotland's travelling fans were more often congratulated for their good behaviour on the continent. In Scotland itself the hooligan problem declined after 1980, and the horror of Heysel allowed Scottish fans to express a certain sanctimonious attitude towards the brother enemy south of the border.

English teams were more successful in Europe than their Scottish counterparts, but the record of their supporters was deplorable, as they ran up what John Williams described in 1986 as 'a grim checklist of locations and dates which charts the violent and destructive passage of the English football fan abroad: Rotterdam '74 and '83; Paris '75 and '84; Luxembourg '77 and '83; Turin '80; Oslo and Basle '81; Anderlecht and Copenhagen

'82; and Bruges '84' (*Off the Ball*). Such was their reputation for mindless violence that notably brutal police squads, such as the CRS in France and the *Policía Nacional* in Spain found themselves in the unusual situation of being praised by the locals as they laid into the visiting English with relish. In such circumstances, Heysel came not as a surprise, but as a natural conclusion.

Beyond Bradford and Brussels

It was easy in the 1970s and 1980s to see in hooliganism an 'English disease': despite the attempts by Dutch and German hooligans to emulate their cross-Channel counterparts, there was something peculiarly English, or British, about the islanders' propensity to wage war against other fans. Hooliganism on the continent was of a different nature, and there and in Latin America it was more likely to be sparked by an incident on the field, leading to pitch invasions, attacks on referees and players, or simply fights between fans, often with weapons. Moats, spectator fencing and riot police are a permanent monument to such problems. It was the behaviour of crowds in the inter-war period that gave rise to such precautionary measures, but little in the post-war period has indicated a change in attitude. And today, while many fences in Britain have come down after Hillsborough, they remain in place in most Latin countries.

The most serious disturbances have taken place in Latin America. It is there that the worst fan-related disaster took place, at Lima, Peru on 24 May 1964, in an Olympic qualifier between Peru and Argentina. With only a few minutes to go Argentina were winning 0–1, when the home team scored a goal which was disallowed by the Uruguayan referee. A few spectators scaled the perimeter fencing to persuade him to change his mind, and they were followed by others, causing the referee to end the game. The police then went on to attack the fans, firing teargas and even bullets into the crowd and setting dogs on them. In the ensuing panic 318 people lost their lives and more than 500 were injured in rioting that continued for hours outside the ground. A state of emergency had to be declared. Most of the dead were killed in the crush when locked exit doors prevented them fleeing the police. Demonstrations followed, against the police and against the government, with serious clashes between police and students at the university. On 26 May most of the dead were buried in a mass funeral, and along with demands that respect be shown to the dead appeals were made that the game be replayed.

South America's next major disaster came at the end of a River Plate/ Boca Juniors derby in Buenos Aires in 1968, when celebrating fans dropped lighted papers on those below them, setting off a panic that led to

74 deaths when stampeding fans found the exit gates locked. In a variation of such practices from the wealthier spectators, drunken fans urinating from the stands at a Deportiva Cali/Club América game in Cali, Colombia in late 1982 set off a stampede that resulted in 22 deaths and over 100 injuries. A year earlier, at Ibague in Colombia, 18 were killed and 45 injured when a wall collapsed during a game between home team Deportiva Tolima and Deportiva Cali.

In Mexico in 1985, sandwiched between the Bradford and Heysel disasters, ten fans were killed in a crush in Mexico City. On 5 June 1991 ten fans died and 128 were injured in street violence in Santiago following the victory of Colo Colo against defending champions Olímpia of Paraguay in the South America Club Cup. None of this was directed against rival fans. Several South American teams have died in air crashes, which in itself is hardly surprising given that air is often the only way of conveniently covering some of the vast distances over difficult terrain. One of these crashes, however, that which caused the destruction of the Alianza of Peru team in December 1987 was thought to have been caused by a terrorist bomb.

Alongside these major tragedies came regular reports of deaths on a smaller scale. As Colombia geared up to host the 1986 World Cup, one incident among others that lost them that honour was when police broke up a pitch invasion by firing on the crowd, killing two, including a young boy shot in the back. Two men were beaten to death and others were taken to hospital in a serious condition. In August 1990 FIFA declared that all Colombia's national and club matches against foreign opponents be played outside Colombia, because the safety of the officials could not be guaranteed: the drug bosses were involved in football teams, for gambling and money-laundering purposes, and had simple ways of dealing with those who crossed their path. In Argentina in the Videla years, the police were accused of encouraging violence on the field and in the stadium as a form of political safety valve. In Brazil police were said to have given up arresting violent fans because the judges let them off too lightly, while in Chile the police were accused of acting with too much ferocity towards violent fans. A feature of many of these incidents in South America is the participation of coaches and managers, joining the players in brawls and attacks on referees. During a radio debate in Brazil in late 1991, high-ranking officials appearing before a national audience threatened to kill each other, but only got so far as throwing chairs.

In Europe the 'Latin temperament' was often given as the reason for the wild antics particularly of Italian fans, whose anger was as likely to be turned on their own team as on their opponents or referees. In the mid-1950s there were several incidents involving fans and attacks on referees, and visiting supporters have often had to complain of knife attacks, but there have been no major tragedies: indeed, more workers were killed in the frantic rush to prepare stadiums for Italia 1990 than in all football-related violence there. In Spain and Portugal there have been no major catastrophes.

France's worst tragedy came in May 1992, when a temporary stand at the Furiani stadium in Bastia, Corsica, erected to accommodate the demand for the semi-final game in the French Cup between the local team and Marseille, collapsed shortly before the game began: fourteen were killed, over 1300 injured. The game was put off and players vowed not to continue in the competition for that year. There was no question of hooliganism.

In Greece violence between fans is common, and may have taken a turn for the worse after the introduction of open professionalism in 1979: derby games between Olympiakos and AEK were even banished to the island of Rhodes to help combat this problem. Again, however, it was a crush against locked doors that had the most serious consequences. This was on 8 February 1981, when fans surging towards an exit at an Olympiakos/AEK derby in the Stadio Karaiskaki, Piraeus, found the exit closed. Twenty-one young Olympiakos supporters were crushed to death.

When Greeks play Turks some form of violence can be expected, and the appropriate measures are taken in advance, with the military backing up the police. In Turkey itself the treatment of Kurds and the perceived grievances of other minorities has given rise to provincial tensions that frequently threaten to break out in violence. This was behind the worst riot in Turkish football, although the spark was a simple incident in the game between the two teams of the neighbouring provinces, Kayseri Spor and Sivas Spor, in September 1967. A Kayseri player was ordered off for continual foul play, but a shower of stones and verbal abuse from the home fans convinced the referee that he should change his mind. This incensed the reported 3–5000 visiting fans from Sivas, and fighting with knives and broken bottles broke out, pistols were fired and there was panic on the way to the exits. Reports claimed 40 to 44 were killed, with 600 injured in fighting which continued for two hours around the ground before police with fixed bayonets restored order. Civil war threatened to break out between the two provinces, and the army was drawn up along the border. In Sivas businesses belonging to people from Kayseri were picked out for retaliation, and cars with Kayseri number plates were attacked.

Elsewhere in Europe, in the Balkan powder keg, the bitter rivalry of Croat and Slav found expression on the sports field. The wonder of the Yugoslav game was that despite the deadly hatreds of Serbs, Croatians and other ethnic minorities, football not only continued, but produced some of Europe's finest teams, at club and national level. Only now has civil war caught up with them, and football stadiums have been used to store the dead, and players have been sold to earn money to buy weapons. Despite all this, one of the worst riots in recent times had nothing to do with ethnic differences: on 7 March 1992 rival fans at a Pelister Bitola vs. Vardar Skopje brought the game to an end at half-time: both teams were due to join the new Macedonian League.

In northern Europe, where politics are usually more stable, the Dutch and the Germans caught severe doses of the 'English disease'. The behaviour of these hooligans continued throughout the 1980s with increasing ferocity as well as sheer lunacy as individuals sought in the anonymity of the crowd to vent their pathological hatreds. Dutch fans throwing home-made bombs introduced a novel element. All of this led to justifiable fears of a major confrontation between the English, Dutch and German fans at the European Championships held in West Germany in 1988. In the event, the Dutch found more fun in watching their team win the competition, and despite the attempts by some reporters, especially from television, to get fans to live up to their reputations, the sensation seekers were disappointed. There was massive damage in Düsseldorf when organized German hooligans outflanked the otherwise vigilant police and attacked some destitute English followers congregated around the railway station. There were other incidents, often involving proto-fascists among the English and the Germans, but devout English patriotism won over the sort of Anglo-German union so desired by Hitler before he engaged in his European rampages.

In the Soviet Union, evidence of spectator violence could be found in the ring of soldiers occupying the front row seats of Soviet stadiums, a precaution which followed a riot at Leningrad in 1937. In pre-glasnost days disasters were kept secret. Thus it is less than surprising that news of two of the world's worst sports disasters was kept under wraps for years. The first was in 1979 when seventeen players and officials of the Uzbekistan first division side, Pakhtakor Tashkent, on their way to a league match in Minsk, died with 237 others in a mid-air collision with another plane. The match was cancelled, but all the public knew of it was in a short note, buried on the inside pages, that the game had been postponed. The other took place at the Lenin Stadium in Moscow, on 30 October 1982, when more than sixty people met their deaths in an accident similar to the 1971 Ibrox disaster. The match was a UEFA Cup game between Spartak Moscow and Haarlem of Holland. It seems that spectators were leaving the ground with Spartak leading 1–0, when another goal encouraged them to go back, some of them slipped in the treacherously icy conditions, and others fell over them. Seven years would elapse before it was reported in the Soviet press: *Sovietsky Sport* claimed that the official in charge of the exit gates was found guilty of negligence and sent to a labour camp for 18 months: the stadium managers were acquitted.

The nation that gave the world the Tiananmen massacre has been unable to prevent hooliganism. The worst incident was when China was eliminated by Hong Kong from the World Cup in May 1985. Some of its long-suffering citizens took the chance to vent their frustration in riots that were picked up with delight by the western press, to titillate their anti-Communist and anti-soccer readers. Since China was host to the Under-17 World Youth championship that year the government immediately embarked on a good behaviour campaign, with crowds awarded points for orderliness and politeness towards their opponents and punishments for being rude. Anti-social behaviour, like jeering in unison, throwing objects on the field and letting off firecrackers were punished with points being deducted. Damage to property, littering and spitting were also punished in this way.

In the 'third world' countries the toll of deaths at football matches makes bleak reading. Rival fans have killed each other, and been killed by police, but the vast majority of deaths have come from overcrowding in inadequate facilities and bungled administration. At the Nepal national stadium on 12 March 1988 at least ninety-three people were trampled to death and over one hundred injured when thousands of fans fleeing a hail storm came up against locked exit doors, which the police refused to open without the proper authority. In Libya a few days earlier knife-wielding fans set off a panic in which twenty died when part of the stand collapsed at a Libya vs. Malta match in Tripoli. The game was continued, to the consternation of the players, until an ambulance came speeding on to the pitch with its siren blaring. In Cairo in 1974 more than forty people were killed in a panic with a twist to the usual tale. Egypt were due to play Dukla Prague in the 100,000 capacity Nasser Stadium, when ticket holders were told at the last moment that the game would be held in the much smaller Zamalek Stadium instead, allegedly for their 'greater comfort'. In the rush of ticket holders to get into the ground while there was still room, a stampede developed with tragic results. The worst riot in black Africa came in 1980 when the lights failed at a match between the Nigerian teams the Bendel Insurance and Canon; but the worst death tolls have been in travel to games in crowded transport: fifteen players were drowned crossing Lake Victoria for a local match in Kenya in 1985, and in 1980 in Zambia nine players and officials were killed and thirteen seriously injured when their mini-bus crashed on the way home from a game.

From elsewhere in Africa came stories of spectators killed in crushes, or killing each other, or being killed by government troops: in Cameroon on 31 October 1976, the President, who was watching the game on television, sent in his paratroopers by helicopter to break up a riot that broke out during a World Cup qualifying game against Congo. This began when the Congo goalkeeper attacked the Gambian referee for awarding Cameroon a penalty, and was joined in his outrage by the spectators. Two people were killed by the troops. In South Africa, on 13 January 1991, more than forty people were killed and more than fifty injured when fighting broke out at a pre-season friendly between Kaizer Chiefs and Orlando Pirates, at the Ernest Oppenheimer Stadium. A referee's decision sparked the trouble, and knives were waved and bottles thrown, but the deaths came when panicking spectators were crushed against a spectator fence.

The melancholy tally could be continued, and to it could be added innumerable tales of tragedies in which football was incidental, like the landslide in Libreville, Gabon, during a Gabon/Congo–Brazzaville international where nine were killed and thirty injured. More often it has been merely a catalyst, as in celebrations that went wrong, of drunks who fell off balconies toasting their team's triumphs on television or traffic accidents due to the lifting of normal restraints in post-match euphoria. Or suicides after defeat. And always the deaths from heart attacks from people watching big games, live or on television, and before that while listening to the radio. Again there are those simply linked to personal problems, like the French woman who shot her husband because he would not answer her questions while he was watching the World Cup; on a larger scale there are deaths related to vendettas, like the Karen insurgents in Burma, still resisting the attempts of the government to assimilate them into the new Burmese society, who on one occasion invited rivals from a government faction to a football match in 1955 and then massacred them.

Mirror or motivater?

Football, like sport in general, can bring out the best and the worst in its followers and participants. That some people are happier with hate than love is not football's fault. It was Liverpool fans who taunted Manchester United fans with the chants, referring to the 1958 Munich disaster, 'Who's that lying on the runway?' But in Italy Torino fans congratulated Liverpool on the 39 Juventus fans they were said to have killed at the Heysel, while in Africa at a game in Nigeria between the national team and Ethiopia in a World Cup qualifier, the home support threw bread on to the pitch to mock the Ethiopians; in the return match the Nigerians were pelted with missiles and then attacked when they were said to have insulted the crowd by making begging gestures, pointing to their mouths and rubbing their stomachs. This is a sickness of the soul that knows no national boundaries and is unrelated to any particular sport.

In societies where violence is endemic and/or where ethnic groups live under what they consider to be oppression or injustice, it would be unreal to expect them to play soccer like gentlemen. In countries where basic facilities for daily living are lacking, the failure of football grounds to safely accommodate the tens of thousands who want to watch the game might be a cause for alarm, but not surprise.

What surely is a cause for both alarm and surprise, is that in the country that gave the world the game, the first country to become fully industrialized and the country that once prided itself on its democratic traditions, there have been more deaths at football matches than in any other except Peru. To this statistical fact can be added the subjective judgment that it has also provided the most disreputable football followers.

Taken together, the deaths from tragedies and riots at soccer matches throughout the world must exceed those at all other sports combined. The incidences of spectator violence with less drastic consequences are equally notorious. This has led, in countries where soccer is a minor sport, in the United States and Australia, for example, to the game itself being blamed for the violence. The Argentine Juan José Sebreli (*Futbol y masas*) has also claimed, from isolated examples of football violence in South America, Europe and then England, that the Latin violence was merely the early seed 'of an irresistible tendency in football.' Like Gerhard Vinnai in *Fussball-sport als Ideologie* – translated into several languages – Sebreli is a sociologist with more interest in fashionable theories than serious analysis.

In the non-soccer countries pundits point to the low scoring, and claim that it leads to boredom, relieved presumably by the fans making their own entertainment; on the other hand, they claim that because soccer is non-violent it lacks the catharsis of body contact sports and so the fans have to let off steam by attacking the players, the referee or each other. More reasonably, it can be agreed that soccer is a simple and open game, in which legal or illegal violence is difficult to disguise, and because of its low scoring nature the referee's decision as regards off-side or a penalty is often more vital than in other codes. But this still does not explain why players should brawl, spectators invade the field or rival fans attack each other. Kyle Rote Jr., one of America's first home-grown soccer heroes, in his otherwise sensible *Complete Book of Soccer*, puts forward the simple and simplistic view that soccer fans had such an obsession with the game, that under 'its spell, reasonable men could turn into savages.'

Soccer is not unique in the violence it has attracted. In French rugby in the 1920s and into the 1930s the fighting among players and attacks by spectators on referees were so bad that the British associations refused to play there. Cricket in India and the West Indies has had its riots, and the bloodiest encounter at the 1956 Olympics in Melbourne was in the water polo, when the Soviet Union played Hungary shortly after the suppression of the Hungarian uprising. Ice hockey games have known deaths in the rink and riots in the stadiums. In the United States, the apparent absence of violence around sporting fixtures is in marked contrast to the violence in daily life. Comparisons with the States in regard to violence and to sport are almost pointless: its sport culture is like no other on earth, and its violence in daily life is also related to peculiarly American developments. This has a natural effect on even its best sports analysts when they comment on soccer violence. During its coverage of Italia 1990 the esteemed *Sports Illustrated* reported an attack by English on Dutch supporters which resulted in minor property damage and ten people being hospitalized, with the comment that only in soccer 'could such an ugly scene qualify as relatively good news' (25 June 1990). In the same issue, William Oscar Johnson reported the story of the celebration of the Detroit Pistons' second straight NBA title in which eight people were killed 'in a night of madness brought on by the success of the local professional basketball team.' A leading investigator concluded that those who died would have done so in any case, since 'When your time is up, your time is up'. The celebrations of the Pistons' supporters was far from a one-off event, and other tales could be told of rape, looting and pillage – cheered on by joyous fans – in other 'celebratory' disorders after basketball or American football games. The 'celebratory' nature of these disturbances has to be emphasized, however, and much of the trouble is caused by thugs taking advantage of the situation. Most soccer related violence involves people who are deeply involved in the game.

Violence surrounding other sporting events or those in other countries in no way alters the reality of the violence and deaths that have been associated with soccer. None of it, however, tells us anything about the game, only about the people who play it and watch it. The popularity of soccer is such that it far surpasses all other sports. Its popularity is based on its simplicity, its economic democracy, and hence its appeal to the poor, the illiterate, the working-classes: people who are more likely to settle their difference and express their grievances with fisticuffs rather than through lawyers and letters to the editor.

The popularity of soccer is such that it is spread throughout a variety of cultures, many of which are violent in themselves, and more so when they come into contact with each other. Such political, religious, ethnic and other hostilities cannot be forgotten in a game of football. Soccer is played where governments rule with little sense of justice towards their people, and so notions of Fair Play in daily life are as irrelevant as Fair Play on the football field. In Britain, the game's worst excesses came in the 1980s, during the decade of rule by a government that preached that 'greed is good'.

The violence at soccer matches has less to do with the game than with the political and social tensions and prejudices in which it is played. Those who like to claim that there is something in the game itself that inspires its followers to commit terrible acts of savagery have to explain why the game as played in Great Britain between about 1920 and 1960 was watched by tens of millions of people in an atmosphere as close to sporting perfection as could be expected.

The people's game?

Football more than any other sport is 'The people's game'. This is not to say that ordinary folks own and control it – they have never done that – but rather that they have supplied the vast majority of its players and those who follow the game, week in week out. In the 1980s increasingly profit-oriented directors sought personal wealth out of what in many cases had previously been a spread of family shares; private executive boxes came to take up the space often occupied by standing spectators; and players themselves enjoyed salaries that lifted them well beyond the economic class they had come from. The idea that clubs belonged to the people was becoming hard to sustain, but it was never given up. Even when the English game was at its nadir, in 1985, came two related movements that showed that some followers of the game in Britain were not prepared to let it fall into the hands of its would-be destroyers: not just the hooligans on the terracing, but those among the directors and in the gutter press. The first of these was the Football Supporters' Association, founded in August 1985, in direct response to Heysel. The other, a sort of media adjunct to the FSA, was the fanzine movement, a spontaneous blossoming of publications put out by fans concerned about the direction the game was taking, and fed up with the banal fare served up in the official club magazines and the sensationalism of the tabloid press.

The Football Supporters' Association is a modern version of the attempts through the years of ordinary supporters to keep in touch with their club and feel that they were part of it. Unlike previous supporters' clubs, the FSA was an active body unwilling to sit back and do what it was told. Such was its success that it was granted legal representation during the Taylor Inquiry into the Hillsborough disaster. In this fight-back by the fans, Britain showed itself once more in a leadership role.

As early as the 1880s fans had gone to extraordinary lengths to follow their club, and before the turn of the century some had organized themselves into associations to follow their team to away games. Among the first were Celtic in Glasgow, who made deals with the club on season tickets, travelled to the games on horse-drawn brakes, later motor-driven coaches usually with a large banner depicting one of their heroes and a bugler announcing to all in the vicinity that they were loyal followers of the club. They would also organize social evenings and invite players along.

From the earliest days, in addition to what they paid through the gate, supporters had raised money to help their team. This reached such embarrassing proportions in some cases, especially in the 1930s, and only among the smaller clubs, that delegates from the supporters' club were given representation on the board. In the 1960s, as spectators in Britain no longer saw it as inevitable that the only way to follow the team was from a windy and rain-swept terracing, the supporters themselves often helped to improve amenities and build social clubs at their own expense on the club's premises. On the continent and South America many football teams actually were 'clubs', open to any member who could afford the membership fee. Unlike Britain, too, many of the best grounds in Europe were in municipal hands, leased out to the football club. More typically in Britain the club owned its own premises. Thus when the 'greed is good' philosophy started to predominate from the 1960s the reality of this private ownership showed its more callous side, as supporters' clubs were looked on as a mere commodity.

In the mid-1960s, on the basis of a 'gentleman's agreement', Coventry City supporters used their own money and voluntary labour to build a social club on the club's premises, only to be told after spending nearly £30,000 that they had no rights to it. A similar fate met Ipswich Town supporters, who spent even more time and money at their club's ground, only to be told in 1967 that a new supporters' club had been formed and they were no longer wanted. There were many other similar cases, most notably at Manchester United, where David Smith, who had built up the Manchester United Supporters' Club into a respected and profitably run organization, was dismissed in 1987 because he stood in the way of the club's commercial expansion. For Smith it was the last act in the 'betrayal of a legend' that went back to the days of Matt Busby. In the world of the eighties loyalty and goodwill meant nothing unless it could be transmuted into cold cash. Few took notice of the 'Millwall in the Community' project which brought club and supporters together and resulted in a remarkable turnaround in the behaviour of the Millwall supporters.

With the apparent subsiding of hooliganism on the part of the British fan, and with improvements in technology, the idea first raised by Ray Sonin in 1951 of an international supporters' club could perhaps still be realized. At Italia 1990 the English FSA provided an alternative source of information for fans, and played a big role in the English fans' relatively trouble-free World Cup. By then the best examples of good behaviour came from the Danish fans known as the 'roligans', from the Danish word, 'rolig' for 'laughter'. Beginning about 1985, Danish supporters came to games in fancy dress, drowned out their more obnoxious fans with their own brand of humour, and got pleasantly drunk. In 1986 they formed themselves into the Danish Roligans Association, with 1100 members,

45% of whom were women. Sponsored by the Carlsberg Brewery and the Danish Dairy Industry they brought laughter even into defeat, and at the 1988 European Championship insisted on singing the alternative national anthem rather than the more militant official one, thus entering into unofficial competition with the German band playing under instructions. In response to the anti-Turkish riots of late 1992, German and Italian clubs made their opinion on racism clear. In Germany shirt advertising was replaced by the slogan: 'My friend is a foreigner', while in Italy on that same day, 12 December 1992, banners were paraded around the grounds declaring war on racism and proclaiming that fans should unite against it.

Attempts to get the clubs to accept greater social responsibility were vigorously pursued in the fanzines, the first of which appeared in 1985. These publications, initially very amateur in their production, were produced by supporters frustrated or angry at the way they had been kept at arm's length by clubs that seemed to be turning their backs on the traditional supporters. Unable to express their views through the official organs of the club, because most of them were vitriolic in their criticism of the directors, and aware that the daily press was too tied to the clubs to be overly critical, these fans, taking advantage of cheaper photocopying and eventually desk-top publishing, founded their own organs of opinion. There had been unofficial supporters' papers back in the 1960s, such as *The Shamrock* put out by dissident Celtic supporters, and from 1972 to 1976, *Foul* magazine was produced on the presses of *Private Eye* as a deliberate spoof on such saccharine publications as *Goal* and *Shoot*. The more immediate origins of the fanzines, however, were in the music fanzines of the early 1980s.

The first specifically football fanzine was *Off the Ball*, whose first numbers in 1985 were wildly erratic in quality; hardly surprising in that it was open to the expression of any opinion. From a mere handful in the first two years, the fanzines burgeoned into a full flowering with over ninety by the end of 1988, and double this number within five months. By 1990 it was calculated that two hundred fanzines were selling a million copies. By then just about every team in the English and Scottish leagues had their own fanzine, some as many as four. Many sold only a few dozen copies, but one of the first, *When Saturday Comes*, was selling more than 17,000, a much more professional publication than the first roughly photocopied pages put out by Mike Ticher in 1985. *When Saturday Comes* was committed to the game as a whole, and despite its commercial success it has not lost its democratic edge. Like the FSA it has appealed to the best in spectators, and organized trips to Albania to see the England team and to Dakar in 1992 to see the African Nations' Cup finals. In Scotland *The Absolute Game* covers the Scottish scene, while Glasgow Celtic's *Not the View* – a direct shot at the official *Celtic View* – quickly became the best selling fanzine in

Britain with sales of over 11,000. *Born Kicking* is a fanzine brought out by women for women. The organ of the FSA suitably sums up the spirit of the fanzine movement: *Reclaim the game*. Other sports have taken up the idea, which has also spread abroad.

Whether football clubs belong to the fans, the local community or are a commercial proposition is a debate that is as old as the game. Clearly the clubs are private concerns, but historically they have grown with the fans and would be nothing without them. Today the players acknowledge the presence of their supporters in a way that was unknown in the past, at least in Britain, although this could be an attempt to bridge the class gap that exists now as it never did before. To the management, the supporters are little more than a source of revenue and vocal encouragement for the team, and an embarrassment when they caused trouble. Nowhere is the insult to the ordinary fan more starkly evident than in the executive boxes, where people often with little interest in the game can improve their business contacts in return for a fat fee to the club. Directors have always used clubs for such purposes, but in other days it was a small recompense for the money they put into the club with no financial return. And apart from a good position in the stand, softer seats and a roof over their heads, they watched the game in the same atmosphere as those crushed in behind the goals. These who need to watch football behind glass with room service and a private television set should hire a room in a hotel and watch the game from there.

The relationship between the club and profit-oriented directors has been brought dramatically into focus in recent years, and has been given further emphasis by the selection of the United States to host the 1994 World Cup. Off the field the competition is shaping up to see what happens to the 'people's game' in the hands of the unashamed champion of sport for commerce's sake. In the meantime, in Asia and Africa, the game was flourishing as never before, so that more than ever it will be the world as much as the world of football, that will be on display in the United States in 1994.

Endnotes

The best analyses of the hooliganism phenomenon are in the various works of the sociologists from the University of Leicester, funded by the Sir Norman Chester Centre for Football Research. Of their many works the most thorough is:

Eric Dunning, Patrick Murphy and John Williams, *The Roots of Football Hooliganism. An Historical and Sociological Study*, Routledge and Kegan Paul, London and New York, 1988.

Their most recent work, which should be consulted for a more detailed bibliography, and from which I have borrowed some contemporary newspaper references, is:

Patrick Murphy, John Williams and Eric Dunning, *Football on Trial. Spectator violence and development in the football world*, Routledge, London and New York, 1990.

For an excellent participant observer study see:

John Williams, Eric Dunning and Patrick Murphy, *Hooligans Abroad. The behaviour and control of English fans in continental Europe*, Routledge and Kegan Paul, London, 1984. Second edition, 1989.

Williams and Wagg, *British Football and Social Change* and
Lanfranchi, *Il calcio e il suo pubblico*

are of particular use for this chapter. See especially the articles by Rogan Taylor, Stephen Redhead and John Williams in Williams and Wagg. For a full account of the Football Supporters' Association, see

Rogan Taylor, *Football and its Fans. Supporters and their relations with the game, 1885–1985*, Leicester University Press, Leicester, 1992.

On Manchester United and its supporters, see

Michael Crick and David Smith, *Manchester United. The Betrayal of a Legend*, Pelham Books, London, 1989.

Phil Shaw, *Whose game is it anyway? The book of the football fanzines*, Argus Books, Hemel Hempstead, 1989,

is a compilation of extracts from the best of the fanzines, with a short but informative introduction.

An American perspective on hooliganism is in

Bill Buford, *Among the Thugs*, Secker and Warburg, London, 1991

while for a delightful set of confessions from an individual fan bitten by the football bug

Nick Hornby, *Fever Pitch: a fan's life*, Gollancz, London, 1992,

is one of the best books written on football.

CHAPTER EIGHT

Third World, New World

The World Cup final of 1974 was an all-European affair, won by host nation West Germany against the Netherlands in a game controlled by an English referee. Yet off the field new forces were transforming soccer into a truly global game. Just a few weeks before the World Cup the nations of the 'third world' had exercised their democratic rights to elect a President of FIFA who was committed to promoting the game in their countries. Ironically, the transfer of power away from its European, and particularly Anglo, influence, came at a time when Europe itself was about to take an unhealthy grip on the field of play, attracting to its domestic leagues, particularly in Italy and Spain, the cream of world soccer talent: not only from Latin America but parts of the world not hitherto known for their soccer, above all from Africa.

It was at this time, too, that the headquarters of the world's two great sporting empires, FIFA and the International Olympic Committee, were transformed from modest premises in Zurich and Lausanne into luxurious offices as befits the world's most important international sporting bodies. This transition from modesty to grandeur came during the presidency of two men whose backgrounds were in marked contrast to those of their predecessors. In 1974, Jean Marie Faustin Godefroid Havelange, better known as João Havelange, Olympic representative for Brazil in swimming in 1936 and water polo in 1952, president of the Brazilian FA, recipient of a multitude of titles, and multi-millionaire businessman, replaced Stanley Rous, one time schoolteacher, esteemed referee and long-time secretary of the FA, as president of FIFA; in 1980, Juan Antonio Samaranch, faithful follower of Franco then ambassador to the Soviet Union after the dictator's death, replaced the Irish journalist Lord Killanin as president of the IOC.

Behind the presidential success of the two men lay the business and political acumen of Horst Dassler, owner of the Adidas sporting goods empire, which he had inherited from his father, Adolph, better known as Adi. Horst also inherited the famous 'shoe war' that began in 1948 when his uncle broke from Adi Dassler to found the rival Puma company. Adidas supplied shoes for runners at the Nazi Olympics in 1936, boots for the Wehrmacht in the Second World War, and after 1948 Puma and Adidas tried to outdo each other in giving away footwear and other accessories to high profile sports people: to footballers at the 1954 World Cup in Switzerland, but above all to Olympic athletes, provoking a near crisis at

Mexico in 1968 for the gifts and contracts they offered amateur athletes. Horst effectively won the 'shoe war' with his success in establishing the power bases of Havelange and Samaranch: in return his company won rights to the world's great sports festivals. Adidas now have the contract as sole suppliers of sporting apparel and equipment for the World Cup which will take them into the next century.

Dassler's deal with FIFA came after the election of Havelange in 1974, when the challenger, expecting an easy victory, was almost beaten by the influence wielded by Dassler on behalf of Rous. Shrewdly, the new president brought Dassler into his own camp. Dassler then showed Havelange how to finance the promises he had made to the third world countries as part of his election platform: in essence by winning over Coca-Cola to a massive sponsorship deal that financed the new world youth tournaments introduced by FIFA to help the under-developed football countries. Dassler then went on to show Samaranch how to convert the five rings of Olympic peace and purity into commercial gold, by engaging in a similar sponsorship programme offering exclusive use of the sports world's best known logo to selected multi-nationals.

Samaranch is Spanish, Havelange Brazilian, and Dassler, who died of cancer in 1987, was German. All of them shared a dislike of the 'anglos' and their pre-eminence in the sporting world. But they were also men whose time had come. Joao Havelange became president of FIFA after canvassing far and wide to win the support of the newly emerging nations of Asia and Africa, with promises of improved facilities, better coaching and medical services, the promotion of junior football and additional places in the World Cup. More immediate benefits were said to have been offered to delegates voting for the new president, and according to Keith Botsford in an investigative article in *The Sunday Times* of April 1974 'small brown envelopes' were said to have been pressed 'into large black hands.' However that may be, Rous's time was up: despite his contributions to the game at every level, by the 1970s he was out of his depth, a man whose old-world values were out of place in the post-colonial world.

Global expansion

In Asia after 1945, and in Africa from 1960, most of the countries that had been under colonial domination opted for independence, and at the same time as they sought to build their new constitutions they applied for membership of FIFA. In the 1970s the countries of the Middle East suddenly showed that they were a force to be taken note of: setting off a panic in many capitalist countries by suddenly lifting the price of crude oil in 1973, and upsetting the traditional soccer market by dipping into the apparently bottomless buckets of oil money to attract star football players and coaches with Aladdin-like contracts. Together with the Communist bloc countries, the new football powers brought approaches to the game that were beyond the ken of old time colonial administrators.

In the mid-1950s FIFA had eighty affiliated members, only eighteen of whom were from Asia and five from Africa; two decades later, when membership had almost doubled, to one hundred and forty-one; there were thirty-nine countries from Africa (including suspended members South Africa and Rhodesia) and thirty-three from Asia; by 1990 there were one hundred and sixty-six member nations, forty-eight from Africa and thirty-six from Asia. By then soccer was represented in every part of the globe, with FIFA presiding over six regional confederations. The first of these had been formed in South America in 1916 (CONMEBOL), the others came much later, Europe not forming its UEFA until 1954. In that same year the Asian Football Confederation (AFC) was formed, and three years later the Confédération Africaine de Football (CAF). The north and central American powers finally came together to form CONCACAF in 1961, and four years later the last outposts of the football world were brought under the international umbrella when the islands of Oceania agreed to federate in 1965–66.

The biggest of these confederations, by far, is Asia, where nearly fifty-four million players were registered with FIFA in 1990. But it is Africa, with its five million registered players, that has made the soccer world sit up and take notice: African players are present in many of Europe's best teams, and it was the brilliance of the Cameroon team in Italia 1990 that effectively gained the African nations an extra place in the World Cup to be held in the United States in 1994. Asian nations and Asian players, despite their numbers, have yet to make a major impact on the world scene.

The growth of the game in Asia and Africa has seen the construction of stadiums to accommodate the crowds and the ruling vanity. In 1991, according to FIFA figures, which seem to be exaggerated, and are subject to constant change as seating takes over from standing room, Brazil was still the home of monster stadiums, and the Maracana, despite being somewhat dilapidated and reduced to a capacity of 165,000, is still the largest in the world. Four other stadiums in Brazil have capacities of over 115,000. Second to the Maracana in world terms, however, and again according to FIFA figures for 1991, is the Rungnado Stadium in Pyongyan, North Korea, which holds 150,000; the fourth biggest, with 120,000, is in Indonesia, the Senayan Main Stadium in Djakarta. The biggest stadiums in Africa are in Egypt, where the Nasser Stadium in Cairo holds 100,000. The stadium of Arab Contractors, however, sliced out of a mountain by the construction company owned by the man who founded the team in the mid-1970s, millionaire entrepreneur Osman Ahmed

Osman, is said to hold 120,000. After Korea and Indonesia, the two biggest stadiums in Asia are in India, the Corporation in Calicur and the Eden Garden in Calcutta; the biggest stadium among the Middle-Eastern countries, Tehran's Azadi Football Stadium, also holds 100,000, although there were said to be 130,000 present in 1978 when Iran qualified for the World Cup in Argentina. Most splendid of all, although it has a capacity of only 75,000, restricted to men only, is the futuristic King Fahd Stadium in Riyadh, Saudi Arabia. These stadiums were not always built solely for soccer, but it is soccer that is most likely to fill them.

The impact of the Afro-Asian nations was not to the liking of some European commentators, and when they were granted an extra place each for the 1982 World Cup FIFA was accused of giving in to clamorous voices out of tune with their footballing ability: sixteen teams from Africa and Asia withdrew from the 1966 World Cup because they were awarded only one place between them (and Oceania): this was increased to two in 1970. Havelange promised to double this, and did so by having the finals of the World Cup enlarged from a comfortable 16 teams easily divided by four, into a cumbersome 24 that resulted in a crowded fixture lists. Havelange was also said to have called in a political favour from Samaranch to bring about this change. Havelange used his influence with third world members of the IOC to get Samaranch elected as its president, and in turn Samaranch was said to have suggested to the Spanish organisers of the 1982 World Cup that they increase the number of participants.

By then Havelange had gone a long way towards fulfilling another of his promises: to promote the game in under-developed countries. However dubious the role of Dassler in this, and whatever the fears about commercial intrusion, the partnership of Coca-Cola and FIFA in the expansion of various world competitions outside the World Cup and the Olympic Games has been a spectacular success. There had been many regional competitions under the control of their particular confederation long before this, of course, but the age of jet travel and instant communication by phone, fax and satellite meant that these could be expanded to a worldwide basis.

The first international soccer competition outside the major nations was held in Asia in 1913, as part of the first Far East Championship Games organized by the Philippines. Japan and China were the other two main participants, occasionally joined by the Dutch East Indies. These games were held every two years until 1934, when tensions between China and Japan were close to breaking point. Soccer was also part of the first continent-wide sporting gathering at the Asian Games held in New Delhi in 1951, and thereafter on a quadrennial basis from 1954. The first purely soccer competition in Asia on a continental basis was the Asian Cup, held in Hong Kong and won by South Korea in 1956. It is played every four years, with a regional group deciding which countries (four, later eight) should proceed to the finals, but it has never been without its political problems. The Asian Champions' Cup competition for club teams had an even more troubled history. It got under way in 1966–67, but was plagued with problems of distance and politics, as well as a comparative lack of enthusiasm in Asia for club as against national or provincial teams, and was suspended between 1972 and 1985. From 1959 a particularly successful Asian Youth Cup was held every year until 1980 when it became biennial. Some of the most successful competitions in Asia have been organized on a regional basis, in Seoul, Bangkok and Kuala Lumpur in particular, with invitations extended to teams from other parts of the world.

In the Middle East, which for FIFA purposes is included in the Asian confederation, there have been a host of Gulf, Arab and other club and national competitions. Most recently Saudi Arabia has staked a claim to be the venue for a regular Inter-continental nations' cup for the champion nations of each confederation. It is possible that a new confederation will have to be formed to include the Middle East countries and those of the former Soviet Union that now fall into the Asian sphere. The AFC could then be reduced to a more manageable size.

The African nations have not been without their problems of politics and distance, but under a powerful controlling body, the Confederation of African Football, (CAF) a series of continental competitions for clubs and nations, as well as a host of regional competitions, have reflected the passion for the game throughout Africa.

By contrast, the Oceania Football Confederation is something of an anomaly, with its members, usually island nations, scattered throughout the Pacific Ocean. Its first members, Australia, New Zealand, Fiji and Papua New Guinea were small fry on the world scene, while the additions since then, countries like Solomon Islands, Tahiti, Vanuatu and Western Samoa, are even smaller fry. Smaller fry still, as Paul Moon has shown in his remarkable coverage of the continent, play the game on the islands and atolls of the South Pacific without becoming members of FIFA. Australia, easy prey for the sharks of the larger confederations, have usually been too strong to play in the regional competitions of the Pacific, and have not always maintained their membership of the OFC.

Stanley Rous had been one of the first to encourage youth football, and had shown a paternalistic interest in 'colonial' countries. But it was under Havelange that such competitions were introduced on a worldwide basis with a deliberate bias towards countries outside the European and South American confederations. Many of the regional competitions were given a new lease of life in this way as they acted as a qualifier for the world cups. Havelange's first chance to deliver on the promises that secured his election was when he inaugurated, with the sponsorship of Coca-Cola, the first

World Youth Cup, for players under twenty years old. The first tournament was held in Tunisia in 1977, the second in Japan in 1979, where a young Maradona showed the prodigious and precocious skills that were to astonish the world. In 1981 the tournament, played in Australia, became an official Championship, the FIFA/Coca Cola World Youth Championship, and although it was won by West Germany, the revelation was tiny Qatar, who notched up famous victories on the way to the final, most notably 2–1 against England. From this time on the Championship has gone from strength to strength: the established soccer countries started to take it more seriously and massive crowds turned out, especially when the host country was doing well. In Mexico in 1983, 110,000 watched Brazil beat Argentina in the final. The Soviet Union provided the sombre venue for the next competition, where the host nation drew in the final with Nigeria, who were awarded the trophy on penalties. Chile was chosen for 1987 where the final, between Yugoslavia and West Germany, was again drawn, and at Saudi Arabia in 1989 Portugal beat Nigeria 2–0 in the final. As the home nation in 1991 Portugal survived a brilliant Brazilian onslaught to retain the trophy on penalties before 127,000 adoring fans, the biggest crowd at a FIFA competition since Brazil in 1950. Australia's remarkable success in that competition won it the right to host the 1993 championship, where Brazil and Ghana contested a superlative final, won by Brazil by the narrowest of margins.

The Under-seventeen World Championship began as a schoolboys competition. In contrast to the World Cup where the majority of places in the final are reserved for Europe and South America, each of the five major confederations is allocated three spots, the sixteenth nation coming from Oceania. Europe and South America, with only six representatives, at first did not take this competition seriously, but this is changing, as the potential World Cup hopes of eight years hence go on show. More to the point, however, is that the quality of play has attracted large crowds to watch them. Now the finals would not be complete without the agents from Europe with their open cheque books.

Nigeria won the first final in China in 1985, played before enthusiastic crowds, but in Canada two years later they lost on penalties to the Soviet Union, in near anonymity. Scotland was the venue in 1989, and the Scots turned out in their tens of thousands after a cool start, to see their young hopefuls draw 2–2 in the final against a suspiciously blue-chinned Saudi-Arabia, who were awarded the Cup on penalties. The 1991 competition, now officially a championship (the FIFA Under-seventeen World Championship), was switched from Ecuador to Italy as a result of a cholera epidemic, and since the home team did not proceed beyond the first rounds in Tuscany, so the crowds were down. But not the standard of play, and for those around the world watching the final on TV the performance of the Ghana team, who beat Spain with a late goal, was a triumph of justice and attacking football. Present, too, were agents from the top European teams, their eyes set particularly on the young Africans. At Japan in 1993 Nigeria beat Ghana in an all African final.

The problem of over-age players is obvious in such competitions, and FIFA have come down hard on known abuses. In the case of some Africans there is a problem in that often they do not have a recognized birth certificate, and a Costa Rica player was discovered to be over-age in the 1985 competition only when he registered his real age for the World Cup in 1990: Costa Rica were then suspended from all age competitions for two years. Zambia were banned until 1993 from all age competitions for violations in 1991, and the success of the USA in getting to Italy was in part at least because their usual nemesis, Mexico, had been banned from all international competition for particularly serious violations. Nigeria and Iraq have also suffered long suspensions. At the 1991 World Youth Cup the only sour notes were struck by Argentina, and to a lesser extent Uruguay, with displays of the brutality and poor sportsmanship more usually associated with their senior teams. Uruguay punished their errant representatives; Argentina unsuccessfully appealed the fines and suspensions imposed by FIFA. At the under-seventeen competition in Italy, however, Argentina won the Fair Play award, emphasizing again the dual nature of Argentine football that has been the joy and despair of connoisseurs since they first took up the game.

Soccer at the Olympic Games has always posed problems: besmirched with professionalism, but too popular and too much of a money-spinner to be left out. From 1930 the major soccer nations lost interest in them, but from 1952 the state amateurs used them as a world forum. In 1978 FIFA tried to get rid of some of the anomalies of star professionals appearing in the Olympics at the same time as it sought to win the favour of the Afro-Asian countries, by decreeing that any European or South American who had represented his country would be banned from the Olympics. This, however, did not apply to the other confederations. The countries of the state amateurs, whose players floated freely between Olympic and World Cup selection, were the most affected, and the most indignant, but the Afro-Asian countries still placed more emphasis on the World Cup. The issue was finally resolved by decreeing that from 1992 soccer at the Olympic Games would be restricted to players under twenty-three years old, a sensible solution that has offended the inglorious ambition of the Olympics custodians to see every sport represented in the Olympic Games at the highest level, regardless of whether they already have their own world competition. The success of Australia and Ghana in reaching the last stages of the Barcelona Olympics, to play off for third spot showed the success of the tournament in encouraging the weaker nations, but to the relief of the money-mad organizers it was only the presence of Spain in the final, against Poland, that guaranteed a sell out crowd in the final.

FIFA introduced an international five-a-side competition in 1989, but this is unlikely to interest anyone other than those directly involved. On the other hand, the FIFA Women's World Cup promises to win as much interest as the youth competitions. First held in China in November 1991, it was played before capacity crowds of over 60,000 and millions more who watched on television, despairing when the home team was eliminated in the quarter finals. China were beaten by Norway, who reached the final only to lose to the USA, that most under-developed of soccer nations, who were run-away winners in all their games until they came up against Norway. The football was open and attractive, with teams playing to win rather than not to lose. The goalkeeping, however, was uniformly abysmal. One of the more welcome additions to the Atlanta Olympic Games in 1996 will surely be women's football.

The world game has gone its own way even outside the direct control of FIFA. Each year in Sweden the Gothia Cup is played in a spirit of youthful exuberance, by boys and girls from all over the world, aged from eleven to nineteen, and playing in various grade competitions. The boys and girls bed down in school classrooms with sleeping bags, and the games proceed from 8 am to 10 pm every day, in two halves of twenty-five minutes. In 1991 there were nine hundred youth teams representing forty countries. An equivalent to the Gothia Cup in Sweden is the Dallas Cup in Texas. This international soccer tournament was first held in 1980, and has gained steadily in prestige: for the twelfth competition in 1991, one hundred and forty-four teams from eighteen countries took part in various age groupings under nineteen which included girls as well as boys. Indeed it would appear that soccer is well on the way to becoming the leading international team sport for women.

The first champions of the Third World

FIFA's campaign to develop soccer around the world has also brought soccer from around the world to those who were unaware that soccer was being played throughout Asia and Africa long before its recent successes. The impact of Africa on the world game, which must be left to a separate discussion, is so recent that as late as the mid-1980s only Asian nations could claim to have done well in the final stages of world competition: North Korea at the World Cup in England in 1966, and Japan's bronze medal in the Mexico Olympics of 1968. Before 1939 the only African nation to take part in the Olympics or the World Cup was Egypt, while Japan, China and Korea (albeit in Japanese colours) all made some impact:

today these are the three nations making claims to be the first Asian nation to host the World Cup in 2002.

Egypt, the first country from Africa or Asia to join FIFA (1923), were the leading third world soccer power in the years before the Second World War, and the dominant power among the Arab and African nations until the 1960s. French and British influences were strong in the development of football, which was soon taken up by the Egyptians. In the 1890s games were being played in Cairo by British residents doing what British residents did, and by 1903 they had founded several clubs. As elsewhere this was soon followed by the founding of local clubs, the first and most famous of which was Al-Ahly. Founded in 1907, Al Ahly, or National, are one of the most successful African teams, fanatically supported by an estimated seventy per cent of the soccer-mad population. Like Zamalek, they are an elite club: a wide social gulf separates them from their supporters, and the tens of thousands of youngsters crowding the streets of Cairo, and so stuck for space that they can be seen playing on the inner lanes of the highways, have more chance of being killed on the roads than passing through the doors of the upper-class, amateur club they support.

Egypt had a thriving domestic competition under royal patronage by the 1920s, when they also entered the international soccer arena. In 1920 at the Antwerp Olympics they surprised everyone by holding Italy to a 1–2 loss, and in a meaningless complementary game dreamed up by the organizers after the Czechoslovakia walk-off in the final, beat Yugoslavia 4–2. At the Paris Olympics in 1924 they more than surprised when they won their first round game against a sulking Hungary in dispute with their management, by 3–0, but were brought back to earth with a 5–0 loss to Sweden in the next round. They came fourth in Amsterdam in 1928, and since then Egypt have performed well in subsequent Olympics. They were a foundation member and dominant force in the formation of CAF and the introduction of the African football championships.

Japan were one of the sensations of the 1936 Olympic Games when after being 2–0 down at half-time they swamped the powerful amateurs of Sweden in a 3–2 victory. It is a victory that is remembered by Swedes even today from the radio commentary of the game with an excited Swedish commentator calling out 'Japanese everywhere . . .! Japanese every-where . . .!' In their second game, however, Japan were trounced 8–0 by Italy. Since then a bronze medal in the 1968 Olympics has been their only success on the world stage. Japan were expelled from FIFA along with Germany in 1945, and readmitted in 1950. In this time the predominantly US influence saw soccer upstaged by baseball. In the Hiroshima area, where Americans were less than welcome and the face of the occupier was more often British, soccer prevailed over the American game. Sumo remains the national sport.

Football is said to have been brought to Japan by a British school-teacher in 1874, but its first entry into any type of serious competition came in 1917 when Tokyo hosted the third Far East Games. In 1921 the Japanese FA was founded (Nippon Shukyu Kyokai) and a national cup competition was introduced that same year. In 1929 Japan entered FIFA, but it was not until the 1960s, and the performances of Kunishige Kamamoto, that the public was attracted to the game. Unprecedented crowds of 50,000 came to see the new star at the Tokyo Olympics of 1964, and in Mexico four years later, Japan won the bronze medal. Kamamoto is said to be the best soccer player born in Asia, but despite tempting offers from European clubs, he spent his long and distinguished career in Japan. When he left the scene soccer lost much of its popularity.

As a result of the enthusiasm shown for soccer in 1964, a national league was set up the following year. Made up of teams that read like a listing of the world's top multi-national companies – Nissan, Mazda, Mitsubishi, and others – Yomiuri, although they were backed by the powerful Shimbun communications empire, was the only team that operated on the western model. For most footballers in Japan before professionalism the only ways to succeed were through a factory team or a college team. Outside these, potential talents were left to die unseen, while those who went through a works team or a college team had to let their ambitions rest there. By 1982 league attendances, which had been as high as 7500 in 1968, were down to an average of just over 2000. Japanese teams relied on imports, especially from Brazil, and its competitions like the Japan Cup, introduced in 1978 and later called the Kirin Cup, included teams invited from abroad. Japan also rescued the World Club Championship in 1980. Renamed the Toyota Cup, it is played regularly before capacity crowds of 62,000.

Since the late 1980s the domestic game has taken immense strides, with soccer taking over from baseball as the most popular game, especially with the young. Furukawa and Yomiuri won the Asian Champions' Cup in 1987 and 1988, while at the national level Japan won the Kirin Cup in 1991 and the Asian Nations' Cup for the first time in 1992, preventing Saudi Arabia making it three in a row. All of this was a promising lead up to the introduction in May 1993 of a full-time professional league: the J-League. Although backed by industrial concerns, the teams do not play as such: Grampus Eight, whose signing of English international Gary Lineker brought them unprecedented publicity, are connected to the Toyota company. This deliberate attempt by Japanese businessmen to create a professional soccer league in what was once barren ground, has echoes of the ill-fated North American Soccer League: in its cowboy commercial-ism, with everything that can be sold having a J-League logo attached to it and the American style names, while in the league itself draws have been eliminated, with shoot-outs to decide games drawn after extra-time. However, the promoters have limited foreigners to three per team, and do not expect a return on their investments, which include the construction of some 100,000 all-seater stadiums, for many years. The seriousness of Japan's intent in regard to its soccer future was pledged in its bid to host the 2002 World Cup.

Alongside Japan at the 1936 Olympics was China, but they made little impact, being eliminated by Britain in their only game. Caught up in full-scale war with Japan the following year, constantly involved in revolution-ary wars until 1949 and revolutionary politics thereafter, China has seen little success on the soccer scene since then. In 1990 it had 21 million registered footballers, more by far than any other country, with only the United States coming close to them – a comment on statistics rather than the strength of soccer in these two countries. Like Japan, China has made a bid to host the 2002 World Cup, but unlike Japan, with its mere two and a quarter million registered players, there is little evidence so far of China reaching world status: on the contrary, although they showed as hosts to the 1985 World Youth Cup and the Women's World Cup in 1991, that they were capable of running an international event with efficiency and colour, there have been occasions when the administration of the domestic game under the communists makes the worst blunders of other federations look like inspired efficiency.

As in Japan, China had a long-standing local form of football, and the association game was brought by the British through the port towns, several of which had formed clubs by the turn of the century. The Chinese contempt for things European began to change, and a national team was formed in 1912 after the revolution of that year. In the following year a team of Chinese students played in the first Far East Games, a competition which they won on every occasion but the first. Over the next decade or so China sent teams, mainly of students, to play against neighbouring countries, as far away as Australia and New Zealand, but most frequently against the Philippines and the far from neighbourly Japan.

The military and the missionaries formed teams, and the treaty ports soon had active competitions: Shanghai and Hong Kong had teams representing various nationalities, including German, Portuguese and French, while Jews were represented in the Jewish Recreation Club of Shanghai. The Chinese formed their own teams, the most notable of which was South China Athletic Club, and many games, at times inflamed by 'anti-foreigner' passions, ended in brawls and attacks on the referee. At the National Games in Shanghai in 1935, where teams came from Malaya, Java and Liaoning (Manchuria) as well as the Chinese provinces, 90,000 watched the final between Hong Kong and Canton. In a basically peasant country, suffering debilitating poverty, most of the players were middle-class. The Chinese team that went to the Olympic Games in Berlin in 1936, and held out against the British eleven before conceding two goals and leaving the competition beaten but not disgraced, comprised several clerks in the pay of wealthy employers who covered their costs, a merchant, the owner of a fleet of trucks, three pilots, two soldiers and a traffic policeman.

After the revolution of 1949 many of these middle-class players and millionaire supporters of the game, left the mainland, and Hong Kong Chinese became prominent in the foundation and early days of the AFC. On the mainland the new governing body for sport, the All China Athletic Federation organized a series of local competitions; one of the first winners of the national championship was the team of the People's Liberation Army, thus adding a soccer medal to their triumphs in the Long March and the defeat of Chiang Kai-shek. The new regime was recognized as a member of FIFA from its inception, since the geographical area it controlled was that of the pre-existing China, but it kept clear of capitalist sporting ventures. On the island of Taiwan soccer played second fiddle to baseball and basketball, but it served to cause confusion when Taiwan, calling itself China, was admitted to FIFA in 1954. Four years later the People's Republic resigned in protest. The communist regime was not to allow its sporting flowers to bloom in the free market, and its footballers had to be content at first with games against communist neighbours North Korea and the USSR, at least until the great split, which then restricted competition to its European ally, Albania.

Sporting contacts opened out to games against countries like Tanzania and other African countries where China was trying to exert influence, but disappeared when the ideological fanatics of the 'cultural revolution' took over from 1966 to 1970, and the domestic game all but went out of existence. Then came the 'ping-pong diplomacy' of the early 1970s, which saw China anxious to re-enter the world body of football. This posed a problem for FIFA, since its rules forbade its members from playing against unaffiliated countries. However, Havelange had made it clear from 1974 that he wanted communist China brought into the FIFA family, an ambition shared by the Hong Kong millionaire businessman Henry Fok, who won the support of the Middle East countries by pledging his opposition to Israel. In 1974 the AFC expelled Taiwan to allow China to enter its confederation, and this faced FIFA with the even greater problem of having to expel the AFC, its biggest confederation. Nelsonian diplomacy continued to prevail, as FIFA bartered the fate of Israel, also expelled, by moving it to Oceania if Taiwan could be restored.

None of this prevented teams from England, Portugal, Italy and elsewhere visiting the People's Republic in the late 1970s, while teams from China were invited to play games around the world in return. This was in breach of FIFA's rules about playing with non-members, but was overlooked. China was even allowed to enter the draw for the 1982 World Cup before it became a member of FIFA. Other, much smaller, nations, had been expelled for not paying their dues. It would not have happened in Rous's day.

Some of China's respected visitors predicted that China and the USA, then at the height of its soccer boom, would soon be among the world's best soccer nations. Basketball and volleyball were then more popular than soccer in China, but despite the determination of the regime to see China shine on the international soccer stage, and despite the great surge of popularity in the 1980s, success has been thin, even in tournaments like the Great Wall Cup, initiated in 1983 and open to teams from outside China. Attendances at domestic games rose dramatically in the 1980s but dropped off when entry costs, in the spirit of that capitalist decade, went from a mere 30 fen (about four cents) to four yuan – about $1.50, or two days labour. Injudicious showing of highlights of the Italian and English football leagues at the expense of the local game also did not help.

The integration of China into the new world of crumbling ideologies can be seen in the naming of the Marlboro Dynasty Cup introduced in July 1990 for invited foreign teams, the finals played in the Workers' Stadium in Beijing. It will, however, need more than a mixture of capitalism and Confucianism to overcome the muddle that has characterised football in China recently, where weird rule changes regarding scoring have been introduced supposedly to brighten the game. In the manner of other state amateur teams, too, China pampered its national team, the Olympic selection, taking players from other teams and entering it in the national league. Teams thus deprived were awarded special points, but when the Olympic team won the league and the AFC refused to recognize it as a club team, so ruling it ineligible for the Asian Champions Cup, the books were cooked to show that the second-placed team had really won.

When Japan annexed Korea in 1910 it also annexed its sporting talent. In 1935 the Korean team Keiyjo won the Japanese championship, and the following year many Koreans starred, against their wishes, in the colours of Japan. The most famous of these was Kitei Son (or Kee Chung Song), the marathon winner, and although it has been claimed that the Japanese soccer team that caused such a sensation in 1936 was made up mainly of Koreans, there was in fact only one Korean in the team.

Soccer was brought to Korea by European missionaries and technicians: the crew of a British warship are said to have played the first game in 1882. A Korean FA was formed in 1938, under the control of the Japanese, and entered FIFA in 1940. After the war a team representing Korea played in the London Olympics in 1948, but suffered humiliating defeats. More were to follow when South Korea qualified for Switzerland in 1954, and while South Korea performed well in Asian competitions, winning the first two Asian Cups in 1956 and 1960, they fared poorly on the international stage. The North was less prepared to put itself on show, but when it did in 1966 at the World Cup in England, it caused a sensation, defeating Italy 1–0 and drawing with Chile to go through to the quarter-finals where they found themselves 3–0 up against Portugal only to fall before Eusebio at his goal-scoring best in a 3–5 turnaround. In the tradition of state amateurs, this team had been trained for years, playing against select opposition in secret until show day in 1966.

Both Koreas were members of FIFA resulting in the inevitable problems. In 1945 the FA of the Democratic People's Republic of Korea was formed, and joined FIFA in 1958. The South became a member of FIFA in 1948, and when both Koreas qualified for the finals of the Olympics in Japan in 1964, North Korea withdrew in protest at the presence of the South.

Despite South Korea's reputation as one of the strongest soccer countries in Asia, in terms of spectator interest it fell behind professional baseball in the late 1970s. The influence of the Americans and their high-profile presence accounts in part for this; it may also have played some part in the revival of soccer in the form of the Hallelujah soccer team. Made up of evangelical Christians, they became Korea's first professional team, in 1980, and devoted their efforts on the field not just to making money, but to promoting God. Further American influences can be seen in the names of the eight teams that made up the full professional soccer league in 1983: Bulls, Dolphins, Tigers, Elephants and Royals being appended to more pedestrian commercial names. South Korea has been called the 'Yugoslavia of Asia' for the way it lost players to other countries, usually in Asia. To discourage this a ban was placed on players who went abroad, but this rule was relaxed in the 1980s, and when South Korea qualified for Mexico in 1986 they included Cha Bum-kun, the best Asian to play in Europe, who starred in the Bundesliga for a decade from 1978. He was also a devoted Christian.

South Korea performed creditably in Mexico, but the Superleague, created as a fully professional league in 1984, suffered huge drops in attendance as players were taken from their home team for national duty. Hallelujah were forced to turn amateur as a result and later dropped out of the league. South Korea made it to the finals of the World Cup again in 1990, but failed to match the feats of North Korea in 1966. Against Asian competition only the Middle East countries have proved consistently able to beat South Korea. With the approaching unification of North and South, first symbolized in the Korean team that went to the Under-twenty World Youth Cup in Portugal in 1991, and having already staged a most impressive Olympic Games in 1988, Korea must be seen as the major Asian competitor to Japan to host the 2002 World Cup.

Fair play in colonial Asia

Amidst the ravages of the Second World War, games continued to be played in Asia, not least football. The football associations of colonial Asia, as elsewhere in the colonial world, owed their allegiance to the colonial power first, and FIFA second – in the case of Britain's colonies, FIFA wasn't recognized at all. This changed with independence. The British, with their control over the Indian sub-continent and surrounding countries, and with their trading links elsewhere, were the dominant European power in Asia before the Second World War. Their attitude to their colonial subjects, in soccer as in other matters, was essentially that of the amateurs of the Old Boy mentality. The game was for fun and the teaching of good manners, and in the spirit of the muscular Christians of the early days football was used as one of the vehicles through which the Word of God (and the British) was to be spread. Throughout Africa and Asia, wherever the British flag was planted the Bible followed with a ball to back it up.

The partnership of ball and Bible was not always a pleasant one, although few missionaries could have been as crass as the ineffable Tyndale-Biscoe, who in 1926 set down his reminiscences of his days as a missionary, in *Kashmir in Sunlight and Shade*. Here this man of God tells how he forced football on the schoolboys in his care in 1891. The boys, being Brahmans, were forbidden by their religion to touch leather, but Biscoe set about overcoming such superstitious nonsense by getting the teachers to drive them to the playing area with singlesticks, pickets and other weapons. He personally brought up the rear with his riding crop. Thus this 'dirty, smelling, cowardly crew' were driven to the pitch, where again they refused to touch the leather ball. Again, as Biscoe proudly recalls, sticks won the day and the boys were beaten into action. In his scornful picture of the ensuing fracas, Biscoe takes some sadistic pleasure in the case of one boy who received the ball full in the face, and thus defiled, was reduced to tears. All eyes were then turned to Biscoe, but a serious incident was averted by the brave Christian telling the others to 'take the fool down to the canal' and wash him.

The role of the military in spreading football in India, however inadvertently, was much more important than that of the missionaries. Soldiers played for their own enjoyment, but they also allowed the locals to join in, and they in turn formed their own teams. When one of these local teams beat a regimental team in 1911 it went down as one of the great events in Indian colonial history. This was in Calcutta, the most fanatical football centre in India, when Mohan Bagan won the Indian FA Shield. As Tony Mason has shown, this victory had lessons for master and subject, as each tried to outdo the other in sporting conduct; but the joy of the locals could be borne by the British in the knowledge that such small setbacks helped maintain their hegemony.

The game in India was played in the early evening when the hot and humid conditions were more bearable, and lasted only 30 minutes each half. British civil and military personnel introduced the game, and from kick-around games between officers and men, and then with the locals, teams and leagues were formed. In 1888 the Indian Football Association (IFA) was formed, and with it the Durand Cup, probably the oldest knock-out tournament outside the United Kingdom, which has lasted from colonial times until today. In 1889 the Trade's Cup was introduced for competition between locals and Europeans. In 1898 the Calcutta League was founded with eight teams, five military and three civil. In 1902 a Bombay League was founded. By this time young Bengalis from the colleges were playing the game regularly and had formed their own teams: one of these was Mohan Bagan.

Mohan Bagan were founded in 1883, and were to become the best supported team in India, held in such veneration that in 1989 even their bitter rivals East Bengal and Mohammedan Sporting did not object when the Indian government proclaimed them 'The national team of India'. On their first executive committee were three maharajahs and a knight, while their founder was a millionaire landowner among whose properties was Mohan Bagan Villa, from which came the name of the new team. After three changes of ground Mohan Bagan, wearing the green and maroon of national independence, took up part of the public area of the Maidan, where they soon attracted thousands of admirers, especially when they won the Trade's Cup three years in a row from 1906. As a result of this success they were invited to take part in the IFA Shield in 1909, a competition which had grown in such stature as to be seen as a sort of national championship.

In 1911 came their historic victory. In the semi-final against the Middlesex Regiment team there were re-enacted scenes reminiscent of the early days of the game in Britain. Thousands began to roll up hours before the kick-off, many having walked many miles to get there. As they crowded around the ground those at the front were pressured from behind and fights broke out as they tried to maintain their place. The trees surrounding the ground were thick with spectators and several were injured as branches proved incapable of supporting their weight. This game ended in a draw, but a 3–0 victory in the replay took Mohan Bagan through to the final. This was played against the East Yorkshire Regiment on 19 July, before 50–60,000 spectators, and the British team was defeated by the odd goal in three.

Great was the rejoicing as the players were chaired from the field, although some commentators thought this rather unseemly, and the celebrations were muted by reminders from the victors that they owed much to the help from their many friends in India and Britain. The British teams had not always been exemplars of fair play in some of the early games, resorting to a brutal physical style when things were going against them. There were also odd incidents of straight bad sportsmanship by individual Britons unable to accept defeat, but by and large they took it well, and the small-circulation Calcutta daily, *Nayak*, could praise the 'magnanimous equanimity of the Englishman' refusing to react to the taunts of exultant Bengali youths. This same paper had a political message for its readers, pointing out that 'the rice-eating Bengali is capable of learning everything to perfection and beating even his teachers. Teach him warfare and he will prove as clever and indomitable as the Japanese.'

Football continued to prosper in India, and by 1929 the IFA had 154 clubs, only fourteen of which were European or Anglo-Indian; few were racially mixed. In 1914, Aryans and Mohan Bagan were admitted to a newly created second division of the Calcutta league, and Mohan Bagan were promoted two years later. The British military teams continued to dominate until Hitler forced many of them to return to Europe, but in 1934 Mohammedan Sporting, founded in 1891, won the Calcutta League championship, which they dominated for some years.

In 1937 the first real national association, the All India Football Federation (AIFF), was formed. In that year, as the Islington Corinthians discovered during their world tour, the game was followed with fanatical passion. One of the Corinthians players described the intense excitement of the crowds of up to 100,000 who came to watch them play in India. He testified that ethnic and religious divisions were overlooked in the hope of beating the Europeans, while the players might take the field in football boots as a courtesy to their guests, but removed them as soon as the game got tough. In *Sportsmen of Punjab*, Sarwan Singh describes how the Bengalis

> discuss football while eating, travelling in the tramcars, attending public meetings and taking out processions. It is beyond the prowess of an ordinary man to procure a ticket for a good football match in Calcutta. The Bengalis queue up for the tickets even up to two days ahead of the commencement of the issue of tickets.

In the world arena, however, the best India could do was a fourth place at the Melbourne Olympics in 1956. By the 1960s India had lost even its dominant place in Asian football. After independence Mohammedan Sporting and East Bengal, but above all Mohan Bagan, carried off most titles in the Calcutta League, which remained the strongest in the continent, and also in the nationwide competitions.

In recent years the dominance of the big three has been broken, with teams like Kerala Police and Mahindra and Mahindra, the team of the jeep makers from Bombay, challenging for top honours. By world standards, however, the standard of play is poor, corruption is rife and brawls on the field frequent, so that Indian football, with more than eight million registered players, has not reached the international heights of hockey and cricket, sports favoured by wealthier Indians. Nevertheless, a reminder of India's role in Asian soccer can be seen in the Nehru Gold Cup, which began in 1982. This tournament, open by invitation to nations from around the world, is the most successful on the continent, with crowds averaging 80,000.

Elsewhere on the sub-continent, Pakistan were a major soccer power shortly after independence, but hockey, cricket and squash, and the hostility of the ruling elite, reduced soccer to a minor sport. On the other hand, East Pakistan, which became Bangladesh in 1971, is a major soccer stronghold, and the derby between its two top teams, Mohammedan Sporting and Abahani Krira Chakra, has nothing to learn from the great derbies elsewhere in the world. Bangladesh joined FIFA on independence, and part of its means of reconciliation with Pakistan was to enter into football competitions with it. Sri Lanka, the former Ceylon, has a vigorous domestic competition, but has made few efforts to join the international scene.

Burma, later known as Myanmar, was initially one of the most successful Asian soccer nations: the only team said to have beaten the Islington Corinthians on merit during their 1937 tour was from Burma. Its football 'golden age', however, came in the decade after 1964: Burma won the Asian Games tournament in 1966 and shared gold with South Korea in 1970, qualified for the Munich Olympic Games in 1972, returning with honourable defeats. Even during its political isolation from the rest of the world, Myanmar maintained its affiliation with FIFA.

Of the other former British colonies in Asia, Malaysia distinguished itself with the organization of the Merdeka (Independence) Tournament. This competition for invited national teams was introduced in 1957 to celebrate independence the previous year, and remains one of the best run competitions in Asia. The Malaysians have an overwhelming interest in the game, fuelled by a mania for betting, and professionalism was introduced in part at least to eliminate the worst aspects of corruption that went with this. Malaysian clubs, helped by the government, have encouraged foreign stars to play there. Inder Singh from the Punjab claims that he was offered 300,000 rupees by the Prime Minister, Tenku Abd-ur-Rehman to play there for five years, as well as providing comfortable living and citizenship for his family. Punjabi patriotism prevailed, and this offer he refused; he also refused offers from Mohan Bagan and SC Vancouver.

In Hong Kong a professional league was set up in 1969–70, backed by millionaire businessmen. Crowds of nearly 30,000 flocked to the games, but like the great American experiment, the Hong Kong league, based on imported professionals and personal profit, eventually failed. The all-Chinese champions of long standing, South China AA, remained amateur until 1980, but still won several of the early leagues: Rangers were the only non-Chinese team, while Bulova and Seiko played out the rivalry of two brother watchmakers, in an Asian version of the Dassler saga.

Chinese expertise ensured that Singapore would have the best-run administration in Asia, but the base from which it draws its players was too small to make it a strong soccer power, other than as an organizer of tournaments.

In those parts of Asia under French control, soccer was never a major sport. As a colonial power, the French were influential in spreading soccer, but in Africa rather than Asia. Even before the wars that racked Indochina after 1945, soccer was a minor sport, although an FA was formed in Saigon in 1923 controlling the southern part of the peninsula. After the war France encouraged international matches with the mother country, but the nationalists refused to be diverted from their aims. In 1948 the Cochinchoise FA gave itself a Vietnamese name, and in 1952 was accepted into FIFA despite being under colonial jurisdiction.

Football continued to be played until partition, and after 1954 South Vietnam took part in the first Asian Cup in 1956. They won many of the tournaments played in the area, including the first South-East Asian Peninsula Games, played in Bangkok in 1959, and their club teams, Vietnam Customs and Vietnam Police, played in the Asian Champions' Cup. Football was not so well established in the North, and the FA of the Democratic Republic of Vietnam was not formed until 1962. It became a member of FIFA in 1964, but because of the presence of South Vietnam did not become a member of the AFC until after reunification in 1975. Fighting a war and refusing to join a confederation which welcomed the enemy limited North Vietnam's soccer experiences, and since then playing football has not been a priority. A tournament was held in 1978 to celebrate 35 years of Communist rule, and included army teams from the Soviet Union and east Europe, as well as Laos and Angola. This SKDA Tournament, effectively for army clubs of the socialist countries, became an annual event. More important, a national league was founded in 1980, and the top team came from Hanoi: the Army and Sport Club, founded on 10 October 1954, the day France withdrew from Vietnam.

Laos and Cambodia made little impact on the soccer scene, although each had its own FA, Cambodia formed in 1933 and Laos in 1951 after its liberation. Cambodia's FA joined FIFA as the Fédération Khmère de Football Association in 1953, and despite the wars in the region ran a successful domestic competition and enjoyed some international successes. In 1975 descended the blight of Pol Pot and football became a total irrelevance. But not a thing of the past: in December 1984 a team from Cambodia (Kampuchea) played in the fifth SKDA Tournament in Vietnam; but in its first entry, Cambodia lost to Vietnam B and Cuba.

Indonesia should be one of the most powerful soccer countries in Asia, but the popularity of the game at local level has not been matched by the necessary administrative expertise (or honesty). Soccer is the popular passion, but badminton has provided the international success. Soccer began under the Dutch, and it was as the Dutch East Indies that Indonesia was represented in France at the World Cup in 1938. In Europe they played many friendlies in the Netherlands before being bundled out by Hungary in the first round. Indonesia's best performance on the international stage was at the Olympic Games in Melbourne in 1956 where they forced the Soviet Union, the ultimate winners, into a replay after holding them to a 0–0 draw in the first round. Indonesia's main stadium, despite a capacity limited to 110,000, has packed in as many as 150,000 for the final of the national football championship. Indonesia successfully ran the Asian Games in 1962, but it is better known for its organization of the less successful political Games of the Newly Emerging Forces (GANEFO), which it hosted in 1963. In Mercu Buana, the 'Light of the Universe', it has perhaps the most grandiloquently named team in the world.

Thailand was the only Asian nation to escape serious foreign intervention, but it could not escape the traders, and a few of them – British – were behind the formation of the FA of Siam in 1916. The Thai's enthusiasm for soccer has yet to be matched with international success, and Thailand is perhaps best known for the King's Cup, held annually in Bangkok since 1968 for invited nations in the region. In the Philippines, soccer made a promising beginning, but the Spanish influence was soon nullified by that of the USA. When it escaped in 1946 from what was characterized by one unsympathetic observer as '300 years in a Spanish convent and 40 years in Hollywood', baseball and basketball were more popular than soccer. A national championship was founded in 1911, and in 1913 the Philippines founded the Far East Games, and won the first Asian soccer international when they defeated China. After the First World War, however, the US influence increased and soccer faded away as the Philippines failed to win even one of the small regional competitions.

Deserts and mountains have proved little obstacle to the spread of the game in Asia. In Nepal an All-Nepal FA was founded in 1951 and joined FIFA in 1970, the AFC the following year. The game was given a boost in 1951 when the Rana family who had run the country from India were sacked by the Shah King who then included football in his programme of modernization. Even in the wilds of Afghanistan organized football is played, a carry-over from the long British military presence. The

Afghanistan FA was founded in 1922 and a league was operating in the 1930s; in 1948 it joined FIFA and was one of the six soccer countries at the first Asian Games in 1951. In even more remote Mongolia, the largest country in the world never to have been a member of FIFA, soccer is played by 35,000 players in twenty-eight tournaments each year, although wrestling and equestrian competitions are more popular. Top team in the Mongolian People's Republic is the police team of the capital, Dynamo Ulan Bator (or Khuch), with Friendship Darkham, the Soviet military team, a close rival. This is changing with the collapse of the Soviet Union, and the venerable state of Mongolia is now in line with the new nations of the world waiting to be accepted into FIFA.

Tibet became an unwilling part of China in 1949, and the fate of soccer there is but just one of the unpleasant secrets of the colonized province: in April 1985 a team from Tibet played in the All-Nepal FA Cup. It would appear that the standard of play was not very high, as Tibet were beaten in the final by a young team from the US, Brooklyn College, the Americans qualifying after defeating the host nation in a game that ended in a brawl with two minutes to go.

Political games

There were six countries represented at the football tournament of the Asian Games in 1951. Absent were Pakistan, which refused to set foot in New Delhi, and China, which refused to play in a competition that included Taiwan. Further political complications were involved when Israel joined the AFC in 1956, and the grouping of pro-Chinese athletic forces and their anti-Israel allies demanded that Israel be isolated. The world game could not expect to escape the world's problems, and politics, present in the corridors of power at FIFA from its inception, merely took on global proportions.

In the late 1960s the Middle East nations came to dominate the soccer competitions of the AFC, bringing with them petro-dollars and an intense hatred of Israel. In view of their proximity to North Africa, and their shared religion, it would make more sense if these nations formed a seventh confederation. The historical development of football in Africa, however, has linked the north African muslim nations to the continent as a whole.

The countries of the Middle East were never colonized but they were unable to avoid the interference of western governments and entrepreneurs, usually British protecting their trade routes from other colonial powers, or seeking control of the oil reserves. In the waves of nationalism that swept the world after 1945 many Arabs reacted against foreign ownership and the way their local rulers sold out to them. Religion and anti-westernism were at the core of Arab nationalism, but football continued to flourish. Some of the ruling Islamic regimes were hostile to the game, but it proved impossible to convince the ordinary people that they should give it up. When Ayatollah Khomeini tried to return Iran to a medieval monastery in which games were shunned, football proved stronger than ideology.

Iran, a non-Arab country, has been the most successful soccer nation of the Middle East. The Persian Amateur FA, under the sports programme of Reza Shah the Great in 1925, made soccer into one of the principal sports, and this was encouraged by the Shah's son, who played for his high school in Switzerland, and came back to his country won over to the game. In 1939 the Amjadiyd Stadium was built in Tehran, but Persia did not enter serious international competition until 1950. In 1962 the Shah introduced a revolution from above that involved a series of social reforms, and the creation of the first national soccer league. European and Brazilian coaches were employed on lucrative contracts, while the players, technically amateurs, received rich rewards: in 1973 football became semi-professional. Derbies between Persepolis FC and Taj FC in Tehran could now regularly pack 100,000 into the Aria Mehre stadium. Iran dominated the Asian Nations' Cup, but the big prize came in 1978 with Iran's qualification for Argentina in the World Cup. A year later came the Ayatollah Khomeini.

One of the Ayatollah's first pronouncements was to prohibit games. Boxing and draughts were immediately banned, but football was too big to come under such censure, so the revolutionary council of mullahs tried to force the players to wear trousers to hide their knees. Women were banned from all sporting stadiums. Rather than resist the tide, the rulers went with it, and insisted that in team photographs a portrait of the Ayatollah be prominently displayed. Star footballers were shown in army uniform, defending the nation against Iraq, but inside the sports stadiums fans found one of the few areas where they could voice their discontent with the regime.

Kuwait (1980) and Saudi Arabia (1984, 1988) took over where Iran left off as winners of the Asian Nations' Cup when Iran was left in the turmoil of its internal revolution and the war with its neighbour, Iraq. These countries in turn would be involved in the crisis of mid-1990 when Iraq invaded Kuwait and threatened Saudi Arabia. Throughout this time Iran and Iraq remained part of FIFA and played against other nations, but there were restrictions on their home games.

Kuwait, with a population of just over a million, but oil rich like Iran, also used its wealth to import coaches, encourage the game at the local level and influence results when the national team was playing. Vast expenditure paid off when Kuwait qualified for the World Cup in Spain in 1982, where their best result was a 1–1 draw with Czechoslovakia. Soccer had been played in Kuwait as far back as 1889, when Britain arrived ostensibly to protect it from the Turks, but stayed on in any case until 1961. The sailors and civil servants sent to 'guide' the Kuwaiti rulers were joined by a major influx of other British personnel after the discovery of oil in the 1930s, and they played among themselves until well after the war. The Kuwait FA was formed in 1952, but did not enter FIFA until 1962. Football was introduced to Kuwaiti schools in 1948, and throughout the 1960s the domestic programme was consolidated before Kuwait went on in the 1970s to establish itself as the most powerful soccer country in the Arabian Gulf.

Saudi Arabia took over from Kuwait as the leading Gulf soccer power in the mid-1980s. As befits the host to the holy cities of Mecca and Medina, the Saudis were lukewarm in their initial reactions to football, and as an independent kingdom from 1932 they were freer to impose their own ideas. The ruling royal house eventually gave its official blessing to the game when the King's Cup was inaugurated in 1959. By the 1970s they were importing foreign coaches, but could not buy immediate success; this finally came under a Saudi coach.

Most Middle East countries, despite being awash with money and paying vast amounts to coaches, were nominally amateur. Iraq, however, made frequent lavish gifts to successful teams (and occasionally others who might help in this way), and when they qualified for the Mexico World Cup in 1986 all of the players were rewarded by Saddam Hussein with the gift of a house and car. Had they lost a different reward would have come their way: in the morning of the match against Syria that ensured qualification, an Iraqi sports daily proclaimed: 'In case of loss, God forbid, the people will not stand idle but will pelt those who disappoint their hopes with tomatoes and bottles.' When Egypt narrowly qualified for Italia 1990, with a 1–0 victory over Algeria, immigrant workers in Baghdad who allowed their joy to show provoked an attack by Iraqis which ended with 100 seriously injured.

The British brought football to Iraq when they came as a mandatory power, and then stayed to keep an eye on its oil. The Iraq FA was founded in 1951, and after the successes of the 1980s, Iraq gained its most expensively won trophy in 1991, when as a result of the Gulf War it pillaged the Gulf Cup. Despite what would appear to be a domestic policy conducted by coup and massacre, and a foreign policy based on contempt for near neighbours, Iraq has stood out as the leader of the moral crusade against Israel.

Israel was created in 1948 and the boycotts and violence that have accompanied its attempts to establish itself as a soccer power are as nought compared to its attempts to establish itself as a nation. And at times, too, its soccer representatives have honed to a perfect edge the cynical sporting dictum about getting your own retaliation in first. Israel has been one of the most successful Asian nations in soccer, but like the Jews of biblical lore they have had to wander the world in search of a confederation that would accept them. Rejected by Africa and Asia, and an anomaly in Oceania, Israel was the sole unaffiliated nation in FIFA until in 1991 it was agreed that it could join UEFA.

Israel formed its FA as Palestine in 1928, started a Challenge Cup that year and entered FIFA the following year. Football was first played by the British in the First World War but its strength came from the immigrant Jews of central Europe. A league was formed in 1932, and although Hapoel Tel Aviv, the team of the workers, and Maccabi Tel Aviv, the team of the Israeli nationalists, were to emerge as the main rivals, the first title was won by Palestine Police, a British team. There were no Arab teams. The league and cup competitions were continued throughout the Second World War, but could not survive the terror campaign between 1946 and 1948 that led to independence. Restarted, they were again suspended in the first of the Arab-Israeli wars that broke out almost as soon as the state of Israel was created.

As Palestine, Israel entered for the 1934 and 1938 World Cups, but were eliminated in the preliminaries on both occasions. Israel's first victory in an international (5–1) was in a friendly against Lebanon in Tel Aviv in 1940, but future internationals would have to wait until 1948, when the Palestine FA became the Israel FA (Hitachdut Lekaduregel Beisrael). Israel's problems were not long in emerging: in the preliminary rounds for the 1950 and 1954 World Cups, Israel lost on the field of play, but in 1958 off-field politics posed a bigger problem when some African nations, followed by Turkey and Indonesia, refused to play against them. At this stage Israel looked like going through to the finals on forfeits, but FIFA decided they had to play someone, had a lottery of second-placed teams and came up with Wales, who beat Israel home and away. At the 1968 Olympics in Mexico, Israel had their first major successes. Morocco refused to play them, and were replaced by Ghana, who lost 5–3 in a brawl that began on the field and was continued back in the Olympic Village. Israel then beat El Salvador, but drew with Bulgaria in the quarter finals and were eliminated on the toss of a coin. The Mexico experience paid off when Israel, having eliminated South Korea and Australia, qualified for the 1970 World Cup finals, where they enjoyed their greatest success before or since: they lost only 2–0 to Uruguay and went on to hold Sweden and Italy to draws.

Israel entered the AFC in 1956, and with Iran, was the most successful nation in the Asian competitions until they were banned. In 1963 the Games of the Newly Emerging Forces staged in Indonesia were a sign of the future for Israel; their competition in Asia became restricted, leading to expulsion from the AFC when they found themselves faced by the organized Arab nations and the Communist bloc. Among the competitions of the Arab nations the Palestine Cup, founded in 1971, was a political statement aimed at Israel, comprising as it did a Palestine team, and various other Arab nations. When an Islamic Soccer Tournament was arranged to take place in Kuwait, FIFA objected to what seemed like a too pointed attack on Israel and banned it. Kuwait then sued FIFA for £3 million.

The various Arab and Gulf countries have organized less politically motivated competitions. One of the most prestigious of these is the Arabian Gulf Football Tournament, a biennial event founded in 1970. Bahrain, Qatar, the United Arab Emirates have all taken part, with Kuwait and Saudi Arabia the most successful. Qatar made a remarkable impact on the soccer scene under their Brazilian coach from 1979, supported by the Emir who, in contrast to some of his predecessors, saw that soccer could serve a useful social purpose. Solid gold cups and pitches of grass rather than sand rolled with crude oil helped to popularise the game.

Brazilian coaches, vast expenditure and concentration on the national team have similarly brought some good results for the UAR. The Arab Cup, founded in 1963 as part of the Pan Arab Games came under the Union of Arab FAs, to be played every three years. The Palestine Cup's lack of general popularity at least allowed such teams as Syria, Jordan and Lebanon the odd chance of winning a game in official international competition. It is now run as a youth tournament.

Football is played in all the Arab countries. Even in Lebanon, football has survived the war; one of the few times the guns fell silent during the Civil War was during the World Cup telecasts. In Syria and Jordan, as well as in Oman and North Yemen, despite lack of success at the national level, the game is still popular.

With all its problems, football in Asia, above all in the Middle East, has shown remarkable progress. Apart from the continent-wide competitions that have had mixed success, there exist a host of regional competitions, from the Merdeka Cup to the Arab Cup, the President's Cup held annually in Seoul and the King's Cup held each year in Bangkok. And others less grand, like the Melanesian Cup. In 1990 this tournament was held in New Caledonia, where the hosts came second and the winner of the previous two competitions, Fiji, came third. Filling in the last two places were Solomon Islands and Papua New Guinea. The winners were Vanuatu, better known as the New Hebrides before gaining independence in 1980. This was their first ever victory in international soccer, with two wins and two draws. In recognition of the occasion the tiny island's ruler, Father Walter Lini, declared a national holiday.

Mining colonial gold

With a population half that of the entire world, it is hardly surprising that Asia has half the world's registered football players. What is more surprising is that so few of them have made it to the top ranks. This is all the more striking when compared to the success of the Africans. These two continents represent vastly different cultures, but both have large-scale poverty, and both have caught the soccer fever. Unlike Africans, gifted Asian players can earn a comfortable living in Asian football, and the cultural attractions of Europe are less appealing to them, but it is still surprising that more Asians have not appeared in the major European leagues.

Cha Bum-kun from South Korea is generally regarded as the best Asian to play in Europe: *Kicker* magazine was prepared to place him among the world's best. He won two UEFA Cup medals and a German Cup-winners medal in his long stays with Eintracht Frankfurt from 1979 to 1983 and Bayer Leverkusen from 1983 to 1988. South Koreans have also played for PSV Eindhoven and in the North American Soccer League. Thailand has lost players to South Korea, as well as Japan, and at least two to Europe: Laohakul to Hertha Berlin in 1980 and Vorawan Chitawanich to Denmark in 1989. Fandi Ahmad went from Singapore to Holland via Indonesia, with mixed success in the mid-1980s. The Japanese Yasuhiko Okudera, who made 234 Bundesliga appearances for Köln and Werder Bremen between 1977 and 1986, was almost as good as Cha Bum-kun. Despite some problems with the language and the fans, and being described as 'ponderous' he established his place in what was then one of the toughest leagues in Europe. Kazui Ozaki also played in the Bundesliga, for Arminia Bielefeld, between 1983 and 1985. Kamamoto, who never played in Europe, was reckoned by Glanville and Rous as being of the top rank. Rous also claimed in 1967 that the Punjabi player Jarnail Singh was 'fit for selection for any world football team.' Singh's travels, however, did not take him any further than Calcutta. With the lifting of controls in China, some of their players have tried their luck abroad, two leaving for Partizan Belgrade in the late 1980s, and from 1987 Guangming Gu has been playing for Darmstadt 98 in the German Second Division.

Other Asian players are arriving in Europe, and it is the very fact that some do succeed that raises the question of why more do not. In the last few years African players have arrived in Europe in droves, and have made it to the top of the toughest leagues in the world. France has always been willing to import sporting talent from its colonies, and even before the Second World War there were many Africans playing in French football: in 1938 came the first great African star, the Moroccan Larbi Ben Barek. Many others followed, and even today France has more African players in its league (and national team) than any other country. From its Asian connections, however, France has received no imports, although New Caledonia and Tahiti have provided players of the top rank.

Portugal was as willing as France to take advantage of its colonial football talent. Its two most famous players came from Lourenço Marques, capital of Mozambique: Mario Coluna, who arrived in Portugal in 1954, and Eusebio, born in 1942, who starred in the great Benfica and Portugal teams of 1961 to 1966. There were forty-eight Africans playing in Portugal in 1991, but since the Portuguese colonies outside Angola and Mozambique were small it is hardly surprising that none of its Asian colonies have produced class footballers.

Belgium has been one of the main countries snapping up talent from the underdeveloped football world, and not just Africa. There were fifty-six Africans playing in its teams in 1991. Spain had long since lost its colonies by 1960, and Germany had forfeited its colonies as punishment for the First World War. Spain's Africans numbered only seven in 1991, while West Germany had ten. Of the other Africans in Europe at that time ten were playing in England, ten in Switzerland and others were scattered in the Netherlands (five), Greece (four), Denmark (two), Turkey (two) and Czechoslovakia (one). Since the *World Soccer* survey that provides these figures, dozens more Africans have arrived to play football in Europe. The Netherlands includes some Moluccans from Asia among its professionals, but two of its greatest-ever players, Gullitt and Rijkaard, and more recently Aaron Winter, world stars of the highest order, are of Surinamese origins.

Great Britain, the world's leading colonial power, virtually ignored the athletic talent among its non-white colonial subjects, apart from organizing Empire and Commonwealth Games where rulers, ruled and once-ruled could compete against each other. The British generally administered their colonies with a paternalistic disdain that saw them encouraging football among their charges without any thought that one day they might have something to offer in return.

Most of the blacks playing in Britain today are of Afro-Caribbean origins; none have come from its substantial Asian population, although they have supplied a couple of referees. By the 1990s, when blacks made up about 1.5 per cent of the population, they comprised 12 per cent of England's top footballers. The vast majority of them were born in England of Caribbean parents. There had been blacks in nineteenth-century English football; in 1909 Walter Daniel Tull, born in England of a West Indian father and English mother, was signed as an apprentice with Spurs. He went on to play regularly with Northampton Town. Jack Leslie, born in 1901 and a regular with Plymouth Argyle, was said to be good enough to play for England but never got the chance. After the Second World War, Lindy Delapenha made a name for himself with Portsmouth. A few blacks appeared in the 1960s, South Africans and the Bermudan, Clyde Best, among others, but the explosion came in the mid-1970s. These were the sons of the immigrants from the West Indies who had begun to arrive in 1948 and in increasing numbers throughout the 1950s. In 1978 Viv Anderson became the first black to play for England; Laurie Cunningham went from Nottingham Forest to Réal Madrid for £800,000; and when Bobby Robson received racist abuse for including several blacks in his squad for the 1982 World Cup he said that he would play a team of blacks if they were good enough.

In other countries where Asians represent a significant ethnic group, as in Africa, and South Africa in particular, their success has not matched that of Africans. Football is far from the epitome of all human endeavour, but it is surprising that more of the poor in Asia have not found in the world game the path to wealth and recognition chosen by others with no more than a talent for controlling a ball. It highlights the question rather than answers it, but when Bert Trautmann, the legendary German who came out of a POW camp to play for Manchester City, later devoted his time to coaching in Asia and Africa, he was struck by the eagerness of young Tanzanians to learn about life in Europe. Despite his attempts to point out the benefits of their own way of life he could not convince them that the apparent wealth of Europeans concealed pressures and drawbacks that made life there far from fulfilling. Apparently his young charges, like thousands of others, were not convinced; those in the Asian countries where he coached were as keen on football, however, but not on going to Europe.

Endnotes

There has been little written on football in Asia, and much of this chapter has been based on scattered information.

Henshaw's *The Encyclopedia of World Soccer* was particularly useful for the period up to the late 1970s, and *World Soccer* for the period since then. Above all, two handbooks that go well beyond straight statistics, and which take Asian and Oceania soccer to 1986, are

Paul Moon and Peter Burns, *The Asia-Oceania Soccer Handbook*, Oamaru, New Zealand, 1985.
Paul Moon and Peter Burns, *Asia-Oceania Soccer Yearbook*, Oamaru, New Zealand, 1986.

Paul Moon is the main contributor to the Asian section of *World Soccer*. I would also like to thank him for his helpful comments and corrections on this chapter.

A recent collection of essays on Sport in Africa and Asia reveals how much work is still to be done. This is also reflected in the rather patchy nature of the collection, particularly in regard to soccer, which despite its importance merits only casual references:

Eric A. Wagner (ed.), *Sport in Africa and Asia. A Comparative Handbook*, Greenwood Press, New York, 1989.

For the historic 1911 game in India see

Tony Mason, 'Football on the Maidan: cultural imperialism in Calcutta', *IJHS*, Vol 7, No 1, May 1990, pp. 85–96.

For the Sikh footballers

Sarwan Singh, *Sportsmen of Punjab*, Publication Bureau, Punjabi University, Patiala, 1984.

Ken Knight, *Soccer in China*, 1991, is a desktop publication with the usual faults of these amateur productions, but it contains unrivalled material on the role of the Chinese in soccer in Asia.
For blacks in Britain,

Dave Hill, *Out of his skin. The John Barnes phenomenon*, Faber and Faber, London, 1989,

incorporates information from the earlier books by Al Hamilton and Brian Woolnough. See also the article by

John Williams, 'Having an away day: English football spectators and the hooligan debate', in *British Football and Social Change*.

For Trautmann's comments,

Alan Rowlands, *Trautmann. The Biography*, Breedon Books, Derby, 1990.

On Dassler, Havelange and Samaranch, see the savage attack in:

Vyv Simson and Andrew Jennings, *The Lords of the Rings*, Simon and Shuster, London, 1992.

Samaranch responded to the accusations in an article by Phil Davison of *The Independent on Sunday* (19 July 1992), claiming that the book was part of a conspiracy to replace him with Princess Anne, and that 'Britain believes people of Latin origin have no right to these positions.'

CHAPTER NINE

Out of Africa

In the early 1960s the enthusiasm for football in west and central Africa was so great that Walter Winterbottom, then a high ranking adviser to FIFA, forecast that Africa would produce world champions before the end of the century. For two decades, however, African football remained something of an exotic curiosity, and Winterbottom's prophecy seemed misplaced as progress proved bumpy in a continent coming to terms with poverty and modernization amid the ruins and uncertainties of a post-colonial world. Then in the 1980s came the first international successes by African teams at the national level, crowned by the brilliant victories of Cameroon in Italia 1990. Now the doubters, who had ridiculed as excessive the demands of Africa for more places in the World Cup, warmly welcomed the extra place they were granted for the World Cup to be held in the United States in 1994.

All eyes were now on Africa and at the African Nations' Cup held in Senegal in January 1992 the continent as a whole seemed to have come of age, with TV cameras beaming all the games direct to a European audience, the venture consecrated by millions of dollars of sponsorship money. This was the first time the finals had been held in January, and the changed date was in order to meet the requirements of most of Africa's best players, who played in Europe and had a better chance of being released during the mid-winter break. The scouts and coaches of Europe were there, too, of course, ready to pick from the shop window of future champions. At youth level Ghana has done particularly well, winning the 1991 Under-seventeen World Youth Championship, and at the Under-twenty Youth Championship in 1993 they played scintillating football to come within an ace of taking the gold medal. A remarkable progress, and the much quoted phrase from Pliny the Elder 'Out of Africa, always something new', was now applied to its football.

Football in Africa today is a game of skill, violence and ebullient spontaneity. The richness of this talent has not been matched by the administrative expertise to bring it to full fruition, and the inefficiency and even corruption in football are often no better than in the political regimes. The new nations also have to battle against a poverty of natural resources, and their uneven distribution where abundant: in Zambia copper, and in Nigeria oil, funded many new stadiums in the 1960s, but two decades later they have fallen into disrepair. For countless numbers of young Africans the best road to wealth and recognition is through football . . . but only by playing abroad: almost the entire Ghana team in the 1993 Under- twenty World Youth Championship were contracted to European teams. Aspects of football in Africa today are reminiscent of the game in Britain before the turn of the century and Europe through to the 1930s: inadequate spectator facilities, resulting in frequent crowd encroachments; teams failing to turn up or leaving the field in protest at poor refereeing; referees and winning away teams having to have police or military protection to escape the wrath of the locals; and as elsewhere deaths due to crowding and even hooliganism. Like Europe, too, competitions have frequently been interrupted by wars. And if the 1992 Nations' Cup is any indication, success threatens to dull the game.

The organization of African football

Organized football came to Africa in the familiar form of traders and missionaries, and then with soldiers wearing the uniforms of various nations in two world wars. It was the most popular sport in Africa by the Second World War. Nevertheless it was only after 1960, when most countries in Africa had gained their freedom, that the game flourished in black Africa. At that time it had taken firm root north of the Sahara, mainly under the influence of French settlers, and in the south, where the British had established the game before forsaking it for more socially acceptable pursuits. In black Africa south of the Sahara, as in Latin America, the local populations watched it being played, formed their own teams, and occasionally were invited to play with or against the Europeans. No sooner had they gained their independence than they were forming their own league and cup competitions and applying to be accepted by FIFA and CAF, their own confederation.

The African Football Confederation, known by its French acronym, Confédération Africaine de Football/CAF, just as the Nations', Champion Clubs' and Cup-winners' Cups are officially known by their French titles, was founded by idealists who hoped to create a united Africa. In this the foundation of CAF in 1957 preceded its overtly political counterpart, the Organization for African Unity, by six years. There were four nations present at the meeting in Khartoum on 8 February 1957 to form a body to control football in Africa and initiate a regular international tournament: Sudan, Egypt, Ethiopia and South Africa, which would soon be expelled for refusing to accept the principle of multi-racial teams. Ethiopia, due to play South Africa in the semi-final of the new tournament, refused to accept a reorganized triangular tournament when South Africa were expelled, and so went straight into the final.

The first tournament was held in Sudan, to honour that country's independence, by contesting a trophy donated by Abdelaziz Abdalah Salem from Egypt and CAF's first president. Another Egyptian, and another general, Abdelaziz Mostafa, replaced Salem as president the following year, and after the four-year presidency of Dr Abdel Halim Mohamed of Sudan (1968–72), the dominant figure in the development of African football took over as president: the Pan-African militant from Ethiopia, Ydnecatchew Tessema.

Tessema was born in Jima in Ethiopia on 11 September 1921, and combined primary and secondary studies with a passion for football that saw him involved at all levels as a player and administrator until his untimely death in early 1988. Prior to being elected President of CAF, Tessema had been General Secretary from the foundation of that body. Whatever the office, Tessema held it with distinction and high moral commitment. He was married in 1943 and went on to have ten children. In 1943 he also became general secretary of the Ethiopian Sports Confederation when it was re-established after the expulsion of the Italians. In this position he represented CAF at its foundation, and thereafter led a vigorous campaign to see Africa find its place in the football world. He held in equal contempt British arrogance, apartheid and the sponsorship of nicotine and alcohol through sport. But he was also a stern critic of those in African football who could not live up to his high ideals.

There were many regional bodies in Africa before the foundation of CAF. The East and Central African Championship, for instance, went back to the 1920s when European missionaries and civil servants founded an Arab and African Football Association. In 1922 a Kenya team visited Kampala, and in 1924 Kenya and Uganda played for a cup donated by a local soap manufacturer, who gave his name to the Gossage Trophy. Tanzania (then Tanganyika) joined the competition in 1945, and in the 1970s it was widened to take in many neighbouring countries. It became the Confederation of East and Central African FAs (CECFA) and inaugurated the CECFA Championship in 1973. This body was challenged in late 1982 by a rival Confederation of Southern Africa Football Associations, when at a meeting in Malawi, Zambia moved the creation of the new body. The secretary of the Kenya FA accused the southern nations of turning their backs on the welcome offered by their East African brothers, and eventually the dispute was resolved in favour of the older confederation. In 1975 the strongest of the regional federations was formed with the West African Football Union, made up mainly of francophone countries. CAF acted as the supreme arbiter in disputes between these bodies.

CAF's own executive committee was formed in 1963 from two delegates from each of six geographical regions. With its head office in Cairo, CAF was often accused of having a muslim bias, but the anglophone members complained in addition of a bias in favour of francophone nations. These divisions came into the open at the election for a new president in Casablanca on 10 March 1988, where the in-fighting and backstabbing among the 'courageous and brave sons of Africa' revealed power struggles as unsavoury as those of UEFA or the International Olympic Committee.

Despite such problems CAF has established continental competitions that have not only survived, but flourished over the years. In 1964 the continental competition for champion clubs, the Coupe d'Afrique des Clubs Champions was introduced, and in 1975 the Cup-winners' Cup, the Coupe d'Afrique des Vainqueurs de Coupe. The Champions' Cup was played by the league champions of each CAF member nation, on a home and away basis, including the final; the winner received the Kwame Nkrumah Cup. The Cup-winners' Cup, known as the Nelson Mandela Trophy from 1986, was played on the same basis, for winners of the various cup competitions. In 1978 an African Youth Championship was founded, named after CAF president Tessema. The senior competitions were dominated by the black African nations in the early years. This was in part because the nations north of the Sahara were put off by the distances involved, and by their closer affinities with other Arab nations of the Middle East. But they would soon overcome such reservations, not least when they realized that the black nations south of the Sahara offered competition of the sternest mettle.

In the official history of CAF, published in 1988, the problems facing football in Africa were squarely set out. Most of these were similar to large confederations anywhere, and many were similar to those that faced football authorities elsewhere in the world: the incursions of politics, race, tribal or religious rivalries; a biased and sensationalist press; instability with frequent sackings of coaches who failed; ignorance of the laws of the game by spectators and players; corruption of referees; and violence resulting from political and social problems.

Variations on some familiar themes

Africa's troubles on and around the football field, of course, are not merely replicas of those elsewhere. Violence against referees and visiting teams seems to be more prevalent and more deadly, and corruption abounds. Referees have been beaten up for appearing to collude in a fixed result, and they have been beaten up for refusing to do so. One of CAF's worries in regard to violence was the way the police and army often joined in. Even for a body with little liking for the British, CAF had to express its wish that one day it might see its forces of order as trustworthy as those who controlled law and order in Britain. There was one problem highlighted by CAF, however, that seemed to have a more peculiarly African touch: witchcraft.

Superstition is present throughout the world; footballers everywhere have their rituals before getting ready for the game. Some believe in the power of pills and in another age the 'magic sponge' of the trainer was said to have great restorative effects. But belief in the power of witchcraft, like macumba rites in Brazil, is rife throughout many African societies, even among the educated who would scorn the suggestion that they believe in it. Many of the witch doctors employed by the clubs are, or were, well paid, and in Kenya in the early 1970s, one of the strongholds of the practice, the vast majority of its two hundred clubs had a witch doctor on the payroll. In South Africa few teams are without their nyanga, often brought in from surrounding countries, to prepare a stronger muti, a special herbal potion, than that of the opposition. The main role of the witch doctor (occasionally a woman) is to raise the morale of their own players, but just as often it is to lower that of the opposition, through a whole range of spells, chants and potions designed perhaps to make the opposition player see two balls, or see it turn into a snake. Frequently it involves doctoring the pitch, and at least one team has taken the field on bicycles to escape this influence.

None of this has met with the approval of the African authorities, who specifically condemned the practice at the XIIth meeting of the CAF General Assembly in 1976. They appealed to member associations to free African sport from 'all the evils which obstruct the realization of the noble objectives which we have chosen. These evils take the form of tribalism, ju-ju and other primitive magic which have always been encouraged in our countries and among our people by colonialism in the hope of obliterating the African personality and controlling our people.' Whether or not this version of the 'divide and rule' theory relates to realities, fines and suspensions have helped to suppress lingering superstitions.

In 1983 players of Stationery Stores of Nigeria attacked the visiting goalkeeper of ASEC because he was believed to have buried a magic charm in his goal, and on another occasion the players of Police of Senegal were attacked by the crowd for wearing amulets believed to have been (witch-) doctored. In their desire to present a modern image to the world the authorities have come down heavily on such incidents: in the case of Stationery Stores their ground was closed and the players involved placed on a two year ban, while the Nigerian FA was fined $3000. Nor do the authorities show any more sympathy where violence is not involved: when the Abaluhya club of Kenya failed to turn up for an away game in 1968 because their witch doctor had predicted that they would incur too many injuries, they were handed out a stiff fine. Four players of Zimbabwe's first division side Tongogara who urinated along the pitch to remove a spell after their team went a goal down were given a life ban by the Zimbabwe FA for indecent exposure.

Government help and interference in the game in Africa also seems to be worse than in all but the Communist and other dictatorships of Europe and Latin America. Governments have built showpiece stadiums and then let them fall into disrepair, or as in the case of the Cameroon government, to double as parking and storage areas for tanks and other military equipment. More frequently governments have promised glittering prizes to teams that did well in international competitions, and dismissed them when they failed. In 1974 President Mobuto of Zaire, whose advent to power in 1966 was accompanied by a determined effort to raise the standard of football, importing foreign coaches and Africanizing the names of all the teams, promised each of the team who qualified for Germany in 1974 a car, a house and a holiday for two anywhere in the world: on their return after failing miserably they were condemned for what was believed to have been the disgrace they brought on the country. The government of Ghana promised large bonuses and houses to the Ghana team for winning the African Nations' Cup in 1978. According to Faouzi Mahjoub in his history of that Cup, the presidency of I. K. Acheampong survived for another fourteen months as a result of the victory. In this time the players waited in vain for their rewards and two years later they threatened to boycott the 1980 finals in Nigeria as a consequence. Many, in the meantime, had left the country to play where they had more likelihood of being paid what they were promised. When Nigeria won the 1980 Cup on home soil President Shagari rewarded each of the twenty-four players in the squad with an air-conditioned Peugeot 504 and a three bedroomed house. Other gifts included the monthly salary of a grateful government official, a television set from an electronics firm, and 1000 Nigerian naire each from millionaire chief Abiola. Abiola, one of the great patrons of the game, founded his own team, the highly regarded Abiola Babes, and encouraged other millionaires in Africa to do the same.

Such gifts are modest in comparison to what sports stars elsewhere in the world were getting paid at this time, but they stand out amidst more general poverty in Africa. It was for such reasons that they were condemned by CAF president Tessema at the finals of the African Nations' Cup in Ivory Coast in 1984, where he drew attention to the rewards among the elite players who were offered bonuses, salaries, apartments and transport, while others could not afford football boots. He might also have added that not even the elite players could always be sure of receiving their salaries, and often the apparent money-grubbing of African players abroad was based on their experiences in Africa, where cash in hand means much more than the cheque in the post. In 1980 CAF permitted professionalism, but this did little to ease the problem.

Government involvement in football has varied from concern about national prestige to simple love of the game. In 1981 the Zambia FA Executive was dismissed because the team was playing badly; in 1982 Zaire withdrew its national team from all international competition; one of the first acts of the new government in Ghana in 1982 was to reverse the sporting policies of the old dictatorship and enter the African Nations' Cup being held in Libya; and in 1983 the Nigerian government disbanded the entire sporting structure. Dictators seeking national glory have included Idi Amin, who supported Simba of Uganda at the expense of certain other teams. In socialist Guinea President Sekou Touré made no secret of his support for Hafia de Conakry, one of the most successful club sides of the 1970s, and anti-Communist Houphouet-Boigny of Ivory Coast is only one African leader who was proud to give his name to the main sporting stadium. Canaan Banana of Zimbabwe is said to have requested that his ashes be buried in his favourite stadium. Kenneth Kaunda, who presided over the destiny of Zambia from its independence in 1964 was reduced to tears for his people and the game he loved when one of the players of Zambia champions Nkana Red Devils was attacked by his own supporters for hitting the post in the 1990 Champions' Cup final penalty decider and so allowed Jeunesse Sportive Kabyle to win the trophy. Indeed, it is the love of so many Africans at all levels for football that allows it to survive amidst the poverty and corruption, the interference and the poor administration, and which will doubtless help it to rise above myriad difficulties to wrest the crown from the more stereotyped Europeans and Latin Americans.

The greatest problem facing CAF is one that has faced every other football nation, and as such is probably insoluble: the loss of Africa's best players to countries where they are better paid – to Europe, the Middle East, and even, in the heady days of the late 1970s, to the United States. For most African footballers there is little to be made out of the game in their own country. Government expenditure on the sport is still in keeping with a poor country; most players even lose money by playing, as the time lost from work is not always made up in wages. When President Tessema condemned the disparities between the well paid and the near destitute he pointed out that one of the results of this was that many of Africa's best players left the continent. He did not, however, have any solution to offer, other, presumably, than a sense of patriotism that was blind to the pickings other people might have been on to. Bans on expatriates playing in the national team have never been successful in keeping players at home. In their migration in search of reward for their talents the young African is no different to the Irish, Welsh and Scottish hopefuls who crossed the waters or trekked south in search of a higher standard of living in England in the early days of the game in Britain; or the Scandinavian, Dutch, German and

English players seeking lucrative contracts in Spain or Italy. In South America today there is a constant drain of players, not just moving from small clubs in Paraguay and elsewhere to Brazil and Argentina, but from these countries to Europe. Within Africa, the richer countries, such as Ivory Coast before the 1980s, then Gabon, attracted the best players from their neighbours. Ghana and Nigeria in particular have not been able to hold on to their stars, and have had to pay the price of their international success, particularly at youth level. Today, with Senegal and Zaire, they are major suppliers of talent not only to Europe and the Middle East, but even India and other African countries. Italy, which for a long time looked in directions other than Africa for its imported talent, now threatens to deprive it of its youngest players with the new system of 'parking': Torino signed three of Ghana's victorious 1991 Under-seventeen team to play in amateur teams until they decide what to do with them. After five years they become eligible to play for Italy.

Like the stars of another generation, who came out of the back streets of Europe and the beaches of Brazil, often using makeshift balls, so the budding professionals of Africa still come off the streets of the cities and the dusty lanes of the suburbs and smaller towns: present day stars claim to have learned their skills with a ball made of a stone wrapped in banana skin or a grapefruit wrapped up in rags; many of them, like Puskas and Pelé in the 1930s and 1950s, prefer football to school, and ball skills take the place of book learning.

From such beginnings came one of Africa's most precocious talents: Nii Lamptey. When only fourteen years of age he distinguished himself in the Ghana team at the Under-seventeen World Youth championship in Scotland in 1989, attracting so many clubs after his signature that his passport was seized by the Ghana FA to prevent him leaving Ghana on his return. Undeterred he skipped across the border to Nigeria without even telling his parents what he was doing. There he sought the protection and advice of Stephen Kashi, a star of the Nigeria team, then playing in Belgium. Somehow he managed to make it from Nigeria to Brussels and at the age of sixteen was playing for Anderlecht, for whom he made a sensational debut, scoring five goals in five games. The payment of an undisclosed sum by Anderlecht to the Ghana FA and Cornerstone, the team Lamptey had played for since he was twelve, seems to have solved the problem of the irregularities in the young lad's peregrinations.

On the other hand comes Anthony Baffoue, one of the dozen or so Africans who have played in the German Bundesliga since the arrival of the first African, Ibrahim Sunday, who came from Ghana in 1975 to play for Werder Bremen. Baffoue's is another side of African life, for he was born in Bad Godesburg, the son of the Ghanaian ambassador to West Germany, and returned to Ghana only once, when he was thirteen. He was the first black to take part in a German Cup Final, for Kickers Stuttgart against Hamburg. Since 1989 he has been with Fortuna Dusseldorf. Speaking with a cultured German accent he could have been the first black to play for Germany, but did not become naturalised.

The passion of the African supporter for his (and her, since women's football is very popular in parts of Africa) local team is little different from that of his counterpart elsewhere, and the tribal associations of teams do not seem to be markedly different from the ethnic, religious or geographical divisions that mark the rivalries elsewhere in the world. Kenya tried to ban teams using tribal names, but in the case of the top team, Gor Mahia, they had to give in. Gor successfully argued that while the majority of their supporters were of the Luo tribe, the Gor Mahia legend was merely derived from a Luo legend of a figure who was renowned for his magical powers. Luo Union, on the other hand, one of the most successful teams at this time, had to change their name.

The names and nick-names of African teams vary from the exotic to the mundane. The Leopards of Zaire and the Black Stars of Ghana we have already come across, and the 'Indomitable Lions' of Cameroon have blazed their name across the world. Nigeria are known as the Green Eagles, and while the Stallions is a suitably athletic title which has been taken by Burkina Faso, the image conjured up by the Elephants of the Ivory Coast is not the happiest to European ears. In club teams there are the Leopards of Kenya, the Black Rhinos of Zimbabwe and the Green Buffaloes of Zambia; popular names are Simba or Young Africa, or such splendid mixtures as Englebert Lubumbashi of Zaire. Many come from industrial factories and government departments, among whom are Kampala City Council, Bendel Insurance of Nigeria, Port Authority of Sierra Leone, and various Police, Stationery Stores and even Prisons. ASEC of Abidjan are one of the top three teams of the Ivory Coast capital, but unlike CARA of Zaire, whose acronym stands for the resplendent Athletic Society of Renaissance Eaglets, ASEC merely tells us that they are a team of Sporting Clerks (Association Sportive des Employés de Commerce). More overtly political are the many Dynamos and others with dates recalling specific glories, such as Premeiro Agosto (First August) of Luanda in Angola, and in a continent where military sport at national and international level is highly developed, many club teams are the teams of the army and air force, usually under ordinary names. When the Communists took over in Ethiopia in 1974 they banned private clubs in the Addis Ababa league and replaced them with team names as exciting as a Marxist treatise: top of the league in 1984 were Ground Forces, followed by the likes of Insurance, Air Force, AA Cement and at the bottom of the league, AA University. Most heartily missed of the well named African teams, however, must be the former champions of Mauritius, Dodo FC: they last won the championship in 1970, but are now extinct.

Pan-African games

The first African Nations' Cup might well have gone to Africa's oldest football power, Egypt, but for the invasion by the British, French and Israelis following the nationalization of the Suez canal in 1956. Egypt withdrew its football team from the Melbourne Olympics that year and its grounds were turned into ambulance facilities, while top teams like Zamalek and National played games only to raise funds for the war effort. Instead the competition was staged in Sudan.

Sudan had played football at least from the days when Kitchener arrived in Khartoum in 1898, after which an Anglo-Egyptian duopoly took over until 1956 when the first of its new dictators set about building a stadium to house the first African Nations' Cup finals. Into the new stadium crowded 30,000 spectators to see Egypt win both its games against Sudan and Ethiopia. The football was fairly primitive, but already potential stars could be seen, and the agents from Europe were there with their cheque books: the captain of the Egyptian team, twenty-one-year old Rifaat Al-Fanaguili was later offered tempting sums by AC Milan and Barcelona to sign on for them.

The second cup was played in Egypt in 1959, by the same three national teams, in the massive Al-Ahly stadium, the first on the continent to hold 100,000 spectators. Ghana, Nigeria and Uganda had gained their independence by this time, and were members of CAF, but declined to enter. Egypt won again, and their star player, Salah Salim went on to win many more international honours before signing for Sturm Graz of Austria in 1962. The Cup due to be held in 1961 was held over because of the widespread political instability in the wake of new nations gaining their independence, and were held in 1962 instead. This time Ethiopia was the host nation and the games were held in Addis Ababa, at the re-modelled stadium named after Haile Selassie, emperor and football fan.

Ethiopia managed to avoid colonization until the gas bombs and other weapons of western civilization subjected its Christian inhabitants to the rule of Mussolini. The oldest Christian civilization in Africa also had the shortest colonial occupation, a mere seven years before the Italian armies were swept out of the deserts of North Africa in 1942. A gentler Italian intrusion had preceded that of the Fascists, when immigrants arrived in the 1920s and founded their own football teams: there were also teams founded by Greeks, Armenians and Indians, but the Italians were the strongest. When the Fascists took over the Italian teams were strictly segregated from the other teams, and Ethiopians were not only banned from playing against European teams, but were not allowed to play on their grounds. Despite this, interest in the game was growing among Ethiopians, and when the Fascists were removed interracial games were gradually restored. St George Sports Association, founded in 1935, became the first team to fire the pride of the locals when they beat the Italian based team Fortitudo in 1942. The following year the Yeitopia Football Federechin was founded along with the usual accoutrements of a league and cup competition. There were nine clubs in the new FA, seven of which were Ethiopian, one Armenian and one Greek. None was Italian, but the Italian influence in football lived on, and it was an Italian, Luciano Vassalo who guided Ethiopia to their African Nations' Cup victory against Egypt in 1962.

Haile Selassie was there in person to see his nation win the final against Egypt, 4–2 in extra-time. Absent in 1962 for internal political reasons, was Sudan, but present were Tunisia, who came third and Uganda who came last in the four team tournament. To restore the Games to their original biennial schedule they were next played in 1963, with Ghana as the hosts. The increased entries meant that games had to be played in two sections. Sudan returned to the competition, and Nigeria made their first appearance. Ghana won the Accra section, and beat Sudan, who topped the Kumasi section, to win their first Cup. It was in Tunisia in 1965 that the black nations from south of the Sahara came into their own. Senegal in their first appearance came second in their group, which Tunisia won, while Ethiopia came last; the other group was made up of three black teams: Ghana, and newcomers Congo-Léopoldville (later Zaire) and Ivory Coast. Egypt and Sudan were missing from the fifth Cup in 1965, due to a tiff with Tunisia the hosts, and while such political problems would continue to plague the games, from this time on they never looked back.

Ethiopia as host nation won the next Cup, which was delayed until January 1968, whereafter disasters both man made and natural enveloped the country. Eritrea had become part of Ethiopia as an autonomous province in 1952, but ten years later Ethiopia simply took it over and all the complications that went with it. In an act of violent modernization, Haile Selassie was removed in 1974 along with his forty-year-old aristocracy, and although Ethiopia were hosts for a third time in 1976, the competition was played against the background of the civil war in Eritrea. From then on Ethiopia would continue to be in the headlines, but not for its football, in the establishment of which in Africa it had played such a key role. Sudan also faded from the football picture as political interference in Ethiopia and its own domestic dictatorship, along with continuing divisions between the muslim Arabs in the north and non-muslims in the south brought misery that not even football could relieve. By then, too, the best footballing nations were no longer the ones who had established the game on a continental basis. In 1978 Ghana won the Nations' Cup for the third time and so won the right to retain it. From 1980 it became known as the Cup of African Unity.

By this time the Nations' Cup was the continent's premier competition, the greatest of the pan-African games. In 1960, to celebrate the granting of independence to its colonies, France had organized the first Friendship Games (Jeux de l'amitié), in Tananarive, Madagascar, with football as part of the competition. Only Madagascar, Cameroon and a French amateur select took part. Madagascar itself has yet to enter the mainstream of African football, although soccer is the most popular sport. It has achieved an unenviable reputation for failing to turn up for the away legs of competitions where they have fared poorly in the home leg. The second Friendship Games were held in Abidjan, Ivory Coast, in 1961, with English-speaking countries invited to take part, and the third in Dakar, Senegal, in 1963, when twenty-four African nations and their athletes competed with representatives from France. From 1965 the Friendship Games were taken over by the newly formed Pan-African Games, and this gave rise in December 1966 to the Supreme Council for Sports in Africa. The All-Africa Games were mainly concerned about the Olympics and so amateurism and athletics. Its soccer tournament, at least so far as the stronger and more professional teams was concerned, was not taken as seriously as the other continental football competitions. For them the Nations' Cup, the Champions' Cup and soon the Cup-winners' Cup were the true All-African games, football being the one sport that was played throughout the continent.

Football, the French and North Africa

The French were the dominant influence in football in Africa. Even before the Second World War, France had encouraged its colonial subjects to run, box and play for the motherland; the most successful of these was El Ouafi, the Algerian who won the marathon for France in the 1928 Olympics. In 1937, following a poor performance in track and field at the Nazi Olympics the previous year, and inspired by the performances of Jesse Owens and other blacks, L'Auto, in conjunction with the French Amateur Athletic Federation, sent a special mission to its colonies in Africa to seek sporting talent that would match natural ability with European discipline. By then African footballers were already a common sight in French football teams, and some played for the national team. Pierre Lanfranchi has identified 147 Africans in the French first and second divisions in 1938. That was also the year that France's greatest African star, Larbi Ben Barek, arrived from Casablanca to play in Marseille and dazzle a generation of

French football fans with his skills. The year after his arrival the Moroccan won his first cap for France in a game against Italy in Naples, and in a career interrupted by war he went on to gain sixteen more.

When France fell to the Nazis in 1940 and a puppet regime was installed at Vichy, one of the fictions that allowed the collaborationist regime to maintain some sense of pride was that it still held on to its Empire, and despite its own scandalous treatment of the Jews, its propaganda in favour of the Empire proudly proclaimed that peoples of all skin colours were French. On 26 May 1942 the publishers of the weekly journal *Marche* brought out a celebratory issue dedicated to the 'Imperial Fortnight', in which the exploits of athletes from Africa, black and Arab, and from Asia, who took part in the great sporting festival, were highlighted. Among them was Nakache, the great Jewish swimmer, not identified as such, and the cyclist Cohen: within a few weeks they would be banned from all competition and their families on the way to death in Poland by way of the sporting stadiums of northern Paris which served as detention centres.

French colonists brought football to North Africa in the 1890s, and from the 1920s the game was actively encouraged by the government. Metropolitan France sent national selections, usually B teams, to play there regularly, and the French champions also made regular visits. Teams throughout French North Africa played in each other's Cup competitions, and competitions specifically involving the Maghreb countries were also introduced. A North African Championship was started as early as 1919, made up of teams from the five leagues, three in Algeria, one each in Morocco and Tunisia. It continued until 1949, interrupted only by the war years, and revived briefly in 1941. A North African Cup started in 1930 and was also staged annually, apart from the war years, until 1949.

In Algeria, league competitions were set up in the 1920s around the three major urban centres of Algiers, Oran and Constantine, and while teams from each of these leagues played against each other, a truly national league had to wait until after 1962. Football in Morocco probably arrived with the Spanish, but the French Army and the Foreign Legion gave it the first major boost after 1910, when France arrived to seize the last part of North Africa that had not been colonized. The first championship was started in 1916, based around the port towns of Tangiers and Morocco. An FA was founded in 1923 and the Steeg Cup was introduced in 1925. In 1955, the year before its independence, Morocco founded its own FA and joined FIFA the following year. Morocco went to the World Cup in Mexico in 1970, where they gave West Germany a fright with a goal in an opening twenty-minute burst that had the Germans staggering before they recovered to win 2–1. In 1986 they went through to the knock-out stage of the World Cup, only to be eliminated by West Germany on penalties. Tunisia became independent in 1956, abolished its monarchy the following year and joined FIFA in 1960. Despite this unusual ordering of priorities, and a much smaller population, they went on to surpass Morocco's success at the World Cup when in 1978 they held West Germany to a 0–0 draw in Argentina and beat Mexico 3–1, but finished third in their section. As a reward for their success, virtually the whole team was lured to Saudi Arabia to play for clubs there.

As soon as its independence was proclaimed in 1962 Algeria formed its own FA and the following year joined FIFA. Ahmed Ben Bella, the leader of the independence movement, the National Liberation Front (Front de Libération National/FLN), founded in 1951, and Algeria's first president, played for Olympique de Marseille during the war, but was regarded as a somewhat showy and selfish footballer, a style that would reappear in his politics. Many of his followers were soccer enthusiasts who passed their time under arrest playing ping-pong and following the football scores, as well as poring over revolutionary tracts. At the World Cup in Switzerland in 1954 the leaders of the approaching insurrection combined an excuse to watch the football with the convenient cover of nearby Berne to conduct one of their most crucial meetings to prepare the war that they launched on 1 November of that year.

On 15 April 1958 the FLN entered its 'revolutionary eleven' in the struggle. This team, based in Tunisia, was made up mainly of Algerians who had been playing in France, but who left to play for 'Free Algeria': these included stars like Rachid Mekhloufi and Mustapha Zitouni, both of whom would have been certain to be included in the French team for the World Cup in Sweden that year. The FLN XI went on to play fifty-seven matches in fourteen countries over the next four years, mainly against North African and Communist opposition, including China and North Vietnam. They won most matches with ease. For the Algerian revolutionaries the footballers were portrayed as patriotic heroes who had set a fine example for young Algerians, and the FLN even sought recognition by FIFA so that it could enter the team in the coming World Cup.

In France a media black-out was imposed, but not before *Le Monde*, not given to much sporting news, let alone printing it on its front page, commented three days after the departure of the 'ten Algerian footballers', that the loss of Zitouni had made much more of an impact on the French public than the departure of Algeria's political leaders. As well as pressure on the media, the French government tried to get FIFA to ban any association that played against the FLN team. On the other hand, it tried to win over public opinion in Algeria by having class matches played there, most notably, and with the willing help of Franco, between Réal Madrid and Stade de Reims, who had just signed French star Kopa. A semi-final of the French Cup was also played there.

When Algeria gained its independence many of the players of the FLN

team secured good positions in the new regime, but Mekhloufi, despite
threats to his life, returned to play in France, where he became the only
Algerian to win the French Cup as team captain. His return to France was
more the reaction of a professional who needed to play with the best than
an act of treachery. In fact Mekhloufi played for the new Algeria in its first
official game, against West Germany on 1 January 1964, and was the
architect behind their 2–0 victory. Each year on the anniversary of 1
November 1954, he joined with other members of the former FLN team in
commemoration of the declaration of war against France. In 1970 he
became Algeria's national trainer, but as a professional he was frowned on
by the new socialist government, and was not eligible to play for Algeria in
games organized by CAF.

From the start, the revolutionary regime in Algeria used sport, and
particularly football, as a means of winning the youth of the newly
independent nation to its cause. For those born after 1962, and twenty
years later they were the large majority, the sacrifice that can make a fairly
sterile regime bearable had lost much of its meaning, and in October 1988 a
youth revolt shook the regime to its core. Their displeasure had already
made itself known at football matches, where insults were freely chanted at
the president and his wife, Halima. In the many incidents in and around the
football stadiums, as reported by the sociologist Youssef Fates, however, it
would appear that simple bad sportsmanship as much as disenchantment
with the regime was at work, while slogans like 'Long live exile and drugs'
scarcely reveal a developed ideology.

Nevertheless, Algerian football was still charged with the politics that
had been there at the birth, with the difference that instead of the French
coming under fire from Algerian freedom fighters, it was the secular
government of the revolution that was coming under fire from those of a
more dedicated religious persuasion, in particular the Berbers and the
followers of the Islamic Salvationist Front (Front islamique du salut/FIS).
These fundamentalist muslims found in football one way to make their
feelings felt in a regime where freedom of speech was not a high priority.
(The opponents of FIS also let their opinions of the fundamentalists be
known at games.) In the case of the Berbers this came through support for
the football team of Tizi-Ouzou, the capital of Kabylie: Jeunesse Sportive
Kabyle (JSK). The Algerian government was offended by the overtly
political support that was centred around the team and in the early 1980s
they forced it to change its name for a while to JET – Jeunesse électrique de
Tizi-Ouzou. Like the Basques and Catalans in Spain under Franco,
however, whether JET or JSK, the Berbers by any other name reeked just
as much of unwanted politics. FIS supporters took their banners to
football matches, causing a headache to the TV technicians who could
muffle the chants but had trouble editing out banners which proclaimed

the FIS cause in three languages, thus giving themselves a nationwide audience for their message. To combat the fundamentalists a rumour was spread that FIS was against football, and that their leader Abassi Madani would forbid it. It seems clear from the elections of late 1991 and the crowds at football matches that the rumours of FIS being a threat to their football were not listened to: chants of 'Army, People, all with Madani!' filled the air at the Cup final in the stade d'Alger in 1990, and the following year FIS had a landslide victory at the polls. The secular government, however, saw FIS as a threat to their interests and so instituted a *coup d'état* against the verdict of the voters.

In football, Algeria in 1982 went one better than Morocco and Tunisia by defeating West Germany in the World Cup in Spain (2–1), only to come up against European fair play that saw the apparent collusion of West Germany and Austria to keep themselves in the competition and cheat Algeria of a finals play-off. Despite the brilliance of many players, particularly Lakhdar Belloumi and Rabah Madjer, the national team went through the 1980s without winning any of the major prizes. In 1986 Algeria qualified for Mexico, without great success, and failed to qualify for Italy in 1990. In the African Nations' Cup the best they could do was a bronze medal at Morocco in 1988. As host to the Nations' Cup in 1990, however, everything fell into place, and not only was the competition well run, but the home team took off the trophy with a victory over Nigeria in the final. The victory, however, was marred by the lacklustre nature of the competition, fought as it was in the shadow of the World Cup qualifiers, and Egypt insulting it by sending only a B team, a day late, and after threatening to pull out.

The Italians took football to Libya when they took over from the Ottomans, but their passion for football was not shared by the locals. Libyans took up the game after 1945, but without great enthusiasm, performing reasonably well in the occasional Palestine Cup or Mediterranean Cup game. When Colonel Gaddafi came to power at the end of 1969, he set about revolutionizing the country around the Koran, socialism and hatred of Israel. Such mixed messages he evidently carried over to football, which he promoted as an arm of politics in favour of the Arabs: or perhaps more accurately against Israel. The 1978 Nations' Cup quarter-final between Libya and Egypt came just after Anwar Sadat had announced his peace initiatives with Israel, and served as an excuse for Libyan fans and players to attack the Egyptians, causing serious damage. There were reprisals in Cairo. In that same tournament Tunisia walked off the field in their game against Nigeria for third place.

Algeria also fell foul of Gaddafi, and political tensions were stirred up with terrible consequences for a return Champion Clubs' match between Mascara of Algeria and Ittihou of Libya in 1985. Since Mascara had won

4–0 at home there seemed little likelihood of the Libyan club catching up, but they set out to do so, crippling Belloumi, who left the field with a broken leg, and who thus missed the greater mayhem when spectators from the 70,000 crowd joined the players in their attacks on the visiting Mascara team. No-one was killed. Relations between the two countries were improved a few years later when Algeria supported Gaddafi after the US bombing of Tripoli early in 1989. As a gesture of thanks to 'brotherly Algeria', Gaddafi instructed the Libya team due to play Algeria in a World Cup qualifying match for the 1990 World Cup to withdraw. Not exactly what Tom Brown would have seen as a sporting gesture. Nor did the vast crowd gathered for the game see it in this way; they refused to leave until forced to do so by the police, and had to vent their frustration elsewhere.

South of the Sahara

West Africa has produced some of the strongest footballing teams in Africa: apart from Ghana and Nigeria, most were former French colonies. Ivory Coast and Guinea, rivals in football as well as how best to modernize, were contenders for the top honours in international competition in the early days. Guinea, under the guidance of their Marxist football fan and president, Sekou Touré, opted to cut off relations with France after independence, but retained full sporting contacts. In Hafia de Conakry they had one of the most powerful club sides of the 1970s, winning the Champions Cup in 1972, 1975 and 1977, and in 1976 were deprived of the title only through the lottery of the penalty shoot-out. Horoya de Conakry won the Cup-winners Cup in 1978. The Ivory Coast, under the one-party rule of Houphouet-Boigny in what is supposed to be a multi-party state, enjoyed one of the most buoyant of the economies among the African nations. In the capital, Abidjan, it had three powerful teams: Stella, ASEC and Stade d'Abidjan who were African champions in 1966. In 1984 Ivory Coast successfully hosted the African Nations' Cup, although the failure of the host nation to make the finals had the usual result of drops in attendance. This was in part remedied by allowing free entrance to some games. At Senegal in 1992, however, Ivory Coast went through to the finals where they drew with Ghana and then were awarded the trophy as the result of a marathon penalty shoot-out. Senegal itself does not have a particularly distinguished football record, but in Diagne, son of the deputy from Senegal, who played for Racing Club de Paris in the 1930s, it produced France's first black international.

Other nations emerging from French West Africa, like Togo, Bénin and Niger have not made much of a mark, while Chad were expelled from FIFA for continued refusal or inability to pay their dues. Mali came second in the Nations' Cup in 1972 and has produced some top class talent, most notably Salif Keita, the first African Footballer of the Year in 1970. Sierra Leone has no great sporting tradition, but neighbouring Liberia produced in George Weah the African Footballer of the Year for 1989. Unfortunately, the abandonment of international competition as a result of the civil war has restricted his appearances in the national team. Mauritania, one of the larger countries but mainly made up of desert, nevertheless has an active football federation and joined FIFA and CAF in 1968. Upper Volta, now known as Burkina-Faso, short of the odd upset, have mainly made up the numbers.

In what was once French Equatorial Africa, Central Africa was one of the first nations to take up professionalism. Gabon is made up mainly of tropical rain forest, but through its oil is one of the wealthiest countries in Africa. Football is played mainly in Libreville, the capital, and what the country fails to produce in footballers it makes up in referees.

The French Congo, surrounded by Gabon, Cameroon and the Belgian Congo is a small country in comparison to its two larger neighbours, but its footballing prowess has been remarkable. Known simply as Congo after a brief flirtation with Congo-Brazzaville after 1960, it won the African Nations Cup in 1972 and its best team, Club Athlétique de Renaissance Aiglons, or CARA, won the African Champion Club title in 1974. Early influences were a mixture of French and Belgian, due to the proximity on either side of the Stanley Pool of the two capitals: Brazzaville, the capital of French Congo, and Léopoldville, the capital of the Belgian Congo. Clubs from both capitals competed in the league founded by the Fédération de Football Association de Pool in 1924.

In Brazzaville, as the American historian Phyllis Martin has shown, French priests sought through Youth Clubs to occupy the leisure time of young Africans. The motives behind this were similar to those bodies in France at this time, both secular and religious, who were anxious to keep the devil from finding work for idle working-class youths, and the priests in Brazzaville, like those in Europe, seemed to be obsessed with evils such as 'immoral dancing' and 'dangerous companions'. Without necessarily giving up the former, young Africans flocked to the football, playing 'mwana-foot' (child's football) wherever they could, with whatever they could use, and until well after dark if they could get away with it. Teams were formed in townships, schools and Missions, and players and supporters gave freely of their own time to construct playing fields and organize the games. African teams occasionally played in curtain raisers to games between white teams.

The repercussions of the depression in Europe were felt in parts of Africa, and in Léopoldville many workers were laid off and had to return to Brazzaville. The unrest caused by this roused fears on the part of the colonial authorities, and native sports clubs came under suspicion of harbouring nationalist activists. For this reason the Native Sports Federation was set up in 1931, run by whites on behalf of Africans, ostensibly to help them develop facilities, in fact to control them. The Africans, however, saw little reward for their efforts, at the same time as the Marchand stadium expanded the luxury facilities it offered the European elite. Tensions came to a head in the boot controversy of 1936. This arose when a footballer had his leg broken in a football match and subsequently died of complications in the wound. The authorities decided that the death had been caused by the players playing with boots rather than in their bare feet, as was more common among Africans. They claimed also to be concerned at the rising violence in football matches, and sought a solution by forbidding Africans to play with boots.

A pointed and dignified response by the four captains of the African teams pointed out that whites had been playing for years with boots without serious accidents, while it was hypocritical to expect them to appear at work in their offices with shirts, trousers and shoes, but to play football in bare feet. Their request for permission to found their own independent African Football Association was turned down. No more were the Africans allowed to control their own sporting affairs than they were the running of their own country. Both would have to wait until 1960.

Across the water from Brazzaville, Léopoldville had an even livelier football culture. On independence Léopoldville became Kinshasa, the Belgian Congo, Congo-Kinshasa, then Zaire. Before their disappointing venture to Germany in 1974, Zaire under their dynamic and football loving president Mobuto, had won the African Nations' Cup twice, 1968 and 1974, and its club teams Vita of Kinshasa (1973) and Englebert Lubumbashi (1967, 1968) had won the African Champions' Cup.

Football arrived in the Congo with Belgian missionaries as early as 1912, and the colonists had organized leagues by 1918. The first major team of locals were Englebert Lubumbashi, founded in 1936 by missionaries devoted to the Boy Scout movement, and first called Saint George FC. In 1944 they became Saint Paul FC, and only after independence in 1960, did they adopt the more grandiloquent title. With civil war raging in the mineral rich Katanga province, the club relocated to Kinshasa where it changed its name again, to Tout-Puissant Mazembé, then back to Tout-Puissant Englebert. The 'All Powerful' could not live up to their name, however, and like Hafia de Conakry who briefly lit up the African football firmament, the greatness of the early days has yet to be recaptured.

Even before Italia 1990 Cameroon were known to be one of the best footballing nations in Africa, and in Canon of Yaoundé and Union de Douala, had two of the continent's best teams. Cameroon was first colonized by Germany, and it was the Germans who introduced football. In 1916 the German colony fell to the allies and after the war it was placed in British and French trusteeship. But it was the French influence that dominated. Cameroon's rapid rise to success after independence was at first mainly at club level: the teams of Douala, the industrial capital on the coastline of the Gulf of Guinea, and of Yaoundé, the administrative capital, supplied teams to beat the best in Africa. Oryx of Douala won the first African Club Championship, in 1964, Canon of Yaoundé won the first African Cup-winners' Cup in 1975, but it was not until the 1980s that the national team came into its own. At the World Cup in Spain in 1982 they were eliminated without losing a game. Then they won the African Nations' Cup in 1984 and 1988, on both occasions against Nigeria (3–1 and 1–0). In Egypt in 1986 Cameroon drew with the host nation in the final, but lost on penalties. Finally, came Italia 1990, when only their occasional crude fouling spoiled otherwise brilliant performances. Against England in the quarter-finals this naïf violence was punished by the free kicks and penalties that gave England victory.

Under the French in the 1920s the native teams in Cameroon were strictly segregated from the European (French) teams: the French would often play against visiting ships in Douala, while the native teams, made up mainly of students, played among themselves. Only in the 1940s were teams integrated. Spectators, too, were segregated, although this was as much a matter of economics as policy, locals being unable to pay the admission to the better parts of the ground. The preferred leisure pursuits of the European elite were tennis and sailing, as this better protected their social credentials: soccer was left to the administrators, the skilled manual workers and the students. Occasionally, non-Europeans were allowed to play in the French teams, and increasingly they became hard to ignore, particularly as a modicum of education and wealth allowed some of them to buy proper balls and boots. This posed the same problem as in Brazzaville (and elsewhere): football might help keep the Africans amused in their spare time, but their improvement at playing and organization gave them confidence in their own abilities, and this was not a desirable outcome.

Some of the native Cameroon teams took on names with a European flavour, but this was discouraged by the administration, who forbade one Douala team from calling themselves Olympique after Marseille, and another for taking on the nickname 'Diables rouges' after the French team SC Fives. Instead the one had to call itself Oryx de Douala, the other The Leopard Club of Douala. Only when the French left were clubs free to call themselves Santos and Dynamo, while players took on names like Magellan, D'Alembert and Mozart. It was the military might of the west rather than its intellectual gifts that most impressed ordinary Cameroonians, and this is reflected, among other cases, in the name of Yaoundé's Canon, and a player who was nicknamed DC4.

Despite the obvious teething problems, football in Cameroon was booming by the late 1960s. There was an efficient administration and a national league with three divisions, two weekly sports newspapers, and as final proof that football had arrived, football stars were being used for advertising. By the late 1970s Cameroon had two of the best stadiums in sub-Saharan Africa: the national stadium in Yaoundé and the Stade Réunification in Douala. Football was played at all levels, but despite the fanatical interest in the game, its rewards were ill-divided.

Officially football was still amateur, and players in the domestic league were paid less than the average worker's £100 per month, while coaches were on £25/£50. The once impressive stadiums had become slums, with rudimentary changing rooms and pitches ruined by the military. At the official level even important local games could be cancelled at the whim of a bureaucrat, and while star players could be whisked in from Europe on a private jet, they could not be assured of being paid for their performance.

The Portuguese were as brutal as the Belgians in their colonizing, but were happy to use colonial subjects for their own glory. Angola and Mozambique formed FAs in the early 1920s and joined the Lisbon FA in 1932, but while they have supplied star players like Coluna and Eusebio to Europe the domestic game has not flourished. These two largest of the Portuguese colonies in Africa were left to civil war and continual political and economic turmoil on independence in 1975. The influence of the US and Cuba in Angola can be seen in the popularity of basketball, which rivals soccer. Coluna, Mozambique star of the Portuguese national team in the 1960s, returned to his homeland to coach, a political decision encouraged by his activist wife.

As in the larger, so in the smaller Portuguese colonies of Cape Verde and Guinea Bissau, football has captured the popular imagination. So it is in São Tome e Principe, the smallest country in Africa after the Seychelles. Remote and sparsely populated, the inhabitants of these two tiny islands follow the game in Portugal with bated breath, especially to see if they have won a fortune on the Portuguese football pools: the 'Totobola'. The two islands have separate leagues, and the winners play each other for the title champions, but do not enter into the African Champions' Cup or the African Cup-winners' Cup: most of their first division games are played with a rope to separate players from spectators and the only stadium, called July 12th, is appropriately modest. Moreover the cost of bringing teams from the mainland is prohibitive. Nor has the national team, a member of FIFA and CAF since 1986, entered the Nations' Cup, but it has played a dozen games, against the likes of Cameroon B and Angola, chalking up one victory, against Rwanda in 1977. With only 1500 registered players it has not attracted the cheque books of European entrepreneurs, but a few of the local lads have gone off to further their football career in Angola, Cameroon and with the lesser teams of Portugal.

The British in Africa

Until 1978 Ghana could justifiably claim to be the best football nation in Africa, but thereafter the rot set in. Nigeria, with its oil wealth and large population, and despite the disastrous Biafran War, established the game on a firm footing but seems to make a specialty of losing finals. Both countries have produced world-beating youth teams, and both have lost most of their best players abroad.

Ghana, under Kwame Nkrumah, was the first British colony to be granted independence, in 1957, and in part to honour this event Stanley Matthews toured the new nation, playing in several exhibition matches. Ghana's role as a political leader in the early years was complemented by its footballing prowess. It was the first black African nation to form its own FA, in 1957, and the first to join FIFA, which it did the following year. Ghana won the African Nations' Cup, in 1963, and the following year they were the first to qualify for the final rounds of the Olympic Games, in Japan in 1964. In 1976 Ghana refused for political reasons and in solidarity with other African nations, to go to the Montréal Olympics in 1976.

In an interesting twist to the usual story, football is said to have been brought to the Gold Coast by a Jamaican, about 1880. However that may be, and whoever he was, the British established a Gold Coast FA in 1922, and from then until 1939 the game prospered with many native teams, most notably Ashanti United and Hearts of Oak. Hearts of Oak are not only the oldest team in Ghana, but one of the oldest in the continent. They were founded in 1911, but came into their own only after independence. Their perennial rivals are Asante Kotoko, from the inland town of Kumasi. Asante began as the Rainbow Football Club in 1924, but two years later changed their name to Ashanti FC, and Titanics in 1931 before settling on Asante Kotoko in 1935. They soon ousted Cornerstone as the best team in Kumasi, and by the 1950s, in which time they had tried to get rid of their tribal image, they were challenging the best teams in Accra. Like their rivals Hearts of Oak they have made it through to the finals of the major continental competitions, but have more often lost than won. By 1985 they had won only two of their six final appearances. One of their early heroes was Robert Mensah, a goalkeeper with a great flair for the dramatic. It was he who starred in a classical incident in the 1970 Champion Clubs final against Tout-Puissant Mazembé. Mensah refused to leave the field with the rest of his team mates after a disputed penalty decision in the second leg in

Zaire, which could have deprived them of the title. Instead he picked up the ball, placed it on the spot and dared any of the Zairians to take the kick. One tried, and failed. Asante won the Cup. Alas, the great Mensah was to lose his life in a bar-room brawl the following year.

Nigeria, with a population of over sixty-two million in the 1970s, is the most populous of the black African nations, and in 1990 it had the highest number of registered players: 520,405. It has also been the greatest supplier of players to the professional leagues of Europe. Despite this, and in part at least because of disputes about whether or not to recall expatriate stars, it was not until 1993 that they qualified for the finals of the World Cup, although it was only the toss of a coin that saw Morocco and not them make it to Mexico in 1970. Nigeria have won the Nations' Cup only once, when as host nation they beat Algeria in 1980, before 80,000 spectators. This sent Lagos and the rest of the country into raptures for days to come. In 1984, 1988 and 1990 they were losing finalists. In club competitions they were also remarkably unsuccessful at the final stage: when BCC Lions beat Club Africain of Tunis to win the Cup-winners' Cup in 1990 they were the first Nigerian team to win an African club competition in thirteen years, although Bendel United and Ranchers Bees had made it to the Cup-winners' Cup final in the two previous years. Shooting Stars won the Cup-winners' Cup in 1976, and Enegu Rangers in 1977.

Missionaries, schoolmasters and government employees brought the game to Nigeria, and a Lagos and District FA was established in 1931, playing for a cup named after the Baron Mulford, one of those eccentric characters who keep popping up in the propagation of the game throughout the world. In 1938 an international was played against the Gold Coast, but it was the British forces in the Second World War who boosted the game to such an extent that the Nigeria FA was set up in 1945 and affiliated with the FA in the same year. After independence in 1960 the standard of play improved significantly, helped by the importing of European coaches. Nigeria has been beset with serious ethnic divisions; attempts to overcome this by having inter-tribal matches in the early 1950s were a dismal failure. Nevertheless, by 1983 the national league founded in 1972 had grown to three divisions with thirty-nine teams.

None of the other former British colonies have distinguished themselves. Tanzania, Kenya and Uganda all became independent in the early 1960s, and it was hoped that they would form an economic union, but this was never successful. In football, too, each has gone its own way, and none of them very far. The one-time German, later British, colony of Tanganyika, Tanzania since independence in 1961, is the weakest of these three countries, although its club teams Simba, Pan-Africans and Young Africans have had some success in regional competitions. As their names suggest, they are politically inspired, and the biggest stadium, Mao Tse-

Tung in Zanzibar, is smaller than most club grounds among the stronger football powers. Kenya is better known for its athletes, but football still reigns supreme. From 1981 they won the East and Central African Championship three times in a row, and Gor Mahia, their leading team, won the Cup-winners' Cup in 1987. Uganda have done better than Tanzania and Kenya in qualifying several times for the African Nations' Cup, even reaching the final in 1978. Under Idi Amin football was promoted as a way of winning friends and influencing neighbours, even to the point of supplying visiting teams with attractive female companions, but brother Africans soon paled at the atrocities that were committed in their name. Amin himself supported the army team, Simba, and wiped out those that displeased him. The recovery of the country could be seen in its successful hosting of the CECFA Cup in 1982. Uganda won this trophy a record number of times, in 1973, 1976, 1977, 1989 and 1990. In this time the competition had spread out to embrace other countries in the region, such as Malawi, Ethiopia, Zambia and Zimbabwe.

Northern Rhodesia gained independence as Zambia in 1964, and Malawi, formerly Nyasaland and before that the Federation of Rhodesia and Nyasaland, became independent in 1965 and declared itself a republic in 1966. Rhodesia, with its substantial white minority, refused to share power with the blacks and isolated itself from whites outside South Africa, when it unilaterally seceded from the British Commonwealth in 1965. Only after years of stalemate, economic sanctions and revolutionary agitation did the blacks receive recognition, when Rhodesia became Zimbabwe in 1980. In that year the Southern Africa Development Co- ordinating Conference was formed, and with it a football tournament to celebrate the event. In 1990 another tournament was held to celebrate its tenth anniversary.

Football in Rhodesia goes back to the early pioneering days, when former public schoolboys, engineers and miners introduced the game as they developed and exploited the country. Before the turn of the century railway development in particular had helped the game grow, and the Boer War gave it a further boost with the arrival of British soldiers. Scottish and English teams visited Rhodesia on tours of southern Africa, and Rhodesia took part in the South African Currie Cup. The Depression of the 1930s and then the Second World War set the game back, and it was not until the economic recovery of the late 1950s that it began to recover. In this time blacks were excluded from white teams, although it has to be said that as late as 1975, the Callies team of Scottish inspiration, who won the Cup in that year, refused to play Englishmen as well as blacks. With the increasing unwillingness of blacks to accept the insult of racial exclusion, whites increasingly took to rugby, and blacks to soccer, although most black teams had a white coach. In the 1980s Zimbabwe promised to emerge as the strongest of the southern African nations, but in fact Zambia have been more successful.

Zambia became one of the few openly professional nations in the 1970s. They were able to build on the strong base created by the British engineers who arrived early in the century to work on the railroads and the mines in Northern Rhodesia. Zambia was behind the formation of the East and Central African Football Federation Cup, which it did not win, however, until 1984. Zambia's first major success came in 1974 when it eliminated powerful Ivory Coast and Congo to reach the final of the African Nations' Cup. There they met Zaire, who beat them 2–0 after a 2–2 draw. Zaire also beat them to the right to represent Africa in the 1974 World Cup. Like many other African teams, the strongest are linked to the military: Green Buffaloes from Lusaka and Sahbia Army. Kabwe Warriors, based in the copper belt city of that name, and more recently Nkana Red Devils have prospered. The first team to take off an African trophy, however, was the relatively unknown Power Dynamos, who beat BCC Lions of Nigeria in the final of the 1991 Cup-winners' Cup. In 1988 Zambia's Kalusha Bwalya was named African Player of the Year after a brilliant performance at the Seoul Olympics, which included a 4–0 demolition of Italy; since then he has gone the way of all African stars: to Europe.

Deserts, swamps and a small population are not been the ideal breeding ground for football, but despite this Botswana has its FA and it joined FIFA in 1976. Like Botswana, Namibia has suffered under the thrall of South Africa, mainly because of its vast mineral wealth. After independence in March 1990, Namibia entered FIFA and CAF. In southern Africa the economic power of South Africa and Rhodesia affected football as it did other affairs. Nations that had no reason to favour apartheid often found themselves forced to compromise with the white government. And with its apparently stronger economy blacks were often enticed into the system in search of work. Footballers, like other workers, were attracted to the employment and higher standard of living that seemed to be on offer in South Africa. And footballers, like workers, often found that the reality was not up to the advertising blurb. Since South Africa was not part of FIFA, players could be seduced with large signing on fees, but once there, and having cut themselves off from their own countries, they were on their own. It is one of the ironies of the sporting boycott against South Africa, that soccer, the most multi-racial sport in the republic, and the sport with the greatest potential to help the disadvantaged, was also the sport that most rigorously observed the ban.

Football and apartheid

South Africa delayed the introduction of television for a host of reasons, one of which was the potential embarrassment of non-whites being portrayed as normal people, particularly on the sports field. It was one of the last countries to televise the World Cup live, in 1990. At that time there were five million spectators at first division games in the republic's major league and hundreds of thousands of players. Soweto is the main hotbed, and there the Kaizer Chiefs lord it over their main rivals, Orlando Pirates and Moroka Swallows. These latter two teams are the oldest black teams, founded in 1937 and 1947 respectively, and although the Pirates, known as the People's Team, have some white players, their support is all black; the Swallows have more white players than black and were run by an Afrikaans businessman with strong political and rugby connections.

The Chiefs are a much younger team. They were founded in 1970 by Kaizer Motaung when he split with the Pirates, and took many of the younger players with him. Motaung had played in the United States with the Atlanta Chiefs, with whom he was nominated NASL 'rookie of the year' in 1968, hence the name of his team. The Kaizer Chiefs went on to inspire in their fans a dedication as fierce as that more familiarly associated with the supporters of Manchester United. Older 'traditionalists' still look on the Chiefs, also known by the zulu name Amakhosi, as upstarts. In 1979 they signed their first white, Lucky Stylianou, a professional of Greek parents, who literally became one of the best known whites in South Africa. Stylianou had played in Britain and Latin America, but he found support for the game there nothing compared to that of the South Africans.

Jomo Sono, picked by Stanley Matthews as a potential African Pelé when he was coaching there in the 1970s, is another South African who did well in the States and came home to buy a team, in 1983. Sono played alongside Pelé and Beckenbauer for Cosmos, hence the name of his team, Jomo Cosmos. In the late 1980s Mamelodi Sundowns, founded in Pretoria in 1970, emerged as a challenger to the Chiefs. Their strength was based on the lavish expenditure of a certain Zola Mahobe, who believed in high living for himself and his players. Among other extravagances he took his team to Wembley in 1986 to see the Liverpool/Everton Cup Final. Alas, it was discovered that his largesse was based on ill-gotten gains, but when the law caught up with him the financial start he had given the Sundowns was enough to see them through the succeeding years.

The rigorous observance of the ban on sporting contacts with South Africa was in part a reflection of the power of FIFA, but it also reflected the more cosmopolitan aspects of the people's game. Unlike their rugby, cricket and other sporting counterparts, many soccer players have had a genuine disgust for racism in sport. The odd rebel soccer tours were disasters for those who took part in them. Before the strictures on playing in South Africa, Stanley Matthews did great work with the schoolkids of Soweto in the 1970s. He took them on a tour of Brazil, and tried to show them that football was not all about kicking the ball as high as you could and attacking: defending, he had to point out, was not unmanly. In all, the maestro's coaching in Africa, mainly South Africa, spanned a period of seventeen years, but for his efforts he found himself on the UN's list of prohibited persons. Such is the irony of FIFA's ban, but it was supported by the blacks. A rebel tour in 1982 played to sparse crowds, despite the wishes of the soccer faithful to see the internationals in action, albeit players with little or long lost reputations. South Africa's isolation was no doubt a major reason for the fanatical support for the game; with so many black leaders in gaol or exile, sports stars gained an exaggerated national glory. For whites in the regime, too, sport took on an otherwise unhealthy obsession, and the isolation of South African sport, an irreplaceable product, unlike mere economic commodities, played a major role in the ultimate dismantling of apartheid.

South Africa's re-entry into the world game has not been as successful as numbers and enthusiasm for the game would have predicted. Clearly the absence of international competition has affected the quality of the domestic game. It seems only a matter or time, however, before this is overcome, and out of an Africa that has sprung many surprises, more seem certain to be in store.

Endnotes

Henshaw, *World Soccer*, and occasional issues of *Afrique football* provided material for this chapter, as well as contemporary newspapers. I would also like to pay particular thanks to my Kenyan friend, Otieno Ochenko, who discussed many aspects of African football with me.

Essential for CAF's point of view are:

Faouzi Mahjoub, *Le Football africain. Trente ans de Coupe d'Afrique des nations. 1957–1988*, Groupe Jeune Afrique, Paris, 1988

and the official history

Confédération Africaine de Football. 1957–1987, Nubar Printing House, Cairo, 1988.

For black football in South Africa

G.A.L. Thabe, *It's a Goal! 50 years of sweat, tears and drama in Black soccer*, Skotaville Publishers, Johannesburg, 1983.

The paucity of serious works on African football is noted in the introductory comments to

William J. Baker and James A. Mangan (eds), *Sport in Africa. Essays in Social History*, Africana Publishing Company, New York, 1987

where they explain that they were unable to commission any chapters on football, despite it being recognized as 'universally popular'.

Since then, Pierre Lanfranchi has assiduously collected vital data on foreign footballers in France, not least from Africa: see in particular, and for more details on the FLN team:

Pierre Lanfranchi, 'Rachid Mekhloufi, un joueur de football dans la guerre d'Algérie', 'Le héros sportif . . .' (EUI, Florence).

An early work on football in Cameroon is unfortunately spoiled by either a poor English translation or a severe case of sociologese:

R. Clignet and M. Stark, 'Modernization and the game of soccer in Cameroun', *International Review of Sport Sociology*, Vol 9, No 3, 1974, pp. 81–98.

An excellent article is:

Phyllis M. Martin, 'Colonialism, Youth and Football in French Equatorial Africa', *IJHS*, Vol 8, No 1, May 1991, pp. 56–71.

For football in Algeria after 1962

Youssef Fates, 'Jeunesse, sport et politique', *Peuples méditerranéens*, no.52–53, juillet-décembre 1990, pp. 57–72.

For football in Nigeria

S.E.W. Akpabot, *Football in Nigeria*, McMillan, London, 1985

is short but useful.

CHAPTER TEN

Towards 2002

The news that the United States was to host the 1994 World Cup was greeted in the soccer world with a cynicism equalled only by the indifference that followed the announcement in the United States itself. Much of the cynicism on the one hand, and indifference on the other, was misplaced. One of the most closely kept secrets of the Los Angeles Olympic Games of 1984 was that more people went to watch soccer than any other sport. The expertise with which the Games were run surprised no-one, but the interest shown in soccer justified the claims of those who said that the United States, and not Mexico, should have been given the 1986 World Cup when Colombia pulled out. At the venues themselves, 1.4 million went to the soccer, about a quarter of the total attendance of 5.6 million. An average of 44,426 came to see the thirty-two games played in four different venues, with 101,799 to see France beat Brazil 2–0 at the final in the Rose Bowl; 100,374 saw Yugoslavia beat Italy 2–1 to win the bronze medal, also played in the Rose Bowl.

The Olympic Games are not the World Cup, however, and no country to this time had been entrusted with holding it without a proven record as a soccer power. The same year as thousands were coming to watch the soccer at the Los Angeles Olympics, thousands were refusing to watch what turned out to be the last season of the North American Soccer League. The failure of soccer after the boom of the late 1970s reinforced the prejudices of those soccer followers outside the States who see it as the land of fast food and the quick fix. For them the US was no place for a game whose strength lay in its base in a local community, nurtured on popular enthusiasm over the decades, and whose aim was to bring pleasure to the fans who followed it: above all, it was not a game geared to easy scoring and constant breaks, imposed from above by speculators out to improve their fortunes. Less frequently mooted is what the world's greatest sporting nation might give soccer, should it ever divert some of the interest in its ruling passions, and convert the skill and enthusiasm at youth level into mature talent.

Throughout the twentieth century there have been regular predictions that the US was on the brink of becoming a world soccer power. With 1994 looming such optimism is beginning to resurface. But more cautiously this time. Too many previous predictions proved to be merely one more addition to a forlorn list of failed forecasts.

An unAmerican activity

When baseball and football established themselves as the great homespun American sporting activities before the turn of the century, soccer continued to be played in pockets around the country. It was particularly strong in the textile towns of New England, and where there was a demand for skilled and unskilled labour for the steel mills, mines and shipbuilding industries that were making the United States the great employment centre of the world. In this time support for soccer came from mainly British and Irish immigrants, and the teams were associated with the workplace, where the owners provided leisure facilities in the hope of dampening incipient labour troubles.

After the founding of the American Football Association in 1884 a short-lived professional league was introduced in 1894. Already some of the problems that lay ahead for soccer loomed. The major one was that the league was organized by people with no real interest in the game: in fact, by baseball owners seeking a more capital intensive use of their sports grounds. The other was that the participants were mainly immigrants. Whatever progress soccer was making was hit by the depression of the early years of that decade. The enthusiasts struggled along into the twentieth century, however, and their efforts were boosted by visits from such renowned English amateur teams as the Pilgrims, in 1905 and 1909, and the Corinthians, in 1906 (when Fall River beat the tourists 3–0 before a crowd of 8000) and 1911. In 1905 the first Intercollegiate Association League was founded, comprising Columbia, Cornell, Harvard, Haverford and Pennsylvania. By 1912 there were organized leagues in twelve states.

By that year, too, soccer had gained an unusually strong hold in Harvard, strong enough for a member of the Stadium Committee to predict that the new stadium then being built would be needed to house the huge crowds that would be flooding to see the Yale soccer team 'just as they do the English cup finals.' Perhaps he wasn't being too optimistic; three years later America's first $1000 gate for a sporting fixture was for the final of the National Challenge Cup in soccer. In January 1924, Thomas Cahill, secretary of the US Football Association, looked at the progress soccer was making and predicted that 'in the not too distant future [it] would rank only second to baseball as the leading pro game.' In the 1920s soccer in the United States was going through its golden period, but such predictions were still being made in the 1950s when the game was a complete backwater. In Charles Buchan's *Football Monthly* you could read rosy reports of the game's progress: in January 1952, for instance, that soccer was growing so fast in the States 'that it may soon rival "football" '; or in May 1953 that 'America could sweep the world.' Another rush of enthusiasm swept the imagination in 1966 in the wake of the World Cup held in England, this time by more normally sober millionaires hoping, as is the way of millionaires (except in soccer), to make even more millions. It was not to be, but ten years later came the mother of all bursts of optimism, with the crowds who came to see Cosmos and Pelé from 1975. By 1985 it was all over: foreign players had lined their pockets and investors had lost millions. Little wonder, then, that people are being more cautious about the likelihood of soccer taking off in the States with the arrival of the World Cup in 1994.

Soccer, wherever it has become a significant spectator sport, has presented the administrators with the problem of whether the profits from the game should go to the elites or be channelled back into encouraging the game at the lower levels. It is the old problem of professionalism and amateurism that has faced every successful soccer administration. In Britain a split was avoided, in other countries it caused crises and breakaways that were eventually healed, not without leaving their scars. In the States such disputes have generally been purely disruptive and have stood in the way of the development of a strong national federation. This problem has been compounded, even caused, by the ethnic element and its seemingly insoluble paradox: the ethnic teams brought in the money and provided the elite players, but in this way soccer was indelibly branded as a foreign game.

This has not been helped by soccer's failure to penetrate the college system to any degree. In no other country would this be a serious problem, but in the US professional sport is based on schools and colleges: elsewhere, and above all in soccer, schools and universities are the homes of pure amateurism, and would-be pros are picked up from the youth teams and nursery systems which have a formal or informal attachment to a senior team. The very survival of soccer in the States, then, has been where ethnic ties are still strong; in such circumstances, however, the quality of the game can be secondary to the cultural comforts of being with your own people and speaking your own language in an otherwise bland or unfriendly environment.

Lacking a solid base, cut off from the main source of native talent, the normal problems besetting any sporting administration were magnified in the US. The power hungry followed their own interests, some of the disinterested lovers of the game battled on, others left in disgust, while the ethnic teams put their communal interests ahead of the national. With each split or division the chances of a national game receded as Americans lost interest or looked on it as an ethnic curiosity: the most unAmerican of all activities.

The first major split in the administration of soccer in the States was in 1890, when some New York City and upper New York State individuals broke away from the AFA to found the American Amateur Football

Association. The break-away body, whose interests were merely cultural and sporting, objected to the way the AFA was controlled by the industrial teams of New England, and which were not strictly amateur. This dispute simmered on until 1912, when the two bodies sought entry to FIFA, only to be told to come back when they had resolved their own differences. FIFA would recognize only one administration.

In the meantime, soccer had put down roots outside the east coast. The Greater Los Angeles Soccer League was founded in 1902, and the San Francisco league two years later. In the mid-west soccer had some hold in Chicago and Detroit, and above all St Louis, which established the distinction, through until today, of being the home of most native born talent. As early as 1890, indeed, the Kensingtons of St Louis were founded as the first all-American-born team, and distinguished themselves in their first season by never conceding a goal. It was on the east coast, however, that soccer had its firmest grip. In 1905, the same year as the Pilgrims first toured North America, college football was undergoing a serious crisis, and soccer enthusiasts sought to take advantage of this. The American game had become unacceptably violent, many players were killed, and no less a person than Theodore Roosevelt turned his attention to it. It was partly in response to this concern that the Intercollegiate Soccer Association was formed. In 1906 it started a league.

Among the soccer people, however, while support from the White House was always welcome, the centre of the soccer world was London and the FA, or FIFA after 1904. The more professional AFA looked to the FA, but in the purely amateur AAFA Dr G. Randolph Manning, born in England but educated in Germany, favoured joining the international body. The secretary of the AAFA, Thomas Cahill, born in St Louis and a sports executive whose main interest was soccer, represented the AAFA at the Stockholm meeting of FIFA in 1912, while the AFA had F.J. Wall of the FA to speak on their behalf. Wall claimed that since the AAFA did not control the professionals they controlled only a partial interest, but FIFA left the power struggle to be resolved in the States. Back home the AAFA won the allegiance of most local bodies on the east coast, and when, on 15 August 1913, a cablegram advised the AAFA that they had been granted provisional membership of FIFA, the AFA threw in its lot with what now became the United States Football Association. In 1945 'soccer' was added to the title, in recognition that 'football' in the States was not soccer. In 1974, the USFA became the United States Soccer Federation.

The USFA got off to a good start with the knock-out tournament for the Dewar Cup, a trophy collected by Cahill in London on his way back from Stockholm, and named after the Scot, Arthur Dewar, who donated it to help promote Anglo-American friendship. The Dewar Cup, at first open only to amateurs, became the National Challenge Cup in 1913, when it was

made open to professionals and amateurs. It was soon recognized as the
national championship and has remained so until today. In 1922 the
number of soccer teams was so great that another trophy, open only to
amateurs, was introduced. The finals of the first National Amateur
Challenge Cup in 1923 were cancelled because of terrible weather, but
thereafter it established itself as a worthy rival to the older competition.

The two great rivals for the National Challenge Trophy in the early years
were Fall River Rovers, like St Louis one of the few consistent homes of
soccer in the States, and Bethlehem Steel, a sporting arm of the industrial
giant. As war clouds prepared to burst over Europe in 1914, Charles M.
Schwab of Bethlehem Steel was spending a fortune on the construction of a
soccer field and stadium for the company, followed by a raid on the other
clubs to create the most powerful team in the States. The company team
from Pennsylvania quickly assumed dominance, and in 1919 they went on
tour to Scandinavia, where they played fourteen games. Before long their
supremacy was challenged by the team from the factory town of Fall River
in Massachusetts.

In 1916 the final of the National Challenge Trophy, between Bethlehem
Steel and Fall River, was watched by 10,000 spectators at Pawtucket, and
ended in what Americans would soon come to believe was an integral part
of soccer: the riot. Bethlehem won that game by the only goal. Then came
the fracas involving players and spectators. Most of the Bethlehem team
were imported Scots, but the following year the Cup was won by Fall
River with nine native-born players. Bethlehem Steel continued to spend
large sums of money enticing professional players from Britain, often
Scots, who were paid anything up to three times what they could earn at
home. Some of these players, like Alex Jackson, to become one of the
Wembley Wizards, and Tommy Muirhead, were players at the peak of
their career in what was then the world's top soccer nation. Some
Americans in the 1920s claimed that their soccer was as good as that played
anywhere, and they were even touted as favourites to win the first World
Cup in 1930.

There were many opportunities to test this, as virtually every year from
the visit of Scotland's Third Lanark in 1921, a British or continental team
toured the States. Corinthians made another tour in 1924, Preston North
End in 1929, Glasgow Rangers in 1928 and 1930, Glasgow Celtic in 1931.
Generally, however, the touring teams had little difficulty in winning most
of their games. Of the many continental teams who toured, the world-
beating Uruguayan national team did not find things all its own way in
1927. Sparta Prague toured in 1926, and many other continental and Latin
American teams came to the mecca of New World dreams. Visits by
American teams abroad were less frequent, and usually to neighbouring
countries.

The Jewish contribution to American soccer has been significant. Hakoah of Vienna toured in 1926 as Austrian champions, suffered some defeats, but played before record crowds of 25,000, 30,000 and 36,000 in successive games. They returned in 1927, and some of their players stayed behind, to add further quality to the burgeoning Jewish teams in the New York area: in 1929 Hakoah All-Stars of New York won the National Challenge Cup. In 1927 and 1936 Maccabi came from Palestine to play, and in the year of Israel's founding the Israeli national team played three games in the States, a visit that was returned by an American League team in 1951 and 1953. The famous MTK of Budapest, with their strong Jewish component, played eight games in 1930.

The big American teams relied on imported professionals, but among native-born talent a few were emerging to equal the imports: Billy Gonsalves of Fall River and Buff Donelli who was better known as an American football coach, were both offered contracts with foreign teams. Francis 'Hun' Ryan from Philadelphia was American born and although Archie Stark was born in Scotland is usually considered an American. It was with such talent, and a few naturalised foreigners, that the United States made so bold as to enter all the great international soccer tournaments of the 1920s and 1930s: Paris and Amsterdam for the Olympics and Montevideo and Rome for the World Cup.

The first official internationals under the USFA were played in Scandinavia in 1916, when the US beat Sweden 2–3 and drew with Norway 1–1. At the Olympic Games in Paris in 1924 the US beat Estonia 1–0, and then went on to perform the remarkable feat of holding Uruguay to a 0–3 loss. The Paris Games were not without their political problems, and American competitors had to face the wrath of the home crowd for the unsympathetic attitude of the American government to the problems of its ally in the recent war. In tennis and water polo there were angry demonstrations, and during the rugby match between France and the United States the Americans were constantly booed, the playing of the Star Spangled Banner was drowned out, and there was fighting in the stand. The French took the side of Estonia in the first soccer match, but what is more surprising is the way they came around to support the underdogs in the game against Uruguay. When the US were losing 3–0 and then blocked the future world champion's attempts to increase the score, the French crowd applauded their sturdy defence. Ironically, it was a system that would later threaten to kill the game. It was claimed by coach Collins that the defensive success in this game was because he introduced the system later made famous or notorious as 'verrou' or 'catenaccio': he brought a 'sweeper' to play behind a line of four backs, and so upset the Uruguayan forwards.

On the way home the US beat Poland 2–3 and lost 3–1 to the Irish Free

State in Dublin, in both cases before friendly crowds. At Amsterdam four years later Argentina dealt a quick blow to New World aspirations with a 11–2 thrashing, but some consolation was found in a 3–3 draw with Poland on the way home. At the World Cup in 1930 the US team performed admirably, a place in the final being frustrated by a typical Argentine combination of virtuosity and viciousness; in 1934 hopes were cut short by Italy, the eventual winners. At the Olympic Games in 1936 Italy again ended US hopes, and again Italy were the eventual winners. The 1–0 loss, however, was something of a farce: two Americans were crocked and an Italian player, Piccini, was ordered off, but refused to go. To aid him in his recalcitrance the other Italian players, supposedly students, pinned the referee's arms to his side and smothered his face. After a long delay Weingartner, the German referee, continued the game as though nothing had happened. Piccini remained on the field. It is unlikely that the referee was acting on any ulterior motives concerning the forthcoming Axis agreement. Unmoved by politics the German spectators were entirely on the side of the Americans.

In the US team that went to the Berlin Olympics, fourteen of the seventeen were born in the States, some of whom came from the German American community (and were firmly against any boycott). If the strongest teams in the national competition still relied on foreigners, many of the players in the other leagues scattered all over the country, and particularly among the winners of the National Amateur Challenge Cup, were born in the USA.

The best organized and longest lasting of the new leagues was the German-American Soccer League, founded in 1923 and surviving today as the Cosmopolitan League. Even in the 1920s it was not restricted to Germans, but its change of name in 1977 is a reflection of the handicap that ethnic names have been in the acceptance of the game. Each year the German-American League invited a German team to play an All-Stars select, and it was in response to such an invitation that Hakoah were invited.

In 1921 the American Soccer League was founded in an attempt to make the pro game national. It led instead to the biggest crisis since the attempt to enter FIFA in 1912. The amateur administrators of the USFA were suspicious of the aims of the professionals, and incensed when in September 1928, led by their brand new commissioner Bill Cunningham, a refugee from baseball who knew nothing about soccer, they voted to withdraw from the National Challenge Cup. This was on the alleged grounds that it interfered with their league fixtures – which did not stop them later introducing their own cup competition. The ASL forbade any of its teams from taking part in the National Challenge Cup, and when three of them refused to obey its injunction, the ASL suspended and fined

Bethlehem Steel, New York Giants and Newark $1000 each. This led to a head-on confrontation when the USFA took up the cause of the suspended clubs. The bitterness this evoked could not be concealed in the official reports of the 1928–29 season, where the president, Armstrong Patterson, talked of being 'assailed by foes within as well as without' and complained of the time that had to be spent in combating 'the onslaughts of the insidious enemy who sought our destruction.' Tom Cahill in his Secretary's Report denounced the 'well planned insurrection' by 'certain individuals' who believed that 'the dollar is more powerful than an authorised organization to control soccer in the United States.' Their interests, he went on, despite their claims about 'modernization', were purely commercial with no pretence to support sport for sport's sake. Familiar words.

A compromise was finally patched up in October 1929, but in the meantime the 'outlaw' leagues of the ASL and the Southern New York Association, who also left the USFA, tried to take advantage of the British FAs not being part of FIFA to make deals with them. They were ignored. FIFA for its part had been concerned about the American professional leagues enticing European professionals to break their contracts. There were no real winners, and philanthropic sponsors of the game, like H.E. Lewis of Bethlehem Steel and G.A.G. Wood of American Woollen Company became disillusioned and withdrew their support.

Out of Wall Street there came an even bigger blow in 1929. When the Depression hit the mill towns and the heavy industries, soccer's strongholds were badly affected. The big three who were suspended by the ASL in 1928 founded an Eastern Professional League, without great success, as a rival to the ASL. In 1933 a reorganized American Soccer League was founded that has survived until today, but never truly national and never truly professional. At the amateur level, the Los Angeles Olympics of 1932 did not have a soccer competition, the only time soccer has been omitted since its first official appearance in 1908. When Olympic competition was resumed after the Second World War, the failures of the US teams were often catastrophic, and the encounters with professional opposition equally so. It was this that made the defeat of the full-strength England team in Brazil in 1950 all the more incredible. The Americans were so sure of defeat that they spent much of the previous evening drinking and enjoying themselves. The game, played on a dry and bumpy pitch in Belo Horizonte, was overwhelmingly dominated by England, who did everything but score. The Americans, who did little but defend vigorously and valiantly, did score. In the thirty-seventh minute, the Haitian centre-forward Larry Gaetjens, by accident or design, deflected a shot by Walter Bahr past goalkeeper Williams. Other accounts say he scored with a brilliant diving header from a cross by Bahr. It was a piece of sporting trivia that gained less attention in the American media of the time than it did forty years later when the US qualified for Italia 1990.

In the 1940s soccer in the States was a non-event. Even so renowned and comparatively cosmopolitan a sports writer as J.R. Tunis could reveal egregious ignorance on the subject. In his book *Democracy in Sport* (1941) he claimed that Americans were 'by nature an active and outdoor loving race' for whom sport was 'an extremely important form of our leisure', while he dismissed the 'races of Latin derivation' because, with few exceptions, 'rarely do they take instinctively to ball games . . . .' So much for the great Uruguayan teams of the 1920s and other southern neighbours in the Olympics and the World Cup. If a leading sports writer could betray such parochialism tinged with racism, it is hardly surprising that the rest of the population saw both soccer and the people who played it as unworthy of serious discussion.

From the 1940s soccer in the States was restricted more than ever to those neighbourhoods with a large ethnic community. At the end of the Second World War the English-speaking world outside Europe received millions of migrants, the majority of whom were English speaking. In the United States many ex-servicemen returned from the war in Europe with a new appreciation of soccer, but they were outnumbered by the newcomers from Europe, mainly non-English speaking refugees. They gave soccer another boost at the same time as it was further confirmed as the game of foreigners. It was only after 1945 that soccer clubs adopted names emphasizing their ethnic affiliation. It was natural that at such clubs members would speak their own language among themselves, but at some clubs even public announcements were made in a foreign language. Names like Teutonia, Sons of Italy, Polonia and Hungaria openly boasted the allegiance of their teams, and although they could be sweetened by patriotic additions, as in the Philadelphia (or New York) Ukrainians, the New York Greek-Americans, Chicago Croatians or even the San Pedro Yugoslavs, that did not change the underlying reality. Not only the game and the people who played it, but the riots that frequently accompanied it, were profoundly 'unAmerican': in a country where it was soon going to be a crime to be 'unAmerican', soccer was to sport as Communism was to politics, but unlike Communism it was an irrelevance. The players who were chaired by the Brazilians in Belo Horizonte for their victory over England in 1950 went home to total indifference.

Only in America

If all but a minority of dedicated Americans remained in happy ignorance of the round ball game, some were aware of its immense drawing power elsewhere. For them the thought of exciting some of that interest in the States was enough to bring dollar signs to their eyes. Even before the viewing audiences for the 1966 World Cup in England alerted some men on the make to this potential klondike, Bill Cox, sports promoter and one-time owner of the Brooklyn Dodgers pro football team, founded his International Soccer League in 1960. This league had all the ingredients for failure, yet surprisingly it struggled on until overtaken by the events of 1966. It relied on foreigners and was played in summer – indeed, had to be played then to attract European professionals. Cox's idea was that eleven teams from Europe and South America, together with an American All Star team, would take part in a league during the European close season, the American summer. Games were played only in New York City at first, at the Polo Grounds, before crowds of about 10,000, but eventually the league expanded to include games in Los Angeles, Boston and Chicago.

The USFA, suspicious as ever of professionalism, were never happy with Cox's importation of foreign teams and after a stormy relationship cancelled his league in 1965. Cox then hit the USFA with an anti-trust suit and set about re-forming a national professional league, but this time not relying on imports. This was in 1966, and other millionaires on the scent of quick bucks sought recognition from the USFA to run the competitions they wanted to introduce. Suddenly the USFA (and the Canadian Soccer Football Association) found itself in the unique situation of being courted by three different groups anxious to win its approval for the franchises it could bestow. The successful group, later to be called the United Soccer Association, was led by Jack Kent Cooke, owner of the Los Angeles Lakers. The other two groups merged. Bill Cox had founded the National Professional Soccer League (NPSL), and now he was joined by Richard Millen, also from Los Angeles, and equally ignorant about soccer as a game. Deprived of international competition because not attached to FIFA, the pirate NPSL scored an offsetting success with a CBS contract to televise one game per week.

In no other country in the world would it have been necessary for one of the promoters to introduce a soccer ball to the TV cameras and explain what it was. This, however, is how Dick Walsh announced his appointment as commissioner to the United Soccer Association in 1966. From such an unlikely beginning the venture barely recovered. In view of the short time at their disposal to get a league in operation by 1967, the Cooke group, with USFA approval, decided to form its league from existing European and Latin American teams. This was the inauspicious beginning of the North American Soccer League, which in the late 1970s brought crowds to watch soccer that many top European teams would have been happy to accommodate.

In the beginning, however, there were problems. For foreign observers the idea of importing foreign teams and giving them a local name seemed somewhat bizarre. But there were many aspects of American sport that foreigners find incomprehensible. One of these is the franchise system, and the right of one individual, the 'owner', and not the local community, to run the team as his private toy and source of profit. It is a myth, of course, that the local community 'owns' the professional teams of Europe or Latin America, and there have been cases of teams being 'relocated' from one area to another (Arsenal perhaps the most famous example), but for various historical reasons the great soccer teams of the world have been located in a particular region and attempts to upset this have often met with bitter, and successful, action by the fans. Americans, too, have shown fierce loyalty to their local team when it was uprooted, not from one part of the city to another, as in soccer, but from one part of the vast continent to another.

The idea of importing teams and more or less arbitrarily assigning them to an American town was less strange in the US than elsewhere, and it had the precedent of Bill Cox's International League. Indeed from some points of view the new experiment did remarkably well. Armed with its new patriotic acronym, the USA brought in eleven complete professional teams and gave them local names: thus Wolverhampton Wanderers, newly promoted from the English Second Division and who would win the league, were stationed in Los Angeles and fittingly called the LA Wolves; Aberdeen from Scotland, who lost 5–6 in the thrilling final, after extra-time, were placed in Washington as the Whips; Boston were not surprisingly given Shamrock Rovers; America's Italians had to share Cagliari from Sardinia, who were placed in Chicago as the Chicago Mustangs. Canada provided two locations, Toronto for Hibernian from Scotland, and Vancouver for Sunderland who played as the Vancouver Royal Canadians.

The worst prejudices of the soccer world outside the States were confirmed when they heard stories that in the televised games of the outlaw NPSL the referee was wired for sound so that he could stop the game to allow commercials to be run. He might do so by holding on to the ball when it was out of play, or even suggest that players have an injury so that he could hold the game up. In one case it was discovered that a referee had given eleven out of twenty-one fouls so that CBS could run commercial breaks. Nor were the televised NPSL games helped by the commentaries of Danny Blanchflower, Irish internationalist turned sports writer and commentator. His criticisms of the European game could be acerbic enough, but he was just too much for American ears more used to sugar coating than honest comment. In a land where the sponsor rules, the product was sacred, and here was Blanchflower ridiculing it.

In the USA competition the locals came out to see some of the games in

impressive numbers, but their prejudices in regard to soccer were further
confirmed in the low scoring defensive nature of too many games. Then
there were the riots. In New York and Toronto the local Italians used
Cagliari as an excuse for nationalistic outpourings that owed more to
Mussolini than Garibaldi. At the Yonkers Stadium, New York, where
Cerro from Uruguay were located as the New York City Skyliners, two
brutal fouls against Cagliari players provoked the wrath of the Italians, and
some spectators descended to the playing area to make their feelings felt,
not with the Uruguayans who committed the offences, but with the referee
who refused to punish them. Other spectators followed and somewhat
belatedly the police intervened to save Leo Goldstein, a survivor from the
Nazi concentration camps, from being beaten to death. In Toronto,
Cagliari looked like being beaten by Hibernians, so they left the field,
which was then taken over by Italian spectators in pursuit of the referee.
Other upheavals involved the Orangemen from Glentoran, playing as
Detroit Cougars, against the Boston Shamrock Rovers, although their
biggest brawl was against Rio champions, Bangu, playing as Houston
Stars, in a straightforward donnybrook.

A peculiarly American touch was added to the war of the two
associations when the NPSL filed an anti-trust suit against the USA/FIFA
and all who belonged to them. In the US, where sport is a business and
monopolies are banned by law, they were correct in their claim, but some
sanity prevailed and the warring leagues came together. The law suit was
dropped, and in 1968 teams from the US and Canada came together to play
in the North American Soccer League (NASL). The crowds were down on
the previous year, despite the standard of play being up, and over the next
two years the game reached a new low. In this time fortunes were lost and
teams dropped out of the league as the profit motive undercut any
pretensions to the competition being run as a sport.

From the end of 1970 to 1975, however, there was a steady rise in interest
in the game, which suddenly soared to previously unheard of heights when
Cosmos enticed Pelé out of retirement with a contract of more than $4
million, a sum which also obliged him to engage in public relations work.
This he did brilliantly, and at the same time cleared the debts he had
incurred through unwise investments – and without which he might not
have found the American offer so tempting. In a world where ridiculous
sums are given to sports stars, this was one of the few occasions where the
money was well spent. Pelé, joined by Georgio Chinaglio in 1976 and then
by Franz Beckenbauer and Carlos Alberto in 1977, lifted the game to
unheard of levels of spectator interest. Throughout 1977 records fell,
culminating in the 77,691 who came to Giants Stadium to see Cosmos beat
Fort Lauderdale in the divisional championship play-offs. Soccer was
attracting more spectators even than baseball.

In 1978, by which time Pelé had made his emotional retirement in a game between Cosmos and his old club Santos, playing one half for each side, Cosmos never played before less than 33,271 spectators, and averaged 47,856. This was their peak year, although in 1979 (46,689) and 1980 (42,804) average attendances were still very healthy. Then came a drop of 8000 in 1981 and another 4000 in 1982. Although Cosmos were the best supported club, others did very well, most notably Tampa Bay Rowdies and Golden Bay, while Seattle, with average crowds around 20,000 for several years, were a surprise packet. No less so than Minnesota, however, who averaged 30,926 in 1978. A few years later they no longer existed. In Canada attendances went against this trend. Vancouver provided the best crowds, averaging 15,736 in 1978 and rising as high as 29,130 in 1983. The game had also picked up in Toronto, from 7336 in 1978 to 15,040 in 1980 and 11,630 in 1983. Big money came from Lipton's to help the New England Teamen, and Arab money was behind Jimmy Hill and the World Sports Academy which ran Detroit. No amount of money can buy tradition, however, and by 1984 the boom was about to burst, with Cosmos bankrupt and expelled from the league.

New York Cosmos (simply Cosmos after 1976) were founded in 1971 by the Turkish-American brothers, Nesuti and Ahmet Ertegun, millionaires through their control of Warner Communications, but devoted soccer fans. They appointed as president Clive Toye, former Fleet Street journalist and more recently Director of Administration and Information for NASL. They won the championship in 1972, but were struggling until the masterstroke of signing Pelé. Cosmos won the soccer 'Super Bowl' in 1977, 1978, 1980 and 1982, and engaged in world tours which, although not always well advised, attracted massive crowds in Europe, Africa and Latin America. When the Ertegut brothers relinquished their control of the club it was left more to the mercies of speculators whose behaviour on and off the field was at times a disgrace – with even Pelé, on the bench and in civvies, involved in one particularly nasty incident in a game against Vancouver Whitecaps on 15 July 1979.

Cosmos set the fashion for paying large sums for overseas stars. All of the NASL teams relied on foreign imports: some like George Best were beyond their best, but others like Beckenbauer and even Cruyff, were still at their peak as world class internationals. Most players, however, came from the English League on a summer loan basis. This saved the American club having to pay a massive transfer fee, gave the player a healthy summer bonus, but left his club in England fretting about the condition he might be in when the season restarted. And despite the short American season, there was always the likelihood of the seasons overlapping. In 1979 the English League banned the loan system. By itself this was not the downfall of NASL. That lay with its failure to bring on young Americans.

In 1968 only about one per cent of the players in the new leagues were North American, and Lamar Hunt's Dallas Tornado even went on a world tour in 1967 with players who had never set foot in the States until they arrived in Texas to play in an official game for their new club. In 1978 there were still no more than twenty per cent native born players in NASL. The administrators were aware of the problem, and insisted in 1976 that all teams had to have at least six North Americans, one of whom had to play for the entire game. Very few of them were top class, and none caught the imagination of American youth. No Michael Jordan appeared to win over young blacks, and the game remained the preserve of middle-class whites, just one more example of American soccer going against the trends elsewhere. Kyle Rote Jr, son of a famous football father and Rookie of the Year in 1973, represented all that was best in white middle-class sportsmanship, but even he did not live up to the high expectations he excited in the 1970s. Youth soccer continued to grow, but was never linked to a professional league that boasted American stars. NASL, rising like a comet on the tail of Cosmos, died just as quickly.

By 1985 pro soccer in the States was virtually dead. Too many people got too carried away in the euphoria of the late 1970s, so that expansion was all at the top. Like all bull markets, it crashed, a victim of over-ambition and over-reliance on foreign imports. The crowds faded away and the TV cameras lost interest. The indoor soccer league has remained as a semi-pro competition, but it cannot be taken seriously; a fun game for participants, but of little relevance to the real game played on turf and under skies however cloudy or grey.

Soccer had been unable to enter the American soul, and yet at a certain level it was becoming part of American life. At youth level soccer continues to thrive, and has done so steadily from the early 1970s: by 1990 more young people, male and female, were playing soccer than any other sport except basketball. In 1988, according to the Soccer Industry Council of North Palm Beach, Florida, of the more than fifteen million people who played soccer only three million were eighteen years or older. In high schools, where the popularity of American football has been static since 1982, soccer has grown continuously in popularity among boys and girls: for under eighteen-year-olds only basketball and volleyball have more participants, and for under-twelves, only basketball. At college level, however, soccer is a minor sport and does not attract scholarships as easily as basketball, baseball or football. The popularity of soccer, too, is still regional: it is particularly popular in 'fair-weather' states like California, Florida, Texas, St Louis and Maryland, while in Dallas, one of the great hotbeds of American football, soccer has boomed with 82,000 registered players.

What all these figures add up to, however, is lost in national terms. There are not enough scholarships to encourage the enthusiasm at high schools to transfer into colleges, and from there there is no national professional league to attract the best of the college players. The present professional soccer league is neither properly national nor professional. And yet at the youth level the performances of the national team continue to improve. In the Under-seventeen World Championship, the USA could beat only Bolivia in China in 1987, and although they did not go beyond the minor rounds in Scotland in 1989, they did beat Brazil, no mean feat at any level. In Italy in 1991 they won the three matches of the minor round, against Argentina, Italy and China, only to be eliminated by Qatar on penalties in the quarter-final. In the Under-twenty World Youth Championship, the USA first qualified for the finals in Australia in 1981 where they lost to Uruguay and Poland, and drew with Qatar. In Mexico in 1983 they had their first victory, against Ivory Coast, but it was their only success, and they did not make it to the Soviet Union in 1985. In 1987 a solitary victory against Saudi Arabia was their only reward, but in Saudi Arabia in 1989 a win against East Germany and a draw with Mali took the US through to the quarter-finals where they beat Iraq 2–1, only to lose to Nigeria in the semi-final and in the third place play-off against Brazil. They failed to reach the finals in Portugal in 1991, but in Australia in 1993 they opened with a spectacular 6–0 goal-scoring blitz against European champions Turkey that had everyone buzzing. A draw with Korea took them through to the quarter-finals on superior goal difference, but although far from disgraced they were no match for Brazil, the ultimate winners.

The promise is there. US success in qualifying for the World Cup in Italy in 1990 was the first time that a disinterested and even antagonistic media, started to look on the game more favourably. Most of the names of that squad had a foreign sound to them, but in fact they were nearly all native born. For the handful of promising stars in that team the only hope of realizing their potential is to play in Europe. Only there can they play regularly against class opposition. In the States they are on a meagre income and opposition is sporadic and poor. Already the US has won a world soccer crown, but that was the magnificent win of the women in the first Womens World Cup held in China in 1991. None of this talent can be turned to the advantage of USA 1994, but it is part of a changing atmosphere that might help bring about the miracle.

One result of Italia 1990 was that Bora Milutinovitch replaced Bob Gansler as national coach. Since then the US team has prospered. Consigned to the past is the dour defensive and physical game of previous coach Bob Gansler, born in Hungary in 1942, but who came to the States as a youngster and played most of his soccer in the stultifying atmosphere of the colleges, run by coaches with little real appreciation of the game and administered by the NCAA which has neither knowledge of, nor interest in soccer. It is here that some of the worst breaches of the rules are made, especially unlimited substitution, which does nothing to develop skills. The new coach, his English and his personal appearance polished to make him presentable to the TV cameras, has brought from his experience with the Mexico and Costa Rica national teams a more creative flair and more emphasis on technical proficiency. His Spanish, too, might take him into the areas where soccer players have traditionally been found outside the States, rather than in the colleges. No soccer team has yet reached world status with a team of players whose healthy bodies were matched by educated minds: the US team is unlikely to break this mould.

Despite the scorn of the local press, and even *Sports Illustrated* about soccer's prospects, large crowds came to see the national team in many of its games after 1990: 51,000 to see the US draw with the Republic of Ireland, admittedly in Massachusetts, but even for a less attractive fixture in Philadelphia against Sheffield Wednesday, who lost 2–0, 44,261 turned up. Crowds of well over 30,000 came to see games against Uruguay (in Denver), Argentina (in Stamford) and Juventus (in New Haven). The flood of applications to host the 1994 fixtures, complete with (refundable) deposits, surpassed all expectations. More important in terms of playing success, the US team won the first Gold Cup, the CONCACAF equivalent to the European Championship, played in Pasadena and Los Angeles in June/July 1991. A late burst secured a 2–1 victory over Trinidad and Tobago in the first round, followed by easier victories over Guatemala (3–0) and Costa Rica (3–2) in the next two. Then came the major triumph in the semi-final with a 2–0 victory over Mexico. The final was a dour affair played by two exhausted teams, and after neither team could score in normal or extra time the US 'won' on penalties. This was one of the US's best ever performances at the national level.

At the 1994 World Cup the US can expect to do reasonably well, and fears about poor attendances are misplaced. Americans, even if they do not like the game, appreciate a spectacle, and there are still many ethnic strings to play on. The one thing that can be said with certainty is that if the game in the States, with its healthy base at youth level and improvements at the national level, does not result in a substantial lift in its popularity, then it never will. Whether this would be a loss for either the States or soccer is another matter.

Plus ça change?

In the 1980s, soccer was hit by what were claimed to be a series of 'crises', resulting in a plethora of solutions for the sporting body's economic ills. Most of these would have been familiar enough to the American sports fan:

profit-making owners, show-biz players on inflated salaries, television dictating how the game be played, the fan at the ground a secondary consideration to the fire-side fan. The cure threatens to be worse than the disease.

There have been 'crises' in soccer since the game was invented, but in the early 1980s a new low seemed to have been reached. In the latter half of 1981 *World Soccer* ran a series of 'investigations' into the problems facing soccer throughout the world. In 1983 Anton Rippon wrote a book entitled *Soccer in Crisis,* and about the same time Hugh McIlvanney asked rhetorically in *The Observer* whether the game would survive into the twenty-first century. All of this came before Heysel and Hillsborough. Hooliganism was an obvious running sore, but declining attendances, television and television sponsorship were raised as matters for concern.

The problem of declining attendances was virtually worldwide in the 1980s, and many clubs were in financial trouble, some even facing extinction. In Argentina and Brazil, still two of the world's great footballing giants at the national level, chaos seemed to rule in the domestic game, and star players sought their fortunes elsewhere. The South Americans seemed to be in a no-win situation: Argentina's success in winning the World Cup in 1978 resulted in many of their players being sought by clubs in Europe, and when Brazil performed comparatively poorly in 1986, players flocked to Europe in search of better things. In Argentina top clubs have fielded reserve teams in the national competition so that their first team could earn bigger money in tours of Europe. In Brazil, the Maracana that had echoed to the roars of nearly 200,000 was frequently an empty shell, with only the Flu-Fla derby likely to reach the safety-reduced capacity of 140,000: outside the big two the highest average attendances in 1984–85, were a mere 19,000: in Argentina crowd averages were only 10,500, despite River Plate averaging 26,000. The big clubs could still draw the crowds, but too many games were played against mediocre opposition. And with the best players looking to Europe, the standards suffered.

In Europe the top clubs in Spain and Italy continued to fill their massive stadiums, and the 'big five' in England operated from a sound financial basis. In most countries the internationals, the derbies and other class encounters, could still be relied on to play to capacity audiences. But too frequently games were being played before meagre crowds in half empty stadiums: and yet thanks to television more people were watching the game than ever before.

In England league attendances fell by a spectacular 30% between 1980 and 1986, a drop of eight million. Attendances at English football in the 1970s saw average attendances for First Division games drop from over 30,000 to 24,500. In Belgium crowds averaged around 9–10,000, in France

5–7000, and in Germany crowds at the top games averaged between 20,000 to 23,000 in the 1970s and were as high as 27,000 in the 1977–78 season. Crowds figures in Italy only underline how figures can deceive, for in 1980 Milan were relegated to the second division over a corruption scandal, and the Italian game was afflicted by other off the field problems before it emerged in the late 1980s with the best league in the world. In 1984 Napoli signed Diego Maradona, with a consequent increase in average attendances by 20,000 to 77,457. In 1985 average attendances in the Serie A were 39,000. Nevertheless, the top drawing club in Europe – and the world – was Barcelona, who throughout the 1980s were drawing crowds of over 100,000 to all their home games; Réal Madrid averaged 70,101 in 1984–85. In Scotland the signing of Graeme Souness by Rangers and a turnaround in the playing fortunes of the club sent average attendances for Scottish football rocketing. Even before then, however, as *World Soccer* (November 1985) calculated, on a percentage of population basis, Scotland, with 1.79% was the second most football crazy country in Europe. First by a long margin was Albania with 3.74%. So much for figures!

A popular club on a winning run had no trouble attracting the crowds, while the appearance of a genuine star player would always increase the gates, whether it was Matthews in the 1950s, Pelé in the 1960s, Cruyff in the 1970s or Maradona in the 1980s (or a Yamamoto in Japan). Stoke City soon recovered their transfer fee in attendances that multiplied by anything up to five times the previous average when Matthews returned to play for them in October 1961, and when Johann Cruyff returned to Ajax Amsterdam for the 1981–82 season their average attendance almost doubled to 21,847. Pelé and Maradona expected to play before sell-out crowds. These were the players the fans happily paid money to see, and these were the players the sponsors wanted to carry their name.

Despite the falling attendances, players' salaries – and not just those of the superstars – continued to escalate, like prices in the art and antique market. In England Johnny Haynes's £100 a week raised a storm in 1961; twenty years on few eyebrows were raised when Joe Jordan asked for £1000. Even then he was a long way behind the stars on the continent where Maradona with Napoli could earn close to £1 million a year with sponsorship money, a figure that would later be tripled. Even West Germany was losing its best players in the 1980s to Italy and Spain, where the highest paid players were all foreigners: Bernd Schüster (FC Barcelona) and Ruud Krol (Napoli) were on £245,000, with only Maradona earning more: a handful of other foreigners were earning close to £100,000. Entry fees were raised to help defray these costs, but it was increased money from sponsorship that picked up a large part of the tab.

Sponsorship is as old as history: in the arts it was called patronage, and it has been present since the days of amateur football, from Lillywhite's first publishing of the rules of the FA to the names given to various sporting competitions. It was the 'sponsorship' of the Schricker brothers' mother that allowed the visit of the first England team to Germany, and even amateur journals have relied on advertisements to keep them going: in the 1930s, to take only one example, the 1934–35 *English Schools' Football Handbook* had the name of the Ajax Co. Ltd intrude its name and information about some of its products at the bottom, top and even middle of nearly every page. Sponsorship, unlike patronage, is not disinterested: it demands a return on the investment. The modern meaning of sponsorship is hard to distinguish from commercialism, but however defined both have been with the game since its earliest days, with manufacturers' signs on stands and stand roofs, makers' names on balls, advertisements in the press, club programme and year books, players selling their name to this or that newspaper column or commercial product. The problem in the 1980s was that the sponsors' money, through global television coverage, made all previous fears about the problems of commercialism seem trivial.

Before the 1980s television in Europe was usually under the control of the state, with little, or tightly controlled, advertising. There were few television companies competing for the rights to televise football, and where they did, as in Britain with the BBC and ITV, there were informal agreements about how much they would bid. In France, Claude Bez broke through the state monopoly and in Italy Silvio Berlusconi challenged RAI, the Italian national broadcaster, having bought his own Canale 5. This was in the second half of the 1980s, when cable and satellite television, and the adoption of privatization as a new religion, led to an open slather in regard to advertising on televised football. In the early 1980s, while perimeter advertising was permitted at televised games, shirt advertising was not.

Eintracht Braunschweig first entered the field of shirt advertising in 1973, with the name of a local brewery, and five years later only Schalke and Köln of the Bundesliga clubs held out against having their jerseys thus desecrated. The money, as much as £225,000 a year, eventually broke them down. In England, where Arsenal were the last to hold out against commercial graffiti on their famous red and white shirts, JVC broke their resistance in 1981 with an offer of about £500,000 over three years. In Scotland, where the numbering of players' jerseys to aid player identification had been dismissed by the SFA in the 1930s because it reduced players 'to the level of greyhounds', shirt advertising was accepted: even Celtic, who had refused to put numbers on their sacred green and white hooped jerseys, numbering their shorts instead, were bought over by a double-glazing firm – ironically the same one as arch-rivals Rangers, no sponsor in Scotland being willing at that time to be associated with just one of the two Scottish giants.

When Hunter Davies wrote his classic account of a year with Tottenham Hotspur in 1973 (*The Glory Game*) he commented how at the start of the year the chairman had declared that he would never allow perimeter advertising around the ground. Before the start of the next season the first boards had gone up. The TV companies were never so hostile to this form of advertising as shirt advertising, presumably because it is less intrusive. For the sponsors who put up the boards and had their name or logo stuck on the players' chests, the value of their promotion multiplied when television beamed the message into millions of households throughout the world: the players were continually in focus, the advertising boards usually in the background. For the national television stations that dominated in Europe there was a natural reluctance to offer this free advertising. For the commercial stations there was a similar problem, although their objection was not so much to advertising, as getting their full return on it. Eventually even the BBC had to give in, at first with restrictions on the size and placement of logos. From the clubs' point of view, the more their sponsor's name appeared before the viewer, the more they could extort from their sponsor. By the end of the 1980s competition for the rights to televise important football matches allowed the big clubs to ask for more, and usually get it. They were calling the shots for the first time, for despite the attempts by some television companies to claim that television could live without football, they found out that it could not.

It was televised football that saved privatized television in France – the only sporting event to evoke a greater interest for a single sporting event had been the victory of Marcel Cerdan over T. Zale for the world boxing championship in 1948. In Spanish regional television TV3 Catalanis and Euskal (Basque) Telebista drew record viewing figures when a local football match was being broadcast with a Catalan or Basque commentary, and in Britain, which showed more sport than Italy, whereas Italy showed more football, the claim that snooker and some other sports were as big attractions as football were shown to be manifestly false. In Italy there was never any doubt about the popularity of televised football.

In France Claude Bez was a key figure in the revolution in the financing of French football. He refused to recognize the 'reciprocity' agreement between national broadcasters that gave free transmission to the away country in European matches, and allowed the clubs to claim higher fees. In 1984 a new subscription channel, Canal Plus, was started up in France. By 1985 it was nearly bankrupt, and was saved only by the transmission of exclusive live soccer matches. In 1987 the French television channel, TF1, was privatized, and the following year, a new sponsorship deal was hammered out for the French national team. Ten years previously, in 1977, French TV and French football had worked out a deal worth £45,000; for the 1987–88 season it came to £20 million.

Claude Bez, born in 1940 into a wealthy family that had few problems surviving the Nazi occupation, was a footballer in his youth, and in 1974 joined the executive committee of Bordeaux, capital of a region where rugby was also popular. In 1977 he became president of the club and sought to make the 'Girondins' the leading club in France. This he did with his 'policy of stars', and lavish spending, in conjunction with the mayor of Bordeaux, former Resistance fighter Jacques Chaban-Delmas, who saw this as good publicity for the region. The club also engaged in financial speculation outside football, and this led to problems resulting in near bankruptcy and gaol for Bez. Part of Bez's problem was that his relations with the media, whom he treated with contempt, were abominable, and he did not own either a newspaper or a television channel to support his own view. The 1960s had seen the fall from the top flight of the great Rheims team that had starred in the 1950s. Racing-Club de Paris also foundered in the 1960s, to be revived in more modern guise as Matra-Racing, based on a profligate spending policy in the 1980s that bought neither success nor stability. On the other hand, another lavish buyer, Bez's bitter enemy, Bernard Tapie, took over at Olympique Marseille and bought enough talent to challenge AC Milan and Barcelona. His ultimate success in winning the European Cup in 1993 has since been shrouded in gloom with the accusations and revelations that people associated with the club were involved in bribery to win matches. Now Olympique Marseille, too, face an uncertain future.

The pursuit of glory through big spending has tainted the game in dignity as well as honesty. Aesthetics did not enter any of the discussion, but even without the excuse of sponsors some clubs in recent times have adopted flashes and darts and diagonals on their jerseys and shorts that at least some players have admitted are an embarrassment. In Florence enraged supporters unsuccessfully took the club to court for tampering with the club's strip in 1981. Some changes in shirt design, however slight, are simply to force parents to buy a new one every year for their kids. In England a measure of decorum seems to have been preserved in regard to advertising: in Italy and Spain the advertising hoardings threaten to engulf the spectacle, while in France, Austria and some other countries shirt advertising has descended to deplorable depths. At the time of writing, the World Cup, much of it sold out to Adidas as suppliers of equipment, is still without a sponsor's name, and national teams are not allowed to wear advertising on their jerseys. It would be reassuring to think that this is to preserve some sense of pride, but it is just as likely to avoid upsetting rival sponsors in the exclusive deals stitched up with FIFA. Otherwise the last major football competition still to resist a sponsor's name is the oldest, but even the FA is now looking for a sponsor to tarnish the game's greatest institution.

To the clubs with the strength the sponsors have given, and the clubs in turn have kept what they see as theirs. In England from 1983 the home team was allowed to keep all of the income from the gate after expenses, rather than share it with the away club. This concession was granted in part to counter threats of a breakaway league. The richer clubs also forced a redistribution of television money so that they got more than the rest. Directors were given the right to pay themselves large salaries, and some like Martin Edwards of Manchester United did just that. And in 1983, as there had been in every decade before and as there would be in every successive year, there was talk of a Super League: of English clubs, of British clubs, of European clubs. All, like the first league, the Football League, with the aim of keeping money among the rich. When satellite broadcasting began in Britain from November 1987, and BSB (British Satellite Broadcasting) started making overtures to the wealthiest clubs in England, forcing ITV and BBC to enter into independent rivalry, the greed of the various club chairmen thrust every other consideration aside as they fought to get their noses in the trough. Sheer numbers and tradition helped to beat them, for the 'Big Ten' of the mid-1980s who were to be given all the television largesse were not the 'Big Ten' of the previous decade. As Danny Blanchflower pungently pointed out, in the mid-1970s Wolves, Derby and Leeds, who were not considered in the discussions in the new TV deal, were winning trophies, while Manchester United were in the Second Division.

Some form of European Super League, with full television coverage, is now only a matter of time. In the United States such a league has been in operation for nearly thirty years, for the National Football League (NFL) of America is a competition based on the elite teams from an area almost as large as Europe, drawing on almost as large a population. It is a sport that middle-class Americans can watch live, but where the vast bulk of the spectators are at home, watching the eighty minutes of play and as much again in interruptions, on television. This is the ideal towards which some in Europe are looking, but while American 'hype' is repugnant to most soccer fans, even they would agree that there is a need for brighter football.

Adjusting the seamless garment

The call for brighter soccer has been made throughout the history of the game, but with the increasing television coverage and the demands of the sponsors, it has reached a new urgency. The number of goals scored in a game is not a good measure of its attractiveness – the poorest competitions have the highest goal-scoring, while there is one (rather philosophical!) school that says that the perfect game would end with a 0–0 scoreline. But goals are what the fans come to see, and in the World Cup the average number of goals scored has steadily dropped from 4.27 for all finals games through to 1958, to 2.21 in 1990. Those in Italy, played in the finest stadiums ever to host the games, were the dreariest ever seen, in no way comparable to the great games from 1950 to 1970 with the Brazilians at their best. The European Cup of 1991 was probably the most boring ever played, a far cry from the final of 1960 when Réal Madrid captivated the spectators with a team whose manager is known today only by the collectors of trivia.

Shortly after the 1994 World Cup was granted to the United States stories began to circulate claiming that soccer was going to be changed to make it more attractive to Americans and the sponsor. One suggestion was that the game be played in four quarters instead of two halves, and another that the goals be enlarged to make scoring easier. The Americans themselves were in no way guilty of such blasphemies, which turned out to have been dreamed up from within the sanctum of FIFA itself. The idea of four quarters instead of two halves raised further fears of 'time-outs' and other artificial interruptions to suit extraneous interests. This particular piece of vulgarity seems to have been knocked on the head. The suggestion of enlarged goalposts rightly gave rise to ridicule and seems to be safely buried – you could after all get rid of the crossbar and give six (or fifty) points for a goal (and consolation points for hitting the woodwork or near misses) if all you wanted to do was increase the scoring. Nevertheless the problem of over-defensive soccer and low scoring games is a problem. It is not a new one, however, and has to be seen within the traditions of the game.

Since the rules were drawn up before the end of the nineteenth century, the only major change has been to the off-side law in 1925. Changes before and since have been minor, involving such matters as the throw-in and free kicks. The most significant changes have been in regard to the goalkeeper. At the turn of the century he could handle the ball anywhere in his own half, but could take only two steps with it and was subject to a veritable mauling when holding the ball. In 1912 his use of hands was restricted to the penalty area. In 1931 the keeper was allowed to advance four steps without bouncing the ball, but further changes came only when charging the goalkeeper, as was common in Britain, threatened to disrupt sporting relations with the rest of the world. In a more enlightened Britain, too, it was coming to be seen as a relic of the past, and when Nat Lofthouse scored his Cup Final goal against Manchester United in 1958 by charging goalkeeper Harry Gregg into the back of the net, none but the Bolton fans, and not all of them, were heartened by the spectacle. Charging was virtually eliminated and goalkeepers were not allowed to advance with the ball by bouncing it. They soon found other ways to waste time and take advantage of their handling privileges.

The rule change of 1992 forbidding the goalkeeper to handle a ball kicked back by one of his own team has, despite the outrage of such respected critics as Brian Glanville and Keir Radnedge, been a boon to the game. Not because it has led to more goals, or created artificially exciting goal mouth incidents by keepers miskicking, but simply because it has eradicated one of the most boring defensive ploys and the most frustrating way of wasting time.

Less felicitously, FIFA has suggested that the throw-in be replaced by a kick, making the point that this was once the case. In this they show a finer grasp of history than logic, for while it is true that in the early days a ball that went out of play was kicked back into play, such an argument could also take us back to the mauls and mayhem of the 1870s. At most, a case could be made for a kick-in where a ball is deliberately kicked out of play, but even this would be mere tinkering.

Suggested changes in the off-side rule are as old as the game, but the only change that could help would be the abolition of 'passive' off-side – the situation where a player does not receive a pass, but is adjudged to be 'interfering with play'. Even this, like so many aspects of the rules, can be dealt with within the present interpretation, and that anachronistic catch-all, 'ungentlemanly conduct', can cover a host of sins. Nevertheless, pressures on referees are continually increasing, and it is only when direction has come from above that certain unsightly aspects of the game have been removed.

Today's game is undoubtedly faster than ever before, and the level of technical skills is much higher. Average players are fitter and can master basic skills in a way that was beyond most players of the 1950s. The game, too, despite contemporary accusations, is less violent: statistics on red and yellow cards tell us very little about the actual game, but more about instructions given to referees as to what constitutes a bookable offence. Television has played its part in eliminating the thug who was often taken for granted in other eras: the Montis of the continent, the clogger in Britain. There were some abominable fouls committed in the 1960s, and no player today would get away with what the Portuguese did to Pelé in the 1966 World Cup: Schumacher of Germany committed grievous bodily harm on Battiston of France in the 1982 World Cup without so much as a warning or a yellow card, but the TV audience was much less forgiving than the referee, while he paid the price in footballing terms for the goal he gave away against Argentina in 1986 when faced by a similar situation. Like other players who have grossly offended against the game, and despite unsung charitable work, it is his attack on Battiston for which he is remembered.

Before the 1980s the so-called 'professional' foul, the deliberate attempt to stop a player scoring a goal, was standard practice: defenders were expected by their team mates and supporters to pull down a forward with a clear run on goal: tripping, rugby tackles and deliberate hand-ball were all part of the last minute defence of a desperate player. This was not always accepted, of course: the blatant foul by hard man Charlie Colombo of the USA on Stan Mortensen that prevented England equalising in the famous 1–0 game in Belo Horizonte was actually praised by the Italian referee in charge of that game, but looked on askance by some of his team mates. In the British press the issue of a deliberate foul committed to avoid a near certain goal came to a head in response to a tackle by Phil Thompson of Liverpool on Nottingham Forest's John O'Hare in the 1978 League Cup Final replay. The referee gave a penalty kick for what was in fact a foul outside the box. Thompson bleated that he had been cheated, as he had carefully timed his foul to avoid a penalty, but reporters with a sense of justice applauded the referee's action. After much heated debate, which helped to change *attitudes* to the 'professional foul', it was an instruction to referees to expel any player who committed such a foul that finally went towards eliminating it.

As the rewards for the top teams escalate, and the effects of a wrong decision are magnified as a consequence, there have been calls for technology to come to the assistance of the referee. In cricket a TV panel watching replays of difficult decisions has been used, but in soccer there would be more to lose than gain by this; the game is too free-flowing to be held up for a panel discussion, and while the all-seeing TV eye has shown some refereeing decisions to be clearly wrong, the referee has more often had his decisions vindicated: the man in the middle will always be correct more often than the partisan fans on the terracing. There is little doubt that a game could be controlled by a television panel set high in the stand, operating whistles and giving decisions over a loud-speaker system. But football without someone to abuse passionately and irrationally, whatever the code, is unthinkable: half the fun would be taken out of the game. There would not be the same satisfaction in abusing a box hidden away in the stand, and if every decision were incontrovertible there would be no consolation for the fans whose most desperate need when their team loses is to claim that 'We wuz robbed!' The one piece of outside assistance that should be granted the referee is an independent time-keeper: today's referees are more willing to add on time for injuries and wastage, but there are still some obvious anomalies in games that have been stopped right on 45 minutes despite many stoppages.

Administrative changes to encourage attacking play have seen goal average replaced by goal difference, then the awarding of three instead of two points for a win, to make a draw, for one point, less palatable. A draw is an honest result, however, and there is no need to eliminate it in league games. Cup games are another matter, but while the shoot-out has been seen necessary to decide which team should advance to the next round, its use to actually decide the result of the final is a blight on the game. The coach of Red Star even admitted that he ordered his players to play for a draw in the 1991 European Cup, drawn league games in Yugoslavia being decided by penalties. A craven confession, even if he was acting within the rules. If so the time has clearly come to change this rule. In knock-out competitions the penalty shoot-out is much preferable to the toss of a coin, but this said there is nothing else that can be said in its favour. Above all it is nothing short of farcical when an African Nations' Cup Final, a European Cup Final, indeed *any* cup final is decided in this way. And yet in the last ten years this is how an alarming number of major trophies have been decided. Among suggestions for breaking the deadlock were counting corners, as used to be done in the old five-a-side tournaments, or giving the game to the team that kept the ball for more than half the game in their opponent's half. More outlandish suggestions have involved counting the number of yellow or red cards, steadily reducing the number of players on the field . . . or even getting rid of the goalkeeper. FIFA has gone some way to solving the problem with 'sudden death' in extra-time; the first team to score being the winner, with penalties to decide only if there are no goals in the 30 minutes of extra-time. The first official application of this rule came in the Under-twenty World Youth Championship in Australia in 1993 when the host nation went through to the semi-final with a goal in the 100th minute against Uruguay.

In sport in general, and soccer in particular, the romance is in the unexpected, above all when the mighty are toppled by the meek. Such romance is less appreciated by the followers of the big clubs, and with them continuing to increase their power the game grinds remorselessly on to ensure that their financial investments are not upset. Thus cup games are played over two legs, or even replaced by leagues, where the shock of the upset is less important. The levelling effect of uneven or muddy pitches, or the vagaries of wind and rain, could be eliminated by playing on synthetic pitches and indoor arenas. The restrictions on buying players could be lifted, or on the number of foreigners allowed to play for any team at any time, as well as unlimited substitution. Not even the rich clubs have as yet gone this far, and even in the United States unpredictability of outcome has still to be engineered by restrictions at least on the signing of players.

So far soccer fans have shown little enthusiasm for sanitized football: most changes around the stadium have been in seating and improved comfort for the spectator, and that is as far as they want to go. The day of football played like a gigantic video game still seems like a futuristic nightmare, but there are some in power today for whom one person's nightmare is another's dream. And no more can football in the 1990s, like football in the 1890s, stray too far from the bonds of the society in which it is played.

Football in the twenty-first century

Soccer has gone through many crises, but no more than the societies in which it is played. As the world game it has suffered more from politics and deliberate interference than any other game, but it has survived the rise and fall of empires, and is likely to continue to do so, for a long time to come. Writing just before the start of the 1938 World Cup in France, *L'Auto*'s Maurice Pefferkorn described the forthcoming competition as a sporting and social symbol. He showed how football with its athleticism mixed with individual and collective discipline had surpassed the Olympic Games, and claimed that although the day of the Corinthians was long gone any loss in elegance, subtlety and artistry had been compensated in the more professional qualities of realism, power and solid workmanship. If the game had changed it was because conditions had changed:

> It is the spirit of our time that is harsher, greedier, more uncertain, more desperate to succeed. In this football merely reproduces the rhythm of humanity. However all people do not feel the effects of this rhythm in the same way. Those who are subjected to the most severe laws do not always find it easy to escape such influences in the way they play their football. This is something else, perhaps, that the World Cup will show us.

In the harsher and greedier world of the 1980s it was not just the names of players and managers who were making the news in the world of soccer. Three of the best known names in world football today are Silvio Berlusconi, owner of AC Milan; Bernard Tapie, owner of Olympique Marseille; and David Murray of Glasgow Rangers. What they have in common is that they own three of the biggest football teams in the world, another is that none of them is first and foremost a football man. Before 1986 they were virtual unknowns in the football world; today they are trying to direct it towards a European Super League for the benefit of a television audience.

There are other wealthy men who have bought or fought their way onto football boards to imprint their own philosophy of what should be done. Among these are Irving Scholar and David Dein who bought Spurs and Arsenal respectively. Both were passionate fans, but Scholar's investments outside football led Spurs to serious financial troubles. Multi-millionaire con-man Robert Maxwell tried to buy up several clubs, but came up against League restrictions. Neither Derby nor Oxford, whom he baled out of trouble, suffered for his financial crimes – other people had to pay for that. The pop star Elton John worked miracles for Watford, the club he had supported as a boy, before relinquishing control. In Scotland Wallace Mercer of Hearts, with more sensitivity to success than tradition, tried to merge the two Edinburgh rivals in a new Edinburgh United in 1990, but his economic rationalism brought Hearts and Hibs fans together in an uncommon unity of views.

Among the men running football clubs today, the most powerful of them all is Berlusconi, who has created one of the most successful football teams in the history of the game. In this he follows in the line of Bill Struth's Glasgow Rangers and Herbert Chapman's Arsenal of the 1930s, or Hungary's Communist regime that produced Honved and the 'Golden Team', or that of Franco's clerical Fascism that gave us Réal Madrid. Berlusconi's AC Milan is the creation of a multi-national millionaire plundering talent from around the globe in an orgy of conspicuous consumption that has been the hallmark of the 1980s. While the Glasgow Rangers of businessman David Murray can put out a team in the Scottish league in which any one of their players is worth more than that of the entire opposition, Berlusconi, because of the three foreigners limit, often has superstar foreign players worth millions on the transfer market sitting twiddling their toes in the stand.

Berlusconi took over Milan in 1986, and immediately set about clearing up the mess of his predecessors: after the bribery, corruption and match-fixing scandals of 1980, Milan were relegated again in 1982, and when Guiseppe Farina bought out the disgraced Felice Colombo, his own wild and irresponsible spending led to him fleeing the country in 1986. When Berlusconi bought Farina's shares and took over, he immediately put his own businessmen in charge, although wisely leaving football matters to those who knew better. Berlusconi was born in 1936, and after a variety of occupations that took in the law, acting as a tour guide, photographer and even singer, he made his fortune in the north Italian property and building boom of the 1960s. In 1980 he entered the television business, and by 1986 owned Italy's three largest television companies, based on Canale 5 in Milan. Through the parent company Fininvest, owned by his family, he controlled supermarkets, publishing companies and advertising agencies, as well as other interests as diverse as insurance and aerospace. As a result he became richer even than Gianni Agnelli who owned Fiat and Juventus. Juventus had been in the Agnelli family for six decades when Berlusconi bought Milan, but the newcomer immediately set about forming a football team that would reflect his image: an image of excellence.

Within a short time Berlusconi had spent £20 million buying the best players in Europe, above all the Dutch trio of van Basten, Rijkaard and Gullit, who were central to Milan's successes from the late 1980s. Through Canale 5 he took on the Italian national broadcaster, RAI, and broke its monopoly on football, forcing up the bidding for big games. Berlusconi made no secret of his aim to see his ultimate goal in a European Super-League, with his television company controlling it. Indeed football for him was not so much an end in itself as a means, through his footballers, to serve his TV and supermarket interests. While he paid out £20 million in the early years buying players, he spent £425 million to buy La Standa supermarkets. And yet it is AC Milan that makes his efforts worthwhile: ownership of a great football team that is the pride of the neighbourhood will always bring more esteem than being the owner of a chain of grocery stores, no matter how big.

The game has come not so much a long way, as traversed a bumpy road in the century that encompasses its growth from the inauguration of the Football League in 1888. The dream of a Scot working as a small businessman in England is likely to become the reality of an Italian businessman beaming the game into the homes of every household in the world. One can only wonder what McGregor would think of the fate of the game he set up as the 'league of the selfish'. However this may be, the game in Britain and elsewhere prospered outside the Football League, and no doubt it will prosper into the next century whatever changes are made to suit television and the private interests of individuals. The game is still the people's game, played in the parks and spare lots and amateur leagues by people who are never going to see their name in print, let alone have their faces seen on television. The professional game will continue to be plagued by the problems of the age as it will be enlivened by the thrills of competition and the genius of star players. The supporters are as important today as they ever were: even in a league devised for television viewers, cardboard crowds and canned cheers cannot substitute for the real thing. Football will always be the game of the people, and soccer the world's game.

Endnotes

For the section on the United States, other than contemporary journals, newspapers and official reports, see the books referred to in chapter three. In addition to these

Sam Foulds and Paul Harris, *America's Soccer Heritage. A History of the Game*, Soccer for Americans, California, 1979

is short and patchy, but has some fascinating detail, much of it presumably based on oral research.
    An essentially statistical account is

Colin José, *NASL. A complete record of the North American Soccer League*, Breedon Books Sport, Derby, 1989.

One of the best books on contemporary football, which gives a sympathetic view of the recent involvement of millionaire entrepreneurs, is

Alex Fynn and Lynton Guest, with Peter Law, *The Secret Life of Football*, Queen Anne Press, London, 1989.

L'Equipe published a special magazine dossier on the financial problems afflicting French clubs, called, 'Enquête sur un désordre désorganisé', May 1991.

Jean-François Nys, 'L'economie du football en France', 'Le Football et l'Europe' (EU, 103/90)

is particularly good on newspapers and television.

Index

People